AIR DISASTER

Volume 3

Macarthur Job
Artwork by Matthew Tesch

ACKNOWLEDGEMENTS

As I have remarked in previous volumes, no book of the nature of the *Air Disaster* series, encompassing the various disciplines touched upon in analysing diverse accidents to modern airline aircraft, each of them in their own way significant to operations worldwide, could be written without the assistance of many others, themselves authorities in their own particular fields.

First and foremost, I unreservedly acknowledge and applaud the tremendous contribution that artist Matthew Tesch has made to this Volume 3 in the series. Himself a commercially qualified pilot and an expert on the world's airline industry and its aircraft types, his efforts have gone far beyond the artist's role of creating the many graphic illustrations that bring the words of the book to life.

Matthew Tesch has personally chosen the photographs that support his illustrations, as well as providing the content of the highly informative captions and descriptive 'boxes'. In many cases, photographs acknowledged to other publications come from his own former extensive collection and library, accumulated over 20 years, which he had donated to HARS, the Historical Aircraft Restoration Society Inc, based in Sydney. He therefore wishes to thank HARS Hon Sec Gary Squire, librarian Neil Louis and HARS member Robin Mead, for assisting him to access and reproduce these pictures. Acknowledgements to WAFM and WAFN-M, are for photographs originally published in the World Airlines Fleets Monthly and its successor, World Airlines Fleets News Monthly, by Airline Publications in the UK. Other photo acknowledgements are to magazines ATW (Air Transport World) and AW&ST (Aviation Week & Space Technology).

Matthew Tesch also researched much of the source material, over and above that available from national accident investigation authorities overseas, to help 'flesh out' often prosaic official reports. Jeppesen-Sanderson Inc provided authoritative reference material on many of the world's airports and airways, and the unfailingly efficient way in which Ms Georgia Wolf and Mr Durham Monsma, at the company's Denver HQ, responded to requests enriches the book's content. Airclaims (London) and Airclaims (Moscow) also proved invaluable contacts, and Airbus Industrie's David Velupillai (Regional Manager Press Relations) provided much data on some of the tragic events in these pages.

Companies closer to home that contributed to the wealth of information contained in the book include Qantas, Flight West Airlines, United Airlines and Thai Airways International, while Lonely Planet Publications proved a rich source of background material for Chapter 6. Individuals who particularly assisted Matthew Tesch's research include Frau Lilo Hartmann in Germany, Mrs Ilse Tesche and Mrs Karen Elmes in Brisbane, Geoffrey Kelly and Russell Wakely in Sydney, and *Australian Aviation's* well known contributor Gordon Reid in Melbourne.

But without doubt Matthew Tesch's most outstanding research success was his obtaining, from no less a source than the Russian Departament Vozdushnovo Transporta (Department of Air Transport) in Moscow, a copy of the official investigation report into the loss of an Aeroflot Airbus A310 in extraordinary circumstances during a night flight from Moscow to Hong Kong. Although the broad circumstances of this disaster were known in the West, this is probably the first time its details have been made available to readers outside the Moscow-centred Commonwealth of Independent States, so making its inclusion in this volume of *Air Disaster* something of a coup for Aerospace Publications.

He has asked me to acknowledge the invaluable assistance given in this regard by His Excellency the Australian Ambassador to Kazakhstan, Australian embassy staff in Almaty and Moscow, in particular their Mrs Viktoria Ivanova, and Australia's Department of Foreign Affairs & Trade in general.

But it did not stop there. The report itself was of course in Russian, and had to be translated! To the rescue came longtime Tesch family friend, Russian speaking Dr Maria Kravchenko, a retired University of Queensland lecturer. Despite the unfamiliar technical subject, her enormous commitment of time and expertise produced a unique document that has enabled the astonishing story to be told in Chapter 7. Both the Sayakhat Air Company's Chief Pilot, Captain Yuri Gres in Almaty, Kazakhstan, and Omega Aviation's Jim Dedman in Brisbane, helped Dr Kravchenko to clarify many obscure Russian aeronautical terms.

So without Matthew Tesch's quite remarkable contribution to the preparation of *Air Disaster*, Volume 3, the book would have been but a shadow of what it now is. I thank him for all his enthusiasm and commitment in bringing the book to fruition and, on his behalf, I thank all those who assisted him.

For myself, in seeking to adequately acknowledge all who have helped compile a book so brimming with technical detail, it is difficult to know where to begin.

Once again, I am indebted to Australia's Bureau of Air Safety Investigation for providing access to copies of relevant overseas accident investigation reports – in particular to Director Dr Rob Lee, and Data Manager Russell Sibbison, in Canberra, and to Clive Phillips, Manager of the Bureau's Melbourne Field Office.

Aviation industry colleagues upon whose expertise I have continued to draw include Captains John Laming, Trevor Thom and Bruce Widmer, aircraft performance engineer Don McLean, Peter Bacon, former Senior Check Flight Engineer with Qantas, air traffic controller Phil Vabre, pilot and former flight engineer Brian L Hill, aviation historian John Hopton, and pilot and LAME Darryl Gruar. Senior aviation 'statesmen' Stanley Brogden OAM, and John Watkins OBE, have continued to provide much needed encouragement and overall advice, as has Colonel Keith Hatfield, DFC. My appreciation and thanks go to them all.

My thanks also go to Mr John Kennedy of Melbourne, who with his father and brother, were amongst the passengers on the Auckland and Sydney bound UAL 747 that lost nine passengers over the Pacific in a terrifying explosive decompression.

As before, my thanks also go to Jim Thorn at Aerospace Publications for his concept of the project, and to his outstandingly capable and unflappable production manager Maria Davey, for her enthusiasm and unflagging efforts in bringing it to its conclusion on time. Thanks are also due to Aerospace Publication's Deputy Editor, Ian Hewitt, for his role in ensuring that the author's and artist's urgent calls for help in accessing reference material were met promptly.

And finally thanks again to my wife, Esma, for her ongoing literary editorship of all my initial work, ensuring that technical jargon was not unnecessarily imposed upon hapless readers who are not themselves pilots or engineers!

Macarthur Job
Lower Templestowe, Victoria, Australia
October 1998

CONTENTS

★   ★   ★

Published by Aerospace Publications Pty Ltd (ACN: 001 570 458), PO Box 1777, Fyshwick ACT 2609,
publishers of monthly *Australian Aviation* magazine.
Production Manager: Maria Davey

ISBN 1 875671 34 X

Copyright © 1998 Macarthur Job and Aerospace Publications Pty Limited
Proudly printed in Australia by Pirie Printers Pty Ltd, 140 Gladstone Street, Fyshwick 2609
Distributed in Australia by Network Distribution, 54 Park Street, Sydney 2000. Fax (02) 9264 3278
Distribution in North America by Motorbooks International, 729 Prospect Ave, Osceola, Wisconsin 54020, USA.
Fax: (715) 294 4448. Distribution throughout Europe and the UK by Airlife Publishing Ltd, 101 Longden Rd, Shrewsbury
SY3 9EB, Shropshire, UK, Fax (743) 23 2944.

INTRODUCTION

This third volume in the Air Disaster series continues the well established theme of Volumes 1 and 2, analysing the way the modern miracle of jet age international travel – extraordinarily safe and sure as it is – continues to be steadily refined by salutary lessons from the harsh world of practical experience.

To put the contents of this book in context, let it be emphasised at the beginning that the risk of dying prematurely in bed is statistically greater than that of doing so in an airline accident! As with the setbacks and experiences reviewed in the previous volumes, the accidents covered in this book have helped to evolve a global transport system whose safety standards surpass even the hazards of everyday life. Literally thousands of airline flights take place the world over, 24 hours a day, every day of the year, in all types of weather, and the overall standard of safety achieved is beyond any other mode of transport the world has seen.

As before, the instances chosen for inclusion in this book are either notable in their own right, or are representative of a number of problems resulting from similar factors. Their other qualification was that comprehensive reports on the accidents themselves, their circumstances, and their subsequent investigations, were available.

All the aircraft types that featured in Volume 2 happened to be products of Boeing and McDonnell Douglas. This time slightly over half of them are products of Airbus Industrie. Far from being a reflection on the manufacturers concerned, this is simply an indication of progress in the global airline industry, particularly perhaps in the field of new technology and the 'learning curve' involved in crew training. The coverage of these accidents is also a reflection of the expert, frank and open reporting of the investigating authorities whose comprehensive reports enabled the reviews in this book to be written.

Looking back, it is fascinating to see how, in relating the stories behind these operational lessons, the emphasis has changed over the three volumes. Volume 1, covering the first three decades of the jet age, was much concerned with unforeseen airframe and operational problems, brought to light by the environment in which this new high speed, high altitude and high power generation of aircraft operated. In Volume 2, the emphasis in many cases was on engine operation and maintenance in less than favourable circumstances, and the dire consequences for the aircraft and passengers concerned. The book also foreshadowed potential problems inherent in excessive dependence on automated navigational and aircraft systems.

But in Volume 3, there is only one instance of an accident resulting from hardware failure. Although the consequences were horrifying, it initially involved no more than a minor electrical short circuit in the cargo door of an elderly Boeing 747. Possibly the outcome of deteriorating but undetected wiring insulation, this accident, together with others not included in this book, in particular the as yet unresolved TWA 800 inflight explosion, should emphasise to the industry that the condition of aging aircraft electrical wiring is just as vital to safety as fatigue considerations in its structure.

The emphasis in much of the rest of the volume is on human factors and on the interface between pilots and automatic systems – the question first raised in two of the accidents included in Volume 2 – on the effects of computerised operational technology on crew responsibility and flight safety.

The numbers of accidents relating to the same question in this volume show that it has become an increasing problem as high technology, computerised aircraft become the norm in world airline operations. It is notable that in none of the accidents examined was there any suggestion of automatic systems malfunctioning. Although equipment faults are not unknown, experience shows that only rarely do they become a problem to the crew, and there is no doubt that the systems themselves function very well.

Nevertheless, it seems clear that today's automated flightdecks still leave a lot to be desired in terms of pilot understanding and reaction in emergencies. On one hand there is an increasing tendency by pilots to over-dependence on automated systems to fly the aircraft in demanding situations, to the obvious detriment of 'old fashioned' piloting skills, perhaps especially in regard to situational awareness. On the other hand, there is evidence that pilots can encounter difficulties in understanding the response of highly automated flightdeck systems, especially in an emergency where timing is crucial.

In many airlines throughout the world today, stress is placed on the programming of automatic flight control systems *because* they will fly and navigate the aircraft with great accuracy and efficiency, and because they supposedly reduce the workload on the crew. But there seems to be little emphasis given to the pilot's ability to rapidly revert to basic flying skills. As a result, over reliance on automatic systems can become a potential danger.

Inadequate training is often cited as the reason for pilots failing to understand the response of an aircraft's automation when they encounter difficulties. Certainly, thorough training in the aircraft's systems is important – pilots should not only know how to key in information, but also have a broad understanding of how the automated systems work.

Yet some automatic flight systems may perhaps be too complicated, at times taking even highly experienced pilots by surprise. Mode confusion appears to be a particular problem, and there is obviously a need to avoid system characteristics that create high crew workloads in critical situations. Keeping a crew fully informed of what the automatic systems are doing, is also essential.

And, as a counterpart to the pilot's ability to quickly revert to manual flying, automatic systems should be capable of being quickly turned off, or overridden. A programmed autopilot system that cannot be effectively overridden in an emergency near the ground is surely, like the pilot who can only fly by pressing buttons, a potential danger.

Apart from these considerations, the safe programming of automatic flight systems is heavily dependent on adequate crew co-ordination, one pilot cross-checking and confirming the other's actions, regardless of crew status.

This too is an aspect that needs constant emphasis in crew training syllabi, not only amongst crews drawn from traditionally hierarchical cultures with their inherent respect for and deference to the status of seniors and elders, where it is extremely difficult for a junior first officer to 'speak up'.

As some of the accidents examined in the chapters that follow indicate, the relationship between pilots on a flightdeck can sometimes defeat the best designed crew operating procedures. A first officer may suspect or fear the captain is making a mistake, but be reluctant for a number of reasons to challenge his authority. Yet safe crews are the ones where the captain accepts that his actions should be challenged, that laid down operating procedures are to be adhered to, and that the first officer shares the responsibility for the safety of the aircraft.

The transition to today's two crew flightdecks, where two pilots now do the work of the former three crew members, was undoubtedly motivated by the present combination of rapidly advancing technology and economic rationalism. In such a climate, any questioning of these philosophies might be considered 'heretical', but there is one posed by the contents of this book that should not be avoided.

There is no doubt that computerised monitoring systems function just as efficiently, or even more so, than the former flight engineer or second officer. But this aside, has the 'rationalisation' of flight crew functions gone too far? Has the aviation industry too slavishly followed the current all-pervading economic fashion to 'downsize' human resources? Is there still a case for a third pair of eyes on the flightdeck whose function is not so much to keep an eye on the aircraft's engineering systems, but who, from 'outside the control loop', could monitor the overall operation of the aircraft?

As passenger aircraft grow steadily bigger, more complex and more costly, the human and financial consequences of a traumatic accident become proportionately more horrendous. Crewing such aircraft with only two pilots, despite their highly sophisticated automatic flight systems, can be a bit like putting all your eggs in one basket. The industry today is in fact still using the basic airline flight crew concept first introduced in the Fokker Trimotor of the 1920s!

With full two deck widebodies now under consideration for future production, is the time approaching to consider an entirely new approach to flightdeck design and operation? By comparison with the consequences of a disaster to such an aircraft, the cost of a third crew member pales into insignificance. Moreover airlines always seem able to find money to outlay on improved cabin service and customer appeal.

Perhaps the best way to answer that question is to ask: how many of the accidents examined in this book could have been averted if there had been a third responsible monitoring pilot on the flightdeck?

GLOSSARY OF AERONAUTICAL TERMS AND ABBREVIATIONS

ADC: Air Data Computer.

ADF: Automatic Direction Finder. Previously known as radio compass.

AFCS: Automatic Flight Control System.

Aileron: Control surfaces on (usually) outer sections of wing trailing edges, controlling bank and roll of aircraft.

Airspeed Indicator (ASI): Instrument measuring speed of aircraft through air, usually expressed in knots.

Air Traffic Clearance: Approval by Air Traffic Control for aircraft to taxi, takeoff, climb, enter controlled airspace, descend or to land.

Air Traffic Control (ATC): System of directing all aircraft operating within designated airspace by radio. Divided into sectors such as Tower (aerodrome control for takeoffs and landings), Departures, Control (en route aircraft), and Approach.

Alt Sel: Altitude Selector.

Altitude: Height of aircraft as shown on altimeter adjusted to local barometric pressure.

Angle of attack (AoA): Angle at which wings meet airflow.

APU: Auxiliary Power Unit.

Artificial horizon (AH): Instrument displaying aircraft attitude in relation to real horizon.

Asymmetric flight: Multi engined aircraft flying with one engine inoperative.

ATIS: Automated terminal information service. Continuous, recorded radio transmission of meteorological conditions at airport.

Attitude: Lateral and longitudinal relationship of aircraft to horizon.

Attitude indicator: See artificial horizon and flight director.

Bunt: Sudden nose down manoeuvre of aircraft, usually producing uncomfortable negative G.

CDU: Control/Display Unit.

CFDS: Centralised Fault Display System.

"Clean" (aircraft): Aircraft in normal cruising configuration, with high lift devices and undercarriage retracted.

CMD: Command.

Control Area: Designated area of airspace in which all aircraft movements are under radio direction of Air Traffic Control.

Control Zone: Designated airspace encompassing terminal area of an airport in which all aircraft movements are under radio direction of Tower Controller.

Co-ordinates: Latitude and longitude of a position anywhere on the earth's surface, estimated to one minute of an arc.

CRT: Cathode Ray Tube [Screen/Display].

CVR (Cockpit Voice Recorder): Sophisticated, "crash proof" tape recording equipment fitted to airline aircraft to record flight crew conversations and radio transmissions. The tape is a 30 minute closed loop which is continuously recycled, providing a complete audio record of the last 30 minutes of any flight.

Directional gyro (DG): Instrument accurately registering direction aircraft is heading. When aligned with compass, provides immediate indication of changes in magnetic heading.

DME: Distance Measuring Equipment. Radio navigation aid providing pilot with constant readout of distance from selected radio beacon.

ECAM: Electronic Centralised Aircraft Monitoring [System].

EFCS: Electronic Flight Control System.

EFIS: Electronic Flight Instrumentation System.

ELAC: ELevator/Aileron Computer.

Elevation: Height of terrain above mean sea level. Abbreviated AMSL.

Elevators: Control surfaces at rear of horizontal tail (tailplane), controlling nose attitude of aircraft.

Endurance: Time (expressed in minutes) aircraft can theoretically remain in air before fuel is exhausted.

EPR: Engine Pressure Ratio. Measure of thrust developed in turbofan jet engines.

ETA: Estimated time of arrival.

ETD: Estimated time of departure.

FADEC: Full Authority Digital Engine Control.

FAA: Federal Aviation Administration.

FAC: Flight Augmentation Computer.

FADEC: Full Authority Digital Electronic Control.

FBW: Fly By Wire.

Fin: The vertical aerofoil member of an aeroplane's tail assembly or empennage. Provides directional stability in flight. Known as the vertical stabiliser in US aviation parlance (see also rudder).

FCDC: Flight Control Data Concentrator.

FCOM: Flight Crew Operating Manual.

FCU: Flight Control Unit.

FD: Flight Director.

FDR (Flight Data Recorder): Complex "crash proof" instrument fitted to airline aircraft to continuously record operating parameters during flight. Early FDRs using stylus scribing on metallic tape recorded only four parameters – airspeed, altitude, heading and vertical acceleration. Today's digital FDRs (DFDRs) simultaneously record some 70 aircraft performance parameters, including instrument readings, flight control movements, engine performance and secondary control settings.

Flaps: Adjustable surfaces on aircraft's wing trailing edge. When lowered, flaps increase lift of wing, thereby reducing stalling speed, and increase drag, steepening aircraft's glide angle.

Flight Director: Complex, computer controlled flying instrument combining inputs of other flying and radio navigation instruments in single large dial located directly in front of each pilot.

Flightplan: Document prepared by pilot on official form before departure, providing details of proposed flight – track to be followed, waypoints, computations of wind effects, headings and speeds for each leg, all-up weight at departure, and progressive fuel burn.

Flight Level (FL): Expression of height in hundreds of feet, based on standard barometric altimeter setting of 1013.2 millibars. Eg, 12,000 feet on standard altimeter setting would be FL120. Differs from altitude in that the latter is based on actual barometric altimeter setting for a particular area or airport.

FMC: Flight Management Computer.

FMGC: Flight Management/Guidance Computer.

FMS: Flight Management System.

FO: First Officer.

"G" (gravities): Expression of force acting on aircraft and its occupants in flight, measured in multiples of earth's gravitational force.

GMT (Greenwich Mean Time): Standard world time used for navigation regardless of location of ship or aircraft. Now generally referred to as UTC (Co-ordinated Universal Time).

GPWS: Ground Proximity Warning System.

Ground speed: Actual speed of aircraft over ground. May be greater or less than airspeed, according to wind.

HDG: Heading.

HDG/SEL: Heading Selector.

HF (High (radio) Frequency): Radio propagation in the frequency band from 3 to 30 MHz. Permits communication over long distances, but reception can be subject to atmospheric and electrical interference. Used by aircraft operating beyond range of VHF and UHF radio propagation.

HSI (Horizontal Situation Indicator): Instrument on the pilot's flight instrument panel capable of displaying position information in ILS, VOR or NAV modes. When selected in NAV mode, displays distance to the next waypoint in top left hand corner, ground speed top right hand corner, and plan view of aircraft's position left or right of track, thus providing instant information on aircraft's position and speed.

ILS (Instrument Landing System): Electronic approach aid which enables a pilot to carry out an approach for landing when weather conditions preclude visual contact with the ground.

IFR (Instrument Flight Rules): Stipulated procedures for navigating aircraft by reference to cockpit instruments and radio navigation aids alone. Enables flight regardless of visibility. Normal operating procedure for airline flights.

IMC (Instrument Meteorological Conditions): Weather conditions in which visibility is less than specified for visual flying, and in which flight is legally possible only under IFR.

Knot: One nautical mile per hour. Equivalent to 1.853km/h.

LOC: Localiser. VHF radio beacon providing accurate horizontal guidance.

Lowest Safe Altitude (LSA): Designated minimum altitude for particular air route, providing minimum of 1,000 feet clearance above underlying terrain.

MAC: Mean Aerodynamic Chord.

MSA (Minimum Safe Altitude): Altitude below which IFR aircraft may not descend unless specifically authorised to do so by ATC. Takes into account high terrain underlying an air route.

Mach number: Figure expressing relationship between true airspeed of aircraft and speed of sound.

Mayday (repeated three times): Radio telephony version of former morse code "SOS" distress call. Derived from the French "m'aidez" – "help me".

N1: RPM of Stage 1 fan of turbofan jet engine, expressed as a percentage of normal maximum fan speed.

N2: RPM of gas turbines of turbofan jet engine, expressed as a percentage of normal maximum turbine speed.

Nautical mile (nm): Measure of distance used for navigation in the air and at sea. Equal to one minute of an arc of latitude on the earth's surface. Is 800 feet longer than a statute mile and equivalent to 1.853km.

Nav: Navigation.

Navaid: Radio navigation aid.

ND: Navigation Display.

NDB: Non directional beacon. Ground based medium frequency radio transmitter sending continuous signals in all directions for use by aircraft fitted with ADF (radio compass).

NOTAM (Notice to Airmen): Message concerning changes to serviceability of aerodromes, radio and navigation facilities.

NTSB: National Transportation Safety Board.

Octas ("eighths"): Expression of cloud amount. Eight octas (or eighths) represents a completely overcast sky; four octas a half clouded sky.

PFD: Primary Flight Display.

Pitot-static system: System of instruments, connecting tubes and air sensors for measuring altitude, airspeed, and rate of climb or descent.

Precipitation: (Meteorological) Rain, hail, sleet or snow in or falling from cloud.

Preflight (inspection): "Walk around" inspection of aircraft by pilot, usually immediately prior to flight.

QFE: Code expression designating altimeter setting in millibars for particular airport. When set on subscale of altimeter, instrument reads aircraft's height above that airport.

QNH: Code expression designating altimeter setting in millibars – when set on subscale of aircraft's altimeter, instrument reads aircraft's height above mean sea level.

Radial: Bearing to or from VOR radio range.

Radio Compass: See ADF.

Radio Range: Type of radio beacon providing defined aircraft tracks to or from that navigation aid.

Rate One turn: Shallow standard rate turn used in instrument flight conditions.

RMI: Radio Magnetic Indicator.

RMP: Radio Management Panel.

RPM (rpm): Measure of engine speed expressed in revolutions per minute.

Rudder(s): Control surface(s) at rear of vertical tail (fin) controlling yawing movement of aircraft.

SAR: Search and Rescue.

SEC: Spoiler/Elevator Computer.

SFCC: Slat/Flap Control Computer.

Sigmet: Warning signal issued by Aviation Meteorological Service when weather conditions suddenly deteriorate.

Slats: Aerodynamic device fitted to leading edge of wings to delay onset of stall.

Spot height: Height noted on chart showing elevation of prominent mountain peak.

SSC: SideStick Controller.

Stalling speed: Low airspeed at which aircraft wings suddenly lose lift. No connection with engine "stall". Is absolute minimum airspeed at which aircraft can maintain flight.

Stick-shaker: Stall warning device which shakes aircraft's control columns as stalling speed is approached.

Tailplane: Horizontal aerofoil member of an aeroplane's tail assembly or empennage. Provides longitudinal stability in flight. Known as the stabiliser in US aviation parlance (see also elevators).

Transponder: Radio device fitted to aircraft which, when triggered off by certain radar wavelengths, emits a signal visible on ground radar screens. Signal usually includes additional information such as altitude of the aircraft.

Trim: Adjusting control of aircraft in climb, level flight and descent, so pilot is not required to maintain continuous pressure on elevators, ailerons or rudder.

T-VASIS: T Visual Approach Slope Indicator System.

UHF (Ultra High (radio) Frequency): Frequency band of 300 to 3000 MHZ. Aviation use confined mainly to military aircraft.

V (code): Schedule of indicated airspeeds stipulated for different phases of flight (see following).

V_1: Decision speed during takeoff. Aircraft is committed to fly when this speed is passed.

V_r: Rotation speed. Speed at which aircraft is "rotated" into liftoff attitude by raising the nosewheel off the runway.

V_2: Takeoff safety speed. Minimum control speed plus safety margin to allow for engine failure and other contingencies.

V_{ne}: Never exceed speed.

V_{ref}: Flap reference speed. Landing speed for stipulated number of degrees of flap extension.

VASIS: Visual approach slope indicator. System of lights located on ground on either side of runway to indicate correct angle of descent to approaching aircraft.

VSI (Vertical Speed Indicator): Instrument displaying rate of climb or descent in feet per minute.

VHF (Very High (radio) Frequency): In general use for inflight radio communications on air routes. Its frequency band from 30 to 300 MHZ is largely free from interference and static, but range is limited to "line of sight".

VFR (Visual Flight Rules): Stipulated flight procedure for navigating aircraft visually, clear of cloud, in Visual Meteorological Conditions.

VMC (Visual Meteorological Conditions): Weather providing specified range of visibility, making it possible for pilots to use visual means to avoid obstructing terrain and other aircraft.

VOR: Very High Frequency Omnidirectional Radio Range.

CHAPTER 1

"We will do two flyovers to demonstrate the continuity of French aviation..."

– Captain's PA announcement to passengers

Air France Airbus Industrie A320-111 F-GFKC [0009]
"Ville d'Amsterdam" – June 26, 1988

It was a new technology aircraft, with computerised control systems designed to fly it more safely and efficiently than any human pilot. But it was still an aeroplane, subject to the same laws of aerodynamics as any other – and its advanced computers were still subject to the frailties of their human operators.

A minor airshow

For aviation enthusiasts in and around the ancient French provincial town of Mulhouse, in the upper Rhine valley, near the junction of the Swiss and German borders, Sunday, June 26, was a notable date in their 1988 calendar of events.

A local airshow was to be held at Mulhouse's Habsheim airfield, on the eastern outskirts of the town, close to the railway and autobahn leading south to the Swiss city of Basle. It was by no means a major airshow, for Habsheim is a general aviation aerodrome, with grass strips for gliders and small light aircraft and a main paved Runway 02/20 only 1000m (3281ft) in length for bigger general aviation types.

But a varied program of sport flying and general aviation was arranged for the day and, as a special feature of the airshow, the organisers had invited Air France in Paris to display one of its newly delivered Airbus Industrie A320s for the first time. The Airbus would not of course be able to land but, operating from the major Basle-Mulhouse Airport on the northwestern fringe of Basle, only 29km to the south, would be able to make spectacular flyovers

along the runway in use at Habsheim to entertain and impress the public attending the airshow.

The advent of the technologically advanced A320 was keenly anticipated by the airline industry worldwide, and the inclusion of a brand new Air France example of the type in the airshow program was rightly regarded by the Mulhouse organising committee as something of a coup.

From Air France's point of view, the trip to Basle, including the flyovers at Habsheim, would be a public relations advantage for the company. There was to be a press reception at Basle-Mulhouse Airport for

Eager photographers crane through the open door of a hovering Gazelle to record the maiden flight of F-WWAI [0001], the first prototype A320-111, on February 22, 1987. The Toulouse-Blagnac passenger terminal is visible in the misty background. Less than six years after the single aisle design had been defined at the 1981 Paris Salon as a revolutionary 727 replacement, the A320 had generated more than 400 orders and options – and at least as much controversy about its Fly-By-Wire technology! Eight days before this photograph was taken, the aircraft had been launched by the late Princess of Wales at a 'son-et-lumiere' show in a Toulouse hangar filled with 2000 dignitaries. The A320 was re-registered as F-WWFT in May 1991. (Airbus Industrie)

the aircraft and crew on their arrival from Paris, followed by a short sightseeing charter flight for local passengers to publicise the company's new aircraft type, only three of which had so far been delivered by the manufacturer at Toulouse.

Because passengers would be coming aboard at Basle, a normal cabin crew was rostered for the round trip from Paris. To add to the passengers' appreciation of the aircraft, the charter flight would commence with the Mulhouse flyover then, weather permitting, the A320 would fly south, parallelling the mountainous country on the Swiss border to take in a view of Mont Blanc, before returning to Basle-Mulhouse Airport. After the passengers had disembarked, the aircraft and crew would return to Air France's base at Charles de Gaulle Airport, Paris.

The new A320

Smaller than the widebody three crew Airbus A300 series, or its more technologically advanced derivative, the two crew A310, the single aisle A320 had been developed to fill the market gap left in the world airline industry by the aging Boeing 727. Designed to be flown by two pilots only, and to carry between 115 and 180 passengers, the A320 was being touted by Airbus as "the ultimate profit maker", its fuel consumption on a passenger seat basis being only half that of the 727.

The airframe of the A320, while basically of conventional stressed skin design, incorporates many new structural techniques in its non pressurised components. In fact, no previous commercial aircraft had made such extensive use of composite materials: composites are used for the radome and fairings, the entire tail unit, most of the engine nacelles, and many other parts (see graphic).

Powered by two wing mounted CFM56-5 (in Air France's case) or V2500 engines, the A320 is nevertheless fundamentally a conventional aeroplane with conventional control surfaces. But unquestionably its real distinction lies in the design of its extremely sophisticated flying control system. Indeed, its advanced digital avionics, computerised systems and fly-by-wire flight controls have been designed to fly the aircraft in its various automatic control modes more efficiently, accurately and safely than human pilots are able to (also following graphic).

The futuristic flightdeck of the A320 is unlike anything airline pilots have been accustomed to previously – there are no control yokes and almost no traditional instruments. The first conventional commercial aircraft to have such a flight control system, the A320 instead has small SideStick Controllers positioned ahead of each outboard armrest for hand flying the aircraft. Pulling a selector knob on the Flight Control Unit (FCU) display on the glareshield gives the pilot control; pushing the knob transfers control to the

Flight Management System (FMS). Integrating the FMS into the aircraft's Automatic Flight Control System (AFCS) results in the A320 coming under the control of the Flight Management and Guidance System (FMGS). With the aircraft in this mode, the pilots' only role is to monitor the flight! Pull-out chart tables are fitted in front of each pilot position.

The A320's Fly-By-Wire system is multiply redundant, using four independent electronic systems, which makes total failure something that need not be considered. The system operates by transmitting electrical outputs from either of the pilots' SSCs, or from the FMCS, to hydraulic units driving the elevators, ailerons, spoilers, speedbrakes, flaps, and slats. In an emergency (such as pilot incapacitation), either crew member can press a takeover button on his sidestick, which will then fly the aircraft regardless of the position of the other stick. For further redundancy, the tailplane trim and rudder can always be controlled manually.

The A320's power levers are not connected mechanically to the engines, but to a Full Authority Digital Engine Control (FADEC) computer, which optimises engine performance and response at all times, while prolonging the life of the engines' "hot parts".

Each pilot position has an uninterrupted view of two big CRT colour displays directly ahead on the instrument panel, with two more in the centre of the panel. All six CRT

The first of 25 firm orders and 25 options for launch customer Air France, F-GFKA [00051] Ville de Paris, at Charles de Gaulle Airport a fortnight after its handover on March 26, 1988. When Airbus Industrie announced the formal go-ahead for the refined A320 project on March 4, 1984, it was taken for granted that the French flag carrier was to be its 'first cab off the rank'. Commitments from Air Inter and British Caledonian followed swiftly, but other Airbus partner airlines – Lufthansa, British Airways and Iberia for example – took longer to reach a decision. Caught up in the marketing hyperbole that accompanied the new type, Air France broke with past practice to name its A320s after European cities in anticipation of the EC union in 1992. (WAFN-JF Boussuge)

Externally, the A320 has been described as "deceptively conventional". In the ergonomic and aesthetic design of its flightdeck however, the efforts of the Porsche Industrial Design Bureau far outdid the usual superlatives. Unhindered by traditional control columns, the EFIS CRT screens and SideStick Controllers are clearly visible. Simplified system and fuel management controls are on the overhead panels, while the Flight Control Unit selectors and display windows are on the glareshield below the windscreen. The standby flight instruments and the undercarriage selector flank the two system monitoring screens on the central panel. Below them are the screens and input keyboards of the Control Display Units which play a major role in the A320's operation. On either side of the thrust lever quadrant and trim wheels, the Radio Management Panels provide sophisticated preselection and control of the aircraft's communication and navaid equipment. Aft of these panels are the speedbrake (left) and the slat/flap (right) levers. Footrests between each pair of rudder pedals accentuate the 'hands-off' character of A320 flight management. This is further emphasised by the pull-out tables for each pilot (stowed in this picture), wittily described by the British aviation press as "at last" affording pilots the opportunity "to really enjoy lunch". (Airbus Industrie)

displays are identical, but all can be programmed differently. But, as with other modern "glass cockpits", each pilot would normally have one CRT in a horizontal situation mode as a Navigation Display and the other in a vertical mode as a Primary Flight Display, with the central displays showing engine and system data.

Together, the flight displays make up the aircraft's basic Electronic Flight Instrumentation System (EFIS) which, with the two central displays, form a major part of the Electronic Centralised Aircraft Monitoring (ECAM) system. Any desired information can be called up on the screen, and any malfunction is instantly displayed.

Such is the design of the overall aircraft control system, that dangerous flight situations resulting from incipient stalls, overspeeding or overstressing cannot develop in the A320. The FMS computers are programmed to keep the aircraft within

its permitted flight envelope at all times, limiting airspeed, angle of attack and vertical acceleration. As long as the pilot's sidestick commands stay within this flight envelope, they are relayed to the control surfaces without modification; should they go outside it, they are instantly inhibited.

During an approach to land, the Minimum Groundspeed System (MGS) continuously calculates the correct flight regime, using the aircraft's airspeed, groundspeed and the known surface wind entered by the pilot into the FMS. Any deviation from the entered wind automatically triggers a change in engine power to maintain the correct approach speed.

If the aircraft encounters severe windshear, its speed sensors detect it at an early stage and increase engine power and angle of attack (AOA). Should the sensors be inoperative, the pilot can immediately apply full power and haul back hard

on the sidestick and the AOA will rise to the safe limit and stay there to provide maximum lift.

Preparations for the flight

The latter stages of arranging the A320's flight to Basle and on to Habsheim for the flyover were evidently completed with some haste. The request from the organisers of the Habsheim airshow had been duly studied by the relevant department of Air France in Paris, and approval passed to the company's Air Operations Directorate and Flight Safety Department. Air Traffic Control and Basle Tower were advised of the intention to conduct the airshow flyover and, late in the week before the airshow, the file containing the request and its details was finally passed to the A320 Flight Division of Air France in Paris.

Only three of Air France's new A320s had so far been handed over by Airbus Industrie at Toulouse and, for the display trip, the Flight Division selected the newest aircraft, F-GFKC, which would be arriving from the manufacturer on the Friday before the airshow. For the display flight it would be under the command of Captain Michel Asseline, the senior management pilot in charge of the company's A320 training who had already left for Toulouse to take delivery of F-GFKC and ferry it to Paris. As copilot for the display flight to Habsheim, the Flight Division chose Captain Pierre Mazieres, another management pilot and experienced training captain rostered for flying duty from Paris that weekend. Because of the extensive and diverse experience of the two pilots, the Flight Division did not consider making any reconnaissance of the Habsheim aerodrome in preparation for the display flight.

Captain Asseline was away from Paris taking delivery of the aircraft on the Friday, and was engaged in A320 crew training on the Saturday, while Captain Mazieres was off duty until the Sunday. The two pilots thus obtained details of the operation only when they were handed the company file on the airshow request after reporting for duty at Charles de

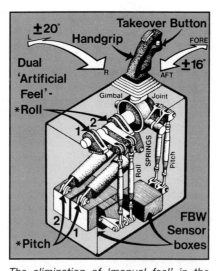

The elimination of 'manual feel' in the A320 was perhaps the most contentious issue of all. As this diagram shows, 'artificial feel' had to be electromechanically incorporated into the SideStick Controllers, which lack any manual reversion linkages to the aircraft's control surfaces. The thrust levers are similarly divorced, commands to the two CFM56-5 or IAE V2500 turbofans being signalled via the FADEC computers. Airbus resolved aircrew suspicions about input conflicts between the left and right SSCs by incorporating a 'takeover button' in each SSC. (Matthew Tesch; Flight International)

Gaulle Airport on the morning of the flight. Even then they were given no verbal briefing on the flyover, or on the details of the aerodrome at which it was being held.

As set out in the crew instructions in the file, the new A320 was to make a normal flight to Basle-Mulhouse Airport, where a press conference and brief reception for the aircraft and its crew would be held. Then, when its sightseeing charter passengers were all aboard, the aircraft would takeoff from the airport, continue the short distance north to Habsheim aerodrome at 1000 feet, lower the undercarriage and some flap, and make a low pass at low speed over Habsheim's Runway 02 for the benefit of the airshow crowd. The A320 would then accelerate and climb to a safe manoeuvring height, turn on to a reciprocal heading, and make a second pass at high speed along Runway 20 to complete the display segment.

The aircraft would then climb normally back to cruising level and make a sightseeing flight south to Mont Blanc and return before disembarking the passengers back at Basle-Mulhouse Airport, thence returning to Paris.

"Airbus likens the fly-by-wire A320 to driving a stagecoach," reported Flight International in August 1986. "Where the coach driver gives a command and the horses take care of the road, the A320 pilot makes a control input and the aircraft takes care of the flightpath." An Airbus engineering test pilot put it more succinctly: "The A320 lives in a box – it can't fly too slow; it can't fly too fast." This graphic combines a much simplified schematic summary of the aircraft's FBW avionics as well as an indication of its use of composites in more than just secondary or fairing structures. As respected commentator Bill Gunston commented of the A320's AFCS, "... pilots have nothing to do from takeoff to touchdown but take an active interest". But, as the Habsheim accident so forcefully demonstrated, the A320 is still a conventional aircraft, and while normal flight regime limits cannot be exceeded with the AFCS functioning, those limits nevertheless exist and can manifest themselves if that electronic protection is inhibited. (Matthew Tesch)

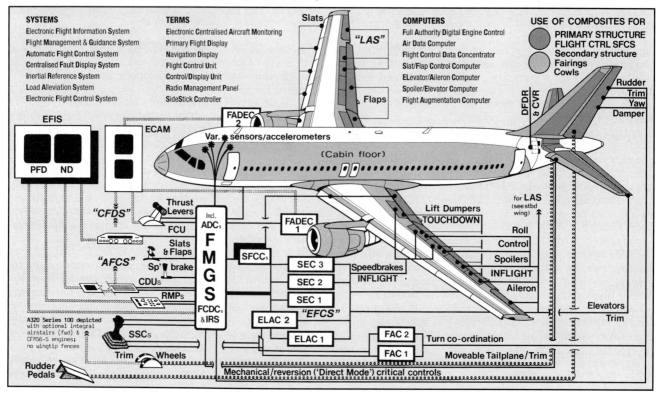

The airshow organisers were conducting a briefing for participating airshow pilots at Habsheim aerodrome that morning, but were not in the least concerned that circumstances did not allow the A320 crew to attend. Air France aircraft had successfully participated in previous Habsheim airshows with similar flyovers on past occasions. In any case the airspace surrounding Habsheim aerodrome would be closed to all other air traffic from the moment the A320 left Basle-Mulhouse Airport, until it completed its display and climbed away enroute to the south.

To Basle-Mulhouse

The late morning half hour flight with the cabin crew aboard from Charles de Gaulle to Basle-Mulhouse was entirely without incident in clear skies. The brief press reception on their arrival was similarly uneventful, both pilots having time to enjoy a fruit juice with the welcoming committee before they had to return to the flightdeck.

The cabin crew had already seated the 130 passengers for the charter flight by this time, and at 12.25pm the copilot called Basle Tower for a startup clearance, followed four minutes later by a request for a taxi clearance.

As the aircraft taxied for the Runway 16 holding point in fine, clear and calm weather, the pilots discussed the procedures to be followed for the flyovers. Neither pilot was familiar with Habsheim aerodrome or even its precise position, except what they had gleaned from their charts. Indeed it appears that they were not even familiar with the pronunciation of its name!

The captain, flying the aircraft from the left hand seat, declared that they would make a normal takeoff from Runway 16, retract the undercarriage and turn right, then with the first stage of flap extended, go "nice and easy" northwards until they located the airfield on the eastern outskirts of Mulhouse.

As soon as they had positively identified it visually, they would extend the third stage of flap, lower the undercarriage, and descend for the low, slow pass along the runway at a height of 100 feet. The captain would decelerate the aircraft down to its minimum flying speed, corresponding to its maximum angle of attack, inhibit the "Alpha Floor" – the function which would otherwise automatically increase engine power when the angle of attack reached 15° (Alpha being the shortened term for angle of attack) – and rely on the

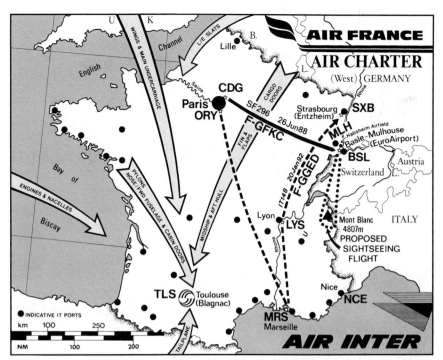

This map provides the setting for two of the three fateful A320 flights described in this chapter, and offers a summary of Airbus Industrie's assembly operations, with particular reference to A320 production. The planned promotional flight of F-GFKC extends southeast from Paris. The truncated IT148 service, initially south from Paris, combines three of Air Inter's then 52 sectors. By the end of the 1980s, rationalisation anticipating the EC Union, as much as the sorry financial state of Air France, had led to increasing amalgamations in the French airline industry, the absorption of UTA being the first of note. By the time F-GGED was attempting its Strasbourg approach in January 1992 (end of this chapter), Air Inter's corporate independence was little more than nominal; shortly afterwards it was renamed Air Inter Europe, only to disappear entirely when its operations were absorbed into "Groupe Air France". (Matthew Tesch)

copilot to adjust the engine power so as to maintain level flight along the runway as the captain held this steep noseup attitude.

On completion of this first flypast, the copilot was to apply takeoff power, and the Airbus would then climb away in a spectacular turn. "I've done it 20 times!" the captain assured his seemingly doubtful copilot.

With the undercarriage and flaps retracted again, the aircraft would then accelerate as quickly as possible to 340 knots while the copilot took over control to position them for a high speed run along the runway in the reciprocal direction. Again they would climb away, then call ATC for a clearance to continue the flight south towards Mont Blanc, about 25 minutes' flying time away.

While the captain was briefing the copilot on the flyover procedure, the Basle Ground Controller called the aircraft to ask what altitude the crew wanted for the short distance to Habsheim. The copilot requested "1000 feet above ground". The controller responded with an airways clearance to turn right after takeoff on Runway 16 and climb to 2000 feet on QNH, which would place the aircraft at about 1000 feet AGL.

The copilot then confirmed that, approaching Habsheim, they would descend for a "low altitude flyover of the airfield" going north, followed by a high speed "second flyby southward towards you", at which time they would require onwards clearance to the south to climb quickly to cruising level.

Replying, the controller informed the aircraft that their further clearance to the south would be passed by Approach Control, and instructed them when ready to call the Tower on 118.3 MHz.

"I've done it 20 times!" Captain Asseline assured his copilot concerning the spectacular climbing turn he proposed after the low speed flyover at Habsheim. In the picture, Airbus Industrie's second prototype, F-WWDA [0002], enacts one of these set piece manoeuvres that were a feature of the A320's public displays at the end of the 1980s. After four years of flight testing, this aircraft became F-GFKQ Ville de Berlin in 1991. (Airbus)

Basle-Mulhouse Airport's stark control tower rises over the terminal facade in this 1986 apron scene (note the Germanic spelling on the terminal roof). In the foreground, A310-308 HB-IPK [412] of Swissair's charter subsidiary Balair is being prepared for its next holiday service. Straddling the 'corner' of the Rhine where its westward flowing headwaters turn north for their long journey to the North Sea, the Swiss city of Basle overlaps the adjoining Franco-German borders. Its French 'twin', Mulhouse, lies 37km by autobahn to the NW, both cities sharing the same major airport on the French outskirts of Basle. (Osprey Books)

The captain then addressed the aircraft's 130 passengers over the public address system in French:

"Ladies and Gentlemen .... Hello and welcome aboard this Airbus 320 – No 3 of the series for Air France – which has only been in service for two days. We shall soon takeoff for a short tourist flight, starting at the Habsheim Flying Club, where we will do two flyovers to demonstrate the continuity of French aviation – and then we shall make a tour of Mont Blanc, depending on the weather conditions and air traffic. I wish you a very agreeable flight."

Prompted by the purser, who informed him some of his passengers were Germans, the captain repeated his message in fluent German.

To Habsheim

After a six minute wait at the holding point because of traffic, during which the pilots completed their pre-takeoff checks, the Tower cleared the Airbus to line up behind an inbound Lufthansa CityLine Fokker 50 on final approach. As soon as the Fokker had vacated the runway, the Airbus was cleared for takeoff from Runway 16. The time was 12.41pm, and the weather remained calm.

The takeoff was perfectly normal. The undercarriage was retracted, but the flaps left at the first detent as the aircraft began its right hand turn on to an initial heading just east of due north (see map), and a minute later the captain announced he was selecting the Open Descent Idle Mode to allow the engine thrust to be controlled manually. Both pilots began looking ahead to the left to identify the position of Habsheim aerodrome in the distance.

Almost immediately, the aircraft crossed the motorway connecting the two cities, about eight miles southeast of Mulhouse, and the captain turned the Airbus to the left to fly parallel with it. Soon after, he began descent, reducing power half a minute later.

COPILOT: You're at eight nautical miles, you'll soon see it [the airfield] – there's the motorway.
CAPT: We leave the motorway to the left, don't we? It's to the left ... no, to the right of the motorway.
COPILOT: It's slightly to the right of the motorway – you leave the motorway on the left.
CAPT: OK – as soon as we identify it, we descend very quickly then.
COPILOT [to Basle-Mulhouse Tower]: We're practically in view of the airfield there.
(B-M) TWR: Roger, you can contact Habsheim 125.25. Adieu.
COPILOT: 125.25. Adieu!
COPILOT: Habzeim? That's it, no?
CAPT: Habsheim. Habs...heim!
COPILOT: Habsheim.
CAPT: There's the airfield! It's there ... you've got it, have you?
COPILOT [Selecting 125.25 on VHF and calling Habsheim Tower]: Habsheim, hello – we're coming into view of the airfield for the flyover.
(HABSHEIM) TWR: Yes – I can see you. You're cleared – sky is clear.
CAPT: Gear down!
COPILOT [to Habsheim Tower as the captain reduces power to flight idle and the Airbus continues its descent at about 600fpm]: OK – we're going in for the low altitude flyover.
TWR: Roger.
CAPT: Flaps 2!
TWR: QNH Habsheim 1012. QFE 984.
CAPT: 984 – put in 984.
COPILOT: 984 – QFE selected!
CAPT: Flaps 3! – That's the airfield, you confirm?
COPILOT: Affirmative!

With the airfield now clearly in view and the aircraft at a height of only 450 feet, the captain saw from the alignment of the airshow crowd that the axis of the flying display was not along Runway 02 as he had expected, but along a grass airstrip aligned northwest. As the aircraft neared the airfield therefore, he gently banked it to the right to re-align its ground track accordingly.
COPILOT: OK, you're at 100 feet – watch it!

At this stage, the crew deactivated the Alpha Floor function, to prevent the computerised control system from automatically applying power as the angle of attack increased.
COPILOT [18 seconds later with the aircraft now only 40 feet above the grass airstrip and still sinking slowly]: Watch out for the pylons ahead – see them?[1]
CAPT [finally levelling off at about 30 feet above the strip]: Yes – don't worry.

But as the aircraft continued over the strip at this height in its steep *(right) The lower of these two maps depicts the track of the final flight of the newly delivered F-GFKC on only its third day's operations in the hands of its new owner. The track distance from Runway 16 on Basle's northwestern outskirts to the forested fringes of Mulhouse by the Rhine-Rhone Canal is only 13nm (24km), and the flight took less than five minutes. The more detailed closeup of Mulhouse-Habsheim airfield (above), brings the final, widely televised seconds of the A320's demonstration flight into clearer focus. (Matthew Tesch; Bureau Enquetes Accidents & Airbus Industrie)*

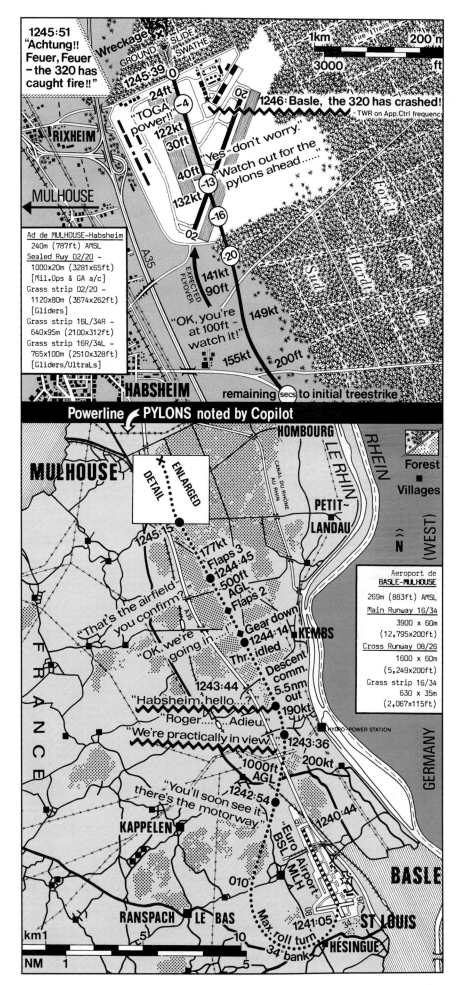

noseup attitude, the pilots suddenly realised that the trees in a forested area beyond the northwestern boundary of the airfield were at least as high as, if not higher than, the aircraft itself.

COPILOT [with alarm]: TOGA power! Go around track!

The crew rapidly applied power, but as the engines began to spool up in response, and the aircraft passed beyond the airstrip, the hundreds of spectators watching the extremely low flypast were horrified to see the underside of the aircraft's tail begin striking the treetops. Slowly the Airbus sank from sight into the trees. Moments later, an orange fireball, engulfed in a column of black oily smoke mushroomed swiftly above the trees as the aircraft, unseen, exploded in flames.

Survival

During the impacts with the trees, the starboard wing was torn off, spilling the contents of the fuel tanks. This ignited immediately, creating a fierce fire on the starboard side as soon as the aircraft came to a stop. Two firefighting vehicles and six firemen, standing by at Habsheim aerodrome to cover the airshow, set off at once to the site of the accident.

A doctor, an ambulance and 10 first aid personnel, also present at the airshow, quickly followed, alerting local fire brigades and hospital emergency services by radio as they went.

On board the crashed aircraft, a number of passengers were dazed by hitting their heads on the back of the seat in front of them, but none were incapacitated by the impact, and the cabin and its fittings remained basically intact. At the front of the cabin, the purser went to announce evacuation instructions to the passengers, but the public address system handset had been torn from its mountings. He then tried to open the port side forward cabin door, but found it obstructed by tree branches.

With the door only partly open, and the emergency escape slide not fully outside the aircraft, it began to inflate, with the result that it deployed partly outside and partly inside the cabin. Together with a passenger and a flight attendant from another airline who had been travelling on the flightdeck, the purser pushed hard on the door. It opened suddenly and the purser and the passenger were catapulted out of the aircraft to the ground, the escape slide falling on top of them.

Taking up a position at the forward door, the flight attendant then began evacuating the passengers in an orderly manner, but their escape route from the aircraft was blocked by tree branches tangled in the escape slide. Passengers following behind them who jumped out alongside the escape slide quickly piled up on top of one another because of the obstructing branches. Halting the egress of passengers for a moment therefore, the flight attendant allowed those who had jumped to quickly extricate themselves and get clear before others fell on top of them.

Outside the aircraft meanwhile, the purser, assisted by another flight attendant, tore away the branches entangled in the escape slide to make a clear path away from the aircraft. The evacuation then continued, the supervising flight attendant remaining at the door until she began suffering the effects of smoke inhalation.

By this time, fire had burst through into the starboard side of the cabin through the breaks in the floor between seat rows 10 and 15. One passenger tried to open the port overwing exit but could not reach it. This was fortunate, because the fires erupting on the port wing had also penetrated into the cabin through broken windows at rows 8 and 9, and opening the hatch would only have increased the danger to those inside.

Beginning to panic, many passengers were now pushing towards the front of the cabin. The flight attendant stationed in the centre of the cabin at seat 12D was thrust into the aisle by a seriously burnt passenger in seat 12F then, as she was trying to assist another passenger whose clothes were on fire, was carried forward by the crush of people trying to escape.

At the forward passenger door, after the last of these passengers had finally left, and the interior of the aircraft was rapidly becoming uninhab-itable, she called back into the cabin to check if anyone was still inside. She received no reply. By this time extremely thick smoke and flame made it impossible to make a visual check. She then left the aircraft herself.

Meanwhile, the evacuation from the rear door had proceeded quickly and relatively smoothly, thanks to reassuring but firm instructions from the flight attendants at the rear of the cabin.

The medical team from the airshow arrived in time to initially examine all the injured and administer first aid to those suffering from burns, while they awaited ambulance and medical reinforcements from Mulhouse.

Ten minutes after the crash, the first of another eight firefighting vehicles arrived at the accident site from surrounding fire stations. But because of the forest, only the smaller vehicles were able to reach the wreckage itself. Access for the bigger vehicles was blocked by the trees, considerably hindering the firefighting effort. Fuel flowing from the port wing fed the fuselage fire, and it quickly spread. Despite the intervention of the fire services, most of the aircraft was consumed by the fire.

Readers who saw the dramatic video footage of this disaster will have no difficulty recalling the awesome moment when the immaculate white A320 began brushing the treetops on the forest verge. But any momentary hopes that the aircraft could power out of its predicament vanished as its red and blue striped fin sank from sight into the forest. An instant later, massive clouds of dark, fire-flecked smoke, billowing into an otherwise clear blue sky, left no doubt as to what had happened. Only the empennage escaped the destruction of blazing fuel from the ruptured wing tanks. (Airliners magazine/Paul Bannwarth photo)

Of the 136 occupants on the aircraft, only three failed to escape. One was a handicapped boy in seat 4F who was apparently unable to move, another a child in seat 8C who was unable to unfasten her seatbelt, and the third was a woman who, having reached the safety of the forward door, went back to assist the little girl and was evidently overcome by smoke. Thirty-four passengers sustained injuries and burns requiring admission to hospital.

Both pilots received minor injuries to the head and collarbones during the aircraft's descent into the trees. As well they were found to be suffering from the effects of smoke inhalation and shock. Both were admitted to hospital for a short period.

INVESTIGATION

The accident site

A forest of young oak and birch trees with an average height of 12m (40 feet) and a base diameter of 20-30cm begins only 60m from the northwestern end of Habsheim's grass strip 34R. Because of its steep noseup attitude and extremely low altitude, the A320 had struck the tops of these trees at the edge of the forest with the rear section of its fuselage and the tailplane.

Fifty metres in from the edge of the forest, indents left by the undercarriage and engines could be seen in the tops of the trees. Because of the thrust of the engines, some of the trees were broken off in the direction opposite to the aircraft's flightpath. Further on, as the aircraft sank into the forest, the wings had cut off the tops of the trees at lower and lower levels.

The aircraft's first contact with the trees was in line with the airstrip's centreline, and the main wreckage amongst the trees also lay on the extension of this centreline, with the tail 270m from the airfield perimeter road separating the airstrip from the forest. Only the relatively undamaged empennage, with the section of the fuselage aft of the rear pressure bulkhead, and the outer portion of the battered port wing, escaped destruction by fire. The burnt out wreckage was surrounded by a tangle of torn and broken trees.

The wreckage trail began 230m from the road, where the starboard wingtip and sections of the ailerons and slats were found. Closer to the main wreckage, there were several more sections of slats, flaps and ailerons, together with pieces broken off the empennage and cowlings, small pieces of skin, and separated engine accessories.

Recovering all these components for investigation along the short wreckage trail required some of the trees to be cut down. The heights of the tree strikes were then measured and plotted, enabling the aircraft's path through the trees to be accurately determined.

Flight recorders

The aircraft's Cockpit Voice Recorder and Digital Flight Data Recorder, both of Fairchild manufacture, were found intact and still on their mountings in the unburnt rear fuselage aft of the pressure bulkhead. Both units were flown to Paris for examination and analysis.

After the first impact with the trees, the CVR continued to operate

for about 1.5 seconds and then stopped. The DFDR continued to operate for about one second, then recorded incoherent data for another two seconds before stopping.

The only explanation for this near simultaneous shutdown of the two recorders was the severing of their power supply cables. Inspection of the tail cone where the recorders were installed showed the break could not have occurred in this section of the aircraft, which suffered little damage. Rather it seemed that the break had occurred further forward, probably in the wheel well area, where the cables would have been most exposed to impact damage.

The CVR tape was initially read out during the night of June 26 at the French Accident Investigation Bureau. The transcription was later improved with assistance from the pilots involved in the accident.

To obtain an accurate chronology of the flight, the tape feed was initially set using the 400 Hz frequency of the aircraft's electrical power supply, and the recorded radio transmissions were then correlated with air traffic control recordings of the different frequencies used, which included time tracks.

The section of the CVR recording covering the final part of the flight, as the aircraft descended from 200 feet AGL, was also examined by spectral analysis, yielding a highly accurate chronology of the final moments of the flight. This also permitted the engine speeds to be determined, and enabled a correlation to be made with a videotape of the accident, the sound track of

Seconds from its horrifying descent into the Forêt de la Hardt Sud, F-GFKC's decaying air speed may be inferred from its extreme angle of attack as it passes the crowds flanking Habsheim's 16/34 grass airstrips at extremely low level. At about this point, the crew suddenly realised that the rapidly approaching darker green area ahead was the edge of a forest – not a continuation of open fields. Their desperate application of TOGA power produced engine spool-ups fractionally faster than their book figures – but it was already too late! (Airliners magazine/Paul Bannwarth photo)

which was subjected to the same type of analysis.

The DFDR was read out by the Brétigny sur Orge Flight Test Centre, also during the night of June 26. The recording showed that the takeoff was made at 12.41pm, on a heading of 155°, and the aircraft left the ground at an IAS of 153kt. A right turn was then held for one minute until the aircraft took up a heading of 010°, and it then flew almost level at 1900ft on QNH (900-1000 feet above the ground) at an airspeed of 200kt, gradually climbing to 2000ft on QNH (see earlier maps).

Progressively, the heading changed to the left to 335-340° and at 1243:44 (12.43pm and 44 seconds), the aircraft began its descent, initially at 300 feet per minute. At 1244.14 the engine power was retarded to flight idle, and the airspeed began to slow by about one knot per second. Three seconds later, the undercarriage was extended and a further 10 seconds later the flaps, which had remained in the first detent, were extended to the second detent. At 1244:45, the 'Flaps 3' detent was selected as the aircraft descended through 500 feet at an airspeed of 177kt, still heading 334°.

At 12.45:06, with the airspeed at 155kt, the aircraft descended through the radio altimeter height of 200 feet. The barometric altitude decreased continuously, while the radio altimeter height oscillated around 200 feet (the terrain over which the aircraft was flying was not flat).

Between 1245:15 and 1245:23, now at a height of 90 feet, the aircraft made a gentle right turn to line up with the grass strip. The maximum bank angle was 13°. The airspeed fell from 149 to 141kt and the aircraft's height decreased from 90 to 46 feet. A fluctuation in the radio altimeter height was evident during this manoeuvre, corresponding to the aircraft passing over a clump of trees on the approach path. Before and after this fluctuation there was perfect agreement between the readings of the radio altimeter and the barometric altimeter.

Three seconds later, still descending, the aircraft passed through a height of 40 feet, with the airspeed at 132kt and falling, and with the engines still at flight idle (29% N_1). At this point over the airstrip, the pilot began a flare to level off, with sidestick pitch movements of low amplitude on an average of 4° nose up. The lowest altitude reached was around 30 feet, during which the sidestick, held at 4° nose up until 1245:30, was brought to 6-7° nose up

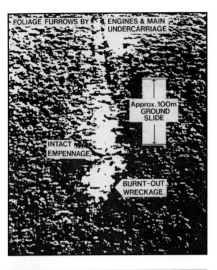

These indistinct reproductions from the French investigation report, both looking back towards the direction of aircraft's approach, at least provide an idea of the swathe cut through the forest by the descending A320 and the access difficulties faced by firecrews. (Bureau Enquetes Accidents; Matthew Tesch)

and held there. TOGA (TakeOff and Go-Around) power was applied at 1245:35, and the aircraft began striking the trees four seconds later.

The crew

Captain

Captain Michel Asseline, 44, had been an airline pilot with Air France for nearly 20 years and was endorsed on Caravelle, Boeing 707, 727, 737, Airbus A300 and A310 type aircraft. As well, for the previous three months, he had been the company's acceptance pilot for the new A320.

He had been an Air France training captain since 1979, and in December 1987 had been appointed to head the company's A320 training subdivision. In this role he was responsible for company policy and technical considerations on training, establishing aircraft utilisation practices, development of the type qualification for the A320, training of the first crews in co-operation with the manufacturer, and aircraft acceptance flights. He had not been involved in any previous accidents.

His flying in the two days preceding

the accident had included the ferrying of F-GFKC from Toulouse to Paris on the morning of Friday, June 24, and flying as an observer on an Airbus Industrie A320 on the Saturday to supervise training being given to Air France pilots. At the end of this day before the accident, he had gone home at about 7pm, spent a normal night, and slept well.

On the morning of the accident flight he had breakfasted around 6am before leaving for Charles de Gaulle Airport, where he arrived at 8.15am for briefing and flight preparation.

Copilot

Captain Pierre Mazieres, 45, was also an Air France management pilot attached to the Flight Division, having been flying with the company since 1969. He had been a training captain for six years and was experienced on Caravelle, Boeing 707 and 737. He qualified as an A320 captain three months before the accident.

He was off duty the day before the accident, spending it at his home in Paris, and had a good night's sleep. On the day of the accident he rose at 5am, had a full breakfast before leaving, and arrived at Charles de Gaulle Airport at 7.30am to prepare for the flight.

The aircraft

The Airbus Industrie A320 was brand new and had been handed over to Air France by the Toulouse manufacturer only two days earlier. It was the ninth A320 off the production line and only the third of Air France's order for the new type to be delivered. Apart from its delivery flight, and crew training trips over the past two days, it was making its first company service.

Fitted with seats for 153 passengers, it was carrying 130 passengers and a crew of six. Its total weight at the time of takeoff was 59,635kg (131,495lb), well within its maximum permissible limit, and its centre of gravity was also within specified limits.

The various parameters of the aircraft's flight, together with its control positions, as recorded on the DFDR, were examined in detail from the point at which the A320 descended through 300 feet until it struck the trees. The examination, which included extensive flight simulator tests, was conducted to ensure the behaviour of the aircraft, its control system, and its response to the crew's control inputs had been normal.

The investigation established that the performance of the flight controls complied entirely with the aircraft type's certification data and that the computerised control systems showed no characteristics likely to have created handling difficulties, even under the unusual conditions of the low level, low speed display flight.

The engines

The response of the engines was questioned by the crew immediately after the accident. The pilots claimed that, after applying TOGA power over the airstrip, the engines failed to achieve the required thrust in time to prevent the aircraft striking the trees ahead of it.

It was established from both the DFDR and the CVR that power was applied between five and 5.5 seconds before impact with the trees. The investigation therefore sought to determine what the engines parameters actually were in response to this sudden power application, and to compare these findings with the certificated performance characteristics of the engine type.

The investigators also had the engines examined in detail by the manufacturer in the SNECMA factory at Melun-Villaroche.

The engine performance after TOGA power was applied at low level over the airstrip was measured from data obtained from three independent sources:
• The engine parameters recorded on the DFDR.
• Spectral analysis of the engine sounds during the final seconds of the CVR recording.
• Eyewitness evidence of the rapid application of power in the final stages of the flyover.

It was determined that power was applied a fraction of a second after 1245:34pm and that five seconds later, according to the DFDR, the N_1 speed of the port engine was 83%, while that of the starboard engine was 84%. The spectral analysis of the engine sounds showed that both engines had reached 91% N_1 0.6 seconds later. The examination thus verified that both the response and performance of the engines was normal, and in compliance with their certification data

Flight preparation

The airshow's invitation to conduct the low level flyovers at Habsheim aerodrome in the A320 had been studied by the relevant departments within Air France, in accordance with internal company instructions. These studies in the main consisted of checking obstacle clearances in case of engine failure, and were carried out with reference to Habsheim's Runway 02/20, over which it

was understood the flyover would be made.

Although French air safety regulations officially required aircraft making such flyovers to maintain a minimum height of 170ft AGL in VFR conditions, it had long been the practice within Air France to conduct tourist and demonstration flights at airshows down to minimum altitudes of 100 feet.

This had not led to any official objections or actions from the French aviation administration or from airshow organisers, and it had become accepted within the company as normal practice.

ANALYSIS

The investigators found that the aircraft was airworthy, that its weight and centre of gravity were within limits, and that there was no evidence of any mechanical or electronic system failure that could have contributed to the accident.

Weather conditions, communication facilities or radio navigation aids played no part in the development of the accident. Both pilots were highly experienced, well qualified to fly the A320, and were medically fit.

The investigation therefore concentrated on the circumstances of the flight, its preparation, and what factors might have led the crew to follow a flightpath disastrously different from what they had planned beforehand.

Control margins

In all earlier aircraft with conventional control systems, pilots are trained to respect the dangers inherent in low speed flight, particularly at low levels. Indeed, the basic principle of maintaining a safe margin above minimum flying speed is almost second nature. It is doubtful if experienced pilots would even consider making a low level demonstration flight in a transport type aircraft close to the stall.

In this case however, the experienced pilots of the A320 did not hesitate to plan the flyover at an extremely low altitude, and at an airspeed lower then the aircraft's normal minimum flying speed. The aircraft's deceleration was planned down to a minimum flying speed, corresponding to the maximum angle of attack permitted by the aircraft's fly-by-wire control system. The captain obviously intended to demonstrate the sophistication of the A320's control system by this low speed, high angle of attack flyover, followed by a dramatic acceleration and climb. The spectacularly low level at which this was to be

carried out could only emphasise the aircraft's remarkable safety characteristics.

The training given to A320 pilots during their conversion to the type emphasised the flight protections which the aircraft's computerised control system provides, in particular the control protections that ensure lift will always be available, no matter how the controls are handled.

But sufficient emphasis was perhaps not given to the fact that, while normal flight regime limits cannot be exceeded with the A320's controls, those limits nevertheless exist. Apart from its highly complex control system, the A320 is a conventional aircraft, and while its operating limits may be approached without the risk of exceeding them and stalling the aircraft, the consequent performance of the aircraft is reduced in the same way as any other conventional aircraft. The load factor available at a minimum airspeed is able to sustain only straight and level flight, and thus precludes any recovery manoeuvres or turns. And the high drag at such low airspeeds, with the aircraft operating on the back side of the power curve, greatly limits any potential climb gradient because of the little available excess thrust.

Hasty descent

In this case it is evident that the aircraft's descent towards Habsheim aerodrome and its positioning for the flyover was conducted with haste and without time to properly stabilise the descent, or to position the aircraft at the correct height, airspeed and power setting. It was also evident that task-sharing by the crew during this time was not as planned.

The aircraft's takeoff and climb to 2000 feet on QNH lasted two minutes, during which both pilots were occupied with the management of the flight. Only at this stage were they able to begin locating and identifying Habsheim aerodrome, which was unfamiliar to them both. As a result, the descent towards the aerodrome only began when the aircraft was less than six nautical miles from the field. This distance was insufficient to both lose height and decelerate in time to stabilise the aircraft at the planned flyover speed and height before reaching the airfield.

In addition, the captain was expecting to conduct the flyover above the aerodrome's 1000m (3281ft) paved Runway 02. It was only when the aircraft was close enough to the airfield for the crew to identify the position of the airshow crowd that the captain realised the axis of the airshow was aligned, not with this runway, but with the grass airstrip 34R instead. Requiring a last minute manoeuvre to adjust the flightpath, this would have further detracted from the task of stabilising the aircraft in its flyover configuration.

The overall result was that, after taking up this new heading to line up with the correct airstrip, far from being airspeed stabilised at the planned height of 100 feet at a constant power setting, the aircraft arrived over the airfield boundary at less than 100 feet, still descending, still decelerating, with the airspeed already falling below 140 knots, and with the engines still throttled back to flight idle.

The aircraft continued to sink well below the planned flyover height as it floated down the airstrip and, as its speed continued to fall, its steep noseup attitude gradually increased. Finally, with its main undercarriage only 30 feet above the airstrip, the aircraft flared slightly to maintain this height. But seconds later, as the

crew suddenly recognised the danger posed by the trees less than 200 metres ahead, they rapidly applied power and full up sidestick.

It was too late. By this stage the airspeed had fallen to only 122 knots, the angle of attack had risen to 15°, and the aircraft had no reserves of energy remaining to convert into height. Five seconds later, as the engines were still spooling up to TOGA power, the rear of the aircraft began striking the treetops, the additional drag finally precluding any remaining possibility of staying airborne.

Engine response

The crew's impression that the engines had failed to respond adequately to the application of full power is understandable in the circumstances. From flight idle thrust, engine acceleration is slower at low airspeeds. In the CFM56-5 engines fitted to the A320, four seconds are required to accelerate from 29% N_1 to 67% N_1, but only one second more is needed to go from 67% N_1 to 83% N_1, the speed the engines had

reached when the tail of the aircraft first struck the trees.

The engine speeds actually continued to increase to 91% N_1, but by this stage the increasing drag of the rear fuselage through the treetops was more than offsetting the increasing thrust being developed, and the aircraft sank into the trees. As it did so, the engines ingested an increasing quantity of leaves and branches, which finally clogged the combustion chambers and shut the engines down.

Inadvertent loss of height

It seemed probable to the investigators that the aircraft's descent well below the planned flyover height, and its consequent dangerous positioning in relation to the trees was entirely unintentional.

In addition to the fact that there was insufficient time to stabilise the flightpath before reaching the flyover airstrip, several factors might have contributed to this error.
• The pilot in command was flying over terrain he did not know, and had no opportunity to study beforehand.
• He had been given only a short time to examine the written documents on the airshow. Not only were these very brief, but they contained no details of geographical landmarks.

(left) The aftermath of F-GFKC's descent into the trees emphasised the need for passengers to be informed of their aircraft's emergency exits and procedures. Preflight safety demonstrations, so often "honoured only in the breach" by experienced air travellers, are more than exercises for the cabin crew! The circumstances of F-GFKC's flight meant that its seats were largely filled by first-flighters without hand luggage – and their unfeigned interest in their surroundings and the safety briefing before takeoff from Basle-Mulhouse undoubtedly saved lives after the basically intact but burning fuselage jolted to a stop in the forest.
In this Airbus Industrie cabin mockup, a representative flight attendant demonstrates the A320's electronic Cabin Intercommunication Data System display. Beneath the door and cabin lighting display (top of panel), keypad options include 'Prerecorded Announcements', 'Boarding Music' selections and other audio programs. Sound and emergency lighting controls are located beneath, with smoke detector panels. Airbus claimed the CIDS software obviated the need to rewire up to 120km of cabling for cabin configuration changes. But it would obviously be of little use after impact forces have interrupted its power supply and the cabin is filling with asphyxiating smoke – as Captain Asseline and his flight attendants unhappily discovered! (Salamander Books; Airbus Industrie)

• Accustomed to demonstrating the aircraft type over airports with runways 2000m or 3000m (6560 to 9845ft) long, and control towers 100 feet or so high, he was suddenly faced with having to do so over an 600-700m grass airstrip with a control tower less than 40 feet high. The scale effect might therefore have given him the false impression that the aircraft was close to the planned flyover height.

• Because of the steep noseup attitude of the aircraft throughout the flyover, the pilot's eye level was considerably higher than the rear of the fuselage. This could have given him a false impression of the aircraft's margin of safety over obstructions in the flightpath.

• As the aircraft was being positioned for the flyover, the crew perceived the forest beyond the airfield only as a colour change from the grass of the airstrip. They identified it as a hazardous obstruction only after the aircraft had descended to its extremely low altitude in the course of the flyover.

Aircraft evacuation

Because of the circumstances in which the round trip to Mont Blanc was taking place, many of the passengers aboard the aircraft were making their first flight. They were carrying little or no hand luggage, and were unusually attentive to the safety briefing by the flight attendants, and their reference to the cabin safety cards, before takeoff.

As a result, when the aircraft came to its abrupt stop amongst the trees, even though neither the captain nor the purser succeeded in their attempts to broadcast evacuation instructions because of the failure of the aircraft's public address system, most of the passengers remembered which was their nearest emergency exit and moved towards it without losing time attempting to recover personal effects.

Even so, a number of passengers had difficulty unfastening their seatbelts because of their unfamiliarity with the mechanism, and it was this factor that ultimately led to the deaths of two of the passengers lost in the accident. The young brother of the little girl whose body was found still in seat 8C told investigators that she was unable to undo her seatbelt. He had managed to unfasten his own, but was carried away by the wave of escaping passengers before he could help his sister.

It was evident that the passenger evacuation proceeded more smoothly and quickly at the rear of the cabin than at the front. Several passengers

Compare this later view of F-GFKA pushing back on a rainy Zurich apron with the post-delivery scene at Paris (earlier page). Although this black and white reproduction cannot depict the altered hue of the French Blue paintwork, other livery variations are apparent. The base of the fin stripes has been raised above fuselage crown level, the EU's emblem of 12 gold stars has replaced the last pair of registration letters forward of the rudder hinge, and the engine nacelles have become uniform white, instead of gull-grey. Following the embarrassing loss of F-GFKC, eight months later F-GFKG [0021] was delivered as a new "Ville d'Amsterdam" and an additional Series 211, F-GKXA [0287], made up the numbers in March 1992. By the third quarter of 1998, total sales of A320s had passed 1800 aircraft. (ATW)

said later that the apparent confidence of the flight attendants at the rear door, and their words of reassurance, helped the passengers to leave the aircraft rapidly and calmly.

Two of the flight attendants had experience of past genuine emergencies, one when an Airbus A300 was hijacked at Brindisi in Italy, and the other aboard a damaged Boeing 747 which was destroyed by fire after an accident at Bombay in India. Their experiences no doubt contributed to the professional manner in which these flight attendants conducted the cabin evacuation.

Findings

• The captain had participated, as Air France's technical pilot, in developmental and test flying on the A320, during which manoeuvres were carried out beyond normal operational limitations. This could have led to overconfidence in the systems of the new technology aircraft.

• The demonstration flight had only been briefly prepared, without real consultation between the departments concerned, or with the crew.

• The presence of passengers on the aircraft probably contributed to the accident. The holiday atmosphere that prevailed amongst the passengers could have been conveyed to the captain, with unfortunate consequences.

• Descent was started 5.5nm from the aerodrome. Throughout the descent, the engines were throttled back to flight idle with the speed reducing.

• At 100ft AGL, the descent rate was still about 600fpm.

• The captain levelled off at a height of about 30ft, engines at flight idle, attitude increasing. He did not have the time to stabilise the angle of attack at the maximum value he had selected.

• Full power was rapidly applied when the angle of attack was 15° and the speed 122 knots.

• The response of the engines was normal and in compliance with their certification.

• The aircraft touched the trees with the rear section of the fuselage, then slowly sank into the forest as a result of the induced drag and the loss of engine power caused by ingestion of trees and branches.

• A violent fire broke out immediately, initially on the starboard side of the aircraft, and flames penetrated the cabin as soon as it came to rest.

• Evacuation was begun immediately by the flight attendants via the forward and rear portside doors.

• Three passengers were unable to leave the aircraft and died in the fire.

Cause

The accident resulted from a combination of the following:

• flyover height lower than surrounding obstacles;

• slow speed, reducing to reach maximum angle of attack;

• engines at flight idle;

• late application of go-around power.

An unusual angle on Indian Airlines' first A320-231, VT-EPB [0045], taken during its maiden flight on March 30, 1989. The aircraft displays its pre-delivery test registration, F-WWDY, forward of the tailplane leading edge, although its wings are already 'correctly' inscribed. After lengthy negotiations and design specifications, Airbus Industrie's first A320 Asian sales success came on March 15, 1986, with India's order for 19 plus 12 options. Worth more than one billion US dollars, even this order was eclipsed less than seven months later by Northwest's commitment to more than 100 A320s. But IA's contracted fleet remained the largest after Air Inter and Lufthansa. IA had been an Airbus enthusiast since the consortium's dark early days in 1973, when it was offered three A300B2s at bargain prices. Unfortunately, the human error aspect of the Bangalore disaster was only underlined 22 months later, when the first of these 'discount' A300s, VT-EDV [034], was involved in a fuel starvation accident in a rice paddy northwest of Madras. Although the A300 was destroyed, fortunately none of its 263 passengers and crew were killed. (Airbus Industrie)

Recommendations

As a result of its findings on this accident, the French Investigation Commission recommended that:

• such display flights be made without passengers and with minimum crew, including only those required to carry out the flight;

• preparation of such display flights include, as a minimum, the standards already provided for in the regulations;

• a comprehensive flight safety brief be prepared, specifying flight parameters to be observed, and procedures to be followed in case of a failure;

• a meeting be held between the crew and the departments participating in the flight preparation well in advance of the scheduled date;

• effective reconnaissance be made of the site where the display flight is to take place;

• where possible, practice flights be made in a simulator, with special attention to critical aspects which could result from non observance of the flight parameters, especially in case of a failure;

• on all passenger carrying flights the use of the seatbelt mechanism be demonstrated during passenger safety briefings;

• such procedures should also be illustrated on the safety instruction card for passengers.

• seatbelt manufacturers be informed of the advantage of unlocking systems in which a single simple action causes both unlocking and separation of the two halves of the belt.

Comment:

The untimely destruction of one of the first of the much vaunted new A320s, immediately after it was handed over to Airbus Industrie's initial and probably most prestigious customer, was a major blow to the morale of the manufacturer.

The fact that the whole flyover sequence, the descent into trees, and the immediate outbreak of fire, was captured on a high quality video camera and subsequently screened on television throughout the world did nothing to help. Even before any more than the barest details of the accident became public, the media and some sections of the aviation press, who perhaps should have known better, were quick to point the finger of blame at the aircraft's revolutionary Fly-By-Wire control system.

Others, perhaps more conscious of Airbus Industrie's misfortune, pointed out that it was the type of accident which could occur in any aircraft when a pilot, under pressure to carry out a maximum performance manoeuvre, made a fatal error of judgement. Indeed, many felt it was the sort of accident that has been recurring throughout the history of aviation whenever exuberance on the spur of the moment has got the better of a pilot's prudence.

And so the French investigation was to prove in due course – but not for a long 17 months, when the final report of the Investigation Commission was at last completed – Airbus Industrie itself doing all it could in the meantime to prove that its fine aircraft and its systems were not at fault.

Even then the manufacturer's reprieve was to be all too short. Less than three months after the publication of the exonerating report on the tragedy at Habsheim, another near new A320 was to come to grief, this time during a normal approach to land in favourable weather. This second accident was to send shock waves, not only through Airbus, but the world airline industry as a whole, some sections of which were anxiously awaiting deliveries of their own A320s.

Tragedy in India

Airbus Industrie A320-231 VT-EPN [079] was delivered new to Indian Airlines on December 22, 1989. Less than three months later, on February 14, 1990 (by which time it had logged only 370 hours), it was operating Flight IC605, a domestic service from Bombay to Bangalore, where it was expected to land at about 1pm local time.

Formed as an autonomous nationalised corporation in 1953, Indian Airlines' route network has become as much regional as domestic, stretching over more than 70 ports from Muscat in the Persian Gulf to Singapore, and from Kathmandu to Colombo. The corporation also offers overnight express mail and cargo deliveries between its four most populous bases. The ill-fated IC605 service to Bangalore operated from one such base at Bombay. Traffic demands from the world's largest democracy impose a ceaseless strain on IA management. By the end of the protracted A320 negotiations in 1985-86, the airline was carrying more than 23,000 passengers on over 210 services every day, and was in fact forced to top-up its 737-200 fleet well ahead of its first deliveries of the sophisticated Airbus in 1989!

With a distinct national service obligation and no small degree of political interference, IA's intense operations and its safety record have come under periodic, if misplaced, criticism. The geographically and ethnically diverse land, with overworked and under equipped air transport facilities, prompts many parallels with Russia and other regions of the former USSR. Numerous doubts were expressed about the wisdom of making the technological leap from proven, rugged Boeings to the hi-tech Airbus A320, and such fears actually led to an announced intention to merge Indian Airlines with Air India under a new identity and a reorganised operational structure. But the 1987 target date came and went, fierce lobbying ensuring the status quo remained – at least until the painful deregulation of the country's airline industry in the early 1990s. (Matthew Tesch)

The Airbus, carrying 139 passengers and five cabin staff, was crewed by two Indian Airlines captains. One, flying the aircraft from the left hand seat, was undergoing his first route check for command endorsement on the A320. The other was his check captain, serving as first officer in the right hand seat. The weather conditions were described as fine, with good visibility, and should not logically have caused any problems.

Bangalore Airport was not ILS equipped but, as weather conditions were excellent, there was no apparent reason why the aircraft could not continue safely, and the crew were cleared to make a visual approach to Runway 09.

On final approach, with the undercarriage extended for landing, the aircraft deviated below the glide path. Descending rapidly well short of the runway at reduced airspeed, the aircraft assumed a steep noseup attitude. At an altitude of about 140ft substantial power was applied, but this failed to check the aircraft's high rate of descent, and it struck the ground heavily with its main undercarriage on a golf course 700m short of the runway threshold.

The airliner bounced, tore its way through a clump of small trees, touched down again on a green, impacted against a stone embankment forming the course perimeter, shearing off both engines, bounced again over a small gully, slid across a road and finally came to a stop close to the airport boundary. It immediately burst into flames.

Ninety-two of the 146 people aboard – including both pilots and two of the five flight attendants –

Another view of F-WWDY (VT-EPB), lifting through V_2 on its maiden takeoff from Toulouse. This picture emphasises the two particular aspects – powerplant and undercarriage – of IA's A320 order. Forsaking not only more conventional and less technologically demanding aircraft types on offer, but also the well proven CFM56-5 engine, Indian Airlines gave the newer, more efficient, but more expensive V2500 engine and its International Aero Engine manufacturers their first major A320 order. IA furthermore insisted on Airbus Industrie's optional four wheel main undercarriage bogie, giving a load spreading advantage over the standard, heavily-weighted twin wheel axles. This was critical for operations on the lower pavement strengths at many of its network ports.

died as a result of the crash and the ensuing fire, which totally destroyed the aircraft. Most of the survivors were injured, 21 passengers and one crew member seriously. Fire crews, who arrived a full 20 minutes after the crash, could do nothing.

The absence of a radio link between the fire service and the control tower increased the response time taken by the emergency crews. A poorly maintained airport road and a locked security gate also hampered the fire and rescue vehicles in reaching the crash scene promptly, a fact which probably contributed to the high death toll.

Check captain unchecked!

Analysis of the CVR tape disclosed that the trainee captain flew the aircraft for most of the flight, with the check captain monitoring his progress. But during the final 30 minutes, the check captain flew the aircraft while he asked questions of the other for training and checking purposes.

The check captain was an experienced airline pilot with some 10,000 hours' airline flying time, mainly on turboprop and Boeing 737 aircraft. But he had flown only some 68 hours on the A320 and Airbus Industrie had not authorised him as a check captain on the aircraft type –

he was one of at least five such Indian Airlines check captains in this situation. The trainee captain was also an experienced airline pilot with a similar number of flying hours, and needed only to be checked out on the A320.

Investigation revealed that the check captain's flight director was in the Open Descent Idle Mode (ODIM), which would have prevented the autothrottle from reverting to the vertical speed mode, the prescribed setting for the approach and landing phase of flight.

The crew were not conducting the landing approach as Airbus Industrie specified. In ODIM, the autothrottle is held at flight idle, with the result that the aircraft could only lose both speed and height. With its angle of attack controlled by its computerised systems, the A320's nose pitched up to try to maintain the correct flightpath, but was unable to do so at idle power. The situation was exacerbated by the lowering of undercarriage and the selection of the 'Flaps 3' position for the approach.

The check captain obviously failed to monitor the safety of the approach as required by the A320 Flight Crew Operating Manual. Neither crew member monitored the aircraft's speed, nor adequately, its

height. At one stage the check captain acknowledged that the aircraft was in ODIM mode and later the trainee captain suggested that the heading/vertical speed mode be used.

Steep descent

But for reasons unknown, the crew apparently continued the approach in Open Descent Idle Mode, in direct contravention of the Flight Crew Operating Manual. The aircraft was by this stage descending rapidly and it should have been obvious that it would not reach the runway. At a height of about 500ft the aircraft's airspeed fell below that recommended for the approach, and continued to decrease down to about 25kt below it.

This situation lasted for about 30 seconds. Neither pilot heeded the four radio altimeter alerts, nor the two sink rate voice warnings, for no recovery action was taken. Only at a height of about 140ft, with the aircraft at minimum speed, maximum angle of attack and at a very steep angle of descent, did the crew finally realise their desperate situation.

The trainee captain shouted "Hey! We are going down!!" and pushed the thrust levers fully forward to the TOGA position. In fact the computerised Alpha Floor activation – the

Rescuers brave the heat and stench of smoking piles of charred debris that, less than an hour before, had been a gleaming, five month old A320. The 13th of Indian Airlines' firmly ordered 19, VT-EPN had been ferried out from France only two days before Christmas 1989. For the unfortunates aboard the A320 when it crashed, the aircraft's relatively low forward speed was nullified by its high descent rate and resulting sequence of hard bounces. Miraculously, more than a third of the A320's occupants survived, but more than half of them had severe injuries. The rate at which IA had been placing its new type in service – one per fortnight throughout the second half of 1989 – meant that the company's check and training captains, far from being accredited by Airbus Industrie, were themselves lacking in type experience. In the eyes of many industry commentators, concerns about IA over reaching its capabilities had been tragically vindicated. This perception of the dangers of operating hi-tech equipment in a low-tech environment did little to allay the qualms of would-be A320 customers. (UPI/Bettmann photo)

F-GGEB [0012], Air Inter's second A320, nearing the holding point for Runway 05 at Nice's Cote d'Azur Airport. The opened cabin air outflow valve (starboard side only) is distinct on the lower aft fuselage, just forward of the rear cabin door. The bold navy 'A320' logo straddling the forward cargo door first appeared on the third A320 prototype on June 18, 1987. As F-WWDB, that aircraft was painted in Air Inter's penultimate triple banded, blue toned cheatline livery during its 2^1/$_2$ years of test and demonstration flying – and the prominent, Airbus applied designation was adopted as a permanent addition. The ill-fated F-GGED first flew on November 4, 1988 in identical colours, becoming the fourth Air Inter A320 in revenue service a few days before Christmas that year. (WAFN-M/Alessandro Maffiodo)

automatic go around mode – had already begun to accelerate both engines with a response that was actually better than their certificated figures.

But it was too late. Both crew members instinctively pulled their sidesticks to full noseup elevator, a control input which, in any other aircraft type, would have resulted in a catastrophic stall. But the computerised flight control system limited the noseup attitude to the maximum permissible angle of attack. Though effective in preventing a disastrous stall, it could do little to check the aircraft's high rate of descent because of the crew's late reaction, and it struck the ground extremely heavily in a noseup attitude.

The accident was finally attributed to incorrect use of the aircraft's highly sophisticated flight control system. The Indian Directorate General of Civil Aviation had previously

advised the airline that the check captain should be "positively monitored" in such areas as operation of the FMGS used on the A320. His own A320 instructors had in fact noted "... numerous small errors and omissions ..." with the FMGS and mishandling of the aircraft's power controls.

Again, despite all the adverse publicity that such a fatal airline accident engenders, prompting the grounding of Indian's A320 fleet pending the outcome of the investigation, Airbus Industrie and the new era A320 had been exonerated of any shortcoming that could have contributed to the accident.

Elsewhere indeed, in different parts of the world, the A320 was proving to be a safe and eminently reliable aircraft when correctly flown within the parameters of its designed flight envelope. But for the Toulouse manufacturer, the problems

with the reputation of the now controversial A320 were not yet over – for even worse was to come.

Back on the doorstep!

Nearly two years later, Airbus Industrie A320-111 F-GGED [015], belonging to France's own domestic airline, Air Inter, was operating Flight IT148 from Satolas Airport at Lyons to Strasbourg's Entzheim Airport on the winter evening of January 20, 1992. Well known as a dedicated Airbus customer since the first days of the manufacturer, Air Inter had no less than 26 A320s and 22 A300s flying its routes.

The aircraft, under the command of Captain Christian Hecquet, a man described as calm, serious and cautious, had arrived at Lyons from Paris and Marseilles at 4.45pm. Its turnaround at Lyons was entirely normal with no maintenance problems reported, and after its 90

Five days after the Bangalore accident, the Indian civil aviation authority ordered the grounding of the 14 A320s so far in IA service, and embargoed outstanding deliveries from Airbus Industrie – an inevitable bureaucratic response to Indian Airlines' overstressed capabilities, rather than an indictment of the A320. The real wonder is that Airbus Industrie kept both its corporate head and its customers' faith during this difficult period. And Indian Airlines can be credited with successfully weathering the storm. The retirement plans for its ageing 737s had to be reversed for a time, but it exercised its dozen Airbus options after all. Its 30 A320s (VT-EPN was not replaced) now make up its primary fleet, together with a number of A300Bs of various marques. (Flight International)

Elegant on its maiden flight in clear Pyrenean skies on January 13, 1989, Air Inter's fifth A320-111, F-GGEE [0016], displays the smartened livery to be adopted fleetwide. Cheatlines and belly grey now deleted, the traditional bright red and French Blue titles and fin flourishes were now accented in a more Groupe Air France house style. The continuous sash of sky blue wrapping around the empennage was a concession to Air Inter's original blue toned image, dating back to its first five Viscount 708s in 1962. At the time F-GGEE was handed over at Toulouse on February 15, 1989, Air Inter's A320 commitment had almost doubled from its initial 12, to 13 firm orders and 11 options, the additions comprising the now almost universal 200 Series aircraft. (Airbus Industrie)

Strasbourg bound passengers had been ushered aboard by its cabin crew of four, it departed in the dark for the one hour flight at 5.20pm.

The European weather was typical for the time of the year, with a north-easterly wind gusting up to 35 knots, three octas of stratocumulus cloud at 1000ft, six octas at 2500ft, and a visibility of 15km in freezing drizzle. There was no high cloud of any significance.

The enroute flight at cruising level was without incident and, nearing its destination, Reims Control cleared the aircraft to descend to Flight Level 70 (7000 feet) and to call Strasbourg Approach on 120.7MHz. This the crew did at 6.08pm, advising they were 22 DME from Strasbourg. The aircraft was cleared to continue descent to 5000 feet on QNH and to report at Andlo, 12nm southwest of the airport. The crew then completed their Initial Approach checklist.

The ATIS at Entzheim Airport (elevation 502ft) was transmitting Information Oscar, reporting Runway 05 in use, the wind 040° at 30kt, visibility greater than 10km, cloud cover three octas at 1100ft and six octas at 2600ft, temperature 1°.

When the crew reported passing Andlo at 7500ft, still descending, Approach Control informed them they were "No 1" for the VOR DME approach procedure to Runway 05.

But the captain, concerned that they were too high and too fast for a straight in approach, indicated they would instead overfly the field to the Outer Marker northeast of the airport, make an ILS approach downwind towards Runway 23, then do a visual circling approach to Runway 05.

Replying, Approach Control told the Airbus to hold at 5000ft, and that they might have to enter the holding pattern over the Outer Marker before manoeuvring for Runway 05 because three IFR aircraft were now in the process of departing from Runway 05.

At this, the captain, anxious to save time said, "We'll go back and do the VOR DME procedure then."

Approach Control then offered to vector the aircraft back to Andlo at 5000 feet, as it would "save you some time".

Vectored while still southwest of the airport, the aircraft was instructed to turn left onto a heading of 230° then to pass Andlo inbound again at 5000ft. The crew were then cleared to establish the A320 on the 051° radial for their final approach. They had selected the second stage of flap and lowered the undercarriage for landing when they were further instructed to report passing over the VOR. Their acknowledgement was the last transmission from the aircraft, and moments later it disappeared from the controller's radar screen.

Isolated peaks rising to nearly 4000ft lie immediately to the northwest of Andlo. As the A320 was completing a left turn to line up on final approach, inexplicably now down to a height of only 2600ft, it struck the pine forested upslope of Mt La Bloss (2700 feet), 10nm southwest of the airport and less than a kilometre to the northwest of the extended runway centreline.

The A320 was destroyed by the impact and the fire that followed, and all but eight passengers and one flight attendant, who were seated in the rear of the cabin between seat rows 28 to 31, were killed.

The subsequent investigation found that the aircraft, while descending at an angle of no less than 12°, and banked about 18° to the left, had struck 25m trees on the western slope of La Bloss, cutting a swathe through the pine forest 120m long. The aircraft was fragmented, only the tailcone aft of the APU firewall escaping destruction.

The survivors, most of whom were experienced air travellers, said they had no warning of the accident, which occurred in total darkness. The descent did not appear to be abnormal, and they had felt no sensation of a rapid descent. All had their seatbelts fastened, as the cabin staff had requested on the aircraft's PA system a short time before.

Those survivors who were not seriously injured helped the ones who were, gathering close to a fire near the tail to keep warm, while they waited for rescue.

Incorrect mode again?

The investigation was unable to determine the exact sequence of events leading to the aircraft's unplanned loss of height so far from the airport, but a primary factor was believed to have been an error in using the Flight Control Unit on the flightdeck glareshield. Either the crew had selected the wrong mode or confused two different modes, resulting in an excessive rate of descent that went undetected.

The FCU could have been inadvertently set in the heading/vertical speed mode instead of the intended track/flightpath mode (recommended by both Airbus Industrie and Air Inter for VOR/DME approaches), with the crew then dialling in "33", believing that they were entering the 3.3° slope command used for the VOR/DME approach at Strasbourg. But the error would have instead dialled in a descent rate of 3300fpm, roughly that of the A320 moments before impact.

It could not be determined why the crew did not detect that a wrong mode had been selected – or that the aircraft was descending at such a high rate, more than four times that of a normal approach.

The modes are selected with a push button on the FCU. When the track/flightpath mode is entered, the letters TRK FPA appear in the FCU's display window band and the mode is also shown on the pilot's primary CRT flight display. Similarly, when the heading/vertical speed mode is chosen, the letters HDG and V/S appear in the FCU display window band, and on the Primary Flight Display.

The comparative inexperience of both the captain and the first officer on A320 aircraft undoubtedly contributed to the accident. Of his total flying experience of nearly 9000 hours, the captain had only 160 hours on the type, and the first officer, with a total of 3600 hours, had only 60. Their co-ordination and communications as a crew also left something to be desired. Neither were wearing headsets, and the captain's decision to make a non precision approach in the existing weather after initially planning an ILS approach probably exacerbated the situation.

The CVR readout showed that the crew had relaxed their attention during the radar guidance by Strasbourg Approach Control, apparently leaving the vertical navigation entirely to the aircraft's automated systems. Their attitude in this regard could possibly have been influenced by the short haul nature of Air Inter's domestic operations, with many landings being carried out automatically. The last words on the CVR were from the first officer with regard to

Early morning startup for F-GHQC [0044], Air Inter's third Series 211 and one of its then 23 strong A320 fleet, ultimately to increase to 32. But only the earlier deliveries of the seven stretched 321s ordered would fly in these Air Inter markings. The balance, plus subsequent A319s, and the remainder of the company's almost exclusively Airbus Industrie fleet were to be reflagged (see map caption earlier in this chapter) before losing their separate identity entirely. In this scene, late in the northern summer of 1991, the parent group's holding makes its corporate mark beneath the flightdeck side windows, and the European flag adjoins the aircraft's registration above the aft cabin windows. Such was the appearance of F-GGED at the time of its loss near Strasbourg shortly afterwards. (Flight International)

the aircraft's alignment with the approach track. A moment afterwards the radio altimeter suddenly sounded "two hundred feet", and the recording then ended with the impact.

As a result of this accident, the Investigation Commission made a number of recommendations with regard to crew training and operations on advanced technology aircraft.

• That operators be informed of the risk of confusion between heading/vertical speed mode and track/flightpath mode, and requested to examine their inflight crew procedures, documentation, and the understanding crews have of the various flight modes.

• That the flightdeck ergonomics of actually handling the flight modes be studied with a view to modifications that would lessen the risk of selection errors, and improve the likelihood of immediately detecting any error. At the time of the accident, Airbus Industrie had already introduced a modification to the Flight Control Unit, incorporating a different display to prevent confusion between the two modes. The manufacturer intended to retrofit all aircraft already in service.

• That regulations be amended to require French public transport aircraft to be equipped with a Ground Proximity Warning System, under the same technical conditions as specified in the Chicago Convention.

Changes were also recommended to existing regulations on emergency locator beacons fitted to aircraft. Because the beacons installed on F-GGED were destroyed in the accident, local emergency services

unnecessarily lost valuable time trying to locate the exact site of the crash. This delay in rescue probably cost the lives of another six victims who had survived the impact but died before help could arrive to attend to them.

A past problem recalled

In a sense, the saga of the three A320 accidents, all related to human factors in operating the type's advanced technology control system, rather than to the integrity of the control system itself, recalled the airline industry's unhappy experience with the outstandingly successful Boeing 727 soon after it was first introduced in the 1960s.

The first of a new generation of jet aircraft, the Boeing 727 was designed for short haul, multi stage domestic airline services. Because of its need to make frequent landings, it had powerful flaps and high lift leading edge devices which gave it far more versatile flight characteristics than earlier, long range jetliners. Yet these very qualities also conveyed the impression to pilots that greater control liberties could be taken with the aircraft.

With the Boeing 727's large flaps, high rates of descent could develop more easily than in earlier jet types, requiring high power, time for the engines to spool up, and ample vertical airspace to correct. Indeed, simply to maintain a normal approach glidepath in the early Boeing 727s with full flap extended required no less than 47% power. And with the engines throttled back to flight idle, the aircraft would descend at more than 2000fpm, a rate impossible to

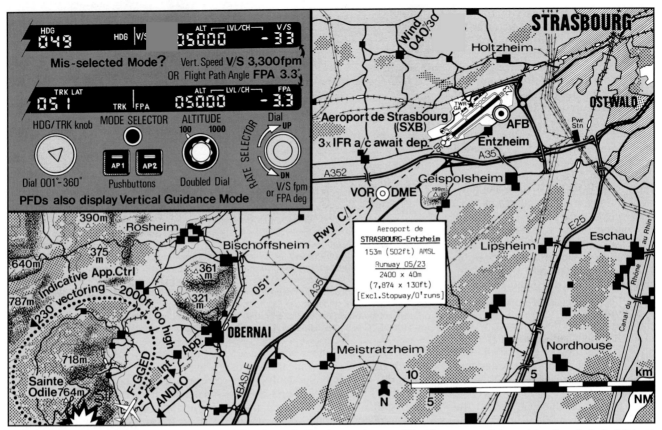

This map of the Alsace plains, from southwest of Strasbourg to the steep outcrops of the Vosges mountains, relates the city to its joint use military airport at Entzheim, and shows the A320's flightpath to the crash site. The inset (top left) depicts a section of the computerised Flight Control Unit on the A320's flightdeck glareshield (refer photograph earlier this chapter) to show the control options so fatally mis-selected by the Air Inter pilots. (Matthew Tesch)

check quickly. The result, in the early years of the type's operations, was a spate of accidents during approaches to land which occurred simply because the crew allowed an excessive rate of descent to develop which they were unable check before the aircraft flew into the ground.

But once this operational problem was recognised, approach techniques devised to avoid unintentionally developing high rates of descent, and crew training implemented accordingly, the difficulty disappeared, and the Boeing 727 went on to become one of the world's most successful and widely used airline aircraft.

The control mode selection problems with the A320 appeared to be in much the same category – a matter that required little more than full recognition of the problem, the measures needed to combat it, and consequent enhanced crew training.

It could also be remarked that, as with some of the early Boeing 727 accidents (see *Air Disaster* Vol 1, Chapter 4), the lack of flightdeck crew co-ordination, task sharing and monitoring – in other words 'Cockpit Resource Management', to give it its vogue title – appears to have played a major part in the development of the three A320 accidents.

And it may not be insignificant that in a number of cases, involving both the Boeing 727 and the Airbus Industrie A320, the aircraft concerned was being crewed by two experienced captains, rather than a captain and a first officer – paradoxically prompting a breakdown in the ordered, systematic flightdeck discipline that is so essential to consistently safe airline operations!

Footnote:
(1) The powerline pylons to which the copilot was referring were 1.5km beyond the aerodrome (see maps for highlighted reference).

Strasbourg: The ancient Alsatian capital has been the seat of the Council of Europe since 1949, and now hosts the monthly sittings of the European Parliament. It was also the fledgling Air Inter's inaugural destination. Formed at the end of 1954 by Air France and the French National Railways as a specifically domestic operation, Air Inter flew its first Paris/Strasbourg service on March 17, 1958. Using a variety of leased aircraft, other routes were added over the following three years on a cautious summer-only basis. Year round operations began four years later in 1962 with the five Viscount 708s mentioned earlier. The midwinter weather prevailing across the continent exactly 30 years later on January 20, 1992 set the scene for a unhappy Air Inter anniversary – shortly before the end of the company's contribution to European aviation history.

CHAPTER 2

"It all happened so fast, no one actually saw it"

– Passenger describing explosive decompression

United Airlines Boeing 747-122 N4713U [19875] (F/n 8313)
– February 24, 1989

To nine unsuspecting passengers travelling in Business Class, it seemed a normal enough international night flight. But a fault in the operating system of the cargo hold door beneath their seats proved a timebomb which sealed their fate.

Honolulu departure

For passengers boarding the United Airlines Boeing 747 at Honolulu in the balmy small hours of a tropical February night – a dark, moonless one with more than the threat of rain – it seemed a routine enough international departure.

They were bound for Auckland and Sydney, aboard the long transoceanic flight which Pan American Airways had pioneered under difficulties more than 50 years before – a service which, apart from the interruption of World War 2, had been operating since 1937, when an island hopping route was developed across the Pacific to New Zealand with four engined Sikorsky S-42 flying boats.

To some of the passengers joining Flight 811 for the first time at Honolulu, the elderly Boeing 747 looked its age, its weather-beaten paintwork and tarnished metal betraying years of hard work on the company's services across the world. But for the many others who had embarked at Los Angeles hours earlier, the scene seemed unremarkable – just another routine reboarding on a long and uneventful night flight, after a stop for refuelling around 1am – and they were eager to resume the rest of their trans Pacific journey.

A few passengers were in fact on this particular aircraft by a late

choice. Originally ticketed to Sydney on a United Airlines direct flight departing from Los Angeles shortly before this one, their long range Boeing 747 had been overbooked, evidently because of a computer error. As it happened, the second flight, via Honolulu, still had empty seats, and United Airlines staff at the Los Angeles terminal had appealed

The vastness of the Pacific is evident in this hemispheric view of Flight 811's planned route. The chain of remote islands that demanded such exacting navigation by early landplane and flying boat crews become little more than waypoints of interest in the INS/GPS era of the Boeing 747. The Pacific Ocean covers more of the planet than all its landmasses combined. (Matthew Tesch)

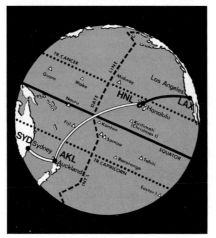

for volunteers to transfer to this aircraft instead. As an inducement, passengers who agreed to do so were offered concessions in exchange for their inconvenience. For a least one Sydney bound passenger, it was a fateful decision.

With a fresh, rested crew aboard for the next leg to Auckland, there was a short delay at Honolulu after all 337 passengers were in their seats – the cabin crew experienced a little difficulty arming one of the cabin doors' emergency exit slides. But finally all cabin and cargo door warning lights were correctly extinguished on the flight engineer's panel, and the aircraft left the gate at 1.33am local time, with the captain at the controls.

Cleared for takeoff from Honolulu's Runway 08R 19 minutes later, the aircraft climbed initially to the left of track, still under surveillance by Approach Control, to avoid thunderstorm buildups which the crew could see from the flightdeck, as well as on the aircraft's weather radar. Because of the thunderstorm activity close to the aircraft's route, the captain decided to leave the passenger seatbelt signs switched on.

Sixteen minutes after takeoff, as they were continuing the climb to cruising level, passing between 22,000 and 23,000 feet, the crew were startled by a sudden thump behind and below them, which shook the whole aircraft. But even before they had time to think, the jolt was followed by an enormous, mind-shattering explosion. The aircraft lurched violently to port, the wind noise instantly intensified to a deafening level, there was an immediate and fierce decompression, with powerful suction, accompanied by a sudden misting of the flightdeck and cabin interior, and the lights went out.

As they were plunged into darkness, the crew's momentary thought was "another Lockerbie!" – and they mentally braced themselves for the worst. But the feared aircraft breakup and loss of control did not eventuate, the emergency lighting came on, then full electrical power was restored.

Moments later the cabin altitude warning horn sounded and the crew grabbed for their oxygen masks – but no oxygen seemed to flow. Throwing the aircraft into an emergency descent, the captain turned 180° to the left to avoid a thunderstorm, and took up a heading back towards Honolulu.

The crew found they were still able to communicate with one another verbally and it was now evident to them that the No 3 engine was rapidly losing power. The first officer dialled in the emergency code on the aircraft's transponder, and declared an emergency to Approach Control. Despite the intense noise level, he experienced no difficulties in communicating with Air Traffic Control. Seconds later, heavy vibration in the No 3 engine, with no N_1 indication, low exhaust gas temperature (EGT), and low engine pressure ratio (EPR) forced the crew to shut the engine down.

All the crews' attempts to contact the flight attendants on the interphone system proved fruitless. So as soon as the No 3 engine had been secured, the captain asked the flight

"Another Lockerbie!" Ten years before this volume went to press, Flight PA103 was destroyed by a terrorist bomb about an hour after takeoff from London. But for the shocked United crew, climbing to cruising level out of Honolulu, the destruction of the PanAm 747 had occurred only 10 weeks earlier, on December 21, 1988. Photographs of its relatively intact nose lying in a Scottish heath, and the massive crater left by the ill-fated 747 in the village of Lockerbie, had been recent front-page news in the world's press. (HARS/MT & ATW)

engineer to check the condition of the passenger cabins himself.

Going back into the upper deck cabin, the flight engineer was aghast to see a gaping hole in the starboard side fuselage skin. The major section missing extended up to the level of the cabin windows, leaving only the fuselage formers and stringers between the cabin and the outside air. Most of the cabin lining had been sucked away by the force of the decompression, leaving the upper deck passengers buffeted by exposure to the intense slipstream and noise.

Hurrying then down the spiral staircase to the lower deck, the flight engineer was numbed by an even more appalling sight – about three metres of the starboard side of the fuselage, from floor to ceiling, had been torn away completely, leaving the main deck business class cabin ('Zone B' – see diagram) wide open to the shrieking elements. More horrifying still, a block of five rows of the double window seats on the starboard side – 10 seats in total – together with the cabin flooring above the forward cargo hold, had

utterly vanished into the night with the fuselage structure, taking with them their unsuspecting but doomed occupants!

The enormous wind noise and draught was deafening and the whole main cabin was in utter chaos. Terrified passengers were shouting and screaming, some hysterically, not knowing what was to happen. Panel linings on the walls and ceilings had been torn loose by the decompression, and accumulated dirt, dust and other debris showered over passengers. Drinking glasses and meal trays had been hurled with such violence by the escaping air pressure that some of them had become embedded in the cabin walls!

Passengers were dishevelled by the battering they were still receiving, and a number were bleeding from injuries inflicted by flying debris. Some were using the aircraft's emergency oxygen masks, but many masks had failed to deploy. Some passengers, more resigned, were sitting still, awaiting instructions. Others, realising the aircraft was going down, had already taken up the crash position, fearfully apprehensive for whatever was to come.

In the midst of the bedlam, hard pressed cabin staff were desperately trying to get passengers to put on their lifejackets – and to stay in their seats. Believing a ditching in the sea to be inevitable, and probably imminent, most of the flight attendants had begun preditching preparations.

From the rear of the aircraft, looking forward from the starboard side cabin windows immediately after the decompression, both engines had appeared to be engulfed in flames. The flames had subsided on the No 3 engine after its shutdown, but now the jetpipe of the No 4 engine was intermittently spitting long tongues of fire, sometimes reaching back as far as the 747's tail.

Running quickly back up the stairs, the flight engineer caught sight of the upper deck flight attendant, now wearing her oxygen mask and lifejacket and strapped into her seat, holding up the aircraft's safety instruction card, and a spare lifejacket, for passengers to see. She had resorted to communicating with her passengers this way because it was impossible to make herself heard over the wind noise.

Back on the flightdeck itself, the flight engineer found the two pilots wanting to shut down the No 4 engine also, because of its high EGT, no N_1 indication, and the flashes of fire it was emitting. At the captain's instructions, when this was done,

The ailing PanAm's sale of its trans Pacific routes was a desperate move by a former giant of the US airline industry. Another giant was the winning bidder, and United made its Australian debut on February 12, 1986. Its 747-122 N4717U [19878] "Edward E Carlson" is seen here after its inaugural Melbourne turnaround, pushing back from Tullamarine's International Terminal. The long-established 811/812 & 815/816 flight numbers were retained, as were the former "Clipper" 747SPs, until the advent of the 747-400. (Aircraft & Aerospace)

the flight engineer proceeded to dump much of the fuel that had been pumped into the tanks at Honolulu a short time before, to reduce the aircraft's weight in readiness for an emergency landing back on the airport. With both engines out now on the starboard side, the crew were holding on left bank to offset the asymmetric drag.

Meanwhile, on the main deck, despite the overwhelming noise and chaotic cabin conditions, flight attendants courageously continued attending to passengers in need, as they went on with preparations for their expected ditching – treating the many minor injuries, helping those having difficulties donning lifejackets, holding up safety cards, briefing able-bodied passengers to assist with the expected evacuation, clearing cabin debris away from all the exits, and instructing passengers in bracing themselves for impact.

As they did so, it became tragically evident that, in addition to the eight passengers lost with their seats when the fuselage structure blew out, one passenger, sitting in a centre block seat closest to the starboard side aisle, had been plucked from his seat and ejected from the aircraft by the explosive force of the decompression – either because his seat belt had not been fastened, or it was not tight enough.

A young woman passenger in the forward economy section later described her own experience:

We had been flying for about 20 minutes and I was listening to my portable CD player when suddenly there was an enormous bang – like an explosion – followed by a tremendous rush of wind and a continuous very loud roaring noise. The cabin lights went out and I didn't know what had happened.

I tried not to panic and, pulling my headphones off, I grappled for my belongings under my feet. I also managed to grab my coat – just as it was being sucked away. As well as this great roar of wind noise and suction, there was an incredible amount of debris flying through the cabin – in front of me I could see the cabin ceiling had just about been ripped right out. I struggled against the rush of air to get my seatbelt buckle done up.

By this time I finally realised what was happening – all the debris flying through the cabin was being violently sucked out through a hole in the side of the aircraft somewhere ahead of where we were sitting. I didn't know how big the hole was – the lights had come on again but I couldn't see it because there was a galley in the way – between me and where the hole was, as I found out later.

It was hard to breathe when it first happened – then the oxygen masks fell down. But only about half of them appeared. It was also hard to hear anything because of the enormous wind noise and

draught throughout the cabin. I had no hope of hearing what was being said on the speakers, but the flight attendants were doing their best to let everyone know to put their lifejackets on – and to stay in our seats.

People all around me were screaming. I thought we were going to ditch into the sea – and horrible visions flashed through my mind of what could happen if we did. I prepared myself for anything, or at least I tried to. As I put my lifejacket on, I thought I'd come to the end of my life – I really thought I was going to die, and I started crying and praying at the same time with my face in my hands.

There was one lady in particular I remember well, sitting in the middle seats just behind me. She was screaming hysterically and had blood all over her clothes from where some of the cabin debris had hit her. The blood really showed up because she was wearing white.

I knew we were coming down, because the air pressure on my ears was becoming intense and the ringing wouldn't stop. I happened to look around and saw a Japanese man stumbling down the aisle. Some other passengers and I tried to tell him to sit down, but he didn't seem to understand. Another Australian passenger from across the other side of the aisle and I finally got him into the empty seat next to mine. Although it had been broken by some flying debris, we managed

Boeing 747-122 N4718U [19879] "Thomas F Gleed" was among the first of United's 339-strong fleet to be repainted after the company's June 1974 livery unveiling (see also Vol 2, pp 39 & 188). It is seen here as it taxis west off Honolulu's main apron, wings sagging with its load of fuel, to depart for Los Angeles. Runway 08L/26R is in the foreground, while behind, framed by the Koolau Range, the control tower can be seen atop the airport's operations building. The 707s beyond the 747's empennage – Taiwanese, Korean and PanAm – date the scene as the mid 1970s. (UAL/APS)

East-facing aerial perspective of Honolulu International Airport as it was in the early 1980s. Diamond Head lies beyond Waikiki (top centre) and Pearl Harbor and its USN facilities are just out of the picture to the left; the entrance channel is also just out of sight in the foreground. A USAF Starlifter waits short of the Runway 08L threshold as a 747 begins its takeoff. The triangle of Hickam's pre-WW2 airstrips is visible on three sides of the massive new apron. After Runway 08R/26L was opened, crews were concerned about lengthy taxi times and overheating brakes – N4713U for example, took almost 20 minutes to taxi to the threshold of Runway 08R for departure. Barely 42 minutes later, the crippled 747 landed back on 08L, stopping on the runway almost opposite the terminal building. (Ian Allan Ltd)

with some difficulty to get his seat belt done up and a lifejacket on him.

Not knowing what was going to happen to us, and still very scared and frightened, I just had to sit still then and be quiet. A few minutes later there was a sudden flash and someone called out that one of the engines was on fire. I didn't know what it was, but both the engines on the right side seemed to be out now and the plane had a terrible lean to the left. I asked my friend behind if she was all right, and did she have any idea of what had happened – we didn't realise that the pilot had already turned the plane around to go back to Honolulu.

Another passenger described the scene in the cabin after the explosive decompression:

When the cargo door burst open with explosive force and the escaping pressure ripped away a large section of the side of the fuselage, the plane shook violently, the lights went out and we were blown about – if you blew up a balloon and then released it, its behaviour would simulate the erratic path of the damaged jet. Nine passengers, eight of them still strapped to their seats, had been instantly sucked through the gaping hole – it all happened so fast, no one actually saw it.

We later learnt that Captain David Cronin initially believed a bomb had gone off and he would soon be joining friends who had perished on the PanAm flight which exploded over Lockerbie, Scotland.

After the lights went out there was only an eerie red glow – from the emergency lighting. The number four engine was ablaze, with a streak of flame coming from the jetpipe – debris had been ingested into the engines.

The noise was absolutely deafening. The great hole in the side of the fuselage channelled the roar of the engines into the cabin. A very courageous but near-hysterical stewardess was running up and down the aisles near us, urging passengers through a megaphone to put on their lifejackets. There was no jacket under my seat. I remember a moment of intense panic – until I realised that if we crashed into the sea, a lifejacket would be of no earthly use.

My wife and I had no hope of

talking to each other because of the intense noise, so we just held hands tightly and waited for the worst to happen. There was no communication from the flightdeck at this stage – our only contact was from the gallant stewardess who was screaming commands through her loud hailer, punctuated by gasping sobs and an occasional, "Oh, my God!"

I knew in my heart that nothing could save us if we hit the water. But just in case, I groped around and found my travelling shoes. This illogical behaviour was based on the premise that I would have something on my feet to kick sharks away – if we survived the crash!

Everyone in the passenger cabin really expected to die. A young steward, unable to cope, sat with his eyes closed, making the Sign of the Cross and waiting for death. One woman, quite overcome by fear, crawled over the seats of others, crying piteously. Although themselves in deep shock, several passengers managed to get her back into a seat and calm her down.

However, most of the passengers remained outwardly calm – people who suffer a prolonged crisis go through a period of "negative panic". They presume the worst and are resigned to the seeming inevitability of death. This utter hopelessness left us nothing to contemplate but a watery grave.

Yet, with 35 years' experience, Captain Cronin was quickly in control and instructed First Officer Al Slader to send a Mayday distress call to Honolulu, advising they were attempting to return to the airport we had left less than 20 minutes before – he knew it was

touch and go whether we would get there.

After another 20 minutes of extreme anxiety for the flightcrew, fear and dismay on the part of the cabin staff, and terror, bewilderment, and in some cases panic and hysteria for the passengers, the welcoming lights of Honolulu hove in sight through misty rain in the distance.

The passenger: *The wind noise had decreased a little, apparently as the aircraft slowed, and with amazement and joy we were able to hear the Flight Engineer's voice over the intercom telling us we were "two minutes to touchdown". It seemed unbelievable and for a little longer we just waited, hardly daring to hope, as the captain went on with his approach.*

The crew had requested that all available rescue and medical equipment be on hand for their emergency landing. Given priority by Honolulu Tower, the crippled 747 was cleared for a straight-in approach to Runway 08. Exercising superb airmanship and drawing on all his accumulated skills to fly the approach asymmetrically with the portside engines only, the captain deliberately maintained a high airspeed of between 190 and 200 knots to ensure he could retain full control.

As he called for the flaps, and they began to extend, the crew had an indication of asymmetrical flap. The captain therefore elected to limit the flap extension to only 10° for the high speed touchdown. Despite the fact that the outboard leading edge slat also failed to extend, the captain retained accurate control, finally touching down very fast but smoothly, close to the runway aiming point. He

then selected idle reverse thrust on the two live engines, relying on heavy wheel braking to bring the 747 to a stop in a little over 2000m.

The passenger: *Then the wheels touched down on the runway – very gently – and there was an immediate outburst of clapping and cheering – and an overwhelming sensation of relief as we braked hard.*

Immediately the aircraft came to a stop on the runway, the captain, using the public address system, which could be heard again now that the aircraft was on the ground, ordered an emergency evacuation.

The cabin crew quickly opened all the exits, deployed all the inflatable escape slides, and the surviving passengers and the crew filed out of the aircraft in an orderly manner, jumping or being pushed into the slides. Even so, a number of passengers and all the cabin crew sustained some injury as they escaped down the long rubber slides to the runway.

After a short time, all were taken in coaches back to the terminal building where they were treated for their injuries and shock. Still uncertain whether the explosive decompression had been caused by a bomb planted in the cargo compartment, agents of the Federal Bureau of Investigation were waiting to question the passengers individually as soon as they were fit to be interviewed. Passengers were also besieged by press and other media reporters in the terminal building.

The passenger's final word: *My wife and I are still in touch with some of the other passengers. The worst affected seemed to be the younger people – it was as though they didn't think they were ever go-*

This final approach view of another United 747 provides a basis for placarding the damage sustained by N4713U – except for the full flap. Captain Cronin elected to use only a 10° setting, with a consequent much higher touchdown speed. The asymmetric flap warning was the result of disabled pneumatics in the starboard wing, the negative response from the outer starboard panels triggering the alarm (see note). In bringing the heavily-laden 747 in on only Nos 1 and 2 engines, the captain and crew demonstrated skills honed over the years in simulator training exercises – but with the added reality of the gaping hole in the fuselage. The 747 was later repaired and returned to United service as N4724U. Finally sold in March 1997, it was at presstime flying with a West African operator. (Matthew Tesch)

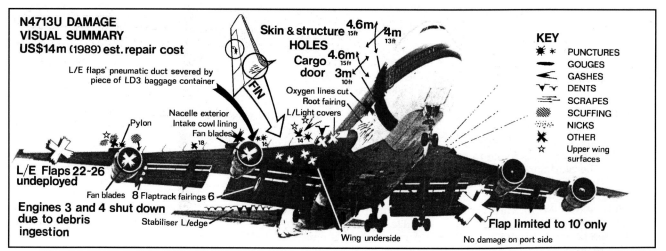

N4713U DAMAGE VISUAL SUMMARY
US$14m (1989) est. repair cost

L/E flaps' pneumatic duct severed by piece of LD3 baggage container

Nacelle exterior Intake cowl lining Fan blades

Pylon

L/E Flaps 22-26 undeployed

Fan blades 8 Flaptrack fairings 6

Engines 3 and 4 shut down due to debris ingestion

Stabiliser L/edge

Skin & structure 4.6m 15ft / 4m 13ft
HOLES
Cargo 4.6m 15ft
door 3m 10ft
Oxygen lines cut
Root fairing
L/Light covers

Wing underside

KEY
☀ * * PUNCTURES
— GOUGES
◄ GASHES
ᴠ ᴠ DENTS
≋ SCRAPES
▦ SCUFFING
⋯ NICKS
✖ OTHER
☆ Upper wing surfaces

Flap limited to 10° only
No damage on port side

Dawn on February 24 revealed the magnitude of the disaster, the gaping hole in the side of the 747 recalling the near-catastrophic failure of the fuselage of an Aloha Airlines Boeing 737 10 months previously while inbound from Hilo to Honolulu (see Air Disaster, Vol 2, Ch 11). Although the area of missing fuselage was similar in both cases – around 35 sq m of the 737, compared to more than 32 sq m of the 747 – the bigger aircraft obviously coped much better structurally. In this early morning photograph, the doors and slides have been tidied up after the passenger evacuation, and, apart from the fuselage damage, only the partly-extended flaps (note outer leading edge) testify to the emergency landing. A JAL 747 stands behind the United 747's tail. N4713U had not yet adopted the enlarged titles of United's 1989 livery modification. (Australian Women's Weekly)

ing to die! And our thoughts are always with the families and friends of those who lost their lives on that awful night.

INVESTIGATION

The search

At 2.10am local time, immediately after the aircraft's emergency call to Honolulu Air Traffic Control, the FAA notified the US Coast Guard that a United Airlines Boeing 747, possibly with a bomb on board, had sustained an inflight explosion and was returning to Honolulu. Forty minutes later the Coast Guard cutter *Cape Corwin* weighed anchor at Maui to search the area of sea over which the accident had occurred, for debris and the bodies of the missing passengers.

Over the following two days, four shore commands, 13 surface vessels and aircraft, and some 1000 operational crew took part in a combined air and sea search and rescue operation. Despite this extensive search, no trace of the Boeing 747's missing cargo door, or any of the lost passengers' bodies could be found, and the search was terminated at 12 noon two days later. Even so, the National Transportation Safety Board was continuing to work with the US Navy for a possible attempt to locate and recover the lost cargo door for examination.

Aircraft damage

When the aircraft was inspected by investigators at Honolulu Airport, the primary damage was found to be a hole in the starboard side of the fuselage about two metres high and three metres long (10ft by 15ft) immediately above the forward lower lobe cargo door. The lower sill and side frames of the cargo door's fuselage cutout were intact, but the door itself was missing. The missing area of fuselage skin extended from the upper sill of the forward cargo as high as the upper deck windows.

Above the cargo compartment, part of the starboard side cabin floor and its structure was missing, together with passenger seats 8GH, 9GH, 10GH, 11GH and 12GH (see diagrams and photograph). The adjoining floor beams inboard of the cargo door were fractured and buckled downwards, and the supply lines for both the flightcrew and the passenger oxygen systems, routed beneath the cabin floor, had been severed inboard of the missing cargo door.

Examination of the structure around the area of primary fuselage damage disclosed no evidence of pre-existing cracks or corrosion, and all the fractures were typical of fresh overstress breaks. There was no damage on the port side of the aircraft, but debris from the fuselage had struck the starboard wing, engines Nos 3 and 4, the starboard tailplane, and the fin.

The wing had sustained damage in a number of places along the leading edge between the No 3 engine pylon and the No 17 leading edge flap, and there was damage to the No 18 leading edge flap.

Aft of No 4 engine, the leading edge skin was broken, with scuffing outboard of the engine.

Inboard, a deep indentation was found above the outboard landing light. The landing light covers were broken, and there were punctures and impact damage on some of the Krueger flaps and the wing leading edge behind them. More punctures were found under the wing, with damage to the fuselage fairing.

A piece of cargo container, lodged between the No 3 engine pylon and the underside of the wing, had severed the pneumatic duct for the leading edge flaps, and there were nicks and punctures on the No 3 and No 4 engine pylons.

All the fan blades on the No 3 and No 4 engines had been damaged by ingested debris. The inlet cowl of the No 3 engine had a large hole in it, as well as tears and scuffs, while inside the cowling the entire circumference of the acoustic panels had been punctured, torn, or dented.

The leading edge of the starboard tailplane was dented in several places, with the most severe three inches (75mm) wide and an inch (25mm) deep. The fin had multiple small, elongated indentations of about ½ inch (12mm) near the base of the leading edge.

Flight recorders

The aircraft was equipped with a Sundstrand model 573 Digital Flight Data Recorder and a Sundstrand model AV557-B Cockpit Voice Recorder.

Examination of the data plotted from the DFDR indicated that the flight was normal from liftoff to the time the forward cargo door blew open. The recorder operated normally throughout this time, but the explosive decompression resulted in a data loss of about 2.5 seconds. When the data recording resumed, all values appeared valid with the exception of the pitch and roll parameters. The lateral acceleration showed a sharp increase immediately the decompression occurred (as the aircraft was literally blown sideways), while the vertical acceleration showed sharp, rapid changes just after the decompression and a slight increase as the aircraft began its descent.

(opposite) Investigators cluster on a Hi-Lift loader for a preliminary examination of N4713U's failed fuselage. Seats 10F and 11F in the centre block can be seen in the middle of the hole, with dangling clusters of passenger oxygen masks above them. Mountings for the side overhead lockers are faintly visible underneath the exposed stringers and tattered insulation of the upper deck. Also visible aft on the broken cheatline is a fuselage frame. Note the distorted floor panels and support beams.
Even more problems for United were to come in the ensuing two months. On March 25, another United 747 lost a fibreglass fairing inflight near Manila. Yet another, outbound from Auckland two days later, shut down an engine. And less than a fortnight afterwards, one of United's ex-PanAm 747SPs made a heavy crosswind landing at Sydney, fracturing a corroded undercarriage bogie and forcing its mountings up through the wing's upper skin. A similar fatigue problem had been discovered on a former "Clipper" 747SP at Sydney only months after the PanAm Pacific acquisition in 1986. (AWW)

The CVR recorded normal communication before the decompression. Just after 2.09am local time, when the aircraft had been airborne for about 16 minutes, a "thump" could be heard on the CVR, about which one of the crew made a comment. About 1.5 seconds later there was an extremely loud bang. Electrical power to the CVR was lost for 21 seconds, but the CVR then returned to normal operation, continuing to record the sounds on the flightdeck.

The aircraft

At the time of the accident the United Airlines Boeing 747 fleet numbered 31, 13 of which, including N4713U, were early 747-122 series aircraft, equipped with Pratt & Whitney JT9D engines. N4713U itself had been built in 1970, the 89th Boeing 747 to come off the production line.

Its actual takeoff weight from Honolulu on the accident flight was 316,845kg (697,900lb), well within its maximum takeoff weight, and its centre of gravity was also within specified limits. It had accumulated 58,815 flying hours in the course of 15,028 flight cycles, and had not been involved in any previous accident. It had always been maintained in accordance with FAA approved United Airlines schedules.

Reproduced from the official NTSB report, this "passenger eye view" shows interior damage as seen from seats 13G and 13H. In the right foreground is a torn-down section of cabin insulation; above it, a segment of carpeted flooring with air duct grills still attached is twisted towards the camera. Immediately aft of the dislocated wall panels of toilet compartment 'B' (top left), the twisted armrest of seat 9F provides a silent epitaph for the unfortunate passenger who occupied it only hours before. And the labels indicating the positions of the missing seats on the right make their own statement on the fate of their occupants. (NTSB)

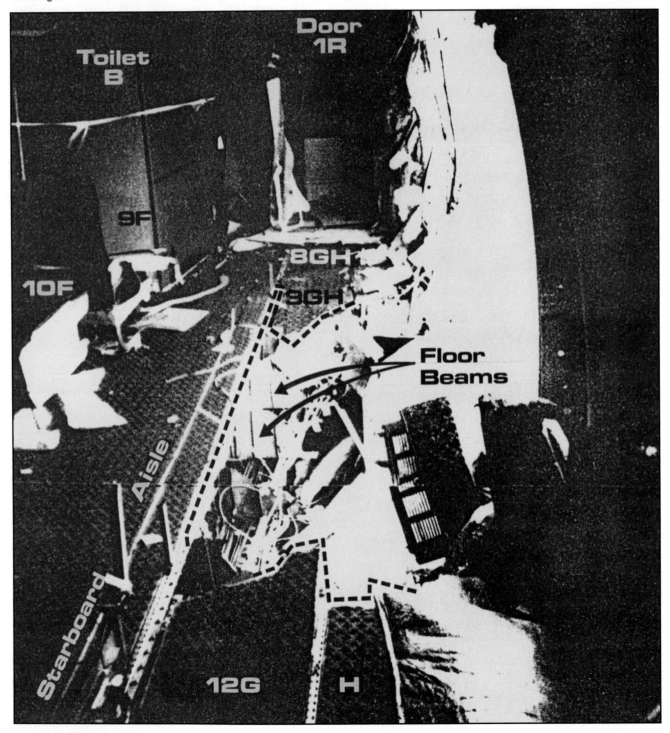

The airport

Honolulu International Airport, seven kilometres west of the city of Honolulu on the island of Oahu, Hawaii, is a "joint use" airport operated by the State of Hawaii and the US Air Force, for military use, the airlines, and general aviation. Rescue and Fire Fighting services are provided by the State and Hickam Air Force Base. To handle its busy and diverse traffic, the airport has two pairs of parallel runways (see aerial photograph).

During its return to Honolulu for the emergency landing, the 747 requested that all available rescue and medical equipment be on hand for the touchdown. When the crash alarm was broadcast, all civilian and military fire units responded at once and, despite the moonless night and light rain, were in position at designated points alongside Runway 08 Left within only one minute.

The crew
Captain

Captain David Cronin, 59, had flown with United Airlines since 1954 and had a total of 28,000 hours' experience. In addition to his 1700 hours as a captain on Boeing 747s, he was qualified on DC-10, DC-8, Boeing 727, Convair 440, 340 and 240, and Learjet aircraft.

First and Second Officers

First Officer Gregory Slader, 48, was another highly experienced United Airlines pilot, having been with the company since 1964. He had a total of about 14,500 hours, 300 hours of which had been flown in Boeing 747s. In addition he was qualified on DC-10, and Boeing 727 and 737 aircraft.

Second Officer Randal Thomas, 46, had been a flight engineer with United Airlines since 1969 and had a total of about 20,000 hours' experience, about 1200 of which were as second officer on B747s. He was also qualified as a commercial pilot with multi-engine and instrument ratings.

The cabin crew

The cabin crew comprised 15 staff – Chief Purser and Aft Purser, both of whom were women, seven female flight attendants and six male flight attendants. All but one, who had become a flight attendant with United Airlines less than a year before, were mature and well experienced.

Survival

The loss of life was entirely the result of the explosive nature of the decompression, which instantly swept nine of the passengers, all but one with their seats, from the gaping hole it had torn in the side of the forward fuselage.

The 15 flight attendants believed they had but a short time in which to prepare the cabin and passengers for what they thought would be an imminent ocean ditching.

During the 20 minutes that elapsed before they realised they would be making an emergency landing back at Honolulu Airport instead, they attended to the injured, fitted their portable emergency oxygen equipment, helped each other and numerous passengers into lifejackets, and held up safety instruction cards and lifejackets to draw passengers' attention to them.

Despite the great difficulty of communication in the noise-swamped cabin, they also briefed "helper" passengers to assist in the evacuation, cleared debris away from the doors and aisles, closed the storage compartments, prepared the cabin for an emergency evacuation, and explained to passengers how to brace for impact.

The lack of a sufficient number of megaphones, limited visibility from the flight attendant seats, overhead storage compartment doors being pulled open by the decompression, and problems with fastening the lifejackets, all added to the flight attendants' difficulties. Another of their problems was that the portable oxygen bottles positioned in the passenger cabins were not immediately usable. Face masks were not attached to the regulators, and they found difficulty in attaching the masks quickly.

Immediately the decompression occurred, the purser in the aft section of the aircraft ran to the flight attendant seat at Door 5L for a portable oxygen bottle. To her dismay, no bottle was there, so she ran back to the jumpseat at Door 4L. By this time she was already light headed from anoxia, but another flight attendant in the seat placed an oxygen mask over her face and she recovered. She later told investigators: *"Considering there was no other available source of oxygen, you can't imagine how horrible I felt going back there needing oxygen, but finding no bottle. It was terrifying."*

Communication between the flight attendants and passengers was extremely difficult because of the intense noise in the cabin, even though the public address system was still working. Although there were flight attendant stations at each of the 10 aircraft doors, there were only two megaphones on the aircraft: one at Door 1L (portside forward main entry door) and another at Door 4L (port door aft of the wing).

The flight attendants assigned to these two doors used the megaphones to broadcast commands to passengers in their immediate areas of the cabin, as well as to other flight attendants as they attempted to prepare the cabin for ditching. All the other flight attendants had to shout, use hand signals, and show passengers how to prepare for the evacuation by holding up passenger safety cards.

A two door overhead stowage compartment, designed to hold a deflated, packed life raft, was located above each cabin door, and contained blankets and passengers' luggage. Some of the doors opened, spilling their contents on to the floor below and blocking the exits. These had to be cleared before any evacuation was possible.

The chief purser found she was not able to adjust her lifejacket's straps around her waist and needed another flight attendant to tighten them for her. Several other flight attendants and passengers also had similar difficulties. One flight attendant in fact helped no less than 36 passengers with their jackets.

Before departure

The 747's second officer said that, before their departure from Honolulu, while the cargo was being loaded and the cargo doors were still open, he used a torch to carry out an exterior inspection of the aircraft. He saw no abnormalities or damage. On going up to the flightdeck, as part of his flight preparation, he carried out a satisfactory operational check of the door warning annunciator lights.

United Airlines staff involved with cargo loading before takeoff said they had closed the forward cargo door electrically. They saw no damage to the door, and verified that it was flush with the fuselage, that its master door latch handle was stowed, and that its pressure relief doors were flush with the exterior.

The United Airlines dispatch engineer, in accordance with company procedures, had performed a final "circle check" (ie a standard walk-around, checking all stipulated points) of the aircraft prior to its departure from the gate. This included his own verification, by torchlight, that the cargo doors were flush with the fuselage, that their master latch lock handles were stowed, and that the pressure relief doors were within half an inch (12mm) of the cargo door's exterior skin.

The cargo doors

The main forward and aft cargo doors of the Boeing 747 are located

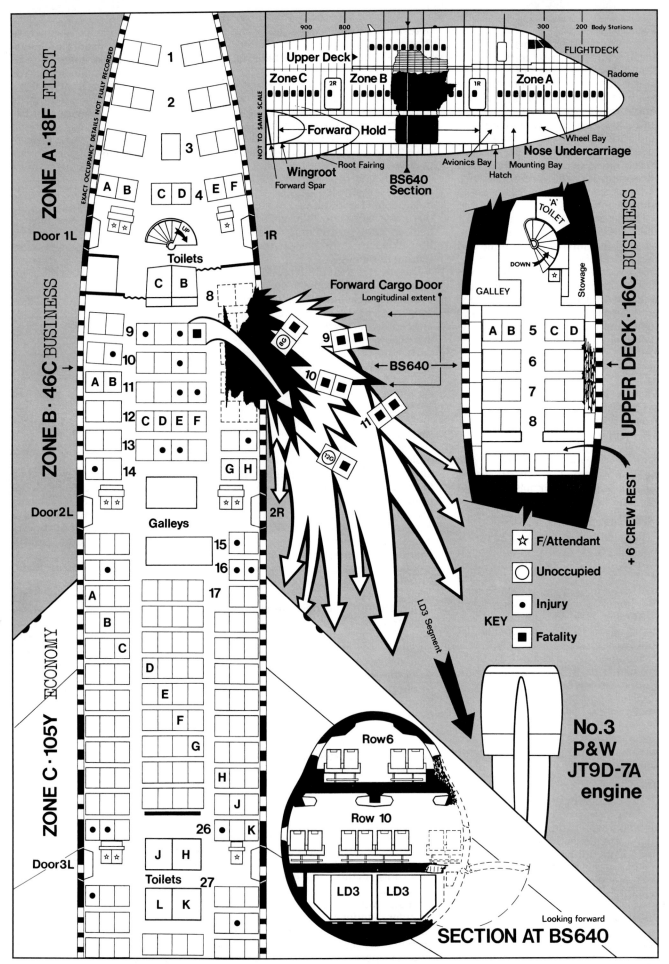

ZONE A · 18F FIRST

EXACT OCCUPANCY DETAILS NOT FULLY RECORDED

1

2

3

A B   C D 4 E F

Door 1L   1R

UP

Toilets

ZONE B · 46C BUSINESS

C B   8

9

10

A B 11

12

C D E F

13

14

Door 2L

Galleys

15

16

A   17

B

C

D

E

F

G

H

J

26   K

Door 3L

J H

Toilets   27

L K

ZONE C · 105Y ECONOMY

Body Stations
900   800   300   200

Upper Deck   FLIGHTDECK
Zone C   Zone B   Zone A   Radome
2R   1R

Forward Hold
Wingroot   Root Fairing   Avionics Bay   Nose Undercarriage
Forward Spar   BS640   Hatch   Mounting Bay
                  Section   Wheel Bay

NOT TO SAME SCALE

Forward Cargo Door
Longitudinal extent

8G   9
            ← BS640 →
10

11

12G

G H
2R

'A' TOILET
DOWN
GALLEY   Stowage

A B 5 C D
6
7
8

UPPER DECK · 16C BUSINESS

+ 6 CREW REST

LD3 Segment

☆ F/Attendant
◯ Unoccupied
• Injury
■ Fatality

KEY

Row 6

Row 10

LD3   LD3

Looking forward

SECTION AT BS640

No.3
P&W
JT9D-7A
engine

Drawings of the forward half of N4713U in plan, profile & cross-section through Body Station 640 (see Vol 2, p 165 for further details of Boeing's "BS" identifier system). All except the nose profile are to the same scale. Injuries caused by flying decompression debris are indicated – the furthest aft injured were passengers in seats 27A & 28J. All the flight attendants also sustained injuries during the evacuation at Honolulu – ranging from abrasions to a dislocated shoulder. (Matthew Tesch; United & Boeing) on the lower starboard side of the fuselage. Both openings are 110 inches (279cm) wide by 99 inches (251.5cm) high, measured around the curve of the lower fuselage. Similar in appearance and operation, they open outwards. Electrical power to operate the cargo doors comes from the ground handling bus of the aircraft's electrical system, which is energised by either external ground power or the aircraft's APU. The design of the electrical system does not allow the engine generators to provide power to the ground handling bus.

APU generator power to the ground handling bus is automatically cut off as soon as an engine generator comes on line after an engine start. If necessary, while still on the ground, the APU generator field switch can be re-engaged from the flightdeck to power the ground handling bus. But if the ground handling bus is still energised when the aircraft becomes airborne, a safety relay automatically disconnects the APU generator from it.

The cargo doors (see accompanying diagram) are designed to carry fuselage pressurisation loads. These loads are transmitted from the piano type hinge at the top of the doors, through the doors themselves, and into eight latches along the bottom of the doors. These consist of latch pins attached to the lower door sill, with matching latch cams on the bottom of the doors.

There are also two midspan latches on the fore and aft sides of the doors, and four door stops which limit inward movement of the door. Two pull-in hooks, on the lower fore and aft of the doors, match with pull-in hook pins on the sides of the door frame.

The cargo doors also have an exterior master latch lock handle, opened and closed manually, which controls both the latch lock sectors, and the two small pressure relief doors. (The next diagram.)

Three electrical actuators operate the doors. The main one moves the door from the fully open to the near-closed position, and *vice versa*. A second actuator moves the pull-in hooks open or closed, and the third rotates the latch cams into the latched or unlatched positions. An internal clutch limits the torque of this actuator.

The cargo doors are controlled by a switch on the exterior of the fuselage, just forward of the door opening, or by a second switch inside the cargo compartment adjacent to the door. The spring-loaded switches return to a neutral position when re-

leased, removing power from the actuators.

To close an open cargo door, the switch is held to "close". When the door reaches the near-closed position, a hook position switch transfers electrical power from the main actuator to the pull-in hook actuator, and the door is pulled firmly closed. The hook switch then in turn transfers power to the latch actuator, rotating the eight latch cams around their latch pins on the door sill. At the same time, the two midspan latch cams rotate around the two midspan latch pins on the sides of the door frame. When all latch cams reach their fully closed positions, power is automatically removed from the latch actuator.

The door is finally secured manually with the master latch lock handle which, through a mechanical linkage, moves lock sectors into place across the open mouths of the eight lower latch cams. The lock sectors are also mechanically linked to two small pressure relief doors on the upper section of each cargo door. Their purpose is to relieve any pressure differential before the cargo doors are opened after landing, and prevent pressurisation of the aircraft should it depart with the cargo doors not properly secured. The position of the lock sectors is indicated by the position of the pressure relief doors. The final positioning of this master lock handle also removes electrical power from all the control circuits, and extinguishes the relevant flightdeck cargo door annunciator light.

The cargo doors may be opened and closed manually through the same sequence of actions, with the actuator mechanisms being turned using a 'half inch' socket driver. Separate socket drives are provided for the door mechanism, the pull-in hooks, and the latches. The cargo doors are fitted with eight small viewing ports, beneath each of the latch cams, for verifying the position of the cams by means of alignment stripes, but visual verification through these viewing ports was not a United Airlines requirement.

Instructions for operating the forward and aft cargo doors electrically were set out in the company's Maintenance Manual. It also contained procedures for dispatching aircraft with a door's electrical system inoperative.

The airline had included a "special maintenance procedure" in its Minimum Equipment List for manual operation of 747 cargo doors. This allowed a special 'half inch' socket drive wrench to be used for opening

or closing the doors. It further authorised an air-driven torque-limiting screwdriver as an alternative to the socket wrench, but its use required special approval by the airline's station maintenance co-ordinator.

United Airlines maintenance

United aircraft were maintained under an FAA approved airworthiness program. All the required major maintenance on N4713U had been carried out at the company's maintenance facility at Oakland Airport, across the bay from San Francisco.

The company's heavy maintenance 'C Check' is scheduled every 13 months and includes:
• structural inspections;
• corrosion repair;
• inspection of critical flight control systems;
• detailed inspection of the cargo doors.

The 'D Check' is scheduled at intervals not exceeding nine years and consists of heavy maintenance to the aircraft structure, engines, undercarriage, interior, and systems, including the cargo doors.

Maintenance records

The aircraft's history showed that the forward and aft cargo doors were original and that neither had ever been removed for repair or replacement. During the last 'C check' in November 1988, the forward cargo door's forward mid-span latch pin had been removed because of gouging of the pin, but a full cargo door rigging check had been carried out. No rigging of the forward or aft cargo doors had been required during more recent checks.

During December 1988, two months before the accident, eight defect reports on the forward cargo door had been recorded, all involving problems with the cargo door's electrical system, which had not always operated. In the weeks that followed, three more discrepancies were noted on the aircraft's maintenance sheets, but all were signed off as having been corrected.

Airworthiness Directives – and a previous cargo door incident

Two FAA issued Airworthiness Directives applied to Boeing 747 cargo doors. The first stipulated an inspection every 1700 flying hours, while the second, issued in May 1988, required an inspection of the door latch locking mechanism "to ensure inadvertent opening of the lower cargo door will not occur in flight". This had been prompted by an incident involving another Boeing 747 cargo door in March 1987.

After taking off from London en

route to New York, the crew of a PanAm 747-121 experienced pressurisation problems as the aircraft was climbing through about 20,000 feet. They descended and the problem ceased at about 15,000 feet. The crew began to climb the aircraft again, but once again at about 20,000 feet, the cabin altitude began to rise rapidly.

The 747 returned to London and it was found that the forward cargo door was open about 1.5 inches (37mm). Even though the master latch lock handle was closed and the flightdeck cargo door warning lamp had extinguished, the latch cams were unlatched.

Investigation revealed that the latch lock sectors had been damaged and would not restrain the latch cams from being driven open. It was concluded that at some time the latches had been opened manually after the door had been closed and locked, without first moving the lock sectors to the unlocked position. As a result, the forced movement of the latch cams caused bending, gouging, and breaking of the sectors.

Tests and research

A number of the accident aircraft's forward cargo door components were despatched to the NTSB's Materials Laboratory for analysis. These included:
• the eight latch pins with pin housings from the lower sill of the door body cutout;
• two pull-in hook pins, with their housings;
• two mid-span pins, one from the forward side of the door frame, and one from the aft side.

Detailed examination of the exposed surface of the pins revealed wear and damage. In general, all the latch pins had smooth wear over the entire portion of the pin area contacted by the cams during normal closing and opening of the door. The pins also had distinct roughened areas with evidence of heat tinting and transfer of cam material to the surface of the pins.

The forward pull-in hook pin was not seriously bent, but the structure to which it was attached was deformed, so the hook pin was deflected outwards. Three of the four bolts holding the aft pull-in hook pin had sheared, so the hook pin was also deflected outwards. Both hook pin ends were damaged, but neither pin was deformed along its length. There was heat tinting on the damaged area of the forward hook pin. The aft mid-span latch pin also exhibited areas of damage.

Inspection of other aircraft

Investigators examined six Boeing 747 aircraft on the ground at Honolulu, watched routine cargo handling operations and assessed the latching of their doors. Generally, the doors functioned normally. But during electrical closing of the aft cargo door on another United Airlines 747, it was found that the pull-in hooks would not pull the door fully closed before the latch cams completed the closure.

As the latch cams operated, the bottom of the door moved circumferentially downward first, and then inboard. A definite "thunking" noise was discernible as the door finally moved to its closed position at the end of the cam rotation. During one cycle, this door refused to open under electrical power. But after the door was "expertly kicked" by a mechanic, and power was reapplied, it opened, apparently normally.

Examination disclosed that the riveted plate holding the aft pull-in hook switch striker was loose, and that the forward and aft midspan cams had heavy gouge marks corresponding to the ends of the midspan latch pins. The aircraft was subsequently taken out of service for repair.

ANALYSIS

The accident was precipitated by the sudden and dramatic loss of the forward lower lobe cargo door, leading immediately to an explosive decompression of the fuselage. There was no evidence of metal fatigue or corrosion in the structure, and all failures were the result of the loss of the door. There was certainly no evidence of a bomb on the aircraft, as first suspected.

The floor structure and seats where the nine lost passengers had been sitting were subjected to the full destructive force of the decompression. The passengers' remains were not recovered, despite an intensive search of the area of sea over which the decompression occurred. Most of the injuries sustained by survivors were the result of the decompression – barotrauma to ears, and cuts and abrasions from the flying debris. Some injuries occurred during the emergency evacuation.

The loss of power on the Nos 3 and 4 engines was the result of ingesting debris ejected from the cargo compartment and cabin by the explosive decompression. Debris also damaged the starboard wing and the empennage.

During the approach, as the aircraft returned to land at Honolulu, all the leading edge flaps extended, except the most outboard sections on the starboard wing. They failed to do so because of damage to the

pneumatic duct, resulting in a loss of pressure to actuate the flaps. The failure of the crew and passenger oxygen systems was caused by deformation and damage to the supply lines adjacent to the failed fuselage structure.

The sudden loss of the cargo door in flight, and the circumstances that led to its loss, became the focus of the investigation.

Loss of the door

There was no evidence of a structural problem within the cargo door itself that could have caused it to fail. Indeed, deformation to the door's latch pins and pull-in hooks, damage to the cabin floor structure near the upper door hinge, as well as damage to the structure surrounding the door, showed that it came off intact. Because the door separated so violently, decompression loads in the cabin broke its floor beams downward as pressure was suddenly released from the cargo compartment beneath it, and the fuselage structure above the door was torn away.

There are no means by which the door locking and latching mechanisms could open in flight from a properly closed and locked position. If the lock sectors are in sound condition, and are over the closed latch cams, the lock sectors have sufficient strength to prevent the cams from vibrating to the open position. So either the latching mechanisms were forced open electrically after the door was secured, or the door was not properly latched and locked in the first place.

Partially closed door?

Examination of the eight latch pins removed from the lower sill of the door revealed smooth wear where the latch cams had been rotating around the pins each time the door was closed. This indicated there had been interference between the cams and the pins during closings of the door over a long period. All eight pins also had roughened areas, corresponding to where the surface of the cams meet the pins as the door closes.

Transferred cam material and heat tinting of the pins was found at this cam-to-pin interface on the roughened areas of all the pins. Indicative of high bearing stress and extremely rapid movement of the cams across the pins when the door separated, this indicated the position of the cams at the time of the separation of the door. All were found to be near to the unlatched position.

The short time between the first thump and the loud explosion recorded on the CVR was undoubtedly the time between the initial failure of the latches at the bottom of the door, and the separation of the door from the fuselage, with its explosive decompression. The door did not fail and separate instantaneously; rather, it first opened at the bottom and then flew open violently. As it did so, it tore away the surrounding fuselage structure as the pressure in the cabin forced the floor beams downward to equalise the loss of pressure in the cargo compartment.

There are only three ways in which the latch cams could have been in a partly latched condition:
• they could have been manually back-driven about 95 turns with a socket wrench after the door had been secured – an utterly unrealistic hypothesis in the circumstances;
• they could have been back-driven electrically after the door was secured, which also seemed highly unlikely;
• the lock sectors had been damaged previously, and the cams were in the open, or nearly open position after the door was "closed". In this case, the door would only *appear* to be locked.

The subsequent pressurisation of the fuselage would have created a load where the cams and pins come in contact. Even with the cams in this unlatched position, this load would have acted to keep the door closed – until the increasing pressure differential as the aircraft climbed finally overcame the friction and the door suddenly burst open.

After the PanAm incident in 1987, it was found that the locking sectors of a Boeing 747 cargo door, as originally designed, could be overcome by the force of the latch cam actuator, either electrically or mechanically. The locking sectors installed as original equipment, including those on the accident aircraft, would thus not hold as intended – they were not sufficiently substantial to unequivocally and finally lock the latches in place.

It thus seemed possible that the numerous malfunctions experienced with the operation of the cargo door in the months preceding the accident could have damaged its locking sectors and contributed ultimately to the loss of the door.

Incomplete latching?

Another possible reason for incomplete latching of the door was that the latch actuator was unable to rotate the cams to the closed position because of excessive friction between the latch cams and pins. This would occur if the cargo door was misaligned, or its pull-in hooks

The Irish character of this picture is excused by its rarity – without cluttering ground equipment and activity – affording a clear view of a 747 open forward cargo door. On the fuselage, the door aperture is flanked (upper left) by a static port and (lower right) by the instruction-stickered external control panel; on the bottom sill of the door the eight lower latch mountings are clearly visible. On the underside of the raised door itself are the two shroud-covered pressure relief doors; less obvious, on the door's bottom edge, the four latch bellcranks with the paired end cams (see accompanying page of diagrams) may just be discerned. The subject of this picture, Aer Lingus's ex-Lufthansa 747-130 EI-BED [19748] "St Kieran" was withdrawn after 24 years' service and broken up in Arizona in August 1996. The presence of 747-148 EI-ASI [19744] "St Colmcille" beyond the belly of "Ciaran" dates this picture in Dublin to 1979. (Flight International)

were not bringing the door in far enough to properly engage the cams around the pins. The smooth wear on the pins was a sign of such interference over hundreds of openings and closings of the door. From this wear, and from the maintenance record of discrepancy reports on the door, it was evident that the door was misaligned and not properly rigged during the weeks and months that preceded the accident.

The wear pattern on the pull-in hook pins also showed there had been interference for some time before the accident. This was further evidence that the door was misrigged, and it is possible that excessive binding of the door mechanism, acting over a period of time, might have finally resulted in a failure of the latch actuator. Whatever the case, the condition of the latch pins and pull-in hook pins clearly indicated prolonged misalignment of the door.

Most of the reported problems with the aircraft's forward cargo door during December 1988 involved difficulties with closing the door electrically. These consistently occurred just before departure, when the aircraft was fully laden. But corrective maintenance, usually performed during overnight inspections when the aircraft was empty, was often found to involve no more than cycling the door and finding it functional.

It is possible that slight flexing of the fuselage with a full load of fuel, cargo, and passengers caused distortion of the door frame, resulting in misalignment between the cams and pins. The pull-in hooks might then not have pulled the door in fully before the cam actuator attempted to latch the door. The wear on the latch pins indicated this had been occurring.

Investigators actually witnessed a similar situation during their inspection of another Boeing 747 in Honolulu. In this case, the aft cargo door was not being pulled in fully by the pull-in hooks, and the latch cams completed the closing cycle with obvious interference and "thunking" sounds. At one stage of this examination, the misrigged door even failed to close electrically.

Ground staff who closed N4713U's cargo doors before departure at Honolulu would have assumed the door closing cycle was completed when they saw the door move to the flush position, and heard the actuator motor stop. As the misrigged forward cargo door *appeared* to close and latch properly, the senior ground handler then closed its master latch lock handle.

Boeing tests during the investigation confirmed that the master latch lock handle could not move *undamaged* lock sectors into place if the door cams were not fully rotated to the latched position. But damage to the sectors could occur in a number of ways. If an attempt were made to open the door manually without first unlocking the master latch lock handle, the mechanical advantage of the socket wrench could drive the cams open, even with the lock sectors in the locked position. But this action would bend and gouge the lock sectors, or even break them off. Such damage could also occur if the door were opened with an air-driven screw driver while the master latch lock handle remained stowed.

Similarly, if the master latch lock switch happened to fail, and ground staff then operated the door open switch with the master latch lock handle still stowed, the electrical actuator would drive the cams towards the open position, bending and gouging the lock sectors.

The circumstances of the 1987 PanAm incident demonstrated that the lock sectors could have been damaged in any of these ways. With the lock sectors thus damaged, they would not restrict the movement of the master latch lock handle to the stowed position, even when the latch cams were not fully latched. Under such conditions, the pressure relief doors would be closed, the flightdeck warning light would extinguish, and there would be every indication that the door was closed and locked.

The accompanying diagrams shows the cams in the fully latched and fully unlatched positions respectively, and the possible position and damaged condition of the cams at the time of the door's violent separation from the fuselage.

United Airlines had not carried out inspections of the accident aircraft's door mechanism after manual operation, as required by the FAA. Thus, any damage to its lock sectors during an incorrectly sequenced manual opening would have gone undetected. It is certainly possible that damage was done to the lock sectors in the months preceding the accident, when there were repeated electrical malfunctions and manual openings and closings of the forward cargo door. Furthermore, scheduled maintenance inspections performed on the aircraft over the preceding 15 months did not include an inspection of the lock sectors. The last time the lock sectors of the forward cargo door would have been inspected was in November 1988, during the aircraft's scheduled 'C check'.

Despite the fact that the missing door from the accident aircraft was not recovered before the investigation was completed, it was concluded that the lock sectors on its forward cargo door had been dam-

aged some time previously during repeated manual operations, when the latch cams were moved without first unlocking the sectors. The damage allowed the master latch lock handle to be stowed. With the pressure relief doors closed and the flightdeck warning light extinguished, there would be nothing to indicate the door was not fully closed and locked.

Design, certification, and airworthiness

The analysis of the accident went beyond determining how the door failed. The investigators also examined the design and certification of the 747's cargo door, and the airworthiness system that should have prevented the accident. As with most aviation accidents, there were many factors involved.

There were multiple opportunities during the design, certification, operation, and maintenance of the cargo door for action that could have precluded the accident. The circumstances that led to it exemplify the need for human factor considerations in regulations, aircraft systems design, and the quality of airline operations and maintenance.

The first opportunity occurred during the design and certification of the cargo door's mechanism, which permitted the lock sectors to be overpowered by mechanical or electrical actuation. The original design was not tested sufficiently to verify that the locking sectors in fact "locked" the latch cams in the closed position. This should have become apparent during both the initial certification testing and the approval process.

Later, when Boeing applied to the FAA to eliminate the requirement for visual verification of the cargo door latch positions via the view ports in the doors, the weakness in the locking sectors should have again become apparent. The failure mode analyses performed by Boeing were based on the assumption that the lock sectors would always prevent the master latch lock handle from being moved to the stowed position when the latch cams were not fully closed. But this assumption was not valid, as demonstrated by the PanAm incident in 1987. The investigators found no evidence that the FAA or Boeing had reassessed the original design and certification of the cargo door at this time.

Several opportunities for preventative action were also missed by United. The Pan American 747 cargo door incident had led to Boeing issuing two Alert Service Bulletins pointing out that latch lock sectors

would, in some instances, not restrain the latch cams from being driven open manually or electrically, and that movement of the latch cams without first moving the lock sectors to the stowed position would cause bending, gouging, and breaking of the sectors.

The FAA then issued an Airworthiness Directive requiring strengthening steel doublers to be installed on the lock sectors to prevent the latch cams from being driven open inadvertently. The Airworthiness Directive also required that, if a cargo door would not operate electrically, a qualified ground engineer, rather than cargo handling staff, was to open and close the door manually. Furthermore, after the faulty cargo door was restored to electrical operation, the lock sectors were to be inspected for any possible damage. But United Airlines had postponed implementing these requirements on the accident aircraft until it was due for heavy maintenance in April 1988 which, as it turned out, was not for another two months after the accident.

It is understandable that an airline would not want to take its aircraft out of service for modifications that do not appear to be "safety critical". There was no implication from Boeing or the FAA that the matter was urgent, and United had scheduled the modifications to take place before the cutoff date in the Airworthiness Directive. United Airlines staff said after the accident that they did not fully appreciate the safety implications of the Airworthiness Directive – or they would have incorporated the modifications much earlier.

Another matter of concern was the effectiveness of the airline's trend analysis. There was nothing to show that the repeated problems with the forward cargo door had "raised a flag" within the maintenance department. An effective

(opposite) Structure and sub-systems of the 747's lower lobe cargo door design. Note: with the exception of the 'External Control Panel' and 'Viewing Port' insets, all drawings are orientated as if the reader is on the inside looking out, with the aircraft's nose to the left. At the top of the page, salient aspects of the door assembly are identified, with an enlarged view of the lower forward corner, accompanied by an exploded view of its skins & structure. Down the left side of the page, the three hook and latch mechanisms are separated for clarity. On the lower right, the locking sectors' scythe-like shapes, and the cam-pin relationships, have been extracted from the enlargement to depict the closing, latching, and locking sequence. (Matthew Tesch; Qantas & Boeing)

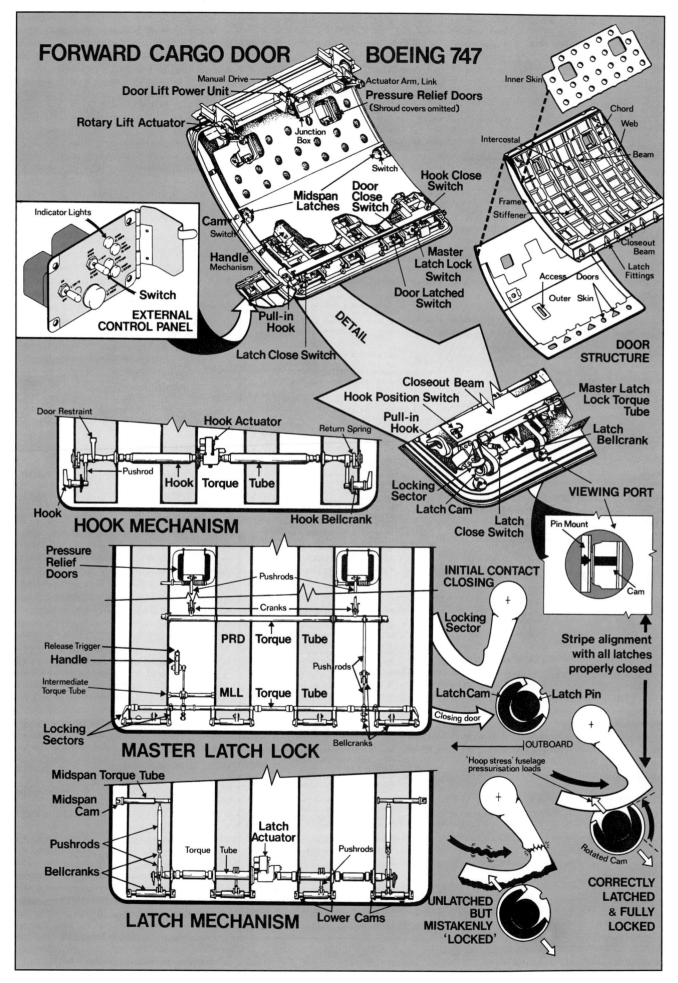

FORWARD CARGO DOOR   BOEING 747

Manual Drive
Door Lift Power Unit
Actuator Arm, Link
Rotary Lift Actuator
Pressure Relief Doors
(Shroud covers omitted)
Junction Box
Inner Skin
Chord
Web
Intercostal
Beam
Switch
Frame
Stiffener
Hook Close Switch
Cam Switch
Midspan Latches
Door Close Switch
Master Latch Lock Switch
Closeout Beam
Latch Fittings
Handle Mechanism
Door Latched Switch
Access
Doors
Outer Skin
Pull-in Hook
DETAIL
Latch Close Switch

DOOR STRUCTURE

EXTERNAL CONTROL PANEL

Indicator Lights
Switch

Closeout Beam
Hook Position Switch
Pull-in Hook
Master Latch Lock Torque Tube
Latch Bellcrank

HOOK MECHANISM

Door Restraint
Hook Actuator
Return Spring
Pushrod
Hook Torque Tube
Hook
Hook Bellcrank

Locking Sector
Latch Cam
Latch Close Switch

VIEWING PORT

Pin Mount
Cam

MASTER LATCH LOCK

Pressure Relief Doors
Pushrods
Cranks
PRD Torque Tube
Release Trigger
Handle
Pushrods
Intermediate Torque Tube
MLL Torque Tube
Locking Sectors
Bellcranks

INITIAL CONTACT CLOSING

Locking Sector

Stripe alignment with all latches properly closed

Latch Cam
Closing door
Latch Pin
OUTBOARD
'Hoop stress' fuselage pressurisation loads

LATCH MECHANISM

Midspan Torque Tube
Midspan Cam
Pushrods
Bellcranks
Torque Tube
Latch Actuator
Pushrods
Lower Cams

Rotated Cam

CORRECTLY LATCHED & FULLY LOCKED

UNLATCHED BUT MISTAKENLY 'LOCKED'

analysis program should have detected the trend and prompted efforts to resolve the repeated difficulties. If it had, the damage to the lock sectors would have been detected.

All these unresolved deficiencies and oversights contributed to the cause of this accident.

Conclusions

• The aircraft had not been maintained in accordance with the provisions of the Airworthiness Directive requiring an inspection of the cargo door mechanisms each time the door was operated manually and restored to electrical operation.

• Multiple intermittent malfunctions of the cargo door in the months prior to the accident led to damaged lock sectors.

• The airline's maintenance trend analysis program was inadequate to detect an adverse trend involving the cargo door on the accident aircraft.

• FAA oversight of the airline's maintenance program did not ensure adequate trend analysis and adherence to the provisions of Airworthiness Directives.

• The wear patterns on the latch pins of the forward cargo door were signs that the door was not properly aligned for an extended period of time, causing interference during the normal opening and closing cycles.

• The design of the 747 cargo door locking mechanisms did not provide for intended "fail-safe" provisions.

• Boeing's Failure Analysis of the door mechanism was not valid, as evidenced by the findings of the PanAm incident investigation in 1987.

• Boeing and the FAA did not take immediate action to require the use of the cam position view ports following the PanAm incident, and did not include this requirement in their relevant Alert Service Bulletins and Airworthiness Directives.

• There were several opportunities for the manufacturer, the airline, and the FAA, to have taken action during the service life of the Boeing 747 that would have prevented the accident.

Probable cause

The National Transportation Safety Board determined that the accident was caused by the sudden opening of the improperly latched forward lower lobe cargo door in flight and the subsequent explosive decompression.

Contributing to the cause was a deficiency in the design of the cargo door locking mechanisms, which made them susceptible to inservice damage, allowed the door to be

HNL Dec.5th	Report – forward cargo door will not open. Corrective action: cranked door latches to close and recycled, checked okay.
HNL 6th	Report – forward cargo door will not open electrically. Corrective action: cranked door latches to close and recycled. Checked okay.
AKL 11th	Report – forward cargo door failed to close fully electrically, manually cranked "pull in" hooks half a turn to close and latches ran okay. Corrective action: adjusted on hook switches Deferred maintenance item 0827 initiated.
HNL 11-12th	Report – door cycled 3 times, opened and closed normally. Corrective action: cleared deferred maintenance item 827
AKL 12th	Report – forward cargo door fails to close electrically. Manually turned hooks to close with door switch selected close until power transferred to latch motor. Hook motor switch requires re-rigging. Corrective action: Deferred maintenance item 831 initiated.
SYD 12-14th	Report – forward cargo door will not latch electrically. When manually closing, latches fail to close sufficiently to close master latch lock after repeated attempts. Corrective action: latches opened manually, door recycled again and operation was normal electrically. (Deferred maintenance item 0831 continued open for future repair.)
AKL 14th	Report – when the aircraft landed, the door operated like the deferred write up. The aft lower corner of the door appears to be trailing. Suspect the hook motor may be over-heating causing the problem. Note: adjusted S-8 door switch, the door operates okay. The adjustment stop for S-8 is bent. Corrective action: (Deferred maintenance item 0831 continued open for future repair.)
HNL 17th	Report – necessary to cycle door 3 times to get it to latch manually. Corrective action: deferred maintenance item 0831 continued open for future repair.
HKG 17-19th	Report – deferred maintenance item 0831. Corrective action: replaced hook position relay K1. Checked door several times. It checked okay. Deferred maintenance item 0831 corrected.
NRT 22nd	Report – prior to departure, forward cargo door inoperative electrically. Manually closed. Corrective action: deferred maintenance item 0835 initiated for future repair.
ORD Dec. 22nd 23rd	Report – deferred maintenance item 0835. Corrective action: operated door several times, could not duplicate. Checked hook closed switch & hook position switch for being closed per MM-52-34-60 procedure 13. Deferred maintenance item 0835 corrected.

unlatched, yet to show a properly latched and locked position. Also contributing to the accident was a lack of proper maintenance and inspection of the cargo door by United Airlines, and a lack of timely corrective action by Boeing and the FAA following the 1987 cargo door incident on a PanAm 747.

Recommendations

As a result of the investigation, the National Transportation Safety Board issued the following recommendations to the FAA:

• Require that manual drives and electrical actuators on Boeing 747 cargo doors have torque limiters that ensure lock sectors cannot be overridden during mechanical or electrical operation of the latch cams.

• Require the installation of positive indicators for outward opening cargo doors on transport category aircraft, independently confirming the position of both latch cams and locks.

• Require that fail safe designs for such non-plug cargo doors on transport category aircraft allow for human error in addition to electrical and mechanical malfunctions.

Postscript to the investigation

Seventeen months after the accident and three months after the National Transportation Safety Board released its report on the investigation, the US Navy made a startling announcement.

For well over a year, using highly sophisticated, deep sea exploration equipment, the Navy had been continuing to sweep the seabed of the Pacific Ocean in the vicinity of the 747's inflight decompression, searching for the missing cargo

NTSB investigators reviewed N4713U's logbooks and maintenance history with their usual thoroughness. During December 1988 the aircraft spent most of its time on trans-Pacific operations, mainly to Auckland and Sydney, but also ventured as far afield as Seattle, Tokyo and Hong Kong. Of the 52 logged turnarounds between the 5th and 30th of that month, 34 were noted "No problem". Seven instances of trouble-free manual operation of the forward cargo door were also recorded. But the eleven "Report" write-ups (reproduced from the NTSB report) and their "Corrective Action", give some indication of the puzzling and frustrating door closing problems being experienced. The Reports show "the problem" either refusing to duplicate itself during trouble-shooting, or apparently righting itself after minor electrical or mechanical adjustments. The USN's successful salvage operation, 18 months after the accident, led the NTSB to withdraw its criticism of UAL maintenance staff and procedures, and warn of "possible ... uncommanded electrical actuation." (NTSB)

door. In July 1990, the salvage team's amazingly skilled and persistent operation was partly rewarded when a section of the door was located in water well over two nautical miles (3700m) deep.

Encouraged by their remarkable find, but still not satisfied, the Navy elected to continue the search, seemingly against overwhelming odds. Three months later again, a second section of the door was found at a similar depth!

When examined by NTSB investigators, the condition of the door's locking mechanism did not support their earlier conclusion that, *because of previous damage* to the lock sectors, the latch cams could have been only partly latched after the door appeared to be closed.

Rather, the investigators' inspection now revealed that *the possibility they had previously considered quite remote had in fact occurred* – the latch cams had been back-driven from the closed position into a nearly open position after the door had been closed and locked. This back-driving of the latch cams had actually caused the deformation of the lock sectors, which of course, had they been strong enough, should have prevented the back-driving.

As a result, the NTSB found it necessary to amend its earlier published findings on the overall accident investigation. The previous conclusion that "multiple intermittent malfunctions of the cargo door in the months prior to the accident led to damaged lock sectors" was deleted from the NTSB report, and the following conclusions were added.

• Short circuits found in the cargo door electrical wiring could have led to unintended operation of the latch actuator. This most likely occurred before the engines were started at Honolulu. There was a small possibility that it could have taken place after this, but only while the APU was running with the aircraft still on the ground.

• Electrical insulation breakdowns found in the recovered cargo door wiring could have resulted in short circuiting. No evidence of arcing was found, but not all the door's wiring was recovered and tests showed that such arcing might not have been detectable.

• An uncommanded movement of cargo door latches that took place on another Boeing 747 in June 1991 was attributed to insulation damage and a consequent short circuit in the wiring bundle between the fuselage and the door. Because of the condition of the accident aircraft's cargo door switches however, movement of its cargo door latches could not have occurred after the door was locked.

In addition, the following sentence was added to the first paragraph of the NTSB's official ascription of "Probable cause" in their investigation report:

"The door opening was attributed to a faulty switch or wiring in the door control system which permitted electrical actuation of the door latches towards the unlatched position after initial door closure and before takeoff."

The revised conclusions, resulting from the US Navy's determined and painstaking efforts over so many months, on top of the NTSB's exhaustive investigation of the operation and maintenance of Boeing 747 cargo doors, doubtless made an important contribution to preventing another such inflight calamity.

But for those who experienced the trauma and terror on board Flight 811 in the early hours of February 24, 1989, the finding nearly two years later that the root cause of it all was an electrical fault in the door rather than a mechanical one, might seem somewhat academic.

CHAPTER 3

"Well, folks, it just isn't our day..."

– Captain's P/A announcement to passengers

Air Ontario Fokker F28-1000 Fellowship, C-FONF [11060]
– March 10, 1989

Snow and ice on the wings – and the need to de-ice before takeoff – is a routine hurdle for pilots in Canada's frozen interior. So why did a highly experienced crew ignore this everyday hazard? The complex answer sends a message to all with a role in aviation – regulatory and corporate, as well as operational.

Frustration from the start

For two Canadian airline pilots, Friday March 10, 1989, didn't even begin well.

Rostered as a crew, Captain George Morwood and First Officer Keith Mills were to fly an Air Ontario Fokker Fellowship on two short return trips from Winnipeg, Manitoba, to Thunder Bay, Ontario. The latter airport serves the twin towns of Fort William and Port Arthur on the northern coast of Lake Superior, and enroute calls were scheduled at the provincial airport of Dryden, also in sparsely settled northern Ontario.

Based in the town of London, 170km southwest of Toronto, Air Ontario was a regional airline, one of several 'feeders' to Air Canada. Bookings from Thunder Bay to Winnipeg were unusually heavy, for it was the eve of a long weekend and the end of the Canadian school term. Schools were breaking for the Spring holidays, and many passengers had connections with Air Canada flights.

At 6:40am Central Standard Time, in readiness for their departure at 7:25am, the crew reported for duty at Winnipeg International Airport. If all went as scheduled, they would complete their day's flying when

they landed back at Winnipeg for the second time at 3:30pm.

The weather forecasts for the day's operations were anything but encouraging. Generally unsettled and deteriorating conditions, with lowering cloud ceilings and freezing precipitation were expected as the day wore on.

Although highly experienced, Captain Morwood had been in command of F28 Fellowships for only two months and had only some 80 hours on type. Air Ontario's Operations Manual applied ceiling and visibility restrictions to takeoff and landings by captains with less than 100 hours in command of F28 aircraft, and the terminal forecasts indicated conditions could deteriorate below the captain's landing limits.

The unfavourable forecasts therefore required the crew to provide for a diversion to an alternate airport. As the only viable alternate was Sault Ste Marie, a town some 225nm further east of Thunder Bay at the extreme eastern tip of Lake Superior, the heavy passenger loadings meant that the aircraft would have to take on fuel at Dryden on each of the return trips.

His flight planning completed,

Captain Morwood reviewed the aircraft's documents, only to find that C-FONF's Auxiliary Power Unit had been unserviceable for the preceding five days, despite efforts to remedy the defect. This posed a further problem – Dryden Airport did not have ground equipment for starting an F28.

For this reason, the Flight Release, issued by the company's Operations Control from its London (Ontario) headquarters to authorise the aircraft's departure, specified that the crew were to leave one engine running during the enroute stops at Dryden. This in turn meant that refuelling would also have to be carried out with the engine running – a procedure known as 'hot refuelling'.

Captain Morwood and F/O Mills then boarded the aircraft, where Purser Katherine Say and Flight Attendant Sonia Hartwick were preparing for departure. In addition to the defective APU, there were several persisting cabin 'snags' – a passenger door that was difficult to close, unserviceable emergency exit lighting, and missing oxygen equipment – and the captain expressed his frustration that these had not been rectified.

Doubtful weather

At 7:49am CST, with only 11 passengers occupying the 65 seat cabin, the F28 lifted off from Winnipeg for the first leg of the initial flight to Thunder Bay. Although the weather at Dryden was now satisfactory for their approach, conditions further on at Thunder Bay had already deteriorated. While they were enroute to Dryden therefore, Operations Control contacted the Dryden passenger agent to ask Captain Morwood to telephone them after landing.

The Fellowship landed at Dryden at 8:19am, 13 minutes behind schedule, parking at the terminal with the starboard engine continuing to run. First Officer Mills remained on the flightdeck, while Captain Morwood went to telephone Operations as requested.

Operations told the captain that, as visibility at Thunder Bay was only three eighths of a mile (less than 700m) in fog, with overcast cloud at 100 feet, the aircraft was to remain on the ground at Dryden pending an improvement in the weather. But when Morwood pointed out that one engine would be consuming fuel throughout this wait, it was agreed that he should call back in 15 minutes.

When Morwood telephoned for the second time, the weather at Thunder Bay was still below his landing limits, but there were signs of it improving. It was agreed that the F28 should now depart, in the expectation that the weather would continue to improve but, if it did not, the flight would divert to Sault Ste Marie as originally planned.

At 8:50am CST, now with 30 passengers aboard and 20 minutes behind time, the Fellowship took off. Conditions did in fact improve during the 40 minute trip above the sparsely settled, pine forested hinterland of northern Ontario, and the crew were able to make an uneventful descent. At 10:30am EST they shut down at Air Canada's Thunder Bay terminal, still 20 minutes behind schedule.

Unplanned load

For the trip back to Winnipeg via Dryden, designated as Flight 1363, the Flight Release issued earlier in the day showed passenger loadings of 55 from Thunder Bay to Dryden, and 52 from Dryden onto Winnipeg. Again Sault Ste Marie was to be the alternate, and the aircraft was required to carry a total of 15,800 pounds (7170kg) of fuel. Some 6190lb (2810kg) were accordingly added to the aircraft's tanks.

After refuelling had been completed however, and all the depart-

F28 C-FONF on the apron at Thunder Bay, barely a fortnight before its disastrous loss. This picture, taken by a passenger, was reproduced in the Commission of Inquiry's final report.

ing passengers and their luggage loaded, it was learned that, as a result of the cancellation of an earlier regional flight, Air Canada had booked an additional 10 passengers on Flight 1363. Air Canada had not informed Air Ontario of the change early enough for the Flight Release to be amended, and this now brought the F28's passenger load up to its total capacity of 65.

Faced with the fact that his aircraft was now overloaded, Captain Morwood told Air Canada's Thunder Bay office he would have to 'bump' (offload) the additional passengers. But when Air Canada conveyed this decision to Air Ontario's Operations Control, the company countermanded the captain's decision, instructing instead that fuel should be offloaded.

Frustrated by the bookings misunderstanding and angry at the company's decision, the captain had 2823lb (1282kg) of fuel pumped from the aircraft's tanks, leaving a total of 13,000lb (5900kg) on board.

The defuelling operation took a further 35 minutes and some Winnipeg bound passengers, with connecting flights to catch, were becoming anxious. Fearing they would miss their connections, they mentioned their concerns to Purser Say and F/A Hartwick, who passed them on to the pilots, adding to the flightcrew's sense of frustration.

At 11:55am EST, now fully an hour behind schedule, the F28 finally departed again for Dryden, where the terminal forecast had been amended to include freezing precipitation. Half an hour later, as they approached Dryden, the crew were informed that light snow had fallen to the west of the town, but the run-

ways remained bare and dry. Just before 11:40am CST, as the jet touched down on Dryden's Runway 29, light snow began to fall on the airport, melting as it made contact with the ground.

Dryden again: more frustration

Turning off the runway at Taxiway Alpha, the main taxiway leading to the terminal building, the aircraft was marshalled on to the apron and came to a stop in front of the terminal. Only the port engine was shut down, the starboard engine being kept running as before.

Eight passengers were leaving the aircraft, with another seven, including two children, joining the flight for Winnipeg. Under a gloomy overcast sky, the snow, gradually increasing in intensity, was now falling in "big wet fluffy flakes" as one witness later described it.

A few minutes after the F28's arrival, Captain Morwood left the flightdeck to telephone Operations yet again, informing them there would be a further short delay while the aircraft took on more fuel. To staff at the Air Ontario counter, Captain Morwood's telephone exchanges appeared to become heated, and he slammed down the handset with some asperity. Speaking then to two passengers who had just left the aircraft, he appeared upset as he apologised for the inconvenience they had suffered.

On the apron meanwhile, a tanker crew were bringing the aircraft's fuel load up to a total of 13,000lb (5900kg) – 6500lb (2900kg) in each wing.

Still on the flightdeck, F/O Mills called Kenora Flight Service (midway between Winnipeg and Dryden – see map) to update the weather forecasts. He told Kenora that visibility at Dryden was "one and a half miles" (slightly less than three kilometres) and described the snow as "quite puffy ... looks like we're going to have a heavy one". Snow continued to fall in big soft flakes.

Captain Morwood returned afterwards, walking quickly through the falling snow from the terminal. As he came up the steps, one passenger thought he looked "disgusted". Neither he nor the first officer conducted a "walk around" inspection of the aircraft.

The doors were closed and, as the pilots started the port engine, a thin film of slush was covering the tarmac, and there was an accumulation of between a quarter and half an inch (6-12mm) of snow on the aircraft's wings.

At 12:03pm, as the Fellowship began to taxi, the snowfall increased. F/O Mills again called Kenora Flight Service to request an

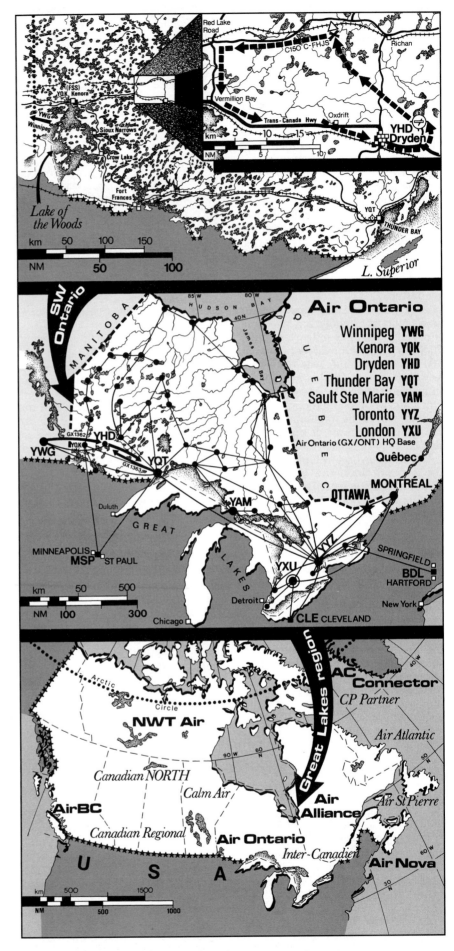

Map references in this chapter. (bottom) Canada, the world's second largest nation in area (after Russia, just bigger than the USA or China) showing the duopoly that developed after airline deregulation in 1986. As Pacific Western and CP Air merged, Air Canada was forced to look to its own traffic base. The ripple effects through many small regional operators led to an 18 month upheaval in the Canadian airline industry. Air Ontario Inc, after its own complex evolution, found itself under the Air Canada Connector banner.

(above centre) Ontario, the most populous of Canada's 12 provinces, showing Air Ontario's route network around the beginning of 1988: the links north and west were formerly Austin Airways' routes; the denser urban corridors south and east those of Great Lakes Airlines. Only the principal domestic ports are shown.

(centre left) Bolder arrows mark the route of C-FONF's eastbound Winnipeg/Dryden/ Thunder Bay flight – and the ill-fated return service.

(top) Southwestern Ontario's topography between Kenora (L) and Thunder Bay (R) is characterised by sub Arctic woodland, numerous lakes and semi tundra. Apart from two east-west rail links, and the Trans-Canada Highway, which connects Kenora and Dryden with Winnipeg, the limited ground communication is evident. Regional centres, as well as many small communities, are heavily dependent on air transport during the long winter months.

(top right) This inset of the Dryden area shows the approximate track of Cessna 150 C-FHJS. Its pilot had intended to continue to the NNW, but the deteriorating weather led him to follow roads back to Dryden. The Cessna's untimely arrival south of the field led to the F28 crew's reluctant decision to hold clear of the runway until the light aircraft landed. (Matthew Tesch; Flight International, Philip's, Rand McNally & the Commission report)

IFR clearance to Winnipeg. But before this could be passed, a Cessna 150 called Kenora FS in urgent tones, reporting 4nm south of Dryden and inbound for landing. The Cessna pilot declared he was having "real bad weather problems" and asked if there were "any chance that plane [the Fellowship] can hold."

Captain Morwood at once called the Dryden terminal on its own frequency to advise they would have to hold: "I can't believe there's a small plane coming in," he declared with exasperation. "God knows how long we'll have to wait." He then repeated the information to his passengers on the PA system, preceding it with the words: "Well, folks, it just isn't our day ..."

By now it was snowing heavily and, with the Fellowship standing at the Taxiway Alpha holding point, Mills transmitted on the Flight Service frequency: "OK – [Flight] 1363's holding short of the active – be advised you are now down to half a mile [visibility] or less in snow."

Minutes later, despite the difficult conditions, the Cessna touched down a short distance beyond the threshold of Runway 29, and the pilot called the F28 to ask: "Are you using Runway 11 or 29?"

"We'll go for 29," Mills replied, and the Cessna pilot let his aircraft roll past Taxiway Alpha to permit the F28 to enter the runway and backtrack for the 29 threshold. Captain Morwood again called the Dryden terminal, this time in a calmer tone: "OK – that small aircraft is down, and we're going to taxi out now." As

the Fellowship continued to backtrack, Kenora passed its IFR clearance to Winnipeg, and the crew lowered 18° of flap.

Takeoff in the snow

Reaching the eastern end of the runway, the crew turned the aircraft through 180° to line up and, holding it on the brakes, spooled up the engines to full power. Mills then transmitted: "Air Ontario 1363's about to roll 29 at Dryden." Fifteen seconds later the brakes were released and the F28 began its takeoff run, an hour and 10 minutes behind schedule. Almost six minutes had elapsed since it had begun holding to allow the Cessna 150 to land.

Snow was continuing to fall with increasing intensity as the F28 accelerated, and the runway was covered by about half an inch (12mm) of wet slush. After a slower than usual acceleration, and longer than normal run of about 3500 feet (1070m), the aircraft was seen to rotate, but struggled only briefly into the air before settling back on the runway. Even so, the takeoff continued.

Rotating a second time, the Fellowship finally lifted off in a nose-high attitude only 100m from the end of the 6000 foot (1830m) runway, passing over the end at a height of only about 15 feet, still with the wings at a high angle of attack.

Down into the trees

Now just visible to those watching the takeoff through the heavy snowfall, the F28 was lost to view behind trees beyond the end of the runway, but its engines could still be heard at

high power. Suddenly there was a brief period of silence – then an intense fireball of orange flames and a mushroom cloud of black smoke erupted from the direction in which the aircraft had disappeared.

One of the airport fire service vehicles, a water tanker, was still on the apron, its driver washing down a small fuel spillage that had occurred when the refuelling hose was disconnected from the F28. Realising the aircraft had crashed, he drove off at high speed towards the western end of the runway. The tanker was quickly followed by the fire chief driving the fire service van. But when they saw the fire was well beyond the western end of the airport and probably in the vicinity of the middle marker beacon, they turned around and headed back towards the terminal and the airport main gate.

The fire chief meanwhile had radioed Kenora Flight Service, reporting the F28 had gone down, and the Dryden police, requesting the municipal emergency plan be activated. The fire chief's van was quickly joined by a rapid intervention fire appliance and the vehicles sped west along the adjoining highway to reach the gate to the access road leading to the middle marker beacon. The fire chief quickly unlocked the gate, waving the other vehicle through first.

Despite the fire crew's rapid response, two civilians were the first to reach the crash site. They too had driven quickly to the access road to the middle marker beacon but, finding the gate locked, climbed over it,

Sistership C-FONG [11070] at Glasgow on December 4, 1988, during its delivery flight on lease from TAT in France. Four months after the Dryden accident, TAT leased this aircraft to Air Niugini as P2-ANY. Having led almost identical earlier lives as the third and fourth of five THY Mk 1000s, both Air Ontario Fellowships came to violent ends. Iran Asseman Airlines bought the former C-FONG in January 1992 as EP-PAW, only to fly it into a mountain near Natanz less than two years later. The fate of another of the Turkish F28s is mentioned in Chapter 5. (WAFN-M/Robert Ellis)

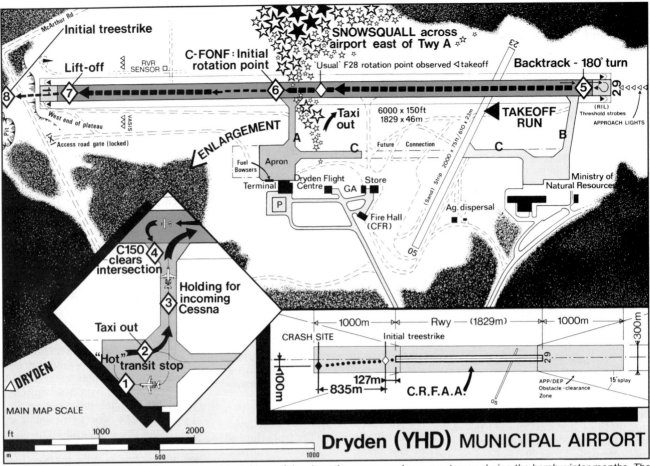

Dryden Municipal Airport at the time of the accident. Many of the airport's access roads were not open during the harsh winter months. The lower right inset shows the Critical Rescue and Firefighting Access Area, as defined by Transport Canada – but it failed to take into account the conditions of the terrain. (Matthew Tesch)

continuing on foot up the road until they were as close as possible to the fire, then forcing their way through about 150cm of snow to the crash site itself. A number of survivors had already escaped from the blazing wreckage, some of them with extensive burns and serious injuries, and all of them suffering from shock. The time was now 12:20pm CST.

Police, ambulances and medical staff were now also arriving at the access road and all possible priority was given to assisting the survivors – tending their wounds, carrying those unable to walk, loading them into ambulances. The 20 to 25 survivors capable of walking were meanwhile making their way to the access road, following the path already forced through the snow. Some were children and all were inadequately clad for the cold.

An hour after the crash, two men were found trapped beneath wreckage, both of them badly injured. Twenty-two bodies, including those of the pilots and the purser, were later recovered from the burnt-out wreckage.

INVESTIGATION

On-site examination

A team of investigators from the Canadian Aviation Safety Board arrived in Dryden aboard two Transport Canada aircraft the morning after the accident.

It was immediately evident that the F28, having failed to climb away after takeoff, had descended into dense pine forest on low snow covered hills *below* the elevation of the airport to the west of Runway 29.

The investigators found that, after leaving the runway close to its western end, the aircraft continued on an almost level flightpath for only 127m, before it began clipping the tops of the pine forest. Barely clearing a tree covered hillock some 600m further on, it then nosed down sharply, cutting a deep swathe through snow covered forest as it demolished trees, caught fire, and struck the ground on the down slope of the hill. Breaking apart and beginning to burn fiercely, the wreckage skidded for a further 80m before lurching to a violent stop, broken into three main sections, almost a kilometre from the end of the runway.

Wreckage examination

The three main sections of wreckage – nose and flightdeck, main fuselage with the starboard wing still attached, and tail section, including both rear mounted engines and the empennage – came to rest upright in the form of a U, with the nose and tail sections pointing back towards the airport (see diagram).

The fire had broken out when the port wing fuel tank was ruptured by tree impacts. The wreckage continued to burn until finally extinguished by the Dryden fire service about two hours later. By this time the flightdeck and fuselage back as far as the rear pressure bulkhead had been consumed. The empennage and the engines escaped serious fire damage.

There was no evidence that the aircraft was on fire before striking the trees, and all the damage was consistent with the tree and ground impacts, and the fire that followed.

At the time of impact the undercarriage was still in transit to the 'up' position. The flaps were extended to between 25° and 27°, the flap setting evidently having been increased from the takeoff position of 18° in a desperate effort to remain airborne.

Examination of both engines and their accessories, together with a thorough investigation of their operating history, showed that both were capable of producing full power. Indeed, it was evident that the engines were operating at takeoff power until after the aircraft became airborne, when it is probable that they were opened to full power. The engine anti-icing system was selected "on".

Although the crew did not leave a completed weight and balance sheet with the company agent, the investigation established that the weight of the aircraft was between 62,600lb (28,420kg) and 64,800lb (29,420kg), well within its maximum structural gross takeoff weight of 65,000lb (29,510kg). The centre of gravity was also within allowable limits.

Overall, the wreckage examination failed to reveal any pre-crash fault that could have contributed to the accident.

The aircraft

The Mk 1000 Fellowship was 16 years old, having been built in Holland in November 1972. For most of its life it had been owned and operated by the Turkish national airline, Turk Hava Yollari. In early 1988 it was bought by the French company, Transport Aerien Transregional, and leased to Air Ontario. It had flown a total of 21,500 hours and had operated 24,600 flight cycles. Its two Rolls-Royce Spey RB183-2 engines had run 9000 and 2300 hours since overhaul, and had been maintained in accordance with approved schedules.

The crew

Captain George Morwood, 52, had been flying from the time he was old enough to become a student pilot in 1953. Two years later he qualified as a commercial pilot and flying instructor, and for the next 12 years he instructed and flew charters for a Toronto based company. In the late 1960s, now with some 13,000 hours' experience, he was appointed a Transport Canada inspector responsible for pilot proficiency checks. In 1970 he became a corporate pilot for a mining company, crewing a Grumman Gulfstream II business jet. Three years later he joined Great Lakes Airlines, the forerunner of Air Ontario, and for the following 15 years flew Convair 440 and CV-580 turboprops. By 1988 he was a highly experienced airline pilot, having served as a company check pilot, chief pilot, and gained management experience. In January 1989 he began line flying on Air Ontario's two newly acquired F28s.

Morwood had more than 24,000 hours' flying experience, but had been in command of F28s for only two months and had only some 80 hours on type. Moreover, the Fellowship was the biggest jet he had commanded, and the only jet type he had flown on scheduled services. He was highly regarded for his operating

Single point adaptor underwing pressure refuelling was a feature of the F28's fast turnaround capability. With the aircraft's fuel control panel only "a few feet" away, all key servicing could be handled from the starboard side. "An important factor in fast turnaround is the APU", claimed Fokker. With C-FONF's APU unserviceable, and the F28 dependent on its No.2 RR Spey for power on the ground at Dryden, the crew was in an awkward position. De-icing with an engine running was specifically prohibited. Moreover, passengers should not have been aboard during a 'hot' refuelling. (Fokker)

standards, sound decision making, and safety consciousness. A fastidious man, he was a stickler for punctuality, with a sense of responsibility for the welfare of his passengers.

First Officer Keith Mills, 35, a pilot for 16 years, had more than 10,000 hours' experience, 3500 hours of which had been gained in jets. After a time as a flying instructor in Toronto, he became a Twin Otter pilot in Canada's far north, later flying light twins and Cessna Citations on air ambulance operations into remote settlements. A year before the accident, Mills gained a command on Air Ontario's Hawker Siddeley HS.748 turboprop aircraft, but only a few months later these were sold. He then applied to become a first officer on the company's newly acquired F28s, and began line operations on the type only a month before the accident. An assertive personality who could be abrasive, Mills had experienced aircraft handling problems on several occasions during his career, necessitating additional training.

Purser Katherine Say and Flight Attendant Sonia Hartwick were qualified and experienced. Both had undergone first aid and firefighting training, and were well regarded by management. Purser Say had not originally been rostered for F28 flights at the time of the accident but, in her supervisory capacity, had been asked to crew them to review the company's cabin service.

Flight recorders

The F28 was fitted with a 19 parameter Sundstrand Universal FDR and a Sundstrand Model V-557 CVR. Both were located in the wreckage and were despatched to the Canadian Aviation Safety Board's laboratory in Ottawa for examination.

Although neither recorder had sustained serious impact damage, both had been subjected to extreme heat, effectively destroying the recording mediums. There was no way the analog information could be recovered from remnants of the CVR tape, and attempts to recover at least some of the digital data on the FDR tape, using scanning electron microscopes, was unsuccessful.

Dryden Airport

Dryden Municipal Airport, elevation 1354 feet, is owned by Transport Canada and operated by the Dryden Airport Commission. Situated 6.5km northeast of the town, its main bitumen surfaced Runway 11/29 is 6000 feet (1829m) long and 150 feet (46m) wide (see airport diagram).

Flight path reconstruction

Because no data was available from the flight recorders, it was necessary to conduct a detailed investigation of the Fellowship's brief flight, using computer generated imagery. The resulting reconstruction did not exhibit any unusual yaw, pitch or roll tendencies before the aircraft's impact with the trees. Moreover, it agreed with the field investigators' conclusions resulting from their assessment of damage.

Witness evidence: the takeoff

Eye-witness evidence was obtained from 10 people on the ground – pilots, fire service staff, airport ground staff and maintenance employees – who watched all or part of the takeoff. Their consensus was that the aircraft's acceleration was slower than usual, that it initially rotated much further down the runway than normal, and that even after it had done so, the main wheels remained on the ground for a considerable time.

It finally lifted off sluggishly after a second, more pronounced rotation, about 5700 feet (1735m) from the beginning of the takeoff. After becoming airborne, one wing dropped and was corrected, but the Fellowship failed to gain altitude, "mushing" through the air in a nose-high attitude.

The evidence of surviving passengers was consistent with these observations. An Air Ontario Dash 8 captain travelling as a passenger said that, after the first attempt at rotation, approximately 4000 feet (1260m) down the runway, the aircraft began to shudder. The nose was then lowered to about half the normal rotation angle, and a second rotation followed.

F/A Sonia Hartwick also recalled the aircraft rotating, failing to become airborne, then rotating a second time. She said that on the first rotation, the aircraft seemed to bounce, fell back on to the runway, bounced again as it rotated for the second time, "jerked to the left with the left wing coming down", and stayed in the air.

Another passenger, a professional engineer with experience in flight testing, said that after becoming momentarily airborne, the aircraft "came back down on to the runway". The noise of the engines then increased and the aircraft finally became airborne. As it crossed the end of the runway, it was only about 15 feet off the ground.

Witness evidence affirmed that the wings of the Fellowship carried a considerable accumulation of snow and "sculptured" ice. One passenger said the amount of snow was such that he "couldn't see the line of rivets". Another declared that, while the F28 was standing at the terminal, the falling snow was "slowly but steadily increasing". A third, in a window seat directly over the wing, said the snow on the wing was melting, but not as quickly as it was falling. At the time the refuelling tanker was by the aircraft, there was an accumulation of up to half an inch (12mm) on the wing. New snow was continually landing on top of melting snow.

F/A Hartwick said that the snowfall intensified while they were waiting for the Cessna to land and that, as they began to takeoff, *the layered buildup of fluffy snow crystallised and turned to ice*. She saw the transformation as it happened.

The window seat passenger said he was looking closely at the wing during the takeoff, hoping the accumulated snow would slide off. As the nose lifted, snow on the rear half of the wing came off with an explosive puff, but that on the forward part quickly froze into rough opaque ice.

Several other survivors, including the Air Ontario Dash 8 captain and an Air Canada DC-9 captain travelling as a passenger, described the ice on the wings as crystalline, layered and rough textured as the F28 accelerated.

Witness evidence: the accident

As the Fellowship finally lifted off after the second rotation, many on

This Fokker picture of one of its F28-1000 demonstrators evokes the takeoff attempt at Dryden. Omit the background and this F28 could be reproducing C-FONF's initial rotation. The wet snow falling in large, puffy flakes was held by the Inquiry to have contributed to the aerodynamic degradation of the Fellowship's contaminated wings. Research by Fokker found that such sticky precipitation would have adhered to the wings' upper surfaces for up to 19% of chord. In other words, potentially a fifth of the F28's wings were accumulating spatterings on top of the existing roughness of the cold-soaked wing. (Fokker)

board sensed something was drastically wrong. The DC-9 captain said that, after the first rotation, the aircraft initially lifted, then "sat back down". Even more engine power was added and the second rotation was to a steeper angle. But although the aircraft lifted off this time, it did no more than maintain this nose-up angle, "mushing through the air".

Even before the initial contact with the trees, a few passengers, realising the aircraft was not flying properly, were assuming a brace position, and F/A Hartwick, seated in the midsection of the cabin, called to passengers to brace themselves.

As the aircraft began hitting trees, Hartwick again shouted to passengers to brace themselves, keep their heads down and grab their ankles. Towards the rear of the cabin, the Dash 8 captain did the same. After the first tree strike, the aircraft levelled out briefly and some passengers thought it would fly away. But it then hit more trees and the banging on the fuselage intensified.

As it descended into the trees, the battering became severe and the noise of tearing metal accompanied passengers' screams and yells. A Royal Canadian Mounted Policeman, one of two escorting a prisoner in the rearmost seats said later: "... the trees kept coming and coming ... I could hear them grinding away at the underside of the aircraft. It seemed to take forever ..."

As the aircraft struck the ground proper, the fuselage broke open. Snow and tree branches were pushed into the cabin, and there was a strong smell of fuel. A passenger looked up to see people being thrown about, luggage tumbling from overhead racks, a spray of jet fuel dousing some passengers, and a sudden flash of fire. Others, bent over in the brace position, saw flame flash from the rear to the front of the cabin. Yet others saw electrical sparks and felt heat from the flash fire.

As the final, violent stop occurred, seats failed at their mountings and were hurled forwards, immobilising their severely jostled occupants. The cabin lighting failed, overhead racks were dislodged, and more fuel was sprayed into the cabin. Black acrid smoke, restricting visibility and rendering breathing difficult, quickly filled the cabin. Burning sections of overhead racks, some already dripping molten plastic, fell on survivors.

Survival

The seating layout comprised 13 rows, each with three seats to the left of the aisle and two to the right (see diagram). The port wing had been fragmented as it cut a swathe through the trees, spilling the contents of its fuel tanks. As a result, passengers in the portside forward seven rows not only suffered the most trauma, but were most exposed to fire. Indeed, only two of the 21 in these seats were to survive. Both pilots, and Purser Katherine Say in her seat immediately behind the flightdeck, also lost their lives.

Those still conscious struggled to release seat belts, and desperately tried to find their way out through the thick smoke. The fire propagated

C-FONF's attempts to become airborne left its mark on the environment. This photograph shows the Rwy 11 threshold and the snowy embankment at the western end of the Dryden Airport plateau. The swathe cut by the aircraft is that defined by "Tree Groups 5-8" in a following diagram. The conifers flanking the swathe were scorched by ignited fuel from the ruptured port wing. (Commission photo)

rapidly, with numerous detonations. Some survivors scrambled over others, some had seat backs pushed on to them by those trying to escape from behind. Yet there was no real panic and many survivors helped one another.

Two men, buried by cabin wreckage in seats 4D and 4E, could hear and feel other survivors escaping over them. After a struggle to free himself, one crawled through a small opening, but then saw his friend was trapped by the legs. While other survivors tripped over them both in their haste to escape, he began removing debris from his friend.

A woman passenger, her body in flames, fell on the trapped man, but was then assisted from the burning aircraft. From the same row of seats, but across the aisle, a young woman holding her baby escaped with the help of the man sitting alongside her, all three suffering burns.

By this time the man attempting to rescue his friend could feel the synthetic fibres of his coat melting. Realising they had little time left and, with the heat now almost unbearable, both exerted pressure on the wreckage together and the man's legs were suddenly freed.

Passengers towards the rear found an impenetrable wall of debris prevented any access to the front of the aircraft, while a curtain of fire blocked their escape through the port side overwing hatch by seat 8A. Only one passenger escaped this way, sustaining severe burns as he did so.

The man in seat 8E was ready to open his starboard side hatch as soon as the aircraft stopped. Though suffering extensive abrasions, he promptly climbed through and was followed by F/A Hartwick, and by a young girl (a daughter of the off duty DC-9 captain).

Other survivors escaped through breaks in the fuselage. One, despite severe injuries, climbed through an opening forward of the port wing before the fire became too intense. Fourteen did so through a gash in the fuselage just forward of the starboard wing, while another six left through the break aft of the starboard wing. Most of the others escaped through the fuselage break near the tail.

One man, travelling with his wife and children, helped his family out, then returned to assist others. Leaving only after ensuring no more were trapped in the tail, he hurried to the burning nose section and helped injured survivors away from the flames. Despite having been doused with fuel, he then returned to try to rescue two more from the blazing port side of the cabin, only to be forced back. *Altogether he helped save 12 passengers in addition to his family.*

When the tail section broke away, the Air Canada captain and another of his daughters found themselves sitting almost in the open, while those opposite them were still enclosed in the wreckage. After removing his daughter from the wreckage, the captain returned to extricate his wife.

The prisoner and one of the police escorting him escaped from the tail

section, but the other constable, his leg broken, fell to the ground between the fuselage and tail and was trodden on by escaping survivors. Recognising his plight, two passengers applied a makeshift splint and dragged him to safety. Undaunted, he sat in the snow waiting for a stretcher, took out his notebook, and recorded details of the crash.

A passenger in seat 2A, pinned by wreckage and the severely injured bodies of those who had been seated near him, was not rescued until an hour after the crash. Badly injured, he was screened from the worst effects of the fire by the bodies of others.

Altogether 47 survivors escaped from the burning wreckage, of whom two later died. There were seven surviving children under 16, all of whom were assisted by their parents or passengers seated next to them. None suffered serious physical injury.

Rescue

The Fellowship had come down in heavy timber, the ground beneath it strewn with dead branches and underbrush. The wet, heavy snowfall persisted for some time after the accident and all the survivors were exposed to extreme cold, most having removed their winter coats when they boarded the aircraft. Eleven, including F/A Hartwick, had lost their shoes.

Safely away from the fire, survivors sought to reduce the suffering of the less fortunate. Some removed their jackets to allow others with no shoes to stand on them, others gave up sweaters to those who were cold. Some performed rudimentary first-aid, some comforted the emotionally upset, others helped those who had difficulty walking.

Sonia Hartwick, despite the shock of losing her fellow crew members, and head injuries which later proved to be a fracture of the skull, displayed courage and leadership in ensuring survivors did not wander off into the forest. She also helped to care for the severely burnt woman passenger.

One passenger, a Transport Canada Flight Service officer, was helping, despite his abrasions, to carry the badly burnt woman from the crash site. He was wet through and his hands were frozen by the time her stretcher was placed in the ambulance. But the ambulance attendant, seeing the Transport Canada security pass still clipped to his shirt, took him for a local airport official and told him to return to the crash site! He did so, helping to load rescue equipment on the way, then met

(left) Wreckage of the port wing, laid out in an Ottawa hangar. The F28 rolled sharply to the left as it descended to the ground. (right) More recognisable parts of the starboard wing centre section lie before the gutted shell of the F28. Note the flap segment, track rail and twisted main undercarriage leg, still attached to the wingroot. (Commission photo)

two more survivors being brought out, and was asked to find an ambulance. But an hour and a half after escaping from the burning aircraft, his legs began to "give out" and he finally was taken to a police car.

The man who helped save 12 passengers in addition to his family, travelled to hospital with the injured police constable in the last ambulance, administering oxygen during the trip. His time as a survivor-cum-rescuer finally ended two hours after the crash when, cold and exhausted, he was reunited with his family.

THE COMMISSION OF INQUIRY

From the witness evidence, the weather at the time, the fact that the aircraft had not been de-iced before departure, the delays in takeoff while heavy snow continued to fall, together with the findings that the aircraft should have been fully capable of flight, it was obvious to the Canadian Aviation Safety Board that the F28 had failed to lift off and climb out normally for no other reason than the wings were heavily contaminated with snow and ice, a condition capable of causing a loss of lift of some 50% (see also *Air Disaster*, Vol 2, Ch 6, p94).

But how could an airline captain of the experience and responsibility of Captain Morwood, a man who had been flying in Canadian weather all his adult life, and a pilot known to be a stickler for flying 'by the book', make such a fundamental error?

Furthermore, why had not F/O Mills, highly experienced in sub Arctic flying, and himself an airline captain, 'leaned' upon Captain Morwood to prevent the rash decision to take off?

On board also were two other airline captains, both travelling as passengers, who were concerned at the condition of the wings, which they could see from the cabin windows. Why had they not attempted to intervene, when their own lives and those of their families were at risk? Even the cabin crew and other passengers were concerned at the amount of snow accumulating on the wings. One with aviation experience even drew it to Purser Say's attention.

At this stage however, 19 days after the crash, responsibility for the investigation was unexpectedly taken out of the hands of the Canadian Aviation Safety Board. The tragic nature of the accident, its perplexing circumstances, the anomalies coming to light in the airline, and even its operational surveillance by Transport Canada, had prompted the Privy Council of Canada to appoint a Commission "to inquire into the contributing factors and causes of Air Ontario Flight 1363 ... and report thereon, including such recommendations as may be deemed appropriate in the interests of aviation safety".

The Commission was not only to make an exhaustive investigation into the crash, *but also into the aviation system that allowed it to happen*. Indeed, the Commissioner, the Hon Virgil Peter Moshansky, a Justice of the Queen's Bench of Alberta, assisted by an impressive team of legal and technical advisers, was granted powers to conduct an inquiry that would be as wide-ranging as he saw fit.

The Commission called 166 witnesses and examined 1343 exhibits, most of them voluminous documents. The public hearings, held in Dryden, Thunder Bay, and Toronto

between June 1989 and January 1991 disclosed numerous deficiencies within Air Ontario, the aviation industry generally, and Transport Canada.

In his preface to the Commission's four volume report, Moshansky declared: "It is my hope that the work of this Commission will have served as a catalyst for change ... I am confident that, if the contents of this report are carefully considered and the recommendations ... accepted and implemented in a timely manner, an important contribution to aviation safety in Canada will have been made."

A summary of the Commission's more significant findings follows.

CORPORATE HISTORY

At the time of the accident, Air Ontario was Canada's third biggest regional airline, serving 15 destinations throughout central Canada and northern USA. But its corporate culture, derived from its modest origins and complex history, retained something of the *modus operandi* of a 'bush' airline. An outline of this history sheds light on some of the factors in the accident.

Austin Airways Ltd

Founded in 1934, Austin Airways was a northern, remote area air service. Forty years later, all its shares were acquired by White River Air Services. Owned by the Deluce family, White River conducted VFR charter operations in northern Ontario during the summer months, using float equipped Cessna, Beaver and Otter aircraft. The Deluce family retained the name Austin Airways.

At the time of the Deluce acquisition, Austin Airways was flying DC-3 and Canso (Canadian built PBY Catalina) aircraft on IFR services on both sides of Hudson Bay as far north as Cape Dorset and Baffin Island. One of the new owners' priorities was to modernise the fleet and, because turbine aircraft operate more effectively in this harsh environment, British HS.748s replaced the earlier types.

Twice, in 1979 and in 1981, the Deluce family expanded Austin Airways by acquiring several smaller airlines in northwestern Ontario and Manitoba. This added 25 scheduled destinations to the company's network, a base at Thunder Bay, some 30 single engine, light twin, and DC-3 aircraft, and a route linking Thunder Bay with Minneapolis, Minnesota, in the USA.

In 1981 the Deluce family made an acquisition of greater significance – a 50% interest in Air Ontario Limited, *the* principal regional airline in southern Ontario. But at this stage there was no attempt to integrate the operations of the two companies.

Meanwhile, more purchases of minor air operators strengthened Austin Airways further, enabling this company to provide services out of Toronto, Canada's busiest airport, with Beech 99s and HS.748s.

Air Ontario Ltd

Incorporated in 1961 as Great Lakes Airlines, Air Ontario operated Convair 440s in more densely settled southern Ontario. In 1975 Great Lakes entered an agreement with Air Canada to take over the latter's Toronto/London (Ontario), route with new CV-580 turboprops. The company thus became the first 'feeder' to Air Canada.

In 1981, Austin Airways, now the biggest airline serving northern Ontario, bought a 50% interest in Great Lakes and changed its name to Air Ontario Ltd. Between 1982 and 1986, Air Ontario expanded its routes considerably, adding more CV-580s to the fleet.

Late in 1986 Air Canada acquired 75% of the shares of both Air Ontario and Austin Airways, with the Deluce family retaining 25% in each. Air Canada's feeder arrangement with Air Ontario had proved successful, and a majority interest in the regional was to ensure the relationship remained intact. For the Deluce family also, the share acquisition provided capital for expanding and upgrading both 'their' airlines. William Deluce was retained as Chief Executive of Air Ontario Ltd, and continued in the same role with Austin Airways.

The two companies continued to operate separately, but within a few months it was clear that a merger would have economic advantages. This was agreed to in mid 1987, with the new combined company operating as Air Ontario Inc from June 19, 1987. Its management was comprised largely of former Austin Airways executives – individuals who had gained their aviation experience in northern 'bush' operations.

Merger

At the time of the merger, Air Ontario and Austin Airways had annual turnovers of some $C35 million each. Yet the two companies were still radically different.

Austin Airways had some 30 aircraft of seven different types – Cessna 402s, Beechcraft 99s and Super King Airs, DHC Twin Otters, DC-3s, Cessna Citations, and HS.748s. Air Ontario, by contrast, operated a homogeneous fleet of 11 CV-580s for its feeder agreement with Air Canada.

Austin ran a diverse range of flights, primarily to remote northeastern and northwestern Ontario – scheduled, charter and cargo services, and an air ambulance using Cessna Citations. Air Ontario on the other hand provided scheduled services between cities in populous southern Ontario and northern USA.

In many respects Austin Airways was still a bush operation, operating in a harsh environment, using unpaved airstrips marginal by 'southern' standards, with navigation aids and weather services of doubtful reliability. Demands on crews in the Canadian North were totally different from those flying heavy airline aircraft in southern, controlled airspace, and the attitudes and experi-

The Dryden investigation made extensive use of computer technology. But with the aircraft's CVR and DFDR both destroyed, data for the computers had to be obtained the hard way. Surveys and maps provided terrain data, but investigators, pacing out the 150m (490ft) wide, 1km (3280ft) long wreckage trail, had to identify and catalogue the positions of all clipped or damaged trees. A plywood baseboard was drilled according to a scaled tree-plan and pencils fixed into it to simulate trunk heights and break-points. To a 1:72 scale model of an F28, investigators added undercarriage and flaps to replicate the configuration of C-FONF. The model F28 was then 'fitted' to the model of each treegroup, and photographed. The results were fed into a computer, and the accuracy and realism of the reconstruction was surprising. This view shows the model F28 entering "Tree Groups 5-8" on the hilltop about 600m (1970ft) west of the runway. (Commission photo)

ence of pilots in the two airlines reflected these differences.

The managements of the two companies also echoed their original operating environments. The non-unionised Austin Airways was less structured than Air Ontario, with executives more interactive with employees: if some facilities were not available at a 'bush' port of call, pilots would do whatever was required, including loading and refuelling. By contrast, in the unionised Air Ontario, formal collective agreements governed employee-management relations, and tasks were clearly defined.

Air Ontario Inc

With the merger, employees sought to establish common representation by the unions concerned and, in the case of the pilot groups, a common seniority was defined. But negotiations with the new company broke down, resulting in a two month pilot strike. The outcome was an agreement applying common work rules to all Air Ontario Inc pilots.

The northern bush routes, dependent for their success on traditional staff versatility, were thus no longer viable and it was decided to sell them to smaller operators. But the decision produced great dislocation, the company shedding some 250 employees in the process.

The merger of the two regionals, the divestment of the northern operations, the staff reduction of almost a third, the merger of two disparate pilot groups, a lengthy pilot strike, the relationship with the new controlling shareholder, the rationalisation of the fleet, and the introduction of jet airliners, all posed challenges to the new management in the 18 months that followed the merger. A high turnover of management personnel also occurred.

The question for the Commission of Inquiry was whether Air Ontario was able to give appropriate priority to flight safety during this period of extreme administrative distraction. For it was in this environment that Air Ontario began its first scheduled jet operations with two solitary F28s.

The fundamental question

The technical findings of the investigation clearly indicated that Captain Morwood erred in commencing the takeoff with snow and ice on the wings. *But why?*

Air accident investigations traditionally involve enquiry into the human aspects of an occurrence – errors that were the immediate cause of the accident – and into other human involvement that did not intervene to prevent the accident. But the Commission's investigation now went further, uncovering regulatory and corporate deficiencies which could have influenced the development of the accident at Dryden.

Regulatory deficiencies

The Commission found that Transport Canada did not:
• have a comprehensive policy for training air carrier inspectors. Turnover in air carrier inspectors resulted in inexperienced staff being pressed into service with little training;
• monitor Air Ontario Inc following the merger and during its introduction of jet aircraft. As a result, Air Ontario operated its F28s for several months without an approved Minimum Equipment List, yet still deferred aircraft unserviceabilities. These discrepancies were not detected, even though Transport Canada approved the F28 training program;
• define criteria for directors of flight operations, chief pilots, and check pilots;
• have clear definitions as to what constituted essential airworthiness items. This left flightcrews uncertain as to when and under what conditions an aircraft should be despatched;
• provide clear guidance regarding the need for de-icing.
• require licensing or effective training of flight despatchers.

A proposed Transport Canada audit of Air Ontario was also delayed. In light of the major changes within the company, a thorough examination of operations was warranted. Even when an audit was eventually

Police vehicles at the crash site, after bulldozers cleared an access path from the Command Post at the intersection of Middle Marker and McArthur Roads, about 250m (820ft) to the southwest. Fire damage blackens the trees behind the empennage; also visible are the battered No 1 engine nacelle and the port main undercarriage. Although the airport's fire chief reached the scene only nine minutes after the crash, with reinforcements from all three emergency services arriving within half an hour, rescue and treatment of survivors preoccupied them all. The last survivors were enroute to hospital before fire-fighting equipment was set up to quell the flames in the still-burning wreckage – an hour and fifty minutes after the crash. But by then both the CVR and DFDR had been damaged beyond their designed protection limits. (Commission photo)

(opposite) This spectacular Matthew Tesch compilation is based on an aerial photograph taken by investigators the morning after the accident, with a sectional elevation of the terrain and flight profile at the top of the page. Treestrikes are related from the profile to the perspective drawing, with databoxes providing the time in seconds from the start of the takeoff, together with the F28's height relative to the runway, its attitude (roll, as '+' to the right, '-' left), and pitch ('+' up, '-' down). The different treestrike modes are depicted in the 'balloons'. In the foreground, the crash site can be related to rescue vehicle access. An enlarged plan of the wreckage is superimposed, but the ordered cabin diagram only indicates survivability – most of the cabin's contents and its occupants were hurled into a heap on the forward port side, with only seats D and E in rows 6,7 and 9 remaining in position. The survival of the passengers in seats 1E and 2A was nothing short of miraculous.

In the absence of DFDR data, the pitch angle of the F28 after liftoff was difficult to determine. It was finally established by the discovery of red glass from the anti-collision beacon on the aircraft's belly between Tree Groups 1 and 2. For the first treestrike to have destroyed the small fitting with such surgical precision, the investigators calculated the pitch angle would have been at least 5.5°. Had it been less, either the nose undercarriage or underside antennae fittings would have been damaged or carried tree debris – but none was found.

ELEVATION

m 50 100   500

◁2762m/58.5 sec

Nose falling
Port wing destroyed
Steepening roll left
Fuel ignited

Rwy
413m AMSL

-5m
-10
-15

-80m

Nose dropping   Stbd wing low   Nose high

From start of takeoff run
◁1927m/47.2 sec

Strip end Threshold   'Liftoff'

Typical F28 Rwy 29
departure

~50m

04m   8 7 6   5

4
McArthur   Road

3   2   1

C-FONF

Tree Group No. 1
Time: 47.2 sec
Altitude: -1.3 ft
Roll: 6.4 deg
Pitch: 5.5 deg

Access
gate locked

Tree Group No. 5
Time: 56.2 sec
Altitude: -10.8 ft
Roll: -10.1 deg
Pitch: -1.0 deg

Tree Group No. 6
Time: 56.3 sec
Altitude: -10.5 ft
Roll: -10.3 deg
Pitch: -1.3 deg

Tree Group No. 7
Time: 56.4 sec
Altitude: -11.1 ft
Roll: -10.5 deg
Pitch: -1.3 deg

Tree Group No. 8
Time: 56.5 sec
Altitude: -10.5 ft
Roll: -13.9 deg
Pitch: -3.6 deg

Tree Group No. 4
Time: 53.2 sec
Altitude: -5.5 ft
Roll: 6.4 deg
Pitch: 3.1 deg

Tree Group No. 3
Time: 50.0 sec
Altitude: -2.3 ft
Roll: 6.0 deg
Pitch: 5.5 deg

Tree Group No. 2
Time: 48.6 sec
Altitude: 2.0 ft
Roll: -1.1 deg
Pitch: 5.5 deg

Airport
plateau

1

2

3

4

Centreline 29 at rwy elevation

C-FONF
Rel. track
Alt./F'path

McArthur Road

5

6

7

8

-8m

-18m

Main
Wreckage   -25m

Bulldozed
Access

Survivors

Middle Marker Road

Burns, smoke
emphasis

13

11 10 9 8 7 6 5 4 3 2

A
B
C

D
E

Survivors

O.P.P. Police cars

Command Post
Roadblock

■ FATALITIES : Impact forces
emphasised here

○ CREW

12A GX Dash-8, 13D AC DC-9 Captains

conducted, it failed to review the most significant change – the step up to F28s.

In summary, the 'safety net' that should have been provided through statutory safety regulation, was lacking.

Corporate deficiencies

Air Ontario's management practices increased the potential for error. Air Canada, despite its controlling interest, did not require Air Ontario to operate to its new parent's 'first level' standards. Deficiencies might have been prevented had Air Canada taken a more active role.

During the Air Ontario-Austin Airways merger and the period leading up to the pilot strike, there was apprehension and animosity between the crews of the two companies. Former Air Ontario Ltd pilots referred to their Austin colleagues as "bush pilots", while former Austin Airways pilots called their Air Ontario Ltd counterparts "401 pilots" – an allusion to the major highway running from Windsor via Toronto to Montreal.

Personnel changes

The period between the merger and the Dryden accident saw substantial changes in personnel. Their number was reduced from 800 to 600, and there was turnover in critical management positions. This lack of continuity impeded standardisation following the merger, and supervision of introductory F28 operations.

Lack of jet experience

Air Ontario did not have experience in jet airline operations. At the time the Fellowship was being introduced, efforts were made to acquire outside management expertise, and representations were made to Transport Canada. A pilot with substantial jet transport experience was engaged but resigned after a month, *declaring he could not function when he did not get the support he needed.* Air Ontario then decided to manage the F28 program internally – using pilots with minimal F28 experience and no previous experience on large jet aircraft.

Operational inadequacies

Fellowship services were initiated without an Air Ontario operating manual. Neither was there an approved Minimum Equipment List until some months later. Crews thus lacked standardised operational guidelines.

Air Ontario's despatch and operational control system failed to provide crews with the same level of support as in the parent organisation. By contrast, Air Canada provided its despatchers with formal training and operational guidelines, including rules forbidding the despatch of an aircraft with an inoperative APU into any airport without groundstart facilities.

Training difficulties

The training of Air Ontario's F28 crews was contracted to Piedmont Airlines in the USA. Piedmont itself was being taken over by USAir which, to achieve standardisation, was converting all former Piedmont personnel to USAir procedures. As Air Ontario had not developed its own manuals, some pilots returned from their training with the Piedmont manual and others with that of USAir!

Another result of the USAir-Piedmont merger was that the Piedmont F28 flight simulator was *not* available to some Air Ontario crews. A number of Air Ontario F28 pilots were trained *in the aircraft itself* by Air Ontario F28 training pilots who were themselves newly qualified.

Air Ontario's chief pilot for both the F28 and the CV-580 was also its Fellowship project manager. He had numerous additional duties, including line flying during the strike, and conducting training and line indoctrination in the F28 for new crews. Yet he himself had little operational experience on either the Dutch twinjet or the American turboprop.

Informal culture

The period in which Air Ontario was introducing Fellowship services was characterised by lax supervision, high management turnover, a despatch system whose staff were inexperienced and lacked knowledge of the F28, and a lack of standard operating procedures.

One incident affecting crew attitudes was the removal of a Fellowship crew from a scheduled trip to be interviewed by the chief pilot for

The 'old guard' is farewelled by the new order in the rain at Toronto International Airport. Outgoing Convair 580 C-GJRP displays the blue and green livery of Air Ontario Ltd. Behind, a new Dash 8, C-GJIG, displays the bold vermilion, silver and white of the Air Canada Connector family. Great Lakes Airlines was a major Convair user, and the retitled Swissair livery of many of its 440 Metropolitans was a familiar sight in the early 1970s. A surprising number of CV-580s remain on the Canadian register as freighters or other conversions. The Dash 8 fleet of Connector members has burgeoned, and numerous leases occur to adjust capacity across the country. Only recently have the aircraft been named: C-GJIG (F/n 801) is now City of Harrisburg. Dryden however, a painful memory, does not appear on the fleetlist. (MT – WAFN-M/ John E Garden)

writing up too many maintenance discrepancies! Instead of entering 'snags' in the aircraft's journey logbook, pilots wrote them on pieces of paper to pass on to relieving crews, thus deferring maintenance and avoiding grounding the aircraft.

Another nonstandard procedure was called "the 80 knot check", *a visual examination of the wing during takeoff to ensure that snow had blown off!* Crews had considerable leeway in deciding whether to take off with surface contamination, and Transport Canada did not discourage this practice.

It was apparent that instructions during F28 training, and in the Fokker manual, that no snow, ice, or frost should be allowed to remain on the wings of the F28, tended to be discounted by pilots who had successfully flown other aircraft in such a condition. In the 'bush pilot' culture of the airline, this tendency might not have been refuted. Rather, the indulgent management environment probably exacerbated such practices.

Another difficulty was that the Transport Canada inspector appointed for the Fokker Fellowship was *himself inexperienced on the aircraft type* and therefore not in a position to assess and impose appropriate standards.

Maintenance

A number of maintenance problems were exacerbated by lack of familiarity with the aircraft and a shortage of spare parts. On the day of the accident, C-FONF was despatched with an unserviceable APU and had three other deferred maintenance items, including roll and yaw modes in the autopilot, and an intermittent fuel gauge defect. Other discrepancies were inoperative exit lights, dim cabin emergency floor lighting, missing oxygen masks, and problems with securing the main door handle because of a missing clip. These reflected haphazard maintenance and added to the crew's frustrations.

Flight attendant training

Air Ontario's flight attendant training did not encourage bringing operational matters to the attention of the flightdeck. It stressed the competence of pilots and fostered total reliance on them. There were inconsistencies in this separation of responsibilities – the company's instruction to the captain to "hot refuel" at Dryden with passengers aboard was one example, – a procedure contrary to the company flight attendants' manual!

Events in Thunder Bay

Decisions by Operations Control resulted in the flight falling further behind schedule. Defuelling at Thunder Bay, just after the aircraft had been refuelled, to carry the extra passengers, caused a further delay of 35 minutes, and Captain Morwood particularly disliked being late. The crew had also to calculate the aircraft's takeoff and landing data over again. In insisting on this action, Operations usurped Morwood's authority to operate the flight as he deemed necessary.

Crew experience

Captain Morwood received 22 hours of F28 simulator training in 1988 and a further 8 hours 20 minutes during his recurrent training in 1989. At the time he began flying the Fellowship as a line captain he had only 29 hours on the type. But all his checks were well flown, and he received only satisfactory comments on his reports. At the time of the accident he had 81 hours on the F28.

Morwood was considered above average as a professional pilot. But despite the best efforts of the Commission, no evidence was found that either Morwood or Mills was fully conversant with the phenomenon of 'cold-soaking' and its potential effect on aircraft contamination by snow and ice. There was also evidence that some Air Ontario CV-580 pilots were not greatly concerned about wing contamination, having taken off at times with snow and ice adhering to the aircraft. Morwood may well have been such a pilot.

Captain Morwood had a strong commitment to on-time operations and a high level of concern for his passengers, numbers of whom that day had expressed concern about missing their connections in Winnipeg. In addition, Morwood had a personal trip planned for the following day out of Toronto. These factors could have increased his determination to complete the trip as near as possible to schedule.

F/O Mills completed 8.3 hours of training and a 1.2 hour pilot proficiency check on the F28 in February 1989, but had no opportunity to train in the simulator. He flew 20 hours of line indoctrination then, with only 29.5 hours on type, began duties as a Fellowship first officer.

Mills had a record of some difficulties with aircraft handling, but met all regulatory requirements. The fact that he did not receive simulator training in the F28, together with Captain Morwood's long experience and reputation as a "perpetual instructor", might have made Mills reluctant to offer operational suggestions. Mills also had personal plans for the next day.

One of the basic premises of airline operations is that crew members support one another in safe and effective flight management. When both crew members are still becoming familiar with the aircraft, the margin of safety is obviously reduced.

Other issues made the pairing of Morwood and Mills potentially stressful. Morwood came from Air Ontario Ltd, while Mills came from Austin Airways. As well, both had been flying as captains previously. The week of the accident was the first time they had flown together and at the time of the accident, their total time as a crew was just over two days.

Other crew and passenger concerns

The question asked repeatedly during the Commission hearings was: why didn't someone bring the buildup of snow on the wings to Captain Morwood's attention? Yet, except for efforts by one passenger, no one made any attempt to check that the captain was aware of the aircraft's condition.

F/A Hartwick felt concern immediately after the cabin door was closed. She had seen the snow on the wings while the aircraft was standing at the terminal and thought it would be de-iced. Walking through the cabin after the door was closed, she heard passengers saying they hoped the snow would blow off.

After the pre-takeoff cabin check, the two flight attendants stood at the back of the cabin as the aircraft taxied away. Sonia Hartwick then became increasingly apprehensive while they waited for the Cessna 150 to land. The snow was now starting to build up on the wings, and one of the two constables in the last row of seats expressed his own concerns to her, asking what the crew intended to do about it.

But a number of factors mitigated against the flight attendants taking the matter to the flightdeck. There was a feeling that pilots did not accept them as an operational part of the crew. On previous occasions Hartwick *had* gone to the flightdeck with safety concerns, only to be told not to worry – even though the pilots conducted no checks at the time to verify her concerns.

An incident involving a HS.748, under the command of the management pilot who was later to become project manager of the F28 program and chief pilot for the F28s, was apparently common knowledge among Air Ontario staff. It resulted from a takeoff in poor weather with snow on the wings, leading to violent vibration on climb-out and the need to make an emergency landing. Before this takeoff the flight attendant had conveyed her concerns about the snow, as well as those of some passengers, to the captain, but was told to "take her seat". Afterwards, neither this captain nor his first officer "had any recollection" of the conversation!

F/A Hartwick's knowledge of this incident, and the manner in which that captain had responded, clearly influenced her while taxiing out at Dryden. Indeed, it was understandable why Air Ontario flight attendants believed that management, and some pilots, were not interested in their comments. Sonia Hartwick's respect for the professionalism of both Captain Morwood and Purser Say was also a factor influencing her decision not to go to the flightdeck.

In the case of the two airline captains travelling as passengers, their lack of affirmative action was unfortunate – to say the least. As professional pilots, they had a clear understanding of the danger, and their indication of concern *would at least have been considered by the usually meticulous Captain Morwood.*

The reasons why they did not raise their concerns differ, but there are two points on which they agree – both assumed the crew was aware of the condition of the wings, and both believed the aircraft was going to be de-iced.

While taxiing away from the terminal and backtracking on the runway, the DC-9 captain thought they were proceeding to the more remote de-icing area near the Ministry of Natural Resources (see airport diagram). This was a reasonable assumption, as Air Canada often de-iced its DC-9 aircraft at locations remote from the gate. There was no doubt in his mind, he recalled, that the aircraft had to be de-iced before takeoff.

The Dash 8 captain knew the de-icing equipment at Dryden was on the apron near the terminal, and expected they were going to return there. If the aircraft was not de-iced, he believed the takeoff would be aborted should the snow not come off the wings during the takeoff run [a highly dangerous practice in itself]. He also indicated that "professional courtesy" precluded an off-duty airline pilot from drawing the attention of the flightcrew to a safety concern.

The inference was that "professional courtesy" among pilots was more important than safety, suggesting an unwritten code that militated against such communications, even when a potentially life-threatening concern was involved.

Other factors could influence an off-duty airline pilot not to make known his concerns: faith in the professionalism of the duty crew; fear of offending and possible rebuke for unsolicited advice; fear of embarrassment if the concern proved groundless; and a reluctance to interfere in the busy flightdeck workload.

Whatever the reason, the evidence before the Inquiry pointed to a general reluctance on the part of cabin crew and off-duty pilots to intervene in the operation of an aircraft, even in the face of apprehended danger.

The Commission believed air carriers should counsel their pilots that not only was it acceptable, but indeed expected, that off-duty airline pilots on board should draw any perceived concerns to the attention of the captain. Considering the complexity – and size – of jet aircraft today, a flightcrew could only benefit from the eyes and ears of all on board, especially from those possessing pertinent skills.

Closer co-operation between pilots and flight attendants in operational safety was also clearly desirable. (A tragic accident to a Boeing 737 in Britain in 1989 might well have been averted if the cabin crew had conveyed their concerns, as well as those of some of the passengers, to the captain over the shutting down of an engine – see *Air Disaster*, Vol 2, Chapter 12.) Such crew co-ordination must, however, be developed through training. A careful balance must be struck between ensuring pilots are aware of operational problems, and discouraging flight attendants from intruding on the flightdeck.

Had the crew of the F28 been exposed to Cockpit Resource Management training, it is likely that a full exchange of information would have occurred at Dryden, and the aircraft might not have attempted its fateful takeoff. For these reasons:
• Cabin crew, after appropriate training, should be encouraged in adverse winter weather to monitor the wings as part of the pre-takeoff routine to supplement the captain's responsibility.
• Pilots should be made aware that concerns raised by cabin crew should be taken seriously.
• Pilots, when travelling as passengers, should never assume the flightcrew is aware of any situation that they themselves perceive to be a safety concern. They should raise such concerns with the cabin crew and request the information be given to the captain.

The overall situation

From all the evidence, it was apparent to the Commission that an array of factors progressively undermined the effectiveness of the F28 crew and increased their level of stress. But a change in any one of these factors could have interrupted the chain of events that lead to the accident. For example:
• A more stringently regulated despatch system should have precluded operations into Dryden on March 10.
• A more stringent regulatory requirement and training program on the effects of contamination, including cold-soaking, would have created a greater awareness of the potential for degraded aerofoil performance.
• A training program in Crew Resource Management could have led to a critical reappraisal of the decision to take off.

It was evident that Captain Morwood, as a result of cumulative delays and frustrations, had concluded it was best to leave Dryden as soon as possible. He was concerned that passengers were anxious to connect with flights in Winnipeg, and both he and Mills had plans for the next day. A long delay at Dryden, during which both engines would have had to be shut down, would have made it necessary to fly in ground-start equipment before the aircraft could depart again. This would have seriously disrupted the airline's schedules, and passenger and crew plans with them.

With wet snow falling, the large fluffy snow flakes and lack of accumulation of snow on the tarmac could have given the impression the snow was melting and would not adhere to the wings. The possibility that cold soaking was causing rough granular ice to develop *under* the snow on the wings apparently did not occur to the crew.

A last chance to save the situation was missed when the takeoff was delayed for the landing of the Cessna in visibility restricted by the heavy snowfall. By this time however, the stress and frustration of the day had finally – and fatally – affected the crew's judgement.

Commission Finding

The Commission found the captain's decision to take off was made with the knowledge that snow was accumulating on the aircraft, but with the mistaken perception that it was not adhering to the wings and would blow off during the takeoff.

As pilot-in-command, Captain Morwood bore the responsibility for the decision to take off. But it was equally clear the air transport system failed him, placing him in a situation where he did not have the resources to make a proper decision.

Inadequate surveillance by Transport Canada

Concerns about unmanageable workloads, and insufficient air car-

THE AFTERMATH

This selection of photographs, from the Final Report of the Commission of Inquiry, provides a glimpse of tasks faced by air safety investigators after a major airline accident.

(top) The damaged port tailplane and the still smouldering wreckage. The complete empennage was lifted from the forest (above) after the port engine (below) had been sawn from its remaining fuselage mountings. The other engine, with the remains of the tailplane, were also then detached for transport.

(top) Fires still burn around the starboard wingroot and overwing exit late in the afternoon of the accident. (above) The same section is lowered inverted on to a railcar for delivery to the Canadian Aviation Safety Board laboratories in Ottawa. (below) The charred cases of the CVR and DFDR. Not removed from the heat of the fire until 24hrs after the crash, their data could not be recovered.

rier and airworthiness inspectors within the Transport Canada organisation, had been raised as far back as 1982. A Commission of Inquiry on Aviation Safety, established in 1979 to advise the Minister of Transport, pointed out the need for increased staffing in several areas of Transport Canada, particularly in inspection of air carrier maintenance and operations.

In 1984 a review committee found that resource shortages in the Aviation Regulation Directorate were adversely affecting its ability to ensure an adequate level of safety. Allocations to regional air carrier operations were insufficient to meet the workload. Bases had been inspected only 70% of the required time, and then only by omitting certain procedures. Initial inspections of new carriers were frequently delayed, and inspections of new aircraft often postponed. As a result, aircraft were operating without meeting the required standards.

The 1984 review team also warned that continued shortage of resources would result in a perpetuation of the unacceptable 'corner-cutting'. Attempts to cope with an unmanageable workload, with continued non-completion of required inspections, could have an adverse effect on safety.

These expressions of concern about the lack of resources could be repeated, word for word, to describe the situation existing at the time of the accident. Transport Canada still did not have sufficient human resources to discharge its mandate. And it had been repeatedly warned about this unsatisfactory state of affairs.

The problem was not simply lack of staff but workloads imposed by a government staff 'freeze', compilation of paperwork, preparation of statements of justification, discussions on implementing restrictions, proceeding with staff actions, cancelling those actions, reactivating the actions, attempting to overcome staff shortages with untrained temporary staff, waste of clerical staff in training short term help, and serious diversion of managers from operational duties to deal with crises arising from lack of staffing – bureaucratic problems hauntingly familiar to the industry the world over.

In summary

The Aviation Regulation Directorate of Transport Canada was not adequately prepared to perform its functions.

The warning flags raised early in the 1980s and repeated throughout

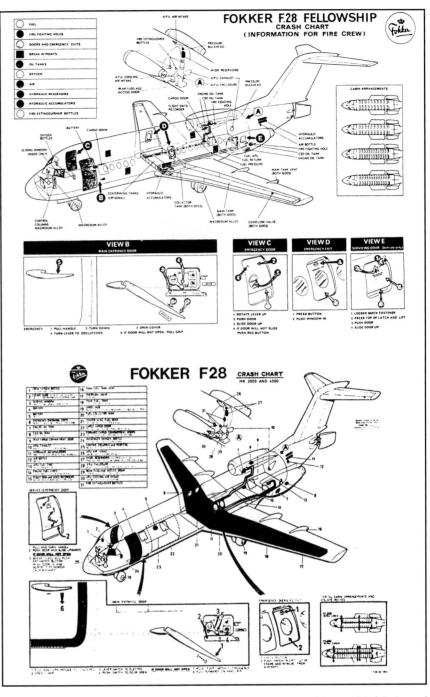

The Inquiry was concerned about other aspects of the Dryden accident which fell short of regulatory requirements. Reproduced here are two versions of F28 Crash Charts produced by Fokker (the Mk 1000 top, and, incorrectly labelled, the Mks 3000/4000, below). Pertinent information is specified for immediate reference by emergency crews. All airports required to maintain a rescue and firefighting capability should have such guides for each of the principal aircraft types they handle. Dryden was handling around 55,000 passengers a year, with regular visits by all Air Ontario's types. Jetstream 31s of the competing Canadian Partner carriers, and Twin Otters of the now defunct norOntair, also used the airport. Yet investigators found only a single, ex Austin Airways HS.748 crash chart in the Dryden Fire Hall.

the decade had negligible effect. It was known that significant increases in personnel would be required, yet such increases were not even authorised, let alone acquired.

Inadequate training failed to ensure inspector competency, and placed new inspectors in positions of responsibility for which they were not qualified. Lack of planning and

managerial direction placed staff in the position of being unable to adequately perform their duties.

Had Transport Canada's Aviation Regulation Directorate been in a position to discharge its responsibilities in an effective manner, some of the factors that contributed to the Dryden accident might not have arisen.

CHAPTER 4

"Nice looking day – hard to believe the skies are unfriendly."

– Captain to First Officer before departure

United Airlines (UAL) Boeing 737-291 N999UA [22742] (F/n 1299)
– March 3, 1991

The crew had no illusions that clear air turbulence generated by standing mountain waves in the area of their destination could be unpredictable – and even vicious. But they never suspected it could become a possible reason for their fatal loss of control.

A long day

For Captain Harold Green and First Officer Patricia Eidson, Sunday March 3, 1991, began routinely enough. United Airlines pilots based at Oakland, California, they were on the second day of a busy two day tour of duty crewing Boeing 737s on a number of domestic flights in the western United States.

The previous day had been a long one. Reporting for duty at Oakland at 5.45am Pacific Standard Time, their day's flying had consisted of a number of legs between Los Angeles and Sacramento, California, finishing with a longer sector to Denver, Colorado, where they landed at 6.30pm Mountain Standard Time (one hour ahead of PST).

By the time they checked into their hotel at Denver, it was 7.15pm MST, their duty time for the day amounting to more than 14 hours. But they were evidently not fatigued, for they invited another UAL pilot, at the hotel when they arrived, to join them for dinner. He had already dined however, and did not accompany them.

In the morning, as the crew were checking out of the hotel at about 7.20am, the first officer spoke to the other United pilot again. Obviously in good spirits, she discussed what she could expect on the trip to Colorado Springs for which she and her captain were rostered – it was to be her first to that airport.

Soon afterwards, she and the captain boarded the 7.30am courtesy bus for the airport. It was to be the captain's last day of duty before he began two weeks' leave.

Short sector

At Denver's Stapleton International Airport, the Midwest's busiest east of the Rocky Mountains, and a major 'hub', the pilots were rostered to take over Boeing 737 N999UA from another crew. The aircraft was operating that morning's Flight UA585 from Peoria, Illinois, to Colorado Springs, via Moline and Denver (see map on following page).

Departing Peoria on schedule at 5am with a normal crew of two pilots and three flight attendants, the Boeing's flight to Moline and on to Denver had been entirely normal, and it had touched down at Denver at 8am, 13 minutes ahead of schedule.

The pilots handing over the aircraft at Denver reported no abnormalities during the flight from Peoria. During his routine exterior inspection of the aircraft, the Denver despatch engineer found the latch on the avionics bay door out of its stowed position. But after checking the security of the door and stowing the latch, he found the aircraft fully serviceable.

The weather briefing the incoming crew were given at Denver included the 7.50am observations for Colorado Springs Airport (elevation 6184 feet). Under the influence of a moderate high pressure system with an approaching wind shift line, the destination weather was reported to be clear, with a visibility of 100 miles, and a temperature of 49°F (10°C). The wind was from 330° at 23kt, gusting to 33kt, and the QNH was 30.03 inches (1016hPa). Fifteen nautical miles away to the northwest, cumulus cloud lay over the Front Range, part of the Southern Rockies mountain chain and some of the highest terrain in the United States, including the precipitous 14,110ft (4301m) Pike's Peak.

After the three flight attendants had seated the 20 passengers booked on the flight, the Boeing made ready to push back from the Denver terminal just before 9am. The captain was handling the aircraft from the left-hand seat, with the first officer responsible for the radio communications.

The aircraft's departure for the 20 minute flight to Colorado Springs was entirely normal. Cleared to taxi for Runway 35L behind another departing United 737 at 9.14am, N999UA was finally cleared for take-off nine minutes later with instructions to turn left on to a heading of 345°M, followed by a further instruction to call Denver Departures on climb to 10,000 feet.

The Departures controller then progressively vectored the aircraft on to a heading of 140° to intercept the designated airway V81 to Colorado Springs and, at 9.26am, directed the crew to resume their own navigation. Three minutes later Departures cleared the aircraft to maintain 11,000ft.

Fateful approach

At 9.32am the aircraft called Colorado Springs Approach Control, reporting its altitude as 11,000 feet, and that it had copied "Information Lima" from the ATIS transmission.

"Information Lima", current for the past 40 minutes, was additionally reporting: "... wind 310° at 13 (kt), gusting 35 ... low level wind shear advisories are in effect; SIGMET Juliet 1 in effect for Wyoming and Colorado, occasional severe turbulence between FL180 to 380 reported by numerous aircraft ... local aviation wind warning in effect calling for winds out of the northwest, gusts to 40kt and above ..."

Approach Control instructed the 737 to proceed to the VOR, then leave it on a heading of 165° in preparation for being vectored to Runway 35 for a visual approach. The controller passed the present wind conditions as "320° at 13kt, gusting to 23kt".

Two minutes later the controller cleared the aircraft to descend to 10,000ft, and issued a further clearance to 8,500ft three minutes later again. When the aircraft reported the airport in sight, Approach Control instructed it to maintain "at or above 8,500 until on base, Runway 35, cleared visual approach, contact Tower 119.9".

F/O (to Tower): United 585 is cleared for a visual [approach] to [Runway] 35.
TWR: Cleared to land – wind 320° at 16, gusting to 29.
F/O: Any reports lately of a loss or gain of airspeed?
TWR: Yes ma'am – at 500ft a 737-300 reported a 15kt loss ... at 400ft plus 15kt, and at 150ft a plus 20kt.
F/O: Sounds adventurous! Thank you!
TWR (half a minute later as N999UA was on its downwind leg): Traffic 11 o'clock, five miles, northwest bound – a Cessna, 7100 [feet], straight in for Runway 30.
F/O: OK, we'll look for him — how many miles are we from him?
TWR: Five miles.
F/O (another half minute later): Where's the Cessna [now]?
TWR: The Cessna traffic is 10 to 9 o'clock now as you're in your turn – passing behind you, no factor.
F/O: Thank you.
TWR (half a minute later again): After landing, hold short of Runway 30 for departing traffic.
F/O: We'll hold short of 30.

This proved to be the final transmission from N999UA.

As the Boeing 737 completed its turn from downwind leg on to final approach at about 1000ft AGL, the wings levelled momentarily. Then, quite unexpectedly, it began rolling

to the right again, at the same time pitching increasingly nose down. Rapidly losing height, it began to dive with increasing speed.

Within seconds, the 737 reached a horrifying near vertical attitude, and it plunged with enormous force into Widefield Park, 3½nm south of the runway threshold, disintegrating in a violent explosion and gouging a crater three metres (15ft) deep.

The fierce conflagration that followed melted much of the fragmented metal structure, as well as scorching nearby trees. There was not the slightest possibility that anyone on board could have survived.

Firefighting vehicles that reached the scene of the crash within minutes could do nothing but quell the intense fire consuming what little remained of the Boeing 737.

INVESTIGATION

Wreckage

The site of the crash lay in flat parkland 6.4km south of the threshold of Colorado Springs' Runway 35, and 315m (1034ft) to the east of its extended centreline at an elevation of 5704ft AMSL. The severe impact had gouged a crater about 13m (40ft) long, 8m (25ft) wide and 3m (15ft) deep. Nearby trees were broken by flying debris and sooted by fire, and grass was scorched.

Except for two pieces of aircraft skin and small debris, the remains of the entire 737 fuselage, exhibiting severe accordion-like crushing throughout its length, lay within the impact crater. The door wreckage was consistent with all doors being locked, and there was no evidence of preimpact fire.

The port wing, fragmented and partly consumed by fire, also lay in the crater. The leading edge devices, although severely crushed, showed evidence of having been extended. No control system components were missing. The outer starboard wing lay outside the crater, its leading edge embedded in the ground, with its chord perpendicular. The outer 2m (6ft) had been torn off by trees as the aircraft struck the ground.

The inboard sections of both wings were mutilated, and some structure had melted. The flaps, separated from their tracks, were recovered and their jack screw positions, symmetrical on both sides, corresponded to the 'Flaps 10' position. The starboard aileron lay about 8m (25ft) beyond its wing.

Severely damaged by impact and fire, the fin and rudder were in the impact crater but the tailplane, in pieces and severely burnt, lay at the

One of United's 100 strong fleet of 737-322s lifts off Runway 08R at Denver. Stapleton Airport's control tower, rising from the sprawling terminal complex, draws the eye to the ramparts of the Front Range and beyond to the uplands of the Southern Rockies on the northwestern horizon. Denver has long been a UAL training centre and hub, second only to the company's headquarters at Chicago O'Hare – as reflected by the liveries in this picture. The ill-fated N999UA was the 70th and last of UAL's 737-200s on strength in 1991, but this marque is virtually the only type not visible here! (Airliners magazine; Andreas Agazzi)

Map of central and eastern USA, showing cities and 737 routes referred to in this chapter. Australasian readers will find it helpful to visualise the UA585 stage lengths as equivalent to Canberra/Sydney/Brisbane/Maroochydore flight sectors. Denver references are to DEN-Stapleton, the city's mammoth new airport not being completed until 1994. (Matthew Tesch)

top of the pile of aircraft debris. The port and starboard tailplane hinge fittings, the centre section jackscrew system, and the port and starboard elevator hinge points were intact, with parts of their respective elevator tab pushrods. There was impact and fire damage to all three undercarriage assemblies, but all were in the extended and locked position.

The badly damaged port engine, buried about 3m (10ft) beneath the port wing, fell apart during its removal from the crater, but examination disclosed no mechanical problems that would have affected its operation before impact.

The forward portion of the starboard engine was buried about 2m (7ft) beneath the starboard wing. Aft of the combustion section, the engine had broken up and its components had scattered – the high pressure turbine rotor was found over 150m (500ft) beyond the impact crater. Again there was no evidence of any mechanical problem that would have affected its operation before the crash.

Damage to the unrecognisable flightdeck defied any useful examination, but there was evidence that both engines had been producing almost symmetric thrust.

Measurements taken at the accident site, together with damage to nearby trees, enabled investigators to reconstruct the complex motion

and attitude of the aircraft at impact – the Matthew Tesch illustration on the next page interprets the quoted NTSB description.

The airport

Colorado Springs Municipal Airport is on the southern side of the city at an elevation of 6184ft. Its three runways are busy, with annual movements totalling nearly 180,000, of which over 10% are airline. The USAF's Peterson Air Force Base alongside the airport shares its movement areas (see map).

Situated at the very foot of the eastern slopes of the vast Rocky Mountains chain, the airport has extensive high terrain in its immediate vicinity. Minimum sector altitudes of 9000ft lie within 25nm of the airport from the north-northwest, clockwise to the south. Even higher elevations, with area minimum altitudes above 16,000ft, lie within 15nm to the west.

Eye witnesses

More than 160 witnesses saw the Boeing 737 turning on to final approach. It appeared to be flying normally until it suddenly rolled to the right and descended steeply. Some saw a white mist in the area of the starboard wing just before the aircraft began its rapid roll.

Many said the aircraft rolled wings

level momentarily as it lined up with the runway, but then rolled to the right until it was inverted with the nose "nearly straight down". Some saw the nose rise as the roll to the right began. Others described the aircraft's motion as "smooth rolling and pitching from normal flight all the way to the ground". No structure separated from the aircraft, evidence supported by a search of the flightpath which located no debris.

One witness about 6nm west of the airport, saw rotor clouds, accompanied by thin wispy condensation, in the area of the accident, 10 to 15 minutes beforehand. Another witness, driving past the area shortly before the accident, also saw "torn wispy clouds".

Weather briefing

The briefing provided to the crew at UAL's Denver operations office

North facing panorama of Colorado Springs Airport, taken from the new terminal, opened in October 1994. The flatness of the mesa on which the city is built, and the Great Plains disappearing beyond the horizon, belie the dramatic terrain out of the frame to the left. Only a few kilometres west of the airport, Pike's Peak rises 7000ft (2100m) above the prairie. Runway 30 (see later map) runs right to left at the far side of the fields beyond the taxiing 727s. Beyond the MD-80 variants at the new pier, the undulating eastern suburbs of Colorado Springs may be discerned above the hangars of Peterson AFB. Although the first sod for the facilities in the foreground was not turned until 15 months after the accident, this camera angle would have provided an excellent view of the approaching N999UA on its downwind leg. (Airliners; Ronald C Hill)

comprised synoptic chart features, the area forecast, Denver and Colorado Springs terminal forecasts, inflight Pilot Reports (PIREPS – see aerial perspective illustration summarising details of relevant reports), and en route NOTAMS.

The synoptic chart section included maximum wind speed and location, the surface pressure centre at 2am, position of the approaching weather front, and the fact that VFR conditions were predicted for the Rockies. The Denver forecast indicated clear skies, 70nm visibility, and northwest winds with gusts to 19kt, The Area Forecast meanwhile, warned of turbulence: "Light occasional to moderate turbulence below 40,000ft, with local strong up and downdrafts over and near the mountains. Isolated severe turbulence at and below 18,000 feet."

The Colorado Springs terminal forecast indicated clear skies, unlimited visibility, and northwest winds gusting from 31 to 37kt. An amendment predicted winds from 340° at 20kt, gusting to 35kt. An Aviation High Wind Advisory, issued by the National Weather Service, was also in effect, indicating northwest winds at 25kt, with possible occasional gusts to 40kt, especially in the foothills.

United's company meteorologists also issue forecasts for Clear Air Turbulence and mountain waves throughout the United States and they had issued a CAT mountain wave forecast at 8.25am covering Montana, Wyoming, and Colorado, for Flight Levels 200 to 390. And SIGMET Juliet 1, an inflight weather advisory current in the area of the accident, warned of moderate to occasional severe turbulence, from 18,000 feet to 38,000 feet, reported by several Boeing 737s and 727s.

Actual conditions recorded at Colorado Springs immediately after the accident were: Clear, with a visibility of 100 miles, temperature 53°F (11°C), dew point 8°F (minus 10°C), wind 320° at 20kt, gusts to 28kt, altimeter setting 30.02 inches Hg (1016 hPa), altocumulus cloud over the mountains to the northwest.

The captain of a Continental 737-200 which took off on Runway 35 about four minutes after the accident, reported gusty winds but no wild gyrations. He said it was a "normal Colorado windy day".

The pilot of a Cessna about 4nm southeast of the airport at the time of the accident, encountered "occasional moderate chop" at 7000ft. Airspeed fluctuations of between 65 and 105kt also occurred, with vertical speed indications of about 500fpm.

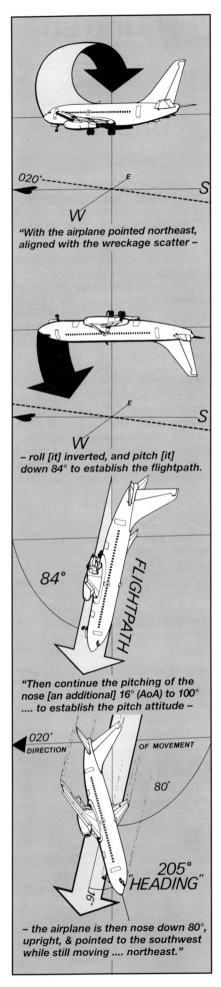

"With the airplane pointed northeast, aligned with the wreckage scatter –

– roll [it] inverted, and pitch [it] down 84° to establish the flightpath.

84°   FLIGHTPATH

"Then continue the pitching of the nose [an additional] 16° (AoA) to 100° .... to establish the pitch attitude –

020° DIRECTION   OF MOVEMENT

80°

205° "HEADING"

16°

– the airplane is then nose down 80°, upright, & pointed to the southwest while still moving .... northeast."

The horrifying train of events that so quickly developed during the apparently normal approach of N999UA were all over in less than 10 seconds, and the limited investigative value of these final seconds on the 737's CVR tape was matched by the few parameters recorded by its DFDR. Similarly, other than a basic assessment of the aircraft's configuration at impact, not a great deal could be determined at the accident site. Eyewitness evidence therefore had to be meticulously sifted. Even so, the NTSB's final derivation of the Boeing's complex gyrations at impact almost defied even this painstaking agency's verbose prose! This Matthew Tesch diagram interprets the relevant quotation from the NTSB report.

Radar data

Radar data recorded by Denver Control covered the 737's flight from its initial radar contact while climbing out at 9.23am, until radar contact was lost only 4nm south of Colorado Springs' Runway 35. The aircraft's last radar data was recorded only 16 seconds before it struck the ground.

It showed that the 737 was approaching the airport from the southeast at about 1700ft above terrain. Its track was consistent with a 45° intercept of the final approach to Runway 35, 4-5nm south of the runway threshold. When about one nautical mile east of final approach, the aircraft began descending to maintain a 3° glideslope. But about 20 seconds later, its descent rate increased to 2200fpm and it crashed about 37 seconds afterwards.

Flight recorders

The Boeing 737's battered CVR and DFDR were both found amongst the wreckage and were sent to the NTSB's laboratories in Washington, DC, for readout and analysis.

CVR

The Sundstrand CVR sustained some structural damage, but its case preserved the overall integrity of the recording tape. Because of the severity of the impact, the tape was creased in several places, and this degraded the quality of the recording. Also, because the unit was ejected from the aircraft into a nearby creek at the moment of impact, it sustained minor water contamination. But it at least escaped fire or smoke damage.

The tape had recorded just over 30 minutes of flightdeck activity and conversation, beginning as the crew made ready to taxi to the holding point at Denver.

It was clear they were mindful that standing mountain wave conditions, with the possibility of extreme rotor turbulence, existed on the lee side of the mountain range to the northwest of Colorado Springs. Soon after they began to taxi, the captain remarked:

The accident aircraft – and its configuration in the Colorado Springs circuit – is represented here by a March 1968 build veteran flying with United until only recently. Following Lufthansa's historic launch order for what turned out to be the short lived 737-130, Boeing's refinement of the slightly longer Series 200 clinched a UAL commitment for an initial 40, opening the floodgates for the so-called Baby Boeing. N9006U [19044] "City of Bakersfield" was, after the prototype, only the 12th 737 to take to the skies, and remained with United until just before its 30th birthday. The livery dates this picture as 1987-88 (see Chapter 2 and Vol 2, Ch 13).
At the other end of the scale, N999UA was the final -200 series example acquired by United. Denver's Frontier Airlines had been a presence in the Midwest and high Cordillera since 1946, with a fleet peaking at more than 60 aircraft. After UAL began moving its flying training activities away from busy Chicago airspace, it dallied with taking over the weakening Frontier during 1985-86, but in the end took only 24 of its 737s – of which N7356F-N999UA was the last. And when Frontier finally collapsed, its remnants were grabbed by Continental. (Hamlyn Books; MT)

"Nice looking day – hard to believe the skies are unfriendly."

This ironic reference to the airline's longstanding advertising slogan, *Fly the friendly skies*, probably reflected his mild concern about forecast conditions. Indeed, after the crew had completed the first part of the pre-takeoff checklist five minutes later, their conversation was about cap clouds and rotor clouds and the danger these could pose, the first officer commenting, "... that's dangerous – could tear a wing off."

The takeoff, climb and en route flight in clear conditions, with the captain flying the aircraft, proceeded normally, except that mechanical turbulence was evidently constant, prompting him to comment that he had "never driven to Colorado Springs and not gotten sick."

The readout showed that at 11,000ft on approach, after the first officer had received Information Lima on the ATIS, and the crew had completed the descent checklist, she briefed the captain on the wind conditions. The following transcription of the crew's exchanges prefixes their timings in minutes and seconds to impact:

10:31 F/O (to captain): OK – they're landing [Runway] 35, wind is 310°, 13, gusting to 35 [kt].
10:27 CAPT (on PA system): Flight attendants prepare for landing.
10:24 F/O: Approach descent checklist complete – got our altimeter set now, wind 310, 13°, gusting to 35 [kt], they're landing on Runway 35 ... and ah ... they're giving a SIGMET and low level wind shear warning re-

port – and then they say also [for] this area that they have a wind warning out for gusts to 40kt.
10:04 CAPT: Oh yeah?
10:03 F/O: So?
10:01 CAPT: So ... ah ... we'll program a 20 knot correction ... we'll make it 135 and 140 [kt].
09:35 Approach Control: Descend at pilot's discretion, maintain 10,000.
08:03 F/O: Springs VOR is 8.8 [nautical] miles from ... the runway ... the airport.
07:57 CAPT: OK.
06:26 APP: Descend at pilot's discretion, maintain 8500.
06:17 APP: Report the airport in sight.
06:12 F/O: Airport in sight!
06:09 APP: Maintain at or above 8500 until on base ... Runway 35 ... cleared visual approach ... contact tower 119.9.
05:42 F/O (to Tower): United 585 is cleared for a visual to 35.
05:34 TWR: Runway 35 ... cleared to land, wind 320 at 16, gusting 29.
05:27: F/O: OK ... we're cleared to land 35 ... any reports lately of loss or gain of airspeed?
05:20 TWR: The last air carrier was the one that reported that ... a 737.
05:14 F/O: Could you repeat it please?
05:12 TWR: Yes ma'am ... at 500 feet a 737-300 series reported a 15 knot loss ... at 400 feet plus 15kt and at 150 feet a plus 20kt.
04:55 F/O: Sounds adventurous! Thank you.
04:52 F/O: OK ... I recommend we hold what[ever] 20kt max is ... and then ... if we get all stable ... I'll watch that airspeed like it's my mum's last minute!

04:41 CAPT: OK!
04:39 F/O: And I'll report [the airspeed] to you.
04:25 F/O: You're abeam the end of the runway right now.
04:23 CAPT: Yeah.
04:17 F/O: The elevation's 6200 feet.
04:15 CAPT: 6172 [ft] ... OK ... we're not gonna be in a rush because we want to stabilise it out here.
04:09 F/O: Yeah ... I feel the same way.
04:01 CAPT: How about flaps to two?
03:58 [Sound of flap lever actuation]
03:45 CAPT: OK ... start around there now ... and wheels down on final.
03:35 [Sound of undercarriage being extended]
03:34 TWR: Traffic 11 o'clock, five miles, northwest bound a Cessna, 7100 [feet], straight in for Runway 30.
03:28 F/O: OK ... we'll look for him ... how many miles are we from him?
03:24 TWR: 11 to 10 o'clock and five miles.
03:15 F/O: OK ... cabin notification completed ... start switches are in flight ... flight and nav instruments are cross checked ... I'll give you the ILS ... it's done.
03:10 CAPT: I got it.
03:09 F/O: OK ... no flaps.
03:06 CAPT: Fifteen flaps!
03:04 F/O: OK.
03:02 [Sound of flap lever actuation] F/O: Gear is down ... three greens ... speed brake armed ... green light ... flaps are five ... green light hydraulic brake pressures are normal ... final descent check complete.
02:57 CAPT: Where's the Cessna [now]?

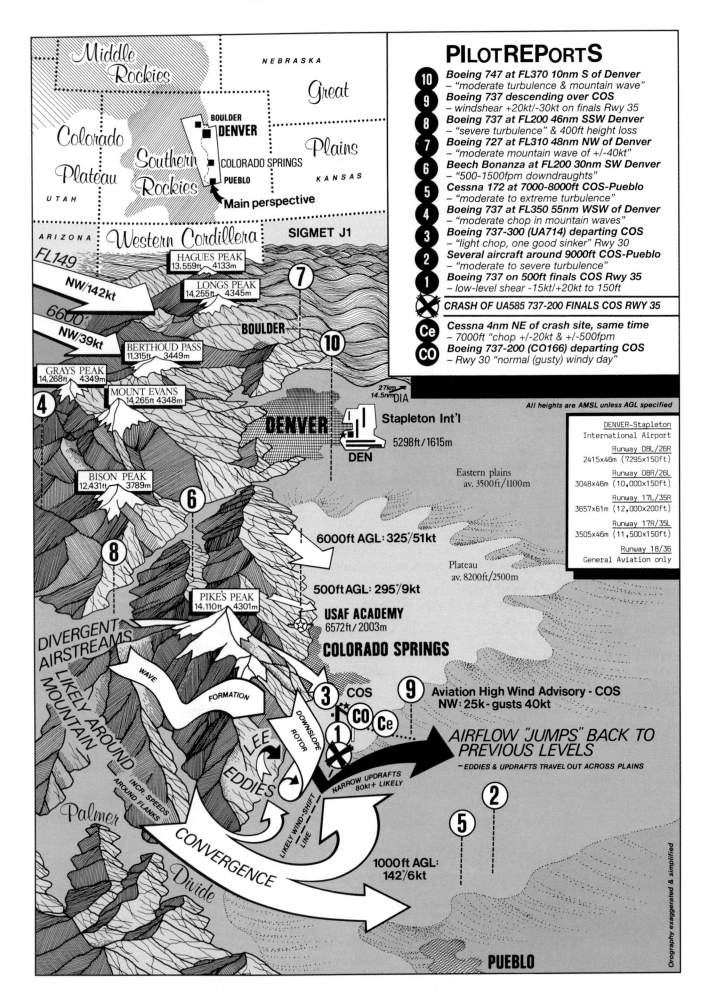

(opposite) North facing aerial perspective of "The Colorado Piedmont" – the urbanised uplands along the eastern foot of the Southern Rockies (see regional inset, top left). More than three quarters of the state's population lives in the corridor extending from Pueblo to Boulder. Atmospheric conditions prevailing on the morning of the accident are indicated. Along the left margin, incoming arrows show the generally northwest airstream, based on forecasts, a SIGMET and other weather advisories issued that morning, and on data recorded at the USAF Academy north of Colorado Springs. PIREPS radioed to ATC are positioned by the various balloons, their numbers sequentially counting down to N999UA's moment of disaster, the final two being logged concurrently with and immediately after the 737's impact. Localised wind effects around Pike's Peak (lower left) are also shown, interpreted from data provided by the National Center for Atmospheric Research. NCAR computer modelling of a January 1989 windstorm along the Front Range was applied to the conditions observed on the morning of the accident, with the depicted results. From all the meteorological evidence uncovered during the investigation, the NTSB found "... significant wind convergence and ... rotation in the area just south of the accident site around the time of the accident". (Matthew Tesch/NTSB)

02:50 TWR: The Cessna traffic is ... 10 to 9 o'clock now, as you're in your turn ... passing behind you ... no factor.
02:43 CAPT: Thank you.
02:21 CAPT: Twenty-five flaps!
02:18 TWR: After landing, hold short of Runway 30 for departing traffic.
02:16 [Sound of engine power increase]
02:11 CAPT: Starting on down.
02:10 F/O (to TWR): We'll hold short of 30. (Then to Capt): That's all the way to the end of our runway ... doesn't mean a thing.
02:02 CAPT: No problem.
01:33 [Sound of 'CO' ident on radio]
01:30 F/O: The marker's identified ... it's really weak.
01:27 CAPT: No problem.
01:12 F/O: A 10kt change there!
01:10 CAPT: Yeah, I know ... awful lot of power to hold that airspeed!
01:03 F/O: Runway is ... 11,000 feet long.
00:59 CAPT: OK.
00:40 F/O: Another 10kt gain!
00:38 CAPT: Thirty flaps.
00:36 [Sound of flap lever actuation]
00:33 F/O: WOW!
00:32 [Sound of engine power reduction]

00:13 F/O: We're at a thousand feet.
00:09 F/O: Oh God!
00:08 CAPT: Fifteen flaps!
00:07 F/O: Fifteen ... Oh!
CAPT: [loudly] OH!
00:06 F/O: ##! [expletive]
  [Sound of flap lever actuation]
CAPT: ###! [expletive]
00:05 [Sound of flap lever actuation]
CAPT: (very loudly) NO!
00:04 [Sound of flap lever actuation]
F/O: OH ###! [expletive]
00:03 CAPT: OH ###! [expletive]
F/O: OH MY GOD! [unidentifiable click] OH MY GOD! [followed by a scream]
00:01 CAPT: [loudly] OH NO ###!! [expletive]
00:00 [IMPACT]

As well as transcribing the voices of the crew and associated flight-deck sounds, the CVR tape was subjected to an acoustic spectral study to measure the rotational speed of the engines immediately before the accident. The study also sought to determine if tailplane trim adjustments made during the final stages of the approach were the result of trim switch actuations on the control column, or were trim inputs from the autopilot.

Aviation came to Colorado Springs in 1919, although its original gravel strip now lies beneath the tarmac of Peterson AFB. Steady, sometimes dramatic, growth since WW2 has not only expanded facilities to the north of Runway 30, but required relocation of the civil terminals, first to the western side of the field in 1966, and again in the 1990s, to the south. The lengths of the original two runways are of note in the high altitude air, and their threshold elevations provide an interesting commentary on the rolling plains of the plateau on which the airport is built. N999UA's downwind leg took it parallel to the work in progress on the new north-south parallel runway, which had the distinction of being the USA's longest civil airport runway when it opened in October 1991.
Locations of the Low Level Wind Shear Alert System's sensors are provided on the airport enlargement, with an indication of their readings around the time of the crash. The drift evident in the aircraft's radar plotted downwind track, as well as the slight zigzagging on the oblique base leg, suggests the effect of the gusty northwesterly winds. The southernmost two sensors recorded the greatest directional variations and the sharpest fluctuations in windspeeds immediately before and after the 737's loss of control. (Matthew Tesch; Jeppesen-Sanderson Inc; Airliners magazine)

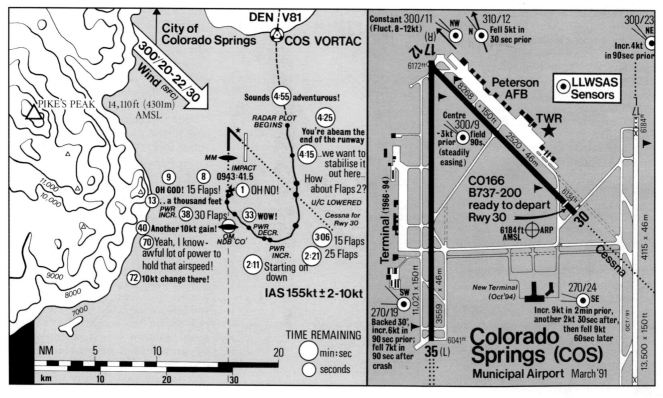

The engine speeds over the two minutes or so before impact showed both engines were operating normally. It was also established that the trim switch actuations were pilot inputs. Continuous engine speed readings during the final 10 seconds of tape were not possible because of the crew's loud exclamations.

DFDR

The Fairchild DFDR had sustained extensive damage, both to its external casings and its electronic components. When the protective casings were cut away, the tape cover was found to be broken and the tape medium dislodged and crumpled. Even so, the tape was not torn, and its data was extractable.

The DFDR had the capability to record a number of parameters but had been installed in N999UA to record only five – heading, altitude, airspeed, vertical acceleration (g loads) and microphone keying.

A readout of its data covering the final minutes of the flight, in combination with the engine data from the CVR, was in agreement with the evidence of eye witnesses. Towards the end of the aircraft's downwind leg at 8500 feet on QNH, the airspeed was fluctuating around 155kt in continuous turbulence.

Cleared for a visual approach, the aircraft began its 180° turn on to final approach a few seconds after 9.40am, and began descending 90 seconds later. As it was converging on the extended runway centreline, the airspeed fluctuations increased to more than 10kt and the turbulence varied between 0.6 and 1.3g.

Half a minute later, the aircraft's heading began changing, the thrust on both engines was reduced from 6000lb to 2000lb, and the aircraft began descending at 2200fpm, a rate greater than required to remain on a 3° glidepath. Seconds later, the thrust was increased to 3000lb per engine. The rate of heading change then increased as the aircraft turned to line up with the runway.

Four seconds afterwards the thrust was increased to 6000 pounds per engine again, with the aircraft straightening out of its turn on to runway heading only briefly before the airspeed and vertical acceleration traces suddenly began to increase wildly. At the same moment the heading changed abruptly.

Within the next four seconds, the heading rate of change increased to nearly twice that of a standard rate one turn and the airspeed rose to more than 200kt as the altitude rapidly decreased.

The impact occurred less than 10 seconds later. The aircraft's vertical acceleration immediately before it struck the ground was about 4g, requiring a 16° angle of attack at 212kt.

The crew

Captain

Captain Harold Green, 52, had flown for United Airlines since early 1969 and had a total of almost 10,000 hours' experience. Of this nearly 2000 had been gained in Boeing 737-200s, 900 of them as captain.

Although this was his first trip to Colorado Springs as pilot-in-command, he had landed there many times as a member of United's flight crew, and from his remarks to the first officer during the flight from Denver, it was certainly not his first experience of turbulence in this area. He had made 14 flights into and out of Denver in the 90 days preceding the accident.

First officer

First officer Patricia Eidson, 42, had been with United for well over two years and had accumulated nearly 4000 hours' experience, including more than 1000 hours as a 737 first officer. She was not scheduled for the trip on which the accident occurred, but volunteered for it

This cutaway drawing of the empennage of a Boeing 737-300 shows the location of the primary and standby rudder actuator mechanisms which so preoccupied the NTSB's attention. Apart from the obvious differences of dorsal fin and tailplane tip extensions on the -300, the details are virtually the same for the 737-200. (Matthew Tesch; Flight International & John Marsden)

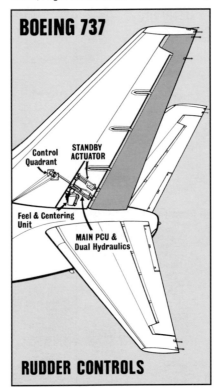

BOEING 737

Control Quadrant
STANDBY ACTUATOR
Feel & Centering Unit
MAIN PCU & Dual Hydraulics

RUDDER CONTROLS

the night before departure without knowing the identity of the captain.

The Customer Service Agent who handled the 737's departure from Denver described the captain as a "real confident type guy" and "very nice fellow" who appeared to be in exceptionally good spirits. He spoke of the first officer as a quiet woman who "had her mind on what she needed to get done." He thought both pilots appeared rested and seemed to get on well.

A member of United's training staff who had greeted the captain around 8.15am outside UAL's Denver operations office, said the captain seemed fine and "didn't look unrested."

The aircraft

The Boeing 737-291 Advanced had been acquired by United from Frontier Airlines on June 6, 1986. Manufactured in May 1982, it was powered by two Pratt & Whitney JT8D-17 engines. At the time of the accident, it had accumulated 26,050 flying hours and 19,734 cycles. The aircraft had taken off from Denver at a gross weight of 35,317kg (77,859lb), with its CofG well within permissible limits.

Maintenance history

The Boeing's most recent C check and Heavy Maintenance Check 4 was carried out by United in May, 1990. At that time it had accumulated 24,004 hours and 18,298 cycles.

A week before the accident, a crew had reported: "On departure got an abnormal input to the rudder that went away. Pulled yaw damper circuit breaker." The corrective action was signed off as: "Replaced yaw damper coupler and tested as per maintenance manual."

The crew said that, at the time, the aircraft was at about 11,000 feet at an airspeed of 280kt in smooth air with the undercarriage and flaps retracted. The first officer, hand flying the aircraft, had just levelled off and was in the process of retarding the thrust levers to a cruise setting when there was an uncommanded yaw of a few degrees to the right. In the time that it took him to adjust the power, everything returned to normal. He could not recall any uncommanded movement of the rudder pedals. The yaw damper was turned off and its circuit breaker pulled before landing.

Two days later, another crew reported "Yaw damper abruptly moves rudder occasionally for no apparent reason on 'B' actuators. Problem most likely in yaw damper coupler — unintended rudder input on climbout at FL250. Autopilot not in use, turned yaw damper switch off and pulled circuit breaker. Two inputs, one rather large deflection." The corrective action was signed off as: "Replaced rudder transfer valve and system checks OK."

Interviews with the crew of this flight established that the first officer was flying the aircraft with his feet on the rudder pedals. While climbing through 10,000ft, he experienced several rapid "jerks" he could not identify. The aircraft was encountering light turbulence at the time.

Continuing the climb between 25,000 and 28,000ft at 280kt in light turbulence, he felt a substantial right rudder input which lasted between five and 10 seconds. He corrected with left rudder and the aircraft resumed normal flight. Both pilots looked up at the overhead panel and saw the No 1 Constant Speed Drive low oil pressure light illuminated. The yaw damper was turned off, its circuit breaker pulled, and the CSD light went out, but came on again five minutes later. The CSD was then disconnected, and there were no more anomalies for the remainder of the flight.

There were no uncorrected maintenance items outstanding when the aircraft took off for Denver on the morning of the accident, and all applicable Airworthiness Directives had been complied with. Required actions not yet accomplished were within the time limits specified.

Hydraulics

The Boeing 737 has three independent hydraulic systems. Although Systems A and B normally provide dual hydraulic power for the flight controls, either can power them alone. Ailerons and elevators can be operated manually, while the rudder can function with the Standby hydraulic system.

The A System, powered by two engine driven pumps, operates the flight controls, undercarriage, nose wheel steering, alternative brakes, inboard flight spoilers, engine thrust reversers, and ground spoilers. The B System, powered by two electric pumps, operates the flight controls, brakes, trailing edge flaps, leading edge flaps and slats, and outboard flight spoilers. Either one of the two pumps powering each system is capable of operating that system.

The Standby System, powered by a separate electric pump, is activated by selecting Alternate Flaps or Standby Rudder A or B on the flightdeck overhead panel. The system can operate the rudder controls and provide an alternative source of power for the thrust reversers and the slats and flaps.

Directional control

The 737's rudder, which has no tab, is hydraulically powered. A rudder Power Control Unit, incorporating dual hydraulic actuators fitted in tandem, is directly connected to the rudder, System A powering the forward actuator, and System B the rear actuator.

Backup power is provided by an actuator operated by the Standby System, and any one hydraulic system will provide control. There is no manual reversion. The standby actuator, not normally powered, is activated by moving either the A or B flight control switch to the STBY RUD position. No more than two hydraulic systems can be used to power the rudder, and at least one side of the PCU remains unpowered when the standby actuator is activated.

Inputs from the rudder pedals or rudder trim actuator are transmitted to both the main PCU and the standby actuator simultaneously. When hydraulic pressure is not available from a particular system, a bypass valve connects both sides of the piston in that system's actuator to the same port of the control valve to prevent a hydraulic lock. Standby activation however, opens the bypass valve, connecting the actuator chambers to separate control valve ports.

The rudder is also controlled by the yaw damper system which operates through System B in the main PCU. Limited to $2°$ of rudder deflection in either direction, the yaw damper is activated by a solenoid controlling B System hydraulic flow through a transfer valve. Electric current through one of the solenoid's two opposing coil windings operates a slide valve, allowing the primary rudder valve to be driven in one direction or the other. The yaw damper operates independently of the pilots' controls and does not feed back to the rudder pedals.

During examination of the main PCU recovered from the wreckage, it was found that electrical wiring to the solenoid was loose and the circuit intermittent. This could have been the cause of the uncommanded yaws experienced on earlier flights. The effect would be erratic deflections of the rudder when the yaw damper was in use. But because the authority of the yaw damper is limited to only $2°$ of rudder travel, it would have had little effect on the aircraft's controllability.

The rudder trim operates via cables connecting the trim control knob on the flightdeck centre pedestal to a mechanical actuator attached to the hydraulic rudder centring mechanism.

Mountain waves

The National Oceanic and Atmospheric Administration informed investigators that atmospheric rotors could indeed develop in the area where the accident occurred – and could be powerful *some distance downwind from the mountains that cause them.*

Rotor clouds form in standing eddies under the crests of the lower layers of mountain waves, and a succession of rotors may even develop downwind from a ridge. Lenticular clouds may be visible above them, but rotor clouds often provide the only visible evidence of a mountain wave. Cloud may or may not form in a rotor, depending on the moisture in the atmosphere, and its turbulence may remain invisible.

In general, the base of a rotor is usually near or below the ridge producing it, yet its top may be considerably higher and may merge with lenticular clouds directly above it. Unlike lenticulars, rotor clouds are strongly and occasionally violently turbulent. Constantly forming on their windward side and dissipating to leeward, they appear to rotate – the upper portion moving forward while the lower portion moves backwards towards the mountain.

A meeting of weather scientists, convened by the investigation's Meteorology Group to examine the possible role of mountain waves and rotors in the accident, agreed on the following points:
• Few measurements of atmospheric rotors exist, but they can form in lines several hundred kilometres long, with the most severe turbulence at the leading edge.
• Horizontal gusts of "60 to 80mph" have occurred up to 40,000ft over mountainous terrain. Damage to a sailplane at such an altitude was estimated to have been caused by a 16g load.
• Mountain wave activity depends on atmospheric stability and wind speed. Small differences in these can produce large differences in atmospheric response.
• Isolated effects, such as produced by Pike's Peak, probably have more influence in a particular situation than wave phenomena generally.
• Rotors can sink to the ground and produce strong surface winds.
• Acceleration of airflow to more than 60kt above 10,000ft occurred over Denver about 7am on the day of the accident.

Observations at the USAF Academy just to the north of the city on the day of the accident, showed rotor clouds to the west between 7am and 9am, but not during the next observation later in the morning.

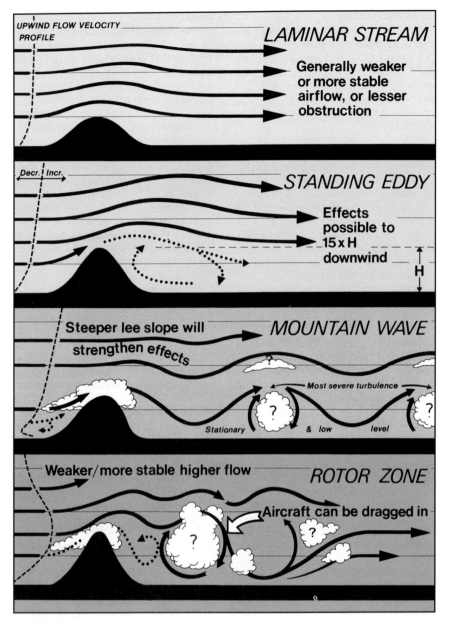

LAMINAR STREAM

UPWIND FLOW VELOCITY PROFILE

Generally weaker or more stable airflow, or lesser obstruction

STANDING EDDY

Decr. Incr.

Effects possible to 15 x H downwind

H

MOUNTAIN WAVE

Steeper lee slope will strengthen effects

Most severe turbulence

Stationary & low level

ROTOR ZONE

Weaker/more stable higher flow

Aircraft can be dragged in

Simplified diagram showing primary effects of airflow over a prominent mountain ridge. These stream effects are broadly applicable, regardless of specific wind or terrain conditions, though lack of moisture in the atmosphere may preclude the formation of the 'give-away' roll or lenticular clouds. Rotor streaming can occur with a only a moderate airflow over a sharp terrain obstacle, or vice-versa. But as NCAR scientists pointed out to the NTSB, particular, localised effects can be beyond the predictability of the most sophisticated computers. (Matthew Tesch; NTSB & AGPS)

Weather staff at Peterson Air Force Base located alongside Colorado Springs Airport to the south of the city, told investigators that rotor clouds had been observed previously in the area of the airport but were uncommon. Peterson's weather radar did not detect any weather returns at 9.50am, but because of strong gusty winds, a Low Level Windshear Advisory was in effect.

Rotor clouds

A sailplane pilot, who flew frequently in the area north of Colorado Springs, told investigators mountain waves and rotors were possible in the area of the accident, but this would be further to the

south than usual. He had flown in many rotors and on one occasion had almost lost control. Glider tugs that had penetrated rotors had been thrown into bank angles of 90°, he said.

Another sailplane pilot, with 15 years' experience in mountain wave flying in the Colorado Springs area, said he was planning to fly at Meadow Lake, 14nm to the northeast, on the morning of the accident. But after talking to another pilot who had terminated his flying because of "turbulent, squirrely conditions," he decided against it. He commented that it was "not uncommon" for rotor clouds to touch the ground at the Air Force Academy,

but although rotors *did* occur south of the city where the airport is located, they were rare.

A glider instructor, who had lived in the area for more than 25 years, said that, around noon on the day of the accident, he was inside a building at a wrecking yard when he suddenly heard the wind roaring. Going outside, he saw a rotor impacting the ground at wind speeds he estimated to be around 70-80mph. Limbs were blown off trees and car bodies were damaged.

He believed the rotor was part of a north-south line of rotors which would most likely have extended to the accident site. The year's weather had been highly unusual, with many days of strong downslope winds and rotors. The rotors could be small or many miles long, and he had experienced vertical velocities of 5000-6000fpm in them. Rotors he had seen impacting the ground had severely damaged houses and railway wagons.

In a subsequent written statement, the instructor told investigators his wrecking yard was about 20km north of the airport and that its elevation was 7300ft. There was unusually strong pre-frontal weather on the morning of the accident, with a sky full of rotor clouds. One rotor system, passing over parallel to the Front Range, extended noticeably to the south. He added that when he had flown gliders into vertical velocities of more than 5000fpm in and around rotor systems, pitch changes of 60° and roll angles of 190° (more than inverted) were not uncommon.

A Continental Airlines pilot, who had flown in the area for 25 years, told investigators that rotors had occurred in the past over the approach to Runway 35 during strong mountain wave conditions. He had seen aircraft roll 45° as a result. He had encountered rotors in T-37, T-38, and Boeing 727 aircraft, but had easily countered any roll with aileron.

Given the right conditions, the pilot said, rotors could exist all along the route from Denver to Colorado Springs. The area further south also had the reputation as extremely rough in which to fly. In certain conditions, a primary wave was located over Manitou Springs (16nm northwest of the accident site), a secondary wave lay just north of the Air Force Academy, and a tertiary wave extended over the airport. At the time of the accident, he had seen a lenticular cloud over Pike's Peak.

Other witnesses

Although most witnesses near the accident site reported light winds generally from the west, the investigators found evidence of a strong rotor in the area at the time of the accident.

One told of a brief westerly gust of "90mph or stronger" about three kilometres east of the accident site, while another reported a 50-70kt gust two kilometres to the east. Another reported a strong gust only a few blocks west-northwest of the accident site.

Still another, on a golf course northwest of the accident site, reported a strong gust, swirling winds, and downdraughts about 5-7 minutes before the accident, with estimated wind speeds of "50-60mph". And about 9.40am, a motorist driving five kilometres northwest of the accident site experienced a gust that almost blew his car off the road. Another, driving a few blocks west-northwest, also reported a brief strong wind about the time of the crash.

One man, about 10km west of the accident site, saw several rotor clouds, accompanied by thin wisps of condensation, within 10-15 minutes of time of the crash. He estimated them to be at 7000ft.

Investigation flight

The day after the accident, a specially instrumented Beech 200 Super King Air belonging to the University of Wyoming flew approaches into Colorado Springs Airport. The general weather conditions, which occur about 10 to 15 days a year, were similar to those 24 hours before. The data it recorded showed a wind shadow existed east of Pike's Peak below 11,000ft, extending from about 10km south of the airport to 5-10km north. In the shadow there were lighter winds and a directional reversal. Vortices and turbulence were also present at the interface between the strong and light winds. Higher up, mountain waves were producing vertical roll. The Super King Air recorded vertical speeds of 800-1000fpm.

The pilot told investigators that, in the area of the crash, he ran into "terrible shear". Flying at 7500ft AGL, the aircraft lost 20kt in airspeed, and 100ft of altitude. He described it as "a very hard hit".

Previous accidents

The investigators documented a number of accidents involving wind shear and rotors over the previous 30 years.

"Pike's Peak or bust!" was the catchcry of fortune seekers heading west in the 1859 Gold Rush. The mountain is named for the army lieutenant who discovered it in 1806. Colorado has no less than 53 mountaintops above 14,000ft – but none above 14,500ft. The prominent Pike's Peak (elevation 14,110ft) however, is noteworthy for more than its proximity to Colorado Springs Airport – it is unique in its isolation between the Rampart Range to the north and the great gap of the Palmer Divide to its southwest. As a result of the accident, the NCAR recommended the establishment of sensor stations on the western and eastern flanks of the peak to provide early windstorm warnings to the controllers in Colorado Springs Tower. (Airliners magazine; Ronald C Hill)

(right) USAF cadets parade before the dramatic architecture of the Air Force Academy chapel. The prestigious USAF Academy was established on the northern outskirts of Colorado Springs in 1958, one of many military installations and defence industry facilities which have become a feature of the region since WW2.

• On January 10, 1964, a B-52 bomber, flying at 14,000ft AMSL (about 5500ft AGL), 5nm east of Colorado's 13,500ft Spanish Peak, lost about 75% of its fin and rudder. The gusts which caused the damage exceeded 140ft per second.
• On March 5, 1966, a BOAC Boeing 707 broke up in flight at 16,000ft, 10nm southeast of the summit of Mt Fuji, Japan. Upper winds from the northwest were blowing at 60-70kt at the time, and there was a strong mountain wave system in the lee of Mt Fuji. Severe to extreme turbulence would have existed in the resulting rotor systems, but it is likely that this would have been intensified by the mixing of air currents swirling around the isolated volcanic cone (see *Air Disaster*, Vol 1, Ch 5).
• Five months later on August 6, 1966, a Braniff BAC-111 broke up in flight at night near Falls City, Nebraska at only 4000ft AGL. Witnesses on the ground saw the aircraft fly over a shelf of cloud preceding a thunderstorm and shortly afterwards saw an explosion in the sky, followed by a ball of fire falling out of the cloud. Violent turbulence associated with the outflow of cold air from the approaching squall line caused the aircraft's fin and starboard tailplane to fail almost simultaneously (see *Air Disaster*, Vol 1, Ch 6).
• On December 2, 1968, a Fairchild F-27B (a licence built Friendship), flying at 11,500ft, broke up in flight after encountering extreme turbulence at Pedro Bay, Alaska. An intense low level mountain wave existed about 5nm downwind from the ridge of Knutson Mountain, with a rotor 2000-3000ft over the northern tip of Pedro Bay.

Weather on the day

Weather conditions on the day of the accident were complicated by a trough over the Rocky Mountains and there was a severe windstorm over the Front Range at the time of the crash. Severe windstorms over the Rockies are caused by low level air flowing over the rugged terrain, generating severe turbulence, rotors and 'jumps'.

Jumps are regions where the airflow rebounds vertically to its original level after passing over the mountains, and can produce updraughts exceeding 40m per second. The widths of the jumps can be quite narrow, resulting in areas of extreme horizontal variation.

Because of the orientation of the complex mountain terrain in the Colorado Springs area, dominated by Pike's Peak and the Palmer Divide, the updraughts could be expected to pass over the airport more or less parallel to the north-south runways. Aircraft approaching from either direction would encounter a rapid increase in upward airflow as the jump passed over. The National Centre for Atmospheric Research informed investigators that Runway 35 had the worst possible orientation in terms of aircraft safety in downslope windstorms. NCAR personnel familiar with the area and its weather believed such conditions were possible on the day of the accident.

The NTSB and Boeing each conducted separate studies to determine possible local wind conditions. Both used DFDR and radar data. In addition, Boeing used a NASA program incorporating known aircraft performance data to calculate vertical winds. The calculations showed large reversals of wind at various positions. Strong vertical currents, peaking at 40-80ft per second down, were derived in the Boeing study.

The strong airflow field that passed over Colorado Springs near the time of the accident could also have produced a series of small but severe rotors. NOAA staff estimated that a typical such rotor could have a rotational velocity of 3.4° per second, with a 1640ft radius and a tangential velocity at the edge of its core of 100ft per second.

Boeing simulations

To examine the effects of various atmospheric disturbances on a 737-200's flightpath, Boeing developed simulator models of the possible accident conditions. The simulator's visuals showed Colorado Springs Airport, terrain features, the rotor, the crash site, and a representation of the flightpath as determined by radar data. The simulator could also be programmed for various control malfunctions.

The simulator was flown by a Boeing pilot as well as by pilots from the investigation team's Operations Group. All attempted to follow the flightpath while encountering atmospheric disturbances or control malfunctions.

In a series of simulations, rotor severity was increased until encounters produced extreme control difficulties. This stage was reached when the rotor's rotation rate approached 34° per second, with a 250ft core radius. Control problems were especially evident at the edge of the core. A more moderate rotor still produced substantial control problems, and even a loss of control, if recovery action was not taken promptly.

Subsequent rudder problems

Sixteen months after the accident, a United Airlines 737-300 captain, taxiing for takeoff at Chicago's O'Hare Airport, found during a flight controls check that the rudder pedals became obstructed at about 25% left pedal travel.

During subsequent testing of the rudder main PCU, binding occurred when the input crank was held against the main PCU body stops and the yaw damper piston was in the extended position. The results ranged from sluggish movement of the actuator piston to a full reversal of piston travel. Thus, a pilot applying left rudder could conceivably end up with a right rudder movement. But this condition could only occur if the pedals were moved rapidly to maximum travel. The failure was attributed to a manufacturing error in the PCU servo valve module.

The corresponding assembly recovered from the wreckage of N999UA was subjected to similar tests. But its manufacturing tolerances were found to be satisfactory, indicating that a reversal of piston travel could not have occurred in this unit.

The Boeing simulator provided further data on the effect of rudder malfunctions. An uncommanded rudder deflection of 7.5° could be easily overcome with the control wheel. But 25 seconds' delay in recovery resulted in the aircraft diving into the ground.

Full rudder deflection resulted in large yaw and lateral excursions, even with full opposite control wheel, and a heading could not be maintained at all if 10-15° of flap were extended. A 20° deflection to the right was found to induce extreme control difficulties and lead to a rolling moment similar to that of N999UA when control was lost.

NTSB simulations

The investigators also used computer simulations to determine what roll and sideslip manoeuvres would produce flightpaths consistent with the radar data, DFDR data, accident location, and impact attitude. But these established that large, rapid rudder inputs near the time of the upset would have resulted in heading angles different from those recorded.

ANALYSIS
Flight path

ATC and DFDR data showed the aircraft intercepted the Runway 35 glideslope a few seconds before 9.42am and began a normal descent. But about 10 seconds later, just before the first officer's "Wow!", a deviation began. Over the next 30 seconds the aircraft descended

Some readers will know of the colourful 'LogoJets' of the now defunct Western Pacific Airlines, headquartered at Colorado Springs. When it filed for bankruptcy late in 1997, its fleet of more than 12 Boeing 737-300s had made marketing mileage as 'flying billboards' – their fins and fuselages 'sold' for corporate advertising, with the airline's logo appearing only over the forward entry and service doors. The city of Colorado Springs utilised the familiar landmark of Pike's Peak aboard N372US, shortly before it was more aptly re-registered as N951WP. An interesting coincidence is that this particular -3B7, originally N351AU [22951], was one of the initial three 737-300s which Boeing first flew in 1984 for type certification and demonstration, before delivery to joint launch customer USAir. (Airways magazine; Bob Shane)

below the glideslope and by the time it was 400ft below, lateral control had been lost. The CVR indicated the pilots were caught by surprise.

Witnesses confirmed the aircraft was banked to the right while turning from the 45° intercept on to final approach. As it became aligned with the runway, it momentarily rolled level, then began to roll to the right again. The roll continued until it was inverted and diving almost straight down. The load factor increased as the bank neared 90°, reaching about 4g immediately before impact.

The CVR showed that the pilots were alert throughout this final nine seconds, and they would undoubtedly have tried to counteract the unexpected roll. The investigators therefore sought explanations for the loss of control and the inability of the crew to recover.

Wreckage

Examination of the engines, as well as the indications on the EPR gauges and transmitters, provided conclusive evidence that both engines were developing power at the time of impact.

All flight control structure was accounted for, and reconstruction of the wing and tail assemblies showed they were intact until impact. The flap jackscrews were selected to 10°, and the leading edge devices were extended at impact. Numerous other wreckage examinations failed to produce evidence of any pre-impact structural problem. The investigators considered the possibility that the "mist" some witnesses saw trailing from the wing was fuel or hydraulic fluid, but there was no evidence of any failure that would have allowed these to escape.

It seemed possible that the loss of control could have resulted from some flight control malfunction. But as it occurred nearly 30 seconds after the flaps were extended to 30°, and after the first officer's unalarmed comment, "we're at a thousand feet", the flap operation at least, was normal.

Controls

With the primary flight controls hydraulically powered, a loss of pressure from either the A or B hydraulic systems would result in a loss or degradation of control functions. But any such problem would have undoubtedly prompted crew comment, and they had the option of selecting the standby system. Examination of the hydraulic components *did* show evidence of contamination, for the most part pieces of O rings trapped in filter housings. But it was determined that this would have had no effect on essential flight control components.

Seen on Boeing's flightline at Renton, Seattle, the three prototype 737-300s were all 737-3B7s. N351AU, later to become the LogoJet mentioned in an earlier caption, was handed over to USAir in November, 1984, but joint launch customer Southwest Airlines inaugurated revenue service with its first example a fortnight before USAir. Both N351AU and N352AU wear the early USAir (ex-Allegheny) livery of orange, red and brown (see illustrations next chapter). N73700 in Boeing livery also has a Colorado Springs connection – it carried out high altitude airfield performance test flying there in early 1984. (Aircraft magazine)

No anomalies were found in the elevator control system. Furthermore, during the attempted recovery from the upset, the aircraft's load factor increased to about 4g – a manoeuvre requiring considerable elevator deflection.

There was no evidence of any lateral control system problem. The aileron power control units were at or near neutral at impact, and there were no anomalies in the actuators that could account for an uncommanded movement. There was also no evidence that a ground spoiler had deployed. Indeed, had either the flight or ground spoilers extended in flight, the aircraft could not have achieved a 4g load factor at 212kt without activating the stall warning stick shaker.

After a later 737 incident in which a pilot found an abnormal rudder response during a preflight control check, it was discovered that excessive manufacturing tolerances in its main PCU assembly could affect its operation. But extensive tests disclosed that several conditions had to exist to produce the malfunction. These conditions did not exist in N999UA's main PCU assembly, and the investigators concluded that its operation was not likely to have been a factor in the accident.

Nonetheless, the investigators were concerned that the potential for this malfunction of the 737's rudder main PCU was not detected during its acceptance tests, and Boeing's test procedures were modified as a result.

Environment

Clear skies and a visibility of 100 miles existed at the time of the accident. The Boeing 737 encountered moderate turbulence below 9000 feet AMSL during its approach to Colorado Springs, and several pilots in the immediate area reported turbulence of moderate intensity.

On the basis of other reports of severe turbulence in the area, the investigators believed a SIGMET and a Weather Advisory should have been issued by the NWS. The possibility of isolated severe turbulence below 18,000ft was included in the Denver Area Forecast, but a low altitude turbulence advisory should also have been issued by United's meteorologists.

Yet these omissions were not factors in the accident. The crew expected turbulent conditions en route from Denver to Colorado Springs, and the investigators believed the turbulence they encountered, even immediately before the loss of control, was no more than moderate. The DFDR showed the 737 was encountering airspeed fluctuations no greater than plus or minus 10kt, with moderate vertical accelerations. These were wholly characteristic of a Colorado Springs day of strong, gusting winds.

Nevertheless, on the basis of the 20kt gain in airspeed experienced by another 737 approaching to land on Runway 35 at 9.20am, the terminal forecast should have been amended to include a Low Level Wind Shear advisory. A warning of LLWS should also have been included in the Area Forecast.

There was evidence of the existence of a rotor in the area of the accident at the time it occurred. The strongest evidence of a rotor powerful enough to pose control problems were witness reports of "a 90mph gust" and "gusts of 50 to 70kt" just to the east of the accident site.

However, these could have been straight line gusts, rather than the result of a rotor contacting the ground. Intense rotors normally produce a distinct roaring, but only one witness mentioned this distinguishing characteristic, and none near the accident site.

The 737 could have encountered disturbed airflow in the form of updraughts and downdraughts, gusts, and both vertical and horizontal vortices. The most likely to have caused the aircraft to roll was the latter – a rotor. The investigators believed the 737 could have flown into a powerful rotor that exceeded its control capabilities, even though data on the DFDR was not consistent with such an encounter.

Combination of factors

Meteorological conditions at the time had the potential to produce control difficulties, and the aircraft's main PCU had design features that, unlikely though it would seem, could have resulted in a loss of rudder effectiveness. Moreover, the standby rudder actuator and yaw damper had anomalies that could have caused minor control difficulties. It also remains possible of course that some entirely undetermined crew factor could have contributed to the loss of control.

As the aircraft was turning from the 45° intercept angle on to final approach, it is possible that atmospheric disturbances rapidly rolled it level against pilot efforts to continue the right bank. If the pilot applied additional control to continue this bank to the right, coincident with an abrupt reversal of the atmospheric rolling moment, excessive right roll could have precipitated a loss of control.

Regardless of available rudder movement, a rotor 10 times as severe as those previously documented would have had to be present to cause the upset. A less powerful rotor, combined with delay in pilot reaction, could also have led to the upset. But the CVR indicated such a delay was unlikely.

The investigators acknowledged that some unsuspected malfunction of the flight controls *could* have remained undetected during the investigation. But, as such a likelihood was extremely low, the investigators considered a powerful rotor the more probable explanation.

Findings

There was no evidence that the crew were affected by illness or incapacitation, fatigue or other personal problems. The flight was conducted in accordance with UAL procedures.

There was no evidence of any pre-impact failure or malfunction of the aircraft or its electrical, instrument, or navigation systems. Both engines were developing power at the time of impact.

Anomalies were found in the hydraulic and flight control systems, but none that could explain an uncommanded rolling motion or loss of control.

Of all the terrain induced atmospheric phenomena the aircraft encountered, a rotor was the most likely to have caused its uncontrollable roll. Yet the DFDR did not conclusively support an encounter with a rotor of the strength necessary to cause an uncontrollable roll.

Either meteorological phenomena or an undetected mechanical malfunction, or a combination of both could have led to the loss of control.

PROBABLE CAUSE

The NTSB investigators, after an exhaustive investigation, could not conclusively explain the loss of N999UA.

Another 737 mystery

The world airline industry, and Boeing in particular, were still perplexed and smarting over the unexplained loss of United's N999UA when, three and a half years later, a remarkably similar upset destroyed another airline 737 in the US – this time a Series 300 aircraft. The apparent initiating factor in this case was not turbulence in the lee of a mountain range, but wake turbulence from a preceding aircraft.

On September 8, 1994, USAir Boeing 737-300 N513AU was operating Flight 427 from Chicago to West Palm Beach, Florida, via a number of en route ports, the first of which was Pittsburgh, Pennsylvania. Nearing Pittsburgh International Airport (elevation 1200ft) towards the end of the 50 minute flight in clear weather, the aircraft was cleared to descend and maintain 6000ft on QNH before being radar vectored for a visual approach to Pittsburgh's Runway 28R.

The first officer, flying the aircraft on autopilot on a heading of 120° with the first stage of flap extended, was levelling off about 15nm northwest of the airport, when, without warning, the 737 flew into invisible wake turbulence. The nearest aircraft ahead was a Delta Air Lines Boeing 727, being similarly positioned about 4nm in front of them.

The encounter threw the 737 into a violent Dutch Roll manoeuvre, rapidly banking it alternately left and right. The rate of roll was far greater than normally experienced in transport category aircraft, but the crew succeeded in levelling the 737 three times before a further violent roll to the left threw it on to its back. The

USAir 737-300s at Los Angeles in 1992 in the red and navy striped, bare metal background livery which took considerable time to apply to the huge company fleet after the takeover of Piedmont and PSA (see also following chapter). N592US [23937] pushing back is a -301, with a -3B7, N517AU [23703] docked behind. USAir's association with the Boeing 737 has been as changeable as its registration blocks and liveries. After doing its bit for the genesis of the -300, it ordered a token 15 Series 200s, decided to acquire more than 70, peaked at a fleet total of more than 200 examples, including the -400 series, then, like United, decided it wanted more than 120 Airbus A319s and A320s as well! Pittsburgh accident aircraft N513AU was one of 16 Boeings delivered to USAir during 1987, three of them in October alone. (Steve Allsopp)

nose then dropped steeply and the aircraft dived at increasing speed, plunging with explosive impact into a wooded hillside. All 132 on board were killed instantly.

As in the case of the Colorado Springs 737-200, the DFDR did not record the positions of the flight control surfaces. But it did show that roll rates and accelerations during and after the upset were substantially beyond those of normal airline manoeuvres. Fourteen seconds after the wake turbulence encounter, when the 737 had lost 500ft, its wings reached their stall angle of attack, doubtless as the crew attempted to recover from the steep dive. And they remained stalled throughout the next 14 seconds, the aircraft continuing to pitch down and roll further to the left until impact.

Investigation

The intensive investigation that followed took more than three years to complete, Boeing alone investing more than 75,000 engineering man-hours in it!

The 737's design and operating history was examined as never before, using new and enhanced simulation techniques to review previous accidents, that at Colorado Springs included. (These incidentally confirmed that the rudder mechanism had not contributed to the N999UA accident.)

Boeing also analysed a large number of 737 upset reports, as a result of which it found that:
• encounters with wake turbulence occur more frequently than previously believed;
• 737 yaw damper failures occur more frequently than previously believed;
• crews, startled by their aircraft's reactions to yaw damper failures or wake turbulence encounters, can perceive such incidents to be more severe than FDRs indicate.

The Pittsburgh 737 investigation sought to identify possible aircraft or crew inputs which would produce the flightpath recorded on the DFDR, and to understand what could have contributed to the crew's failure to recover from the upset. Because flight tests showed that the 737 had the control authority to effect recovery, crew reactions were also considered.

Analysis of the DFDR data showed that the most significant elements leading to the accident were: the unexpected encounter with wake turbulence; a sustained full rudder deflection to the left, the explanation for which could not be determined; and a hard back control column force that held the aircraft in its stalled condition.

Another impact crater, another fragmented mass of aircraft wreckage. Three and a half years after Colorado Springs, another Boeing 737 dived into the ground from relatively low altitude, again during an approach, this time to Pittsburgh International Airport. With the NTSB, restrained by its official mandate, still unable to reach any formal 'cause' for the earlier loss of control, all who held to the windstorm and rotor turbulence theory for Colorado Springs were perplexed by the similarities between the two accidents – for there are no 14,000ft mountains in Pennsylvania. The NTSB's subsequent searching re-investigation of the 737's rudder control design and operation thus fuelled speculation by armchair theorists and media 'experts'. As was the case at Colorado Springs, the barely recognisable 737 wreckage itself offered few leads to what could have happened – as this vertical aerial view of the scarred forest on the Ohio River shows. (Wide World Photos)

Rudder system

Yet another exhaustive investigation was made of the 737's rudder system. All conceivable rudder failure modes that could produce jams, 'hardovers' or reversals were tested and analysed. The effects of extreme thermal conditions, chip contamination, corrosion, and other conditions in the rudder PCU were also examined. The intensive investigation found no evidence of any condition that could have occurred to cause a malfunction of the Boeing 737's rudder PCU.

The NTSB Systems Group, summarising the testing, concluded that the PCU was "capable of performing its intended function," and "was incapable of uncommanded rudder reversal, or movement."

Crew input

Data examined during the investigation revealed that pilots can react to startling upsets with errors in control manipulation (see chapters 7 and 8). Generally any such errors are brief and quickly corrected. Only extremely rarely have such erroneous control inputs been maintained for critical lengths of time. The data showed that pilots:

• can perceive roll rates and roll angles resulting from an unexpected wake encounter to be more extreme than they really are;
• have failed, in several cases, to remove a rudder command after it is no longer needed;
• sometimes operate flight controls independently, or are unaware of the other's inputs.

Both the captain and first officer of the 737 were startled by the wake turbulence encounter which produced an excessive left roll. The first officer responded with a large right control yoke input, which in turn created a large roll acceleration to the right.

It is possible that he then countered the right roll by making a left rudder input, coupled with a reversal of his control yoke from right to left. The left rudder deflection was then sustained until impact.

Thus, in a period of only seconds, the crew experienced large accelerations, potentially confusing feedback, and made large control yoke and probably rudder inputs in a situation that was becoming rapidly life-threatening. In these circumstances, it is quite possible that the first officer could have become

A Boeing flight test program provided NTSB investigators with additional data on the effects of wake turbulence. This included fitting smoke generators to a 727 to make its wake vortices visible. The picture shows a 737-300 being deliberately flown in and around the 727's vortices to determine the effect on controllability. Special instrumentation on board the 737 measured and recorded the resulting data, which was then incorporated into a computer model of the Pittsburgh accident sequence. (Boeing)

• Design improvements have been made to the 737 yaw damper. An operations procedure has been published by the manufacturer, providing a means of minimising the effects of a yaw damper failure, or other system malfunctions that could affect the 737's rudder operation.

Comment:

Although it was assumed in this instance that the wake turbulence that caused the upset was from the preceding Delta Boeing 727, it has to be said that 727s have been operating on busy airways in the US and in many other parts for the world for well over 30 years without earning a reputation for creating hazardous wakes. This is certainly not the case with heavy widebodies (see *Air Disaster*, Vol 1, Ch 10). And the Boeing 757, though not quite in this category, also has a name for leaving a wake to be avoided.

In calm conditions, wake turbulence vortices can evidently persist unseen in the air for surprisingly long periods – as much as 20 minutes. This was found to be so some years ago, when a light aircraft, landing in clear, calm conditions, was destroyed by the wake of a Lockheed Super Constellation which had not only departed, but had disappeared from view into the distance!

The question needs to be asked therefore: could the wake turbulence that led to the Pittsburgh upset have been left by an earlier preceding flight, possibly a Boeing 757 or some heavier aircraft?

A disturbing pattern of accidents and incidents in the USA during 1993, involving Boeing 757 wake turbulence on airport approach paths, was the subject of an NTSB Special Report published at the beginning of 1994. Fatalities resulted from the approach crashes of a Cessna 182, Citation 550 and an IAI Westwind, and a 737-300 and an MD-88 were violently rolled, close to the ground, by unexpectedly vicious 757 vortices. The NTSB found that the 757, although its AUW was just under the "heavy" classification level, generated wake turbulence comparable in strength to that of the bigger widebodies. Its high power-to-weight ratio also made for steeper approach and climbout angles than other traffic, confusing established pilot and ATC assessments for aircraft separation and hazard avoidance.

fixated with handling the control column as the threat of disaster quickly developed, not realising he was still holding on left rudder. This would be consistent with the crew's desperate utterances on the CVR.

Although the official NTSB investigation was unable, as in the Colorado Springs case, to finally determine a definitive cause of the accident, the most significant findings of the overall investigation were:

• Transport crews need to be trained to handle large upsets. Airline pilot training does not prepare crews for recovery from the roll rates and pitch attitudes suddenly encountered by the crew of the Boeing 737. [An observation of worldwide relevance, given the disastrous sequence of events five months earlier, as recounted in chapter 7.]

• The reliability of the 737 yaw damper requires improvement to reduce the likelihood of it aggravating any aircraft upset.

• Highly unlikely potential 737 failure modes can be eliminated as the cause of a control problem.

• The effect of aircraft related or crew input rudder upsets could be reduced by limiting the 737's rudder authority.

• Ongoing research is needed on ways to detect and avoid wake vortices.

• DFDR data from the Pittsburgh accident (as with Colorado Springs) was inadequate because of the insufficient number of parameters being recorded.

As a result of the findings of the Pittsburgh investigation, the following measures have been implemented:

• NASA is conducting research on better ways to detect and avoid wake vortices.

• Pilots are being trained in unusual attitude recovery techniques, and upset recovery training programs are being refined.

CHAPTER 5

"Looks pretty good to me from what I can see..."

– First Officer to Captain, looking out at wings before takeoff

USAir Fokker F28-4000 Fellowship N485US [11235]
– March 22, 1992

As in Canada and Europe, snow and ice on the wings is a routine winter hazard for domestic pilots in the USA, and de-icing before taxiing for takeoff is a regular procedure. But delays on the ground because of airport congestion nullified this vital preflight preparation – with tragic results.

A busy schedule

For two Charlotte based USAir pilots, Sunday, March 22, 1992, was no day off – it was the third day of a scheduled four day tour of duty, and a busy one at that.

For the crew this was nothing unusual. Both were experienced domestic airline pilots, each having served with Piedmont Airlines before their company's 'predatory' takeover by USAir in 1986-87. Their duty period had begun late in the morning two days before on Friday, March 20, when they took charge of one of USAir's Fellowships at Charlotte, North Carolina.

Their first leg that day was to Roanoke, Virginia, departing at 1.50pm, with the captain flying the aircraft. Four more legs followed that afternoon and evening, the pilots alternating their roles as is customary on such services, and they completed their day's work when they landed at Washington's Dulles International Airport at 9.37pm.

The schedule for the following morning, Saturday, March 21, called for an early start and the pilots left their hotel about 6.45am. The early spring morning was cold, with some snow still falling, and while preparing for their first trip of the day, this time back to Charlotte, the crew found it necessary to have the F28 de-iced twice.

But their trip to Charlotte was uneventful, and they landed there at 9.20am. Their next leg was to Mobile, Alabama, where the two pilots had lunch together. At 2.50pm they took off for Charlotte again, arriving just on 4.10pm.

At Charlotte, formerly Piedmont's inaugural 'hub' port and now a regional base for USAir, the crew changed aircraft, taking over N485US, for their next leg to Bristol, Tennessee. Even though VFR conditions prevailed at this destination, the pilots carried out a Category II instrument approach to verify that the aircraft's radio navigation aids were operating satisfactorily.

In company with the two flight attendants, the F28 crew travelled to the Bristol hotel where they were to remain overnight, checking in at 7.30pm. The captain and first officer then had dinner together at a local restaurant, during which they met briefly with one of the flight attendants. They returned to their hotel at around 11.15pm and, with a later start scheduled for the Sunday morning, March 22, were able to 'sleep in' until after 9am.

At 10am, all four crew members travelled back to Bristol's Tri-City airport together. An hour later they were airborne on their first leg of the day, once again to Charlotte. After landing and shutting down at 11.40am, the captain and first officer, using the latter's car which he had left parked at the airport, drove to a restaurant for lunch, returning at 1.30pm for their next leg to Jacksonville, Florida.

The first officer carried out a preflight inspection of N485US and, at 2.45pm, with the captain flying the aircraft, they departed for the one hour flight to Florida.

Touching down at Jacksonville at 3.50pm, they were scheduled to depart again for La Guardia Airport, New York, at 4.35pm. But because of bad weather in the New York area, they were held for a time on the ground. One of the passengers booked to New York then decided to leave the aircraft at Jacksonville, and there was a further delay while his luggage was removed.

But finally, at 5.15pm, after a delay of about 40 minutes, they took off for New York, with the first officer at

USAir concourses at Charlotte's former Douglas Municipal Airport. This May 1990 scene exemplifies USAir's massive expansion in the latter half of the 1980s. Two DC-9s still wear the orange, bright red and brown stripes of the former Allegheny, while the two 737-200s (left, with N204AU [19603], an ex Western 737-247, in the foreground) have had the interim red and blue USAir logo applied to their fuselages and fins. The F28-1000 to the right of N204AU's rudder carries the full USAir livery, but the other Fellowship (left background) is similarly styled to the 737s. (Air International)

the controls. There were no ATC delays in their clearances to La Guardia. But because the weather was still IMC in the New York area, with wet snow falling, and the airport was reporting visibility at its minimum range, the first officer flew an ILS approach. The runway was covered by a thin layer of wet snow, but the aircraft braked normally to taxiing speed.

Tarmac congestion delayed the Fellowship on the ground after landing for about 10 minutes, and it was not until 7.49pm that the crew were able to shut down at Gate 1, an hour and six minutes behind schedule.

La Guardia departure

The aircraft's next leg was to Cleveland, Ohio, originally scheduled to depart at 7.20pm. The crew had not experienced any problems with the aircraft, and the captain told the duty ground engineer who came aboard as soon as the doors were opened that it was "good to go."

The captain then left the flight-deck, and the first officer made preparations for the flight to Cleveland before himself going into the terminal for five minutes to use the toilet.

Snow continued to fall while the 47 passengers booked to Cleveland were boarding the aircraft, but the fall was not heavy. There were no large flakes, and because the F28's windscreen heat was on low, the snow was sliding off it and the nose had a watery layer on it. There was no wind.

The captain returned to the flight-deck about 10 minutes after the first officer. Neither of them carried out a walkaround inspection of the aircraft, nor did USAir procedures require them to do so.

But before the F28 was pushed back from the gate, the crew requested that it be de-iced, a standard precaution in cold weather airline operations in the northern hemisphere. This was promptly carried out by ground crew, using a 50/50 water/glycol mixture from two de-icing vehicles.

The de-icing operation was completed by 8.25pm, but at this stage one of the vehicles broke down, becoming immobilised behind the aircraft. As a result, the pushback was delayed for a further 20 minutes, during which snow continued to fall and collect on the aircraft.

Because of the delay, the captain requested that the aircraft be de-iced a second time. But with only one vehicle now available, it was necessary to first move the Fellowship away from the gate to facilitate the operation. The second de-icing was completed by 9pm, the engines were started, and five minutes later the first officer called La Guardia ground control to request a taxi clearance.

For the sector to Cleveland, the captain was again at the controls, with the first officer conducting the non-flying pilot duties. Cleared to taxi to Runway 13, the crew changed frequency to La Guardia ground sequence control, which they continued to monitor for the next 20 minutes as they inched towards the runway holding point in a line of other departing aircraft.

Traffic congestion was not the only cause for delay on the taxiways. Soon after the F28 had left Gate 1, Runway 04/22 was temporarily closed for sanding as a result of a "nil braking action" report from another aircraft. This created delays for all aircraft using the airport.

The pilots completed the before-takeoff checklist during the taxi,

(opposite) This map of the eastern United States provides some idea of USAir's regional coverage as well as a symbolic portrayal of its ancestry. Ports mentioned in the text are in bold, as are the movements of N485US on the day of the accident. The broad outer arrows link successive developments in USAir's corporate history. Northeastern airline Allegheny traced its roots back to the pre WW2 All-American Aviation, acquiring Lake Central Airlines in July 1968, and New York based Mohawk in April 1972. Headquartered in Washington DC, but restricted by the physical limitations of its National Airport, Allegheny's principal operational base was Pittsburgh. With the disposal of the last of its CV-540s and 580s, it adopted a new livery in 1978 and, after President Carter's signing of the Deregulation Act, its new USAir name and identity a year later – and the nation's biggest local service operator had become one of 'the majors'.

Piedmont, whose territory overlapped the southern fringes of Allegheny's, began services in 1948 in Carolina and the Ohio River valley. From its original Winston-Salem-Greensboro base, it moved its hub to Charlotte in 1981. Long a Fokker Fellowship customer, it was perhaps inevitable that Piedmont should absorb Altair (Philadelphia), then Empire (New York), with their small but compatible F28 fleets. Altair's six two tone blue F28s, and the 10 orange, red and scarlet Empire aircraft, merged into the Piedmont fleet during the first half of the 1980s, joining the company's new Boeing 737-400s and 767s. But just as Piedmont clawed its way to a trans Atlantic presence, it became the target of a protracted takeover by the insatiable USAir.

(lower right) N465AU [11064], one of 12 ex Garuda F28-1000s Piedmont acquired from Fokker in 1985, after the latter had traded-up to the Mk 4000. Snapped on short final (note the deploying tailcone speedbrake), the aircraft still proclaims its former ownership, its new interim titles having been applied over Piedmont's French Blue cheatline. (lower left) This empennage profile shows USAir's ultimate red and navy livery, as carried on the accident aircraft. (Matthew Tesch)

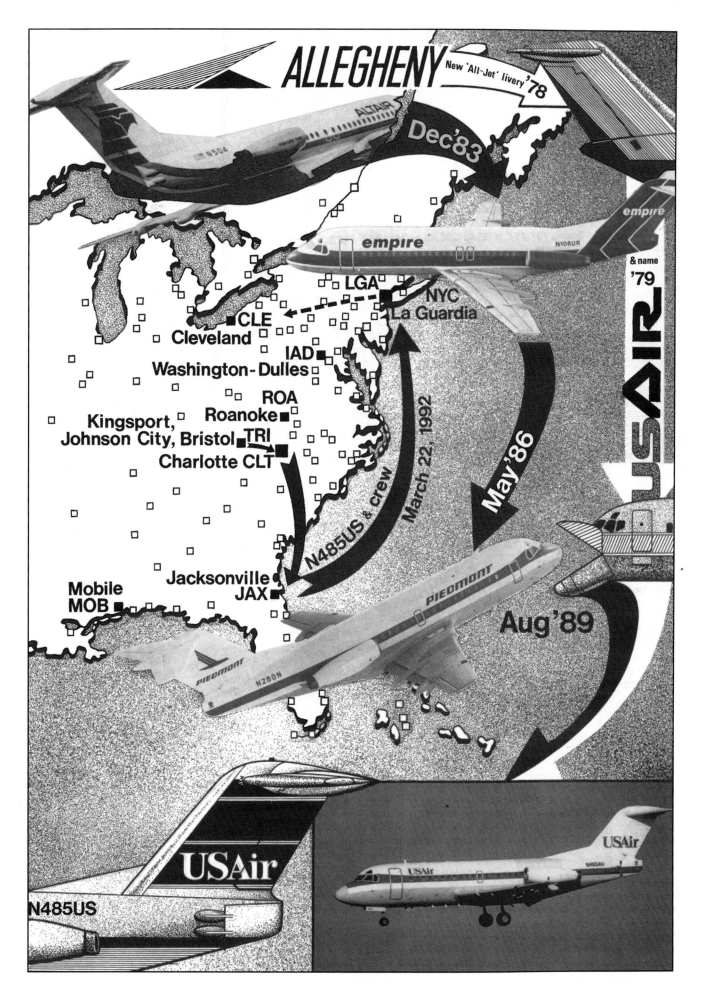

The uncluttered simplicity of the Fellowship flightdeck reflects Fokker's philosophy of appealing to third level and under developed operators – and those upgrading from the highly successful F27 Friendship. The windscreen panels and side windows afford excellent visibility. At the time of N485US's loss, there were eight former Piedmont Mk 4000s under the USAir umbrella, together with the 16 former Altair and Empire aircraft, and 18 of the original Mk 1000s. One-time N465AU (illustrated bottom right on the map page) was sold north of the border in 1992 as C-FXTA, becoming Canadian Regional's Spirit of Fort McMurray. (Matthew Tesch)

selecting engine anti-ice for both engines. Deciding that the flaps should remain up throughout the long taxi, the captain placed his empty coffee cup on the flap handle as a reminder to position them for takeoff when the time came. Though they had no visual or directional control problems, the captain told the first officer they would use USAir's contaminated runway procedures, which included the use of 18° of flap, and that they would use a reduced V_1 speed of 110 knots.

While queuing on the taxiway behind other departing aircraft, the captain announced to the passengers on the aircraft's P/A system: "Folks, we are in line for takeoff, and I see about seven airplanes ahead of us – so it's going to be another eight or nine minutes before its our turn to go ..."

The first officer used the windscreen wipers, and turned on the wing ice inspection light several times to examine the starboard wing, checking the upper surface for contamination, and the black strip on the leading edge for ice buildup.

He saw none, so he did not consider it necessary to seek a third de-icing. The snowfall did not appear heavy, and there was no wind blowing the snow. As they neared the takeoff point, the pilots looked back at the wings several times. Near the time of takeoff, the first officer told the captain: "Looks pretty good to me, from what I can see."

Takeoff – then disaster

At 9.25pm the crew switched to the Tower frequency and eight minutes later they were cleared into the takeoff and hold position on Runway 13. The F28 was finally cleared for takeoff at 9.35pm.

The takeoff at first seemed normal, with no problem evident from vibration, rate of acceleration, ambient noise, or directional control, and the captain lifted the aircraft off with a smooth, gradual rotation to 15° at the normal rate of three degrees per second.

The liftoff itself also seemed normal, with the main undercarriage leaving the runway. But before the first officer could call "positive rate",

the aircraft began to buffet. Then, still in ground effect (see Glossary), it began rolling to the left, the port wingtip momentarily scraping the runway as the aircraft diverged to the left.

With the aircraft now heading off the runway towards the darkened waters of Flushing Bay, the captain desperately levelled the wings and the first officer joined him on the controls, seemingly in consensus that the aircraft was not going to fly.

Striking two of the three outermost VASIS boxes on the left of the runway, then the ILS localiser antenna structure, and demolishing a small pumphouse building, the Fellowship impacted violently against the earthen seawall which protects the runway from the tidal waters of Flushing Bay. Bouncing over the dyke, the fractured wreckage finally came to rest partially inverted on the water's edge, with the forward portion of the fuselage and flightdeck submerged.

Several fires immediately broke out on the water and in the wreckage, but were soon extinguished by the airport rescue and fire fighting service. Rescue operations began almost at once. The time of the accident was a few seconds before 9.36pm.

The aircraft was destroyed by the impacts and fires. The captain, one of the cabin crew, and 25 passengers lost their lives, 15 of them as a result of drowning. Most of the 24 survivors sustained injuries to ribs and arms, burns to the head, hands, arms and legs, as well as multiple abrasions and lacerations.

INVESTIGATION

Wreckage

Initial ground scrape marks, containing aluminium particles and paint chips, and ranging from two to 20 metres in length, were found 1320m from the Runway 13 threshold and about 11m left of the runway centreline. Plexiglass lens cover pieces from the port wingtip were found 65m further on. Two of the three outermost VASIS boxes, 20m from the edge of the runway, were destroyed. Black rubber was evident on the boxes.

Wheel ruts about 60m long, angled 10° to the left of the runway centreline, were found on the wet ground 30m to the left of the runway's edge, with another pair of wheel ruts parallel to the first. Pieces of the aircraft's port wing structure were found amongst the destroyed ILS localiser antenna. Most of the antenna's supporting metal beams were dislodged from their concrete bases.

The grassed earth of the dyke parallelling the left side of the runway

This north facing aerial view of New York's La Guardia Airport characterises America's dependence upon the motor car and aeroplane. Freeway 678 (foreground) passes out of the picture towards Manhattan (lower left), only 7¹/₂ km to the west, substantially closer than the city is to JFK International Airport on Jamaica Bay on the southern side of Long Island (see map). Mayor Fiorello La Guardia secured Glenn H Curtiss (North Beach) Airport for the City of New York in September 1937. A former amusement park, it also became the terminal for Pan American's prewar Clipper flying boats. The yacht basin to the southeast was partly reclaimed for La Guardia's expansion but remains in use. Runway 13, on which N485US made its attempted takeoff, runs left to right across the top of the picture. The paler concrete flanking the runway intersection (upper left) defines extensions built out on piles in Flushing Bay in 1967. Adequate for traffic projections, these became the subject of controversy in 1977-78, when Airbus Industrie was seeking a foothold in the US market. Eastern Air Lines, after trials with the A300B, wanted 24 for its Miami route. But the Airbuses exceeded the load-bearing strength of the extensions, and the Port of New York Authority had to be prevailed upon to strengthen them at a cost of nearly a million dollars! (Ian Allan Ltd)

was scorched, and a nearby pumphouse was destroyed by impact and fire. A section of the F28's port wingtip lay near the water, 80m from the edge of the runway on the Flushing Bay side of the dyke, and pieces of the fire damaged aft cargo door and port wing were found around the remains of the pumphouse. Part of the wing centre section was excavated from the debris of this building. Aircraft structure, found between the pumphouse and the main wreckage, was also damaged by fire, as was a 4m section of the port wing, 63m from the runway's edge. Most of the remaining wreckage was in the water beyond the dyke, about 95m to the left of the runway.

The fuselage had broken into four main sections. The nose, to aft of the fourth passenger window, came to rest upside down and partially submerged in the bay. The pilots' windscreens were still intact, but the lower port side was crushed and the fuselage skin exhibited sooting. The submerged instrument panels were still in place, but the captain's rudder

pedals were displaced upwards about 25cm.

The next section of the fuselage, from aft of the fourth passenger window to the eleventh, was afloat in the water. Its floor was torn and fire damaged, while the roof and port side showed compression buckling and sooting. A short section of the starboard wing remained attached.

The fuselage was partly destroyed by fire from the eleventh passenger window to the aft bulkhead, and the remains of this section lay submerged in the waters of the bay. The empennage was lying on the port tailplane at the water's edge, with the fin and rudder still attached, but showing sooting and fire damage.

Five impact points were evident on the leading edge of the port wing, with the front spar bent rearwards in the strike areas.

The leading edge of the starboard wing had impact damage in two places, with timber embedded in the skin.

The undercarriage was in the down and locked position, and the

flaps in their middle range at about 18°. Elevator and rudder deflections were neutral, with the rudder trim jackscrew in the mid-range.

Engine controls were all at settings consistent with takeoff power. Both high pressure fuel valve levers were at their forward limits of travel, the fuel shutoff valves "on", and both crossfeed valves were closed. All four boost pump switches were selected "on", and the three unburned pumps contained fuel. The fuel gauges showed 7100 pounds (3195kg) in the port fuel tanks and 7600lb (3420kg) in the starboard, and the engine pressure ratio (EPR) gauges were at a thrust index value of 1.74 and 1.75.

The port engine had separated from the fuselage and lay to the left of the runway. The starboard engine, submerged in the water, remained with the rear fuselage. Rotational-type damage was present in both engines.

Nineteen of the F28's double and triple seats had separated from the cabin floor and were scattered throughout the wreckage, six of them damaged by fire. The remaining nine seats were not recovered. Seats near the front of the cabin sustained less damage than those towards the rear.

Flight recorders

The aircraft's Fairchild F800 Digital Flight Data Recorder was not damaged in the impact, but its electronic components and recording medium were affected by water and jet fuel. After being treated in the NTSB's laboratory, the quality of the recording was found to be good, and data from the accident takeoff, as well as from the five preceding flights, was recovered.

The indicated airspeed, magnetic heading and microphone keying information from the DFDR were normal. The aircraft's ground track throughout the takeoff and accident sequence were determined from the data, with a negligible altitude recording.

The Fairchild A100 Cockpit Voice Recorder also yielded good quality information, beginning at 9.04pm when the Fellowship left USAir's Gate 1 at the La Guardia passenger terminal, and ending when electrical power was lost as the aircraft broke up.

Four seconds before 9.35pm, the CVR recorded the parking brake being released, then the sound of the engines spooling up. Thirteen seconds later the captain, and then the first officer called "80 knots". This was followed eight seconds later by the first officer's V_1 (decision speed) call, then his V_R (rotation speed) call. The specified takeoff speeds for the F28's weight and configuration were 124 knots for V_1/V_R and 129 knots for V_2 (takeoff safety speed).

Two seconds after the V_R call, the nose undercarriage oleo strut could be heard extending as the F28's nose lifted, and five seconds later the sound of the 'stick shaker' stall warning began. Five seconds later again the first aural stall warning beep sounded, followed by five stall warning beeps which began another five seconds later. Almost immediately there was the sound of the initial impact, and the recording ended two seconds later.

Examined on a sound spectrum analyser, the recording was used to determine that the engines stabilised at 101% N_1 throughout the takeoff until five seconds before the crash, when they began a slow decrease to 97% N_1.

The aircraft

The medium range Fokker F28-4000, powered by two Rolls-Royce Spey Mk 555-15P turbofan en-

Looking southeast towards the Borough of Queens from above the American Airlines pier, La Guardia's distinctive and futuristic 49m (161ft) high control tower dominates the scene. (Dreamweaver)

gines mounted on either side of the rear fuselage, was designed to carry as many as 85 passengers. It has moderately swept wings, with no leading edge high lift devices[1], a T-tail and no thrust reversers (see also side-box on later page).

USAir's coach cabin in N485US was equipped with 28 double and triple seats for a total of 68 passengers, as illustrated in the accompanying diagram. It also had two single forward facing cabin crew jumpseats, one in the front between the two galley units, with the second in the rear fuselage between the two toilets.

The aircraft was delivered to Piedmont Airlines in August 1986 and acquired by USAir with the merger of the two airlines three years later. It had flown nearly 12,500 hours and over 16,000 cycles, and its maintenance records showed that all required inspections had been carried out. At the time of the accident, both its gross weight of 29,383kg (64,790lb), and its centre of gravity, were within specified limits.

The crew

The captain, aged 44, had flown nearly 10,000 hours and held type ratings for the F28, DC-9, EMB-110

Bandeirante, DHC-7, 737 and the piston engined DC-6. He was qualified also as a turbojet flight engineer and a flying instructor.

He had joined Piedmont Airlines as an F28 first officer in May 1985, and became a 737 first officer 16 months later in September, 1986. He was upgraded to F28 command in January 1989 and to 737 command a year later. Because of a cutback in the airline's operations, he was reassigned as a captain on F28s in January 1991.

The first officer, 30, came to Piedmont Airlines in July, 1989. At the time of the accident he had accumulated 4500 flying hours, but only 29 hours were in the F28. Moreover, his F28 time was his only pilot experience in transport category jets. He also was a qualified flight engineer and a flying instructor, and in addition held an FAA air traffic controller's licence.

The airport

La Guardia Airport serves the New York and New Jersey metropolitan areas and lies on partly reclaimed land four miles east of New York City, close to the northwestern tip of Long Island (see map). It has two principal runways, 04/22 and 13/31. Two thirds of the airport is surrounded by water, with Flushing Bay at the end of Runway 13, and Bowery Bay at the end of Runway 31. Its elevation is only 21 feet AMSL and most of the low lying airport boundaries adjoining the bays are protected by earthwork dykes or sea walls some two metres high and 10 metres wide at their base. Runway 13, the runway from which the accident occurred, is 2170m (7120ft) long and 45m wide.

The terminal forecast for La Guardia at 8.00pm on the night of the accident was for an overcast ceiling of 500 feet, visibility one kilometre in light snow and fog, and an easterly wind from 070° at 10 knots.

Because Runway 04 was closed between 9pm and 10pm, arrivals and departures were restricted to Runway 13. This reduced the airport's movements to 50 aircraft per hour, but 36 arrivals and 22 departures were scheduled during this time. From 9pm until the accident at 9.35, there were 11 arrivals and 14 departures. Another USAir F28 was the last aircraft to land on Runway 13 before the accident.

La Guardia Tower logged N485US's call for a taxi clearance as 9.06pm and its departure time as 9.35pm, an interval of 29 minutes. There were no "Gate Hold" procedures in use, and the Tower could not give a departure sequence at the time of an aircraft's initial call, because of the physical limitations of the airport. To provide guaranteed departure times, it would have been necessary to drastically limit the number of aircraft using La Guardia.

Witness evidence

The surviving first officer said that, using right rudder, the pilots had tried to manoeuvre the F28 back over the runway to avoid descending into the water, at the same time trying to hold the nose up to forceland in a flat attitude. Their control inputs were in unison, but there were no more aileron inputs, nor major control inputs of any kind. Accompanying the buffeting, the nose was pitching up and down, "just like we lost lift," as the first officer later described it.

The first officer did not touch the power levers and the last thing he remembered was an orange and white building disappearing beneath the nose, a flash, an initial impact, then violence as the aircraft tumbled, and a sudden final impact.

Fatally injured passengers were seated between rows four and 11, near the overwing exits, and at row 13 (see diagram). Surviving passengers said they had not assumed the brace position before the impact and, when the wreckage came to rest, many in the forward cabin were upside down. Others, who were upright, were in water over their heads.

Some passengers had difficulty releasing their seatbelts because of disorientation. Some escaped through the holes in the cabin, several assisting others out into the water. Others were assisted from the water by the rescue teams. The surviving flight attendant and first officer escaped through a hole in the floor near the forward flight attendant's position. Some of the survivors waded to the dyke, climbed over it, and slid down its snowy slope to the runway.

A Northwest Airlines Boeing 757 that taxied out for takeoff around 9pm, had queued on the taxiway directly behind N485US and the 757's captain had a good view of the F28. There was just enough snow to "fuzzy" the USAir titles on the forward fuselage, its captain said, but the wings appeared to be clear. He believed the snow had "all but stopped" and he was more concerned about the amount of vehicular traffic on the airport – the sweepers and snowploughs – than he was about the snowfall.

A Boeing 727 operating a shuttle flight had landed at La Guardia at

In this view looking NNE (see accompanying map) a tanker vehicle waits to cross the runway as Delta's 727-232Adv N476DA [20751] taxis past. Although LGA's field elevation is nominally 21ft, the expanse of Flushing Bay flanking its northern boundaries dictates protection for its movement areas, in particular for Runway 13/31. Astride the 2m high seawall on the left is the decking for the Rwy 13 ILS Localiser antennae. Beyond, jetties carry a discharge pipeline and approach lighting for Rwy 22. High speed turnoff Taxiway Tango lies between the runway and the fuselage of the 727. Passing from the picture's left to right, N485US rotated at exactly this point. (Brodie Publishing)

8.45pm, and its second officer said it "picked up a lot of snow quickly during my post-landing walkaround, but by the finish it seemed to be more rain." The snow was sliding off all but the level surfaces and seemed to be sticking more to the side of the aircraft that faced north.

By the time the 727 had been de-iced for departure, between 9.10 and 9.15pm, it had accumulated less than a quarter inch (about 6mm) of loose wet snow. It pushed back from its gate at 9.25pm and was holding on an intersecting taxiway when the Fellowship taxied past for takeoff. The second officer estimated the F28's wingtip passed within 50 feet of the 727's nose. His position was higher than the F28's wing, which was well lit by reflected light from the runway and other aircraft, and he described the Fellowship as "fairly clean". He could not comment on clear ice, but said that its wings and fuselage were clear of snow.

When the F28 was holding for takeoff, the 727's second officer saw its ice inspection light, which was reflected on the wing, come on for about a minute. He remarked to his

other crew members that the light was "blinding him". He did not see any spray during the F28's takeoff roll, but he did see the fireball at 9.35pm. As the ill-fated Fellowship left the runway to gouge its way into Flushing Bay, another aircraft approaching to land on Runway 13 was instructed to go around at a height of less than 300 feet.

ANALYSIS

Flight performance

Headings and airspeeds from the DFDR were used to plot the F28's ground track from the beginning of takeoff to impact. The aircraft's acceleration was then compared with the expected acceleration as calculated by Fokker. The comparison showed the ground performance to be normal – drag resulting from ice contamination is insignificant below liftoff speed.

Data provided by Fokker showed that an F28, without wing contamination, should lift off about two seconds after the start of rotation, assuming an average rotation rate of 3° per second. With the rotation starting at 124 knots, it should lift off at 131 knots, when the pitch attitude would be about 5°. The Angle of Attack (AoA) would reach a peak of about 9° as the aircraft began its initial climb. With a stall AoA of 12° in ground effect, the aircraft would have at least a 3° AoA stall margin during this transition. The margin would increase as the aircraft accelerated and established a climb.

The two distinctive sounds recorded on the CVR as the F28 continued to accelerate after the first officer's V_R call, were the sound of the nose strut extending as the nose-wheel lifted off the ground, and that of the magnetic clicks in the lift dumper indicator on the instrument panel as the main undercarriage struts extended, 2.2 seconds later. The timing of these sounds was used to analyse the speed at which the captain began to rotate the aircraft, and his rate of rotation into the take-off attitude. It was calculated that the aircraft rotated at 119 knots, about five knots below normal rotation speed. The rotation rate was about 2.5° per second in accordance with USAir procedures.

Analysis showed that, by rotating at 119 knots instead of 124 knots, the aircraft would lift off at 128 knots with an AoA of about 5.5°. Under these conditions, the AoA probably exceeded 9° as the aircraft transitioned to a normal climb.

According to Fokker wind tunnel data, roughness on the upper surface of the wing, produced by particles 1-2mm in diameter at a density of only one particle per square centimetre, can cause the F28 to lose a considerable amount of its lift – about 22% in ground effect and 33% in free air.

During the transition to climb immediately after liftoff, the F28 probably reached an AoA beyond the stall, with significant loss of both lift and lateral control. The abrupt roll that occurred was consistent with this analysis.

Tests in the F28 simulator confirmed that, with a contaminated wing, AoAs as high as 12°, well into the stall regime, were reached even when the pilot began the rotation at the correct speed to a pitch attitude of 15°, at a rate of 3° per second.

The design of most aeroplane wings allows the inboard sections to stall before the outboard, ensuring that roll control can be maintained with the ailerons. But ice particles on the wings can create an irregular stall distribution, so that premature stalling of the outboard sections occurs first, with a resulting loss of lateral control. Wind tunnel tests

A typical USAir Fellowship cabin layout. The pairs of economy seats in row 2, behind the four first class seats, are arranged to minimise the aisle offset aft of the cabin divider. The main cabin is otherwise what Fokker called its "Airline Coach" layout, though USAir's triple seat units were to starboard rather than the more standard reverse arrangement. Seats marked with a letter designator only were unoccupied at the time of the crash. (Matthew Tesch)

indicated that, with the 16° sweep angle of the F28's wing, a nose-down pitching moment could also occur.

It was evident that the aircraft could not achieve a positive climb angle in the 11 seconds that it was airborne before striking the seawall. The maximum airspeed recorded by the DFDR was 134 knots. The stick shaker stall warning activated at this time, and airspeed then decreased.

At this speed, the aircraft should have been able to sustain a load factor of 1.5g at the stick shaker threshold AoA, which would have provided a 3° AoA stall margin. The single 'beep' of the aural stall warning immediately after the stick shaker activated would indicate the aircraft momentarily attained an even higher AoA, probably between 12.5° and 15°. But the signal was not immediately continuous, so for five seconds the AoA was evidently less than the critical wing angle at which lift starts to decay and drag increases rapidly. The fact that the Fellowship was unable to attain normal flight during this brief interval was conclusive evidence that the lift capability of its wing was degraded by snow and ice.

De-icing effectiveness

Although the aircraft was cleared of ice and snow during the two de-icing procedures at the gate, 35 minutes elapsed between the second de-ice and the takeoff, during which the aircraft was exposed to continuing snow in below freezing temperatures.

Assessing the time for which de-icing fluid will remain effective is complicated by many variables – fluid qualities (composition and proportions), ambient temperature, moisture on aircraft surfaces, the condition of the airport movement areas, and the snowfall rate during the waiting time before takeoff. Other factors, such as the shape and slope of the aircraft's surfaces, wind direction, and taxiing speed may also affect it.

Aircraft exposure time should be measured from the time that de-icing begins, rather than when it is completed. Twelve minutes is the average time taken to de-ice a large

Ladders extend across foreshore ditches filled with water and aviation kerosene. Apart from the scorched empennage (tailplane upper surfaces towards the camera), little of the wreckage can be identified but the dismembered fuselage structure behind the investigators (centre left, beneath crane boom pulley). Beyond, the far shore of Flushing Bay stretches from The Bronx (left) towards Westchester County. (NTSB)

aircraft using two de-icing vehicles. It could take longer if there is a considerable accumulation of ice, the aircraft is particularly big like a Boeing 747, or if only one vehicle is used.

Given the number of possible variables, it is difficult to know for how long the results of a de-icing operation will remain effective. Certainly in the case of the F28, enough contamination accumulated in the 35 minutes that followed the second de-icing to lead to control difficulties immediately after liftoff.

Crew's takeoff procedures

Although the primary factor in the accident was the reduced performance of the wing, resulting from ice contamination, the investigation sought to evaluate the extent to which the procedures followed by the crew could have contributed to the aircraft's failure to fly.

Neither the captain nor the first of-

ficer performed a walkaround inspection before departure from La Guardia, but the aircraft was de-iced and the condition of the wings checked by ground staff. The fact that the captain requested a second de-icing after a 20 minute delay at the gate, indicated his concern about the aircraft's continuing exposure to the snowfall. After the second de-icing, he was no doubt satisfied the aircraft was free of ice and snow. His decision to taxi from the gate was thus reasonable – and he did not know they would be delayed to such an extent on the way to the runway holding point.

When the aircraft encountered long delays while taxiing because of airport traffic congestion, the crew's remarks to each other indicated their concern about the risk of snow contaminating the wing again. Crews in these circumstances face a difficult dilemma: do they return to the

gate for a further de-icing, only to be confronted with a further delay – or even a cancellation of their flight? Or do they continue the holding point, accept their eventual clearance to takeoff, and trust the contamination will have not become too serious?

The first officer switched on the wing inspection light several times, but his only related comment on the CVR was nearly 30 minutes after leaving the gate and shortly before takeoff, when he said: "Looks pretty good to me, from what I can see."

USAir's guidance to crews recommends a careful examination of the aircraft's surfaces in such circumstances. But even with the wing inspection light, does looking at the wing from 10m away through a flightdeck side window that was probably wet, constitute 'a careful examination'? The USAir guidance should certainly have alerted the

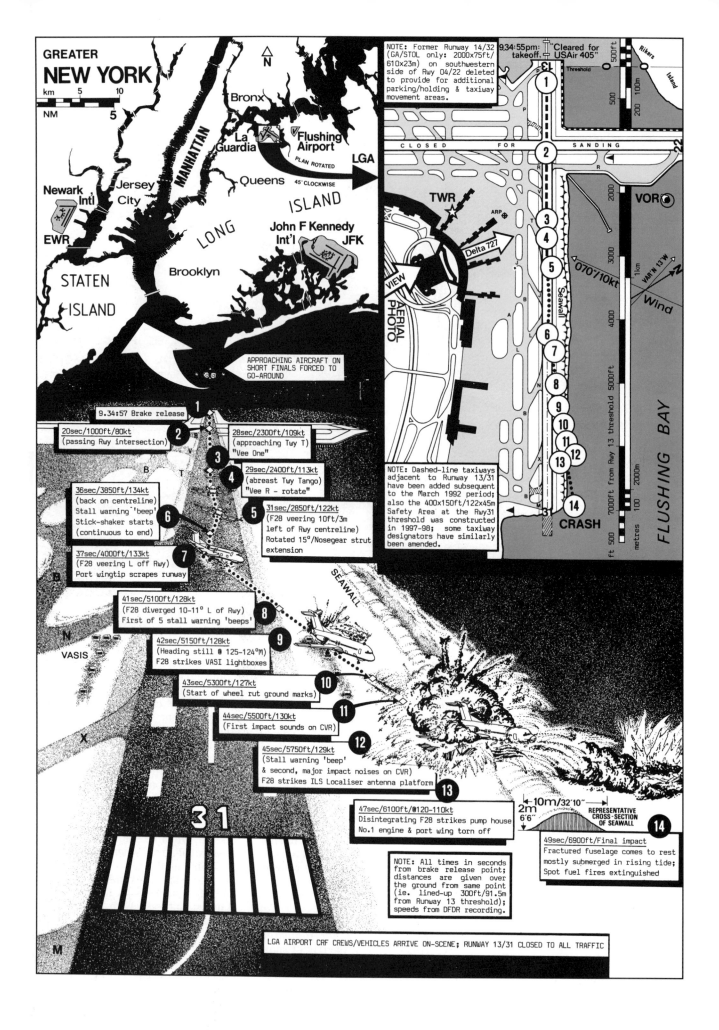

GREATER
NEW YORK

km 5 10
NM 5

Bronx

La Guardia

Flushing Airport
PLAN ROTATED
45° CLOCKWISE

LGA

Newark Intl

Jersey City

EWR

MANHATTAN

Queens

LONG ISLAND

STATEN ISLAND

Brooklyn

John F Kennedy Int'l   JFK

APPROACHING AIRCRAFT ON SHORT FINALS FORCED TO GO-AROUND

VASIS

N

B

X

M

3 1

NOTE: Former Runway 14/32 (GA/STOL only: 2000x75ft/ 610x23m) on southwestern side of Rwy 04/22 deleted to provide for additional parking/holding & taxiway movement areas.

9.34:55pm takeoff.   "Cleared for USAir 405"

Threshold

CLOSED FOR SANDING

Rikers Island

TWR

ARP

Delta 727

VIEW AERIAL PHOTO

Seawall

VOR

070°/10kt Wind

VAR'N 13°W

NOTE: Dashed-line taxiways adjacent to Runway 13/31 have been added subsequent to the March 1992 period; also the 400x150ft/122x45m Safety Area at the Rwy31 threshold was constructed in 1997-98; some taxiway designators have similarly been amended.

CRASH

FLUSHING BAY

① 9.34:57 Brake release

② 20sec/1000ft/80kt
(passing Rwy intersection)

③ 28sec/2300ft/109kt
(approaching Twy T)
"Vee One"

④ 29sec/2400ft/113kt
(abreast Twy Tango)
"Vee R – rotate"

⑤ 31sec/2850ft/122kt
(F28 veering 10ft/3m left of Rwy centreline)
Rotated 15°/Nosegear strut extension

⑥ 36sec/3850ft/134kt
(back on centreline)
Stall warning 'beep'
Stick-shaker starts (continuous to end)

⑦ 37sec/4000ft/133kt
(F28 veering L off Rwy)
Port wingtip scrapes runway

SEAWALL

⑧ 41sec/5100ft/128kt
(F28 diverged 10-11° L of Rwy)
First of 5 stall warning 'beeps'

⑨ 42sec/5150ft/128kt
(Heading still @ 125-124°M)
F28 strikes VASI lightboxes

⑩ 43sec/5300ft/127kt
(Start of wheel rut ground marks)

⑪ 44sec/5500ft/130kt
(First impact sounds on CVR)

⑫ 45sec/5750ft/129kt
(Stall warning 'beep' & second, major impact noises on CVR)
F28 strikes ILS Localiser antenna platform

⑬ 47sec/6100ft/@120-110kt
Disintegrating F28 strikes pump house
No.1 engine & port wing torn off

10m/32'10"
2m 6'6"
REPRESENTATIVE CROSS-SECTION OF SEAWALL

⑭ 49sec/6900ft/Final impact
Fractured fuselage comes to rest mostly submerged in rising tide;
Spot fuel fires extinguished

NOTE: All times in seconds from brake release point; distances are given over the ground from same point (ie. lined-up 300ft/91.5m from Runway 13 threshold); speeds from DFDR recording.

ft 500   metres 100 2000m   7000ft from Rwy 13 threshold 5000ft

LGA AIRPORT CRF CREWS/VEHICLES ARRIVE ON-SCENE; RUNWAY 13/31 CLOSED TO ALL TRAFFIC crew to the risk involved in beginning a takeoff while not wholly certain of the wing's condition.

Detecting minimal amounts of contamination that are nevertheless sufficient to degrade aerodynamic performance is undoubtedly difficult. But going back into the cabin to inspect the wing from closer range would at least have improved the chances of doing so – and in this case might even have prompted the crew to return to the gate. The investigation believed the F28 crew should have taken this action to ensure as far as possible that the wing was contamination-free. Measures taken since the accident provide more specific criteria for wing inspections.

But having decided to continue, the crew should have then made certain their takeoff procedures provided the maximum margins of safety in the circumstances. The same USAir guidance to F28 crews pointed out that the F28's wing, without leading edge devices, was sensitive to the aerodynamic effects of

(right) Airflow patterns over clean and contaminated wings: the F28 is depicted just after rotation, with the main undercarriage off the ground. (top) The arrows indicate designed airflows over and from, a clean wing, whilst the grey screens differentiate aircraft structure and wake vortices. (middle) The effects of the wing fence inboard of the point of sweepback change become apparent as the wing approaches the stall. Its aerodynamic function is simply to prevent the airflow from diverging from its longitudinal lift generation path, thereby restricting stall turbulence from spreading across the wing. A full stall would require a more extreme angle of attack than that shown. On the F28, the stall warning activates at an AoA of 11°, and complete airflow separation, with loss of aileron control, occurs at 19-20°. (bottom) Airflow disruption on a frosted, iced or snow covered Fellowship wing. The little remaining lift generating flow is streamed either side of the wing fence. Fokker research established that a wing with only 1-2mm of surface roughness per cm² would stall at an AoA of only 9-10° – and that a total loss of aileron control could occur! (Matthew Tesch)

contamination, and discussed the use of conservative takeoff speeds and rates of rotation.

While preparing for the takeoff, the captain told the first officer he would use 110 knots as the V_1 decision speed. For this flight however, the specified V_1 speed should have been 124 knots. There was no discussion between the captain and first officer about this reduced V_1 selection and the first officer could not explain why the captain chose it. It can only be assumed that the captain

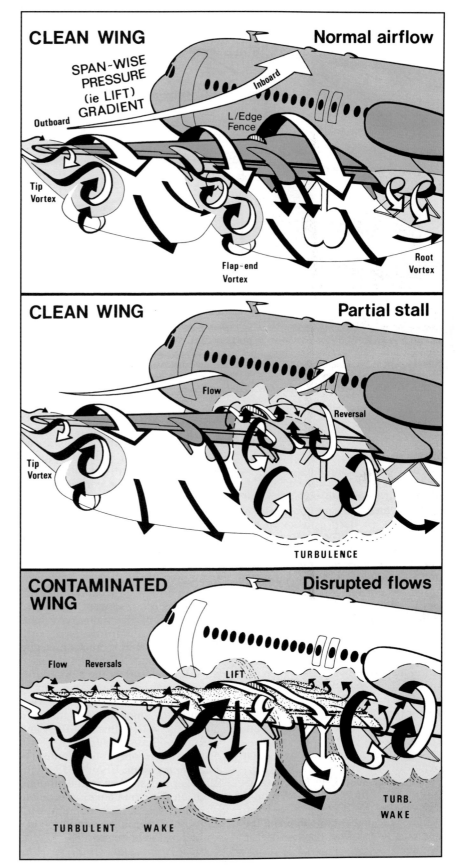

CLEAN WING — Normal airflow

SPAN-WISE PRESSURE (ie LIFT) GRADIENT
Outboard
Inboard
L/Edge Fence
Tip Vortex
Flap-end Vortex
Root Vortex

CLEAN WING — Partial stall

Flow
Reversal
Tip Vortex
TURBULENCE

CONTAMINATED WING — Disrupted flows

Flow Reversals
LIFT
TURBULENT WAKE
TURB. WAKE

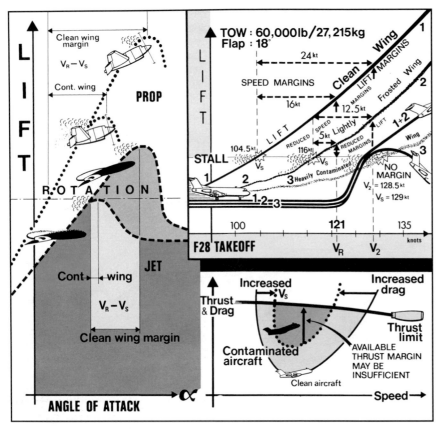

Cross reference to Chapter 3: the contrast in wing performance between turbine powered aircraft and swept wing jets is shown in these graphs. Propeller driven types (Lockheed's L188 Electra being a classic example – with Air Ontario's paddle bladed Convairs not far behind) benefit from the additional prop wash airflow over their aerofoils. The difference in margins is obvious, underscoring the Canadian pilots' apparent lack of concern for their aircraft's contaminated wing capabilities. (Matthew Tesch)

was concerned about his ability to stop the aircraft safely on the relatively short runway in the event of having to abandon the takeoff in the wet and slushy conditions.

V_1 speed is only significant in the context of a rejected takeoff or the failure of an engine, *and the reduced V_1 was not in itself a factor in the accident. But it did lead the first officer to call V_R prematurely. V_1 and V_R are normally the same in the F28, and he inadvertently followed his normal procedure of calling V_R immediately after V_1.*

Because of this, the first officer called V_R at around 113 knots, 11 knots below the correct speed of 124 knots, and the captain began the rotation five knots below this proper V_R speed. As a result, the aircraft lifted off prematurely and at an AoA 0.5° higher than it would have otherwise.

On a normal takeoff with an uncontaminated wing, this small increase in AoA would have been insignificant. But with the wing's performance degraded by contamination, the increased AoA could have made the difference between achieving a successful climb and the immediate stall that resulted in the accident.

Whether or not a successful takeoff could have been accomplished with a rotation at the correct speed remains uncertain. But the captain's early rotation entirely eliminated this possibility, thus contributing to the accident.

It was concluded from the DFDR data that, only seconds after liftoff, the aircraft was in a stall regime from which recovery was impossible.

USAir procedures

USAir's flight procedures met airline standards and were consistent with those of the industry. Flightcrews received information and training on winter operations and their F28 ground school emphasised the critical nature of the F28's "hard" (ie 'non slatted') wing. Also, during recurrent training, USAir pilots were given an examination that included questions on the effects of frost and ice, and pilot responsibilities.

In addition, only four months before the accident, USAir's F28 Flight Manager re-issued an excellent comment on the contamination problem written by a former captain with Empire Airlines, a company absorbed by Piedmont in 1986:

Frost accumulations of as little

as $^1/_{16}$th of an inch, like medium to course sandpaper, on the wing leading edge can increase stall speeds by 30 percent. Uneven contamination across the leading edge will result in wing drop or roll as the stall develops across the wing ... Ice or frost accumulations can appear on leading edges during taxi or takeoff roll – a de-icing beforehand, even on a clean wing, may prevent such accretion.

The captain's memo also explained that slats on the leading edge help to recover the loss of lift resulting from light ice accumulations. It cautioned Fellowship pilots against gaining a false sense of security when, for instance, slat-equipped 727s preceding them took off successfully. With the F28 not equipped with leading edge devices (see sidebox and footnote), its takeoff performance could be quite different.

The memo concluded:

When wing contamination is suspected, despite earlier preventative measures, rotation rates must not be excessive and takeoff speeds may be increased up to 10 knots. Available field length must be accounted for in the decision to rotate more slowly, and to target higher takeoff speeds.

This was in fact a more conservative version of the "unwritten" technique used by Fokker pilots when contamination was possible after de-icing. Although Fokker did not publish the procedure, a Fokker test pilot told the investigators he routinely added a margin to V_R.

Increased V_R was also the focus of an earlier recommendation by the NTSB. Although directed specifically at DC-9-10 series aircraft, it had application to all swept wing jet types without leading edge slats.

Throughout the investigation, pilots acknowledged that the F28, without leading edge devices, was sensitive to contamination. Although they generally acknowledged that, "if necessary, I would examine the wing from the cabin," they universally believed they could detect any critical contamination from the flightdeck. Even USAir's Vice President, Flight Operations, believed crews had as good a view from the flightdeck as they would from a cabin window, even in the case of contaminations as little as $^1/_{16}$ inch in thickness.

In the final Report of the Commission of Inquiry into the similar F28 accident at Dryden, Canada, completed in November 1991 (see Chapter 3), the Commissioner, Mr Justice Moshansky, commenting on wing

Designed as a short haul jet upgrade for the highly successful F27 Friendship turboprop, the F28's airfield performance was always impressive. The minimally swept wing, designed for a 'slow' Mach 0.75 cruise over short to medium haul sectors, with double slotted Fowler flaps across two-thirds of its span, provided excellent takeoff performance characteristics from the start. And the Fellowship Mk 1000's wings needed tip extensions of only 0.75m (2ft 6in) per side to accommodate substantial growth in operating weights and fuselage lengths in later marques.

Its landing performance was vindicated by many test and sales flights, often to poorly developed dirt, gravel, grass and snow covered airstrips in remote parts of the world. The distinctive 'clamshell' speedbrakes of the hinged tailcone (later copied on the BAe 146) permitted speed adjustments above 190kts, and full deflection below that speed. And five lift dumpers on each wing, plus oversize wheel brakes, rendered complex reverse thrust mechanisms unnecessary.

In 1972 Fokker sought to improve its product further. Its hard worked F28 prototype, PH-JHG [11001], was re-equipped with full span leading edge slats and other modifications. Certificated as the 'Mk 6000', this combination of the lengthened fuselage of the 2000/4000, combined with the increased span of the 3000/4000, was intended to enhance the type's airfield appeal, as well offering better economics.

Two Mk 6000s, [11091] and [11092], were

Proof positive that slat equipped Fellowships did exist – for a short time: modified prototype PH-JHG (in Boeing style creamy yellow and brown livery!) displays both its extended leading edge devices and prominent titles. The second of the two purpose-built Mk 6000s, the aptly registered PH-SIX [11092], stands on a wintry Swedish apron during its airline trials. Its applied Linjeflyg titling is not incompatible with its basic two tone blue NLM (Dutch) livery. (MT, Fokker & WAFM/Jenny Andersson)

built for a trial lease to the Swedish domestic, Linjeflyg, then constrained by noise and other limitations at its base at Stockholm's inner-city Bromma Airport, while resisting an inevitable transfer to the more distant Arlanda International Airport. But the improved takeoff performance proved unnecessary for Linjeflyg's needs, and there was concern about the different crew training and maintenance schedules the Mk 6000 would have required. From Fokker's viewpoint also, the slat system's complexity appeared to be a potential burden for its African and South American F28 customers.

In the event, Linjeflyg in 1976 opted for the Mk 4000. The two production Mk 6000s were reconfigured to Mk 4000 specification, while PH-JHG went on to become the avionics testbed for the new Fokker 100 – and the Mk 6000 and its wing devices disappeared into history.

contamination by snow and ice being observed from the cabin, quoted the experience of an Australian Bureau of Air Safety Investigation (BASI) team member:

Mr David Adams [BASI] recounted his personal experience on board an aircraft shortly after he had participated in the ... CASB investigation at the crash site at Dryden ... en-route from Thunder Bay to Toronto, [Mr Adams] boarded an Air Canada 727 ... that had been sitting at the gate overnight. On looking out a window prior to takeoff, he noted that the wings had approximately a half inch of wet snow on them. He was extremely disturbed by this observation, but was initially hesitant to raise the issue with either of the flight attendants or pilots. Finally, he spoke to a flight attendant, requesting her to ask the captain when de-icing would occur. The flight attendant complied with his request and,

approximately one and a half minutes later, an announcement was made that the aircraft would be delayed while de-icing took place.

All this evidence of overconfidence throughout the North American airline industry in regard to wing contamination, showed that crews did not attach nearly enough importance to the need to carefully examine the wings after exposure to weather conducive to accumulations of ice. Such examinations should involve some type of exterior inspection, allowing close or tactile examination, if an aircraft is unduly delayed on the ground after a de-icing operation. And until more advanced technology was available, a further de-icing was the *only* way to ensure wings were free of contamination before takeoff.

Most pilots operating at La Guardia at the time of the accident said they were checking other aircraft near their own for snow and

ice accumulation, and were basing their decisions to take off on the successful takeoffs of other aircraft exposed to the same weather.

Yet such comparisons may be quite invalid. The many variables already mentioned – the other aircraft's ground time, gate exposure, de-icing time and temperature – cannot be known to pilots making the judgement from a taxiway while queuing for takeoff. Moreover, distance and lighting conditions make it virtually impossible to detect the minute amounts of contamination on another aircraft that could adversely affect its takeoff.

It was obvious to the investigation that the crew of the F28, as well as the crews of other aircraft operating at La Guardia on the night of the accident, did not have sufficient appreciation of the effect that even minute amounts of ice can have on aircraft performance, despite their respective company training on the subject.

Another picture as relevant to Chapter 3 as to this one. A Canadian Airlines 737 is de-iced by two cherry-picker vehicles. Two such vehicles usually take 6-10 minutes to cover an F28 or 737 aircraft, one vehicle considerably longer. About 170 litres of glycol mixture, heated to 70°C, is required for an aircraft of this size. (Aircraft & Aerospace)

Optimum takeoffs

Data from simulated takeoffs conducted by Fokker were examined to see if changes in F28 operating procedures could ensure a successful takeoff with ice adhering to the wings.

When the rotation speed was increased 10 knots, the peak AoA decreased from 12° to 9°. In general however, increasing rotation speed could cause problems because of runway length limitations. Alternatively, decreasing the rotation rate to 2° per second decreased the peak AoA from 12° to 8°. *Even so, a pilot could not be expected to control the rate of rotation so precisely.*

A more effective way to limit the wing AoA during takeoff was found to be by *simply decreasing the pitch attitude.* When the target pitch attitude was decreased from 15° to 10°, the peak AoA decreased from 12° to 7° and the rotation rate became less significant. A further advantage lay in the fact that pitch attitude is easily controlled by reference to the attitude indicator.

The engine-out procedures for the F28-4000 recommend a 10° pitch attitude for a climbout at V_2 to satisfy takeoff performance requirements. With both engines operating therefore, the F28 could satisfy climb requirements with an initial pitch attitude below 15°. Further rotation to 15° could occur after the aircraft had climbed out of ground effect. Such a change in operating procedures could give the F28 an increased safety margin during takeoff.

Calculations by Fokker showed that this alternative would also be successful for takeoffs with ice on the wings in the F28's much-developed successor, the Fokker 100. The NTSB believed Fokker should study the effect of establishing a lower takeoff pitch attitude for the F28 and

Fokker 100, and change their operating procedures accordingly.

Reducing the hazard

The La Guardia accident prompted industry wide concerns on the problems of operating aircraft in adverse winter weather. Clearly the lessons of the Potomac River tragedy 10 years before, involving a Boeing 737 with leading edge devices (see *Air Disaster*, Vol 2, Chapter 6), had not been fully absorbed. To better understand de-icing and anti-icing problems generally, and to develop more effective safety improvements, America's FAA sponsored an international conference on the subject in Reston, Virginia.

More than 800 delegates discussed the difficulties and examined possible solutions. The conference produced suggestions to correct existing procedures where they were lacking, and considered possible long term improvements. The focus of the conference was on turbine powered airline aircraft with more than 30 passenger seats.

In addition, the FAA addressed issues relating to airport and air traffic control to reduce the time an aircraft is exposed to freezing conditions between being de-iced and being cleared for takeoff.

Reducing ATC delays

Paradoxically, the very weather conditions that increase the need to expedite clearances for takeoff following de-icing *are those most likely to lead to increased ATC delays.* The FAA acknowledged the need to examine this problem, reviewing existing ATC and airport flow control procedures, as well as procedures such as holding aircraft at their boarding gates until airport controllers are able to expedite their taxiing times to the duty runway.

In this case, the Fellowship took about 20 minutes to taxi from the gate to the area of the departure runway before it even entered the line of aircraft awaiting takeoff clearances. The total time, from completing its de-icing until takeoff, was about 35 minutes, primarily because of traffic congestion.

To guarantee a reasonably timely taxi to the runway holding point for takeoff, effective "gate hold" procedures need to be instituted at congested airports so that the actual taxi time is not prolonged because of other traffic. De-icing operations could then be timed so as not to unduly expose an aircraft to further ice and snow contamination after it has left the gate for the runway.

Another of Mr Justice Moshansky's Dryden Report comments is perhaps relevant here. Commending Transport Canada for its adoption of "new inspection and de-icing procedures", he wrote:

The recently announced intention of Transport Canada to construct at Pearson a remote touch-up de-icing spray facility and a major de-icing/ anti-icing facility, with provision for fluid recycling, estimated to cost C$45 million, is a welcome response to the safety concerns and recommendations outlined in my Second Interim Report [December 1990].

Why such facilities are not more generally available in North America is not known. Some major European airports – and many joint civil/military airports around the world – have them. The aeronautical equivalent of a 'drive through carwash', they are also used for 'decontamination' of military aircraft. In Australia and New Zealand, for example, these gantry-like frameworks are used to spray accumulated brine from the surfaces of P-3 Orions after long range maritime patrols.

Pre-takeoff inspections

The most positive assurance that an aircraft is safe for takeoff in weather conducive to freezing conditions is a close inspection of the wing leading edge and upper surface immediately before takeoff.

US Federal Aviation Regulations require that the wing be clean – but the problem lies in the difficulty crews have in determining whether wings are in fact clean. It is almost impossible to determine by observation whether a wing has a thin film of ice on it – or whether it is simply wet.

While a thin film of ice or frost will degrade the aerodynamic performance of *any* type of aircraft, transport jets that are not fitted with

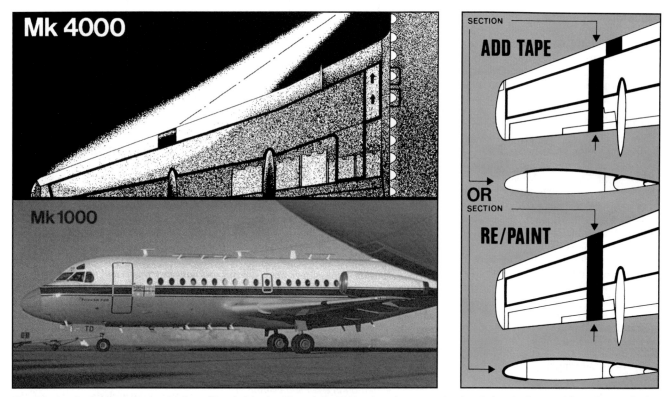

The "black stripe" referred to by the first officer in his checking of the F28's wings for contamination during the long taxi from the terminal to Runway 13 is clarified in these views. (left) This plan view shows the painted mark wrapping around the wing leading edge at the focus of the wing inspection light's beam on either side of the fuselage. Intended to contrast snowflake or ice crystal accretion against the reflected gleam of the natural metal leading edge, the 400mm (15.7in) stripe was recommended by Fokker in January 1984 as a response to changes in US Federal Aviation Regulations on de-icing precautions. The stripe was included on new F28-4000s soon afterwards, and adopted by operators worldwide. (lower left) The stripe can be seen in this picture beneath the second window forward of the engine intake; the inspection light fitting can also be discerned on the grey belly, above the rail aerial, beneath the 5th cabin window. The aircraft in this case is AirServices Australia's former VH-ATD [11047], one of two F28s that were based at Essendon and used for the calibration of the nation's radio navigation aids. (right) In May 1994, following the Dryden and La Guardia accidents, Fokker's earlier recommendation was replaced by a Service Bulletin offering operators a choice of enhanced delineators – either a supplemental adhesive tape application, or a matt black painted stripe from the leading edge rearward over the chord. Few F28 operators have adopted either, preferring the original less obtrusive leading edge mark. (Matthew Tesch)

leading edge devices require special attention. Fixed leading edge wings are more susceptible to lift degradation as a result of ice, frost or snow than a similar wing with extended leading edge devices. Aerodynamic degradation is especially critical during takeoff, since the AoA margin above the stall is less than at any other normal phase of flight.

The critical factor is how close the wing gets to its stall AoA during the takeoff. Even assuming that the percentage lift loss resulting from ice contamination is the same for both types of wings, it takes longer to rotate a 'slatted' aircraft during takeoff, so it has more time to climb and accelerate. And, because aircraft with leading edge devices stall at a higher AoA, the risk of a stall is lower than it is for those with a fixed leading edge. The combination of more altitude, higher speed, and higher stall AoA increases the likelihood of a successful takeoff, so the slatted wing has the greater margin of safety.

Although further study of aerodynamic stall margins and climb re-quirements is needed, decreasing the peak AoA during takeoff would provide an enhanced level of safety for non slatted aircraft in icing conditions. There are far fewer aircraft operating with airlines that have fixed leading edge wings, than those *with* leading edge devices, but nearly all takeoff accidents attributable to ice contamination have involved them. The NTSB believed that the FAA, in conjunction with NASA, should establish a task force to study ways of improving AoA safety margins during takeoff.

However, because some pilots might be led to believe that minute amounts of ice were acceptable on aircraft that have leading edge devices, the FAA was understandably wary about disseminating advice that non slatted aircraft were more sensitive to wing contamination.

The NTSB agreed that operations with wing contamination should not be encouraged with *any* class of aircraft. But because the icing accident record was worse for non slatted aircraft, and differences in aerodynamic stall margins during takeoff could explain the disparity, the NTSB supported a requirement for an external tactile or close visual inspection of the wings of non slatted aircraft immediately before takeoff, whenever excessive ground delays occurred after de-icing.

Technological developments

To avoid having to rely on exterior visual or tactile inspections, modern technology was being incorporated into equipment designed to detect contamination on wings and to indicate an unsafe condition.

Concepts included electro-optical sensing, such as measuring changes in the frequency and amplitude of contamination detecting diaphragms fitted to the wing. The NTSB believed this technology was promising and would in the future detect the presence of ice, snow, or frost.

PROBABLE CAUSES

The probable causes of the accident were the failure of the airline industry and the FAA to provide procedures, requirements, and criteria compatible with departure delays in conditions conducive to airframe icing; the decision by the crew to take off without any assurance that the wings were free of ice after 35 minutes exposure to precipitation; and a takeoff rotation at lower than prescribed airspeed.

Comment:

Though the circumstances leading to this accident were quite different to those which befell Air Ontario's C-FONF at Dryden almost exactly three years before, the aerodynamic 'mechanisms' which prevented successful takeoffs in each case were strikingly similar.

Yet none of the clear object lessons of the Dryden disaster appear to have reached the FAA, the US airline industry or USAir's flight operations office, let alone the hapless USAir pilots concerned. Even the NTSB did not appear to know of the Dryden experience. Certainly, there is no reference to the Canadian F28's loss in the NTSB's La Guardia report.

This seems at odds with the developed Western world's industry practice of openly sharing safety experience. The Canadian Commission's first Interim Report on the Dryden accident was released in December 1989, only nine months after the crash, and less than six months from when Mr Justice Moshansky began public hearings. The second Interim Report was released exactly a year later, just before the hearings concluded in January 1991. The industry media would surely have covered their contents.

There is the question too, of whether Fokker – itself extensively consulted by the Canadian investigators concerning the effect of wing contamination on F28 takeoff performance – communicated the results of its research.

Certainly, the two contaminated wing takeoff accidents which occurred earlier in the career of the Fellowship (see Endbox) were taken to heart. Fokker's own *F28 Flight Handbook* unequivocally spelt out "that all critical surfaces and points be completely clear of snow or ice before takeoff" and, as recently as February 1984, the manufacturer had published *Watch it in Winter*, an article on the operation and maintenance of Fokker aircraft. Three years later, two papers on the same subject were presented at a European aeronautical engineering conference.

Although airline crews might not have had ready access to all these documents, the industry as a whole should not have lacked information.

The lack of thrust reversers on the F28's Rolls-Royce Speys was considered to be of little operational consequence – as this dramatic picture shows! Mk 1000 demonstrator PH-FPT [11994] deploys full flap, lift-dumpers and tailcone speedbrakes on a dirt strip in South America. Oversize wheelbrakes with anti-skid provision enhanced the Fellowship's landing capabilities on substandard airfields. Ironically, this F28 was written-off in a landing overrun at Port Harcourt while with Nigeria Airways in September 1972. Fokker addressed the situation on its subsequent Fokker 100 and 70 designs by fitting clamshell reversers to the aircraft's RR Tays, similar to those on the JT8D engined DC-9. (Fokker)

Indeed, reports on Fokker's simulator and other investigations, carried out as a result of the Dryden accident, were reproduced in full in the Final Report of the Canadian Commission on this accident.

Unfortunately, this exhaustive four volume document was not completed until November 1991, only four months before the La Guardia accident. It was probably still in the process of Anglo-French translation, as required by Canadian law, and printing, when the La Guardia accident occurred.

Even so, there is no doubt that USAir was aware of the F28's sensitivity to aerofoil contamination. Both USAir and Piedmont operations manuals – used by Air Ontario pending the completion of its own F28 manual – were quite clear on the subject.

But it is possible that in-house communication within the vast USAir conglomerate itself may not have been ideal at this time. Having just engorged both Piedmont Airlines and PSA, this huge airline company was now responsible for the operation of an immense but diverse fleet of over 440 jets, and more than 100 commuters, ranging from BAe 146s and Jetstreams to Boeing 737s and 767s, and including 40 Fokker 100s, the enlarged derivative of the F28.

With more than 54,000 employees, USAir had in excess of 4,520 departures every day from a network of over 300 ports – from European capitals to tiny Appalachian communities. And its F28 crews were drawn not only from Piedmont, but also from Empire Airlines and Altair, themselves F28 operators taken over by Piedmont during 1983-1986. In these circumstances, it is perhaps not surprising that the details of the

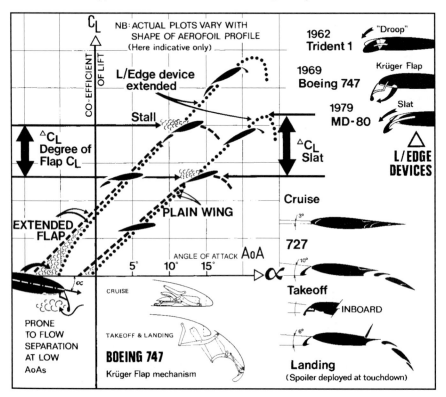

Dryden F28 accident were not disseminated to USAir crews as promptly and as thoroughly as might be expected.

Even so, the La Guardia accident is surely an example of the price that can be paid for failing to communicate safety experience gained in the harsh world of actual flying operations. Had the unfortunate crew of the USAir F28 been fully conscious of the tragedy that overtook a similar aircraft in similar weather less than half a continent away, — as well as the known history of F28 wing contamination accidents — they might well have been more wary of the small amount of snow that had again accumulated on their aircraft's wings — and taken action to deal with it before it was too late.

Footnote:

(1) Leading edge slats, or leading edge devices, as they are more generally referred to in the aviation industry, may be taken to include any extendible highlift devices designed for takeoff, landing or low speed flight. They function by postponing airflow separation from the wing leading edge as the wing's angle-of-attack (AoA) is increased, thus increasing the wing's capacity to generate lift at low airspeeds. Pure-slatted types include DC-9s (except the Series 10), the DC-10 and the Lockheed TriStar, such slats being movable leading edge profiles, sliding forward and down on rails under hydraulic pressure. By contrast, the Boeing 707 and 747 have so-called Krüger flaps which fold out into a cambered profile. They lie flush with the underside of the leading edge, and are driven out, down and forward when extended. Other aircraft types – among them the Boeing 727 and 737 and, to a lesser extent, the A300 and A310 – use a combination of the two. In all cases, the effect of leading edge devices is the same – increasing lift at lower airspeeds.

(left) The first, and shortest lived, of Turkey's five Fellowships.

Fokker Aircraft BV knew of the F28's sensitivity to wing contamination as early as 1969. Barely 18 months after the maiden flight of the prototype, PH-JHG [11001], the fourth pre-production model, PH-ZAA [11004], became the first of four bought by German charter operator LTU. It was delivered to Hannover on February 24, 1969, and spent most of the following day standing in overcast, below-freezing conditions with light snow and drizzle.

Late that afternoon during a preflight inspection, both the captain and a Fokker engineer noted "a thin layer of ice patches" on the wings, but decided it was insufficient to warrant de-icing. At 5.26pm, with the crew and nine passengers aboard, the F28 began its takeoff. Rotating after a 535m (1755ft) run, it rolled to the right, clipping the ground with its wingtip. The F28 then rolled left, then right again, and the captain abandoned the takeoff. The aircraft came to rest off the runway, damaged but still intact, and all aboard evacuated safely.

A Fokker scientist subsequently found that granular ice crystals would have covered the wings and tail surfaces. During the day, the faint warmth of the sun had been sufficient to melt the ice accretions on the port side of the aircraft. But by late afternoon, with the starboard side subject to deep shadow as well as freezing precipitation, the starboard wing remained contaminated – hence the wing drop and ineffective roll control. The stick-shaker activated three times during the brief flight in ground effect.

The aircraft was repaired, returned to service, spent part of 1973 in Italy, and went on to give sterling European service with TAT in France. Not so lucky were the crew and passengers of a Turkish F28, five years later.

Flag carrier THY, with domestic responsibilities in a country with extremes of terrain and underfunded infrastructure, bought five Mk 1000s in early 1973. Almost a year afterwards, on January 26, 1974, the first of the five, TC-JAO [11057] *Van*, after being parked overnight at Cumaovasi Airport, Izmir, on the Aegean coast, was making an early morning departure for Istanbul. Rotating after a takeoff run of 975m (3200ft), the F28 staggered into the air, yawed to the left of the runway and pitched nose-down. With the port wing and belly fairing scraping the ground, the aircraft slid for 100m, struck a drainage embankment, and somersaulted, disintegrating in flames. Sixty-six of the 73 aboard were killed. The aircraft had not been not de-iced, even though the early morning temperature was 0°C, and the relative humidity 95%. The following morning, another F28 overnighting in almost identical weather at Izmir was found to be frosted over.

It is interesting to note in passing that all five of the original THY F28-1000s were to come to grief. Two years later, THY's second F28 crashed into the Sea of Marmara while approaching Istanbul's Yesilkoy Airport. Four years later again, the fifth Fellowship to be delivered to THY struck a hill in fog, 18nm from Ankara Airport. The surviving two, after finally being withdrawn from THY service, were bought by TAT. One then went on to have history repeat itself in the snow at Dryden on the other side of the world, while the other eventually flew into an Iranian mountain late in 1994.

The second F28-1000 to wear the bold red, white and grey livery of Germany's LTU after PH-ZAA, D-ABAX [11006] shows the appearance of the Fellowship damaged in the takeoff accident at Hannover. Disposed of to Italy, then to TAT in France, this aircraft too ultimately went to Canada – as CP Regional's C-GTUU Spirit of Kelowana.

CHAPTER 6

"We will turn back soon ..."

*– Captain to First Officer,
20 seconds before impact*

Thai Airways International Airbus Industrie A310-304 HS-TID [438]
"Buri Ram" – July 31, 1992

It should have been a familiar trip to a familiar airport. But a complex series of seemingly inconsequential frustrations, misperceptions and misunderstandings finally contrived to deprive the captain of 'the plot' – with devastating consequences.

An isolated destination

Since the dramatic conquest of Mt Everest by Sir Edmund Hillary and Tenzing Norgay on the very eve of the coronation of Queen Elizabeth II in 1953, the isolated and impoverished Kingdom of Nepal has found mountaineering and trekking by adventurous visitors from many parts of the world to be a lucrative source of national income.

Indeed, these tourist industries have since become crucial to its economy. But the operationally difficult King Tribhuvan International Airport at the ancient Nepalese capital of Kathmandu, set in the mountainous 'foothills' of the Himalaya less than 100nm southwest of Mt Everest itself, has tended to limit international air services to only a few Asian airlines.

Indian Airlines, Pakistan International Airlines and Thai Airways International all operate regular flights into Kathmandu, for the most part with modern Airbus Industrie widebodied aircraft. Yet the principal departure port for Kathmandu bound international passengers remains Bangkok. The Royal Nepal Airlines Corporation and Thai Airways International in fact share traffic from Bangkok under a bilateral agreement between the two Kingdoms.

Bangkok to Kathmandu

Thai Airways International's Flight TG311 to Kathmandu on the last day of July 1992 was another such trip. Scheduled to depart from Bangkok's Don Muang Airport on a warm and humid morning at 10.30am local time, it was to be operated by Airbus Industrie A310 HS-TID, one of the company's diverse fleet of heavy jet aircraft. With an experienced Thai flightcrew and 12 cabin staff, HS-TID was carrying 99 passengers and was expected to land at Kathmandu's Tribhuvan International Airport three hours later, just after 12.30pm Nepalese time.

The weather was typical for the time of year – late in the first month of the monsoon season. Overcast conditions were forecast for the flight's Bangkok/Rangoon/Calcutta/Kathmandu route, with layers of stratocumulus and altocumulus cloud, and isolated cumulonimbus buildups extending to 40,000 feet.

The Kathmandu terminal forecast for broken cloud also reflected the start of the wet season – three octas of cumulus at 3000 feet AGL, and five octas of altocumulus at 10,000 feet. The wind was expected to be from 210° at 10 knots. The forecast visibility of 10 kilometres could reduce in periods of light rain to three

kilometres, with two octas of stratus at 800 feet, and three octas of stratocumulus at 2000 feet. The moisture laden cloud would probably preclude sightings of the Himalayan peaks further to the north.

The flight progressed normally at Flight Level 350 (35,000 feet) and, at 12.10pm Nepalese time, the crew called Kathmandu Area Control, reporting 150nm southeast, estimating the 'Romeo' reporting point (41 DME from Kathmandu on the 202° VOR radial) at 12.28pm. The controller reported the airfield visibility as greater than 10km, with scattered to overcast cloud layers from 2500 to 10,000 feet and a surface wind from 100° at five knots.

At 12.18pm the crew called Area Control again, requesting descent from Flight Level 350, and the controller advised that the only traffic above FL150 (15,000ft – the transition level for altimeter settings in this Flight Information Region) was a Royal Nepal Airlines service, Flight RA206, inbound at FL370 from New Delhi.

Five minutes later the controller reported visibility to the south of Runway 02 was now only 1.5km. But there were visibilities of 3-4km in other directions, and the Sierra VOR/DME Circling Approach to

Sistership HS-TIA Phitsanulok [415] displays its pink, orange and gold livery on a predelivery test flight in March 1986, after the former Thai Airways Corporation ordered two for its regional operations as a step up from its 737-200s; HS-TIA was handed over at Toulouse on April 29, and delivered to Bangkok on May 7 that year. HS-TIB Ratchaburi [424] followed in early December.
TAC was a government amalgamation formed in 1951, but in 1959 an agreement with Scandinavian Airlines System created the new Thai Airways International. TAC, nominally the parent entity, retained its own domestic identity for nearly 30 years until the two airlines were reunified under the maroon Royal Orchid symbol of "Thailnter" on April 1, 1988, the Kingdom having finally acquired the last SAS holding – but retaining operational and technical links.
By then, Thai was a dedicated Airbus operator, not only of the early A300B4, but the later A300-600/R too. Although the two smaller A310s complemented these, retaining crew commonality, their number was operationally inefficient. So when several ex Canadian A310s appeared on the market in October 1989, Thai acquired a further two from lessor Blenheim – the ill-fated Buri Ram, and HS-TIF Pattani [441]. The latter returned to Canada for the RCAF's Transport Command after the loss of HS-TID. The two original domestic A310s remain with the airline. (ADC/WAFM & HARS/MT)

Runway 20 was available. The crew nevertheless requested Runway 02, which provided a straight-in approach from the low lying Ganges Plain to the south. As the accompanying diagrams show, this was preferable to manoeuvring for a landing in the reverse direction on Runway 20. But the Kathmandu area controller replied that they would have to use Runway 20 because of 'heavy rain' falling on the 02 (southern) side of the airport.

At 12.27pm the aircraft reported over the Romeo fix and was cleared to the Sierra fix (10 DME from Kathmandu and also on the 202° radial) at an altitude of 11,500 feet. Three minutes later the crew again requested the airfield visibility, but the controller simply replied that Runway 02 was "also available" and reminded them to report at 25 DME.

The crew did so, again requesting the visibility, but the controller now instructed them to call Kathmandu Tower. The Tower then cleared the Airbus for a 'Sierra Approach' to Runway 02, gave the aerodrome weather as: "Wind calm, QNH 1010, Temperature 21, visibility towards the south 2500 metres, raining overhead the field", and instructed them to: "Report 10 DME, leaving 9500 [feet]."

Two minutes afterwards, the Airbus crew called again, requesting they maintain 10,500 and divert to Calcutta because of a "technical problem". But before the Tower could reply, they countermanded this transmission, advising operations were now normal and they would like to rejoin the Sierra Approach. The aircraft was cleared accordingly and again told to "report 10 DME, leaving 9500 feet."

The crew replied confusingly: "We can't land this time ... we have to ... left turn back to Romeo again and ... start our approach again." And in response to the controller's request for their present DME distance, they transmitted: "We are 9 DME, 10,500 feet – turn left now?"

Responding a few seconds later to a further request for their DME distance, the crew transmitted: "7 DME now – request clear left turn back?" The Tower replied inconclusively: "Roger, 10 DME, report leaving 11,500."

Half a minute later the crew announced: "We're climbing." To this the Tower replied with the modified instruction: "Report 16 DME, leaving 11,500 for Sierra Approach, Runway 02." The crew's readback of this as "Report 10 DME, 11,500," was but one of several more misunderstandings.

When these were seemingly clarified, the Airbus reported: "We cannot make approach now – we right turn back to Romeo and climb to 18,000 feet to start our approach again."

Told to maintain 11,500 feet because of the conflicting traffic, the Airbus reported it was "13,000" now, and after a further misunderstanding about the altitude to which it was cleared, advised it was "on descent to 11,500, 9 DME from Kathmandu". Several more radio exchanges established the aircraft was finally cleared to backtrack to Romeo and that it was to contact Kathmandu Area Control again.

Nearly three minutes later Area Control asked for the aircraft's DME from Kathmandu and was told "5 DME".

"Confirm 25 DME?" queried Area Control.

"Five ... zero five!" the Airbus replied emphatically.

Some two minutes later again, after transmissions to and from Royal Nepal 206 concerning rain over the field, the Airbus again requested the present visibility. Asked to standby, the Airbus then requested a right turn "back to the airfield".

Nothing further was heard from the Airbus and all further attempts to call it – by RA206, Area Control, and Kathmandu Tower – were to prove in vain.

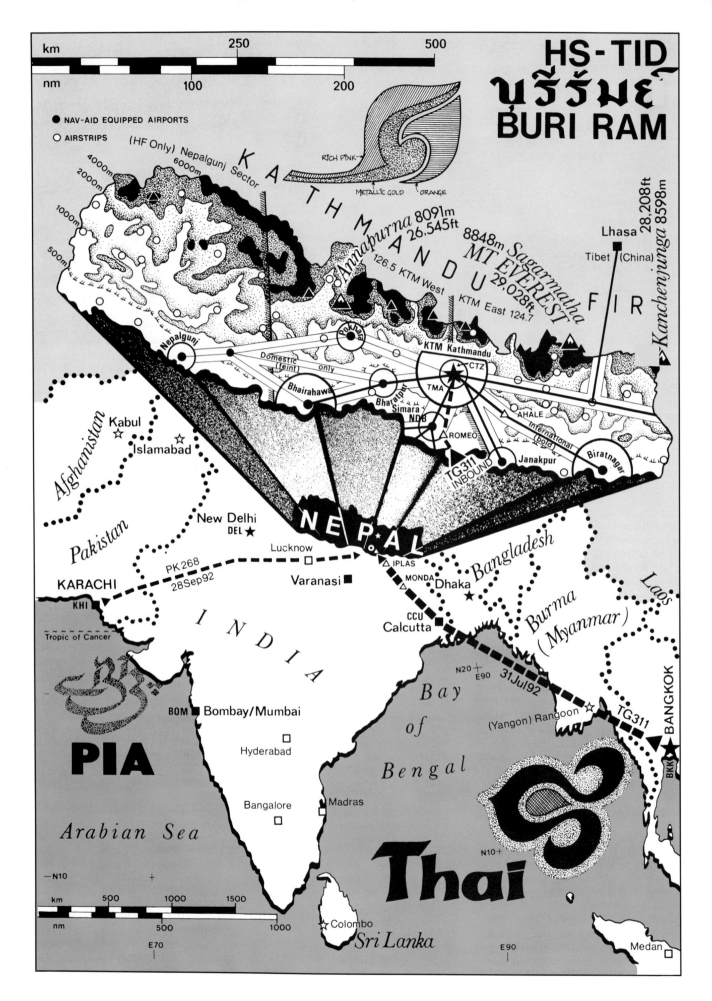

Views of the fertile Kathmandu Valley are evocative of the fabled 'Shangri-la' – on a good day! Geologically isolated, this former cirque (mountain lake) is open to moist monsoonal winds expending their sustenance on the Himalayan ramparts that flank the valley on three sides. But the same terrain, with its expanding population, modern traffic and industrial pressures, can smother the picturesque landscape in morning fog beneath an inversion layer. The Kingdom's population jumped by more than five million to 23m in the four years to 1995 – and the three clustered valley centres – Kathmandu, adjoining Patan, and nearby Bhaktapur – are a drawcard for the rural people of this still poor country. Visibility is at its best in the early months of the year, affording this northward view towards the Thai crash site in the Langtang National Park. (Richard L'Anson & Lonely Planet Publications)

The search

When all attempts to contact the Airbus failed, a search was begun. Because it had last been cleared to the Romeo fix, and air traffic controllers had formed the impression it was manoeuvring to the south, the initial air and ground search took place in this direction. But rain and low cloud made the search difficult throughout the afternoon, and it was not possible to check all likely areas. Nevertheless, a sighting of smoke to the southwest was responded to without success. The failing daylight and rain then hindered further progress.

(opposite, lower) This regional map covers almost 30° of latitude and longitude flanking the Indian Sub-Continent. Routes of both the TG311 and PK268 aircraft are shown inbound to Kathmandu (the latter coming to grief only 59 days after the A310 – see end of this chapter). Cities with solid in-filled symbols are those with scheduled airline services to the Nepalese capital. Thai International was the first airline to operate regular jet services to Kathmandu, leased ex SAS SE.210 Caravelles inaugurating flights there in December 1968.

(above) The enlarged map shows the tiny Kingdom to be a single Flight Information Region. The vast mountain barrier along Nepal's northern borders includes three of Earth's tallest peaks, and a third of the Great Himalaya mountain range. 'Himalaya' is a venerated Sanskrit word meaning "abode of the snows".

(top right) A decorative touch clarifies the TAC orchid symbol, and HS-TID's name. All Thai aircraft are named – and anointed by Buddhist monks before entering service – in Helvetica capitals on the port side nose beneath the flightdeck windows, with corresponding Thai script to starboard. (Matthew Tesch)

The following day, Saturday, August 1, 1992, a review of the ATC communication tapes revealed the startling crew comment "... heading 025". The search was consequently revised to cover the precipitous mountain areas to the north towards the Tibetan border, and later in the day witness reports added weight to the possibility that an accident had occurred in this area.

Ground movements in the spectacular but forbidding mountains to the north of Kathmandu are severely restricted. The high terrain is as steep as it is complex, and although more than 18,000 villagers inhabit many tiny settlements throughout the border regions, ground access is limited to tortuous trekking trails, with the nearest road ending at Dhunche (see maps). Even so, ground troops were dispatched to the area that evening.

Early the following morning, Sunday, August 2, searching aircraft and ground search parties simultaneously found aircraft wreckage scattered down the near-vertical south-eastern face of a mountain ridge, some 24nm north-northeast of Kathmandu.

INVESTIGATION

The accident site

The accident site lay in the 1700 square kilometre Langtang National Park, the nearest of Nepal's nine extensive national parks to Kathmandu. Peaks in the immediate area reach to more than 16,000ft and, only a few kilometres further to the north towards the Tibetan border, rise to well over 20,000ft.

The aircraft had crashed on a steep rock face at an elevation of 11,500ft. The A310 had utterly disintegrated, and it was obvious that no one could have survived.

Although less than three kilometres from the ridgetop village of Ghopte, the site was separated from it by deep boulder strewn ravines, clad in patches with lush vegetation. The wreckage was barely accessible, the altitude and slope making recovery efforts both difficult and dangerous.

Extensive use of the Nepalese Army's Alouette and Super Puma helicopters proved necessary, the machines operating between the base camp at an elevation of 8300 feet, and a landing pad above the site at 12,500 feet. Troops at both the accident site and base camp suffered leech bites and other environmental problems, and a member of the investigation team even died of exposure while attempting the five hour overland trek from the accident site back to the base camp.

The wreckage

The Airbus had struck the 60-70° sloping rock face of the mountain ridge, 23.3nm from the Kathmandu VOR on the 015° radial. Its heading at impact was 005°M, and ahead of its flightpath the terrain continued to rise to more than 15,000 feet over the next 2nm. The aircraft was in the cruising configuration at the time, with slats, flaps and undercarriage retracted.

The wreckage had fallen down the rock face for more than 800m, its scatter consistent with a single, high velocity impact. The starboard elevator and a section of the aft fuselage skin were the only recognisable sections of the airframe.

The impact area was charred, with burned pieces of wreckage consistent with an explosion and fireball. Some 19 tonnes of fuel remained on board at the time of impact, but there was no widespread post crash fire. Witnesses near the crash site reported hearing the crash and explosion, but did not see it because of cloud and heavy rain. Some of the wreckage burned throughout the night following the accident.

Work began immediately to remove the victims' remains, but no autopsy or toxicological examinations were possible. Although a complete cataloguing of the wreckage could not be attempted, both the Flight Data Recorder and Cockpit Voice Recorder capsules were recovered. Later analysis of the FDR and CVR tapes did not reveal any fault with the aircraft up to the time of impact, and such wreckage examination as was possible was considered adequate.

On-site examination of the engines was similarly limited because of the difficulties of the terrain, but the recognisable components located bore evidence of high rotational speed. Engine parameters subsequently provided by the FDR showed that both engines were fully operational and producing power.

The aircraft

The Airbus A310-304 was one of a number built in 1987 for the Canadian charter operator Wardair. Bought by Blenheim Airlease Ltd in April 1990 after Canadian Airlines International had taken over Wardair, it was leased to Thai Airways, together with a sistership, HS-TIF, and ferried to Bangkok in May 1990. In Thai Airways service the Airbus had flown a total of 3949 hours and accumulated 1644 cycles.

The Airbus was fitted with two General Electric CF6-80C2A2 high bypass turbofan engines. At the time of the accident its weight would have been 120,959kg (266,715lb), well under its maximum takeoff weight of 153,000kg (337,365lb), and its centre of gravity within limits.

Airbus A310 aircraft are equipped with a computerised flightdeck in-

The Swiss identity of this long final approach shot of an A310 cannot be denied. But the European Alps, as much as the aircraft type, perhaps assist the perception of what a southerly approach to King Tribhuvan International's Runway 02 must be like – at least in kind weather. Interestingly, snow is rare in the Kathmandu Valley, and the heights above the treeline in the mountains make for drier, barer rock faces than might be expected. Perhaps surprisingly, Kathmandu itself is on about the same latitude as Cairo, Miami and Taipei. With Nepal roughly 1500km closer to the Equator than the European Alps, the Himalaya snowline is correspondingly higher. (Paul Bannwarth/ Airliners magazine, and Lonely Planet)

corporating EFIS (Electronic Flight Information System) displays and integrated Automatic Flight Systems. The type is normally flown using these autoflight systems, with autopilot and autothrottle operation directed by the crew through the Flight Control Unit on the glare shield above the flight instruments.

The aircraft type is also fitted with a computerised FMS (Flight Management System) for both area navigation and aircraft performance management. The FMS's two FMCs (Flight Management Computers) perform the calculations, control the interface with other systems, provide information for display to the pilots, and control inputs to the autopilot and the autothrottle systems. Their memories store information on company routes, waypoints, VOR/DME and ADF stations, airways, airports, runways, and terminal area procedures. Each pilot position is provided with a CDU (Control and Display Unit) for directing the FMS.

Each pilot's instrument panel is also equipped with an ADF RMI (Remote Magnetic Indicator) and a digital DME RMI, referred to as a VOR RMI in A310 aircraft. The VOR RMI displays twin VOR 1 and VOR 2 ra-

dial information over a compass rose, the 'tail' of the needles showing the current radials.

The aircraft has a standby compass which is normally stowed and not visible to the crew unless required as a backup magnetic check.

The airport

Kathmandu's King Tribhuvan International Airport is situated in the Kathmandu Valley at an elevation of 4390 feet AMSL. Mountains surrounding the valley rise to 9655ft only 12nm to the southeast, and up to 8365ft 8nm to the southwest. The terrain is even higher to the north, with a spot height of 11,529 feet 18nm northeast of the airport. Much higher peaks rise to over 20,000ft only another 11nm to the north.

The airport's single paved Runway 02/20 has a length of 3050m and is 46m wide. Runway 02 is equipped with high intensity approach and runway lighting, as well as T-VASIS glidepath guidance lighting.

Kathmandu's Sierra approach, on the 202 radial of the VOR, is a non-precision VOR/DME procedure allowing straight-in approaches to Runway 02 or a circling approaches to the east of the airport to Runway 20. It is defined by eight DME steps from 16 DME and the Locator South NDB at 4 DME, with the co-located VOR and DME 0.6nm from the threshold centreline of Runway 02 (see accompanying diagrams).

An important characteristic of the Sierra Approach is the protrusion of a ridge more than 3500ft above the valley floor (7500ft AMSL), only 9nm from the runway threshold. The site of a Fan Marker 8.3 DME from the VOR, this outcrop of the Middle Hills necessitates descent angles in excess of six degrees, and precise adherence to published DME step altitudes (see diagrams).

The Minimum Descent Altitude for Runway 02 is 5120 feet (800 feet AGL) and the circling MDA is 5,570 feet (1,100 feet AGL). Minimum visibility for both straight-in and circling approaches is 3km. The steepest descent angle, 6.6°, is between 8 DME and 6 DME, and two other DME segments require descent angles of only slightly less.

The Sierra missed approach procedure, complex because of the surrounding high terrain, requires a climb straight ahead to the VOR, with the climb continuing on the runway heading after crossing the VOR until 2 DME on the 022 radial. A right turn is then begun on to the 4 DME arc, which is flown until the 106 radial is intercepted. Continuing to climb, the aircraft then tracks inbound to overhead the VOR and outbound on the 291 radial to reach the point Whiskey at 10 DME at or above 9500ft. At Whiskey the aircraft enters a published racetrack holding pattern (see approach charts).

The crew – Captain

The captain underwent his flying training in the Royal Thai Air Force in 1975 and continued as a service pilot until 1979, when he joined Thai International as a second officer (flight engineer).

In October 1983 he was upgraded to first officer on the Airbus A300B4, A300-600 and A310, and flew in this role until June 1989, when he was promoted to captain. In February 1992 he also became a simulator instructor. At the time of the accident he was a company Acceptance Pilot responsible for test flights on A310 aircraft. He held type ratings for the A300B4, A300-600 and A310-200/300 and, at the time of the accident, had flown a total of 13,250 hours.

He had flown to Kathmandu 24 times in the past 16 months, but had previously made only one flight with the first officer – from Bangkok to Ho Chi Minh City and return. The captain was held in high professional esteem and had no previous incidents or accidents.

First Officer

The first officer was also trained in the RTAF and flew as an air force pilot until 1974, when he was employed by Air Siam, a short lived privately owned airline. In 1977 he joined Thai Airways as a second officer and was upgraded in 1980.

He had been considered for promotion to captain, but was not upgraded because his aptitude tests were unacceptable. Despite this, his performance as a first officer was satisfactory. He held type ratings for the 747-200, A300-600 and A310-200/300.

Three years previously, a simulator instructor had noted he needed to improve his copilot duties and, during periodic emergency training four months before the accident, the instructor commented on his need to follow procedures and basic flight instrument indications, and for emergency actions to be done in sequence. The first officer underwent a further period of emergency training two days later with no reported difficulties.

He had flown to Kathmandu 14 times in the previous 16 months, his last flight there taking place six weeks before the accident. His total flying experience of 14,600 hours was slightly more than his captain's. Like his captain, he too had not been involved in any previous incident or accident.

Typical of not only the Kathmandu Valley, but of 70% of Nepal, is this river gorge, whitewatering its way beneath steep slopes and densely cultivated scarps on seemingly precariously narrow ledges. Since ancient times, the populace's demand for food and fuel, coupled with the lack of arable land, have felled tracts of subtropical forest and endangered many species. But in the timeless Asian tradition, the precious tenable land is richly yielding – all from hand-worked terraces like these. (Time-Life)

Flight recorders

The Sundstrand CVR was found amongst the wreckage on August 4, four days after the accident. Its outer case was severely damaged but the inner tape case was intact. The inner tape case of the FDR, also of Sundstrand manufacture, similarly survived the impact and was recovered two days later. Despite its missing outer protective case, it appeared to be relatively undamaged. Both recorders were taken to the Canadian Aviation Safety Board's engineering laboratory in Ottawa for analysis.

Because the crew had been speaking to each other in Thai, a preliminary transcript was prepared with the assistance of a translator. A review by Thai aviation advisors then improved the transcript and explained some phrases. Further work was carried out in Paris while investigation team members were in France for simulator tests at the Airbus Industrie facility in Toulouse. A final review of the transcript was carried out with the assistance of Thai Airways pilots.

When the inner tape case of the FDR was dismantled, it was found the tape had broken and been damaged. But spliced together and cleaned, it was synchronised with the CVR to obtain an overall 'picture' of the final 20 minutes of flight. Except for the last five seconds of the tape which were missing, and the damaged previous 15 seconds, the FDR record proved to be of excellent quality.

The combined recordings confirmed that at 12.23pm, the area controller reported visibility to the south of Runway 02 as "only" 1.5km, but that the Sierra Approach to Runway 20 was available.

Even so, at the captain's instruction, the first officer requested the use of Runway 02. When this was refused, the pilots discussed the wind conditions on the airfield, and the captain asked the first officer to check the fuel needed to divert to Calcutta, apparently as a contingency.

After reporting over Romeo at 12.27pm and being cleared to the Sierra fix at 11,500 feet, the crew discussed the approach and the missed approach procedure for Runway 20, and again requested the airfield visibility, only to be told now that Runway 02 was "also available". On asking further for the visibility, the controller merely answered, "Go ahead your present DME." Informing the controller they were "25 DME now," the captain repeated his request. Instead of providing the visibility however, the controller

Views of the Langtang National Park close to the Thai Airbus crash site. But what to the recreational trekker may be stunning beauty proved to be a harshly different environment for the unacclimatised investigators!
(above) Gosainkund Lake, a holy pilgrimage site, lies at an elevation of 4380m (nearly 14,400ft) and is one of several similar lakes less than 7km northwest of the village of Ghopte, above the impact site of HS-TID. Held to have been formed from a glacier punctured by a trident-slash by the god Shiva, its waters are said to drain, by unknown subterranean channels, down to a Patan temple a few kilometres southwest of Tribhuvan Airport.
(below) Yaks graze in stonewalled, barren yards above the village of Langtang itself, some kilometres to the north of the crash site. This deceptively bleak landscape yields wheat, potatoes, turnips and other vegetables, and a Swiss venture even produces yak cheeses and dairy products! Langtang village itself is a considerable settlement, with a 'one-way' airstrip, and is the National Park headquarters. Incidentally, the remains of HS-TID now feature in Lonely Planet guidebooks as a point of interest on the trek between Ghopte and the Tharepati Pass. (LP: Stan Armington & Richard L'Anson)

directed the crew to contact Kathmandu Tower.

At 12.31pm they did so, reported they were 23 DME, and selected the slats and flaps to the 15/0° setting (slats 15°, flaps 0°). As the controller cleared the aircraft for an approach to Runway 02 and instructed them to report at 10 DME, leaving 9500 feet, the captain called for "Speedbrake in, flaps 15°" (slats 15°, flaps 15°).

Twenty five seconds later a warning chime sounded on the flightdeck

and a flap fault was recorded on the FDR. Exclaiming that the flaps had not extended, the first officer recycled the flap lever several times but the warning chime sounded again.

"Take it easy," the captain chided him. "Too late to make a landing ... we've got to have the configuration ... we cannot land." This was in keeping with performance requirements, necessitating full flap for the final approach into Kathmandu. It would not now be possible to continue the

The two crew flightdeck – today regarded as industry standard, aircraft size notwithstanding – was a novel and widely resisted concept in the early 1980s. In 1982, Garuda was one of the first airlines to specify the 'FFCC' (Forward Facing Crew Cockpit), with sophisticated computerised electronics and CRT screens on its new A300s. Airbus Industrie was further developing this technology, having already committed itself to FFCC in the smaller, more advanced, A310.

In this contemporary A310 'office', systems controls, previously the domain of the flight engineer, are centralised in the overhead panel. Primary EFIS displays include a pair for each pilot, and a central pair flanking the engine instruments. The crew are engaged in the "Before Engine Start" checks – evinced by the screen display at the first officer's left knee, a plan view of the A310 showing cabin layout and door status. (Interavia & HARS/MT)

Evidently frustrated by the controller's failure to respond to his requests for a left turn, the captain said to the first officer, "answer please – answer please!"

Although they did not realise it, controllers and crew were both referring to the same approach procedure. As evident from the diagrams on these pages, the Romeo and Sierra fixes both lie on the 202 VOR radial, the former 41nm out to the south-southwest, the latter only 10. But as the accompanying reproduction of the approach chart being used by the Airbus crew shows, the reference to the Romeo fix (lower left centre) is not only misleadingly printed close to the 16 DME checkpoint for the Sierra approach, but is also more prominent than the bracketed Sierra annotation at the top right corner of the chart.

The captain's perplexed reaction to the controller's clearance when the aircraft was already so close in, thus becomes more understandable.

"We'll maintain 10,500 feet," the first officer transmitted. Then to the captain: "Are we cleared over Minimum Obstacle Clearance Altitude OK? We can see on our right hand side. How about on our left?"

"Yes, I can see it," the captain responded. Then again he called the Tower: "Left turn now?"

But once more the Tower's response seemed frustratingly equivocal: "Go ahead your DME distance?"

F/O: "Ah … 7 DME now." And again he repeated the captain's question: "Request left turn back?"

CAPT to F/O, evidently with resignation: "We'll climb ahead."

TWR (incorrectly reading back): "Roger, 10 DME copy, sir. Report 16 DME leaving 11,500."

CAPT to F/O: "Climb – continue to climb!"

The crew then began a right climbing turn from their 015° heading, retracted the slats and flaps, and the first officer reported they were climbing. The controller then re-instructed the crew to report at 16 DME, leaving 11,500, for the Sierra approach to Runway 02.

F/O (reading back, but evidently preoccupied by the flap lever's restored operation): "Report 10 … ah … DME … 115."

The Tower's reply further compounded the confusion by altering the distance and height again: "Negative sir, negative. Report 10 DME leaving 9500 feet, QNH 1010, Sierra approach Runway 02, winds light and variable.

F/O (reading back again): "Affirm – report … 10 DME, 9500, 1010.

TWR: "Affirm, affirm."

straight-in approach, because of the steep descent angles required.

The captain then called the Tower himself, requesting they maintain 10,500 feet and divert back to Calcutta "due to … technical". At this stage the Airbus was at 13 DME, descending through 10,800 feet. But just as the Tower acknowledged the request, the flaps extended normally to the position the first officer had selected.

Again the captain called the Tower, advising that operations were "back to normal" and requesting a left turn to join the Sierra approach again. "Can we make a left turn to Romeo now?" the captain asked.

The Tower replied "… clear Sierra approach, report 10 DME, leaving 9500."

His confusing response was to report that they could not land "at this time", and to ask again for a "left turn back to Romeo … and start our approach again."

Working procedurally, without radar, the Tower replied, "Roger … go ahead with your DME distance."

"We are 9 DME, 10,500 feet," reported the captain.

TWR: "Understand 9 DME, 10,500 feet?"

A more accurate idea of each A310 pilot's instrument panel is gained from this close-up. The top EFIS screen is not only an electronic artificial horizon and flight director – it appends much other flight data within its periphery. But more pertinent to the story of the preoccupied Thai crew is the display on the lower screen – the computerised Horizontal Situation Indicator. Note the cross representing the aircraft (bottom centre) and the 85° forward view arc: the aircraft symbol remains fixed, while the track, turn direction, waypoints, beacons, weather and other pictorial displays 're-volve' on the screen as the aircraft's heading changes. Once HS-TID had inadvertently turned through a full orbit on to a 025° heading, the vainly sought Romeo fix to the southwest could not have appeared on the screen. Even so, with the range of 'traditional' instruments surrounding the two screens, the crew were hardly deprived of navigational guidance! (Interavia & HARS/MT)

Nine seconds later, as the turning aircraft passed through a heading of 116°, the captain called the Tower again himself: "We cannot make approach now – we right turn back to Romeo and climb to 18,000 feet to start our approach again."

Meanwhile the Royal Nepal flight, inbound from New Delhi, was intending to join the Sierra approach from the Simara NDB, a few nautical miles west of Romeo.

TWR: "Roger – standby for the time being. Maintain 11,500 feet due traffic for the time being – maintain 11,500 feet."

But by this time the Airbus was climbing through 13,500 feet, so the first officer transmitted: "OK – we maintain 130 now ... we are 13,000 now."

TWR: "OK".

F/O (double checking): "Is that OK?"

TWR: "Ah ... initially maintain 11,500 – initially maintain 11,500 due traffic, RA206, estimating Simara 57 [12.42pm local time] from Delhi, descending to FL150."

An altitude alert warning then sounded on the flightdeck and, as the aircraft's heading passed through 245°, it began a descent from 13,900 feet.

F/O: "Descend[ing] to 11,500 – we are now 8 DME."

TWR: "Roger."

At 12.38pm the captain asked the Tower about the position of RA206 and was again told it was estimating Simara at 12.42pm and was "Flight Level 150 descending".

CAPT: "OK – we are now on descent to 11,500, 9 DME from Kathmandu."

TWR: "Roger – understand still

you like to proceed Romeo to make approach?"

CAPT (with relief that his request has finally elicited a response): "Affirm, affirm!"

Yet again there was a noncommittal reply from the Tower: "Roger."

At this point, with the time at 12.40pm, the Airbus had maintained its shallow right turn through more than 300° and was crossing the 202 radial of the Kathmandu VOR on a heading of 340°.

CAPT (double checking): "Confirm we can proceed to Romeo now?"

TWR: "Roger – proceed to Romeo and contact [Kathmandu Area Control] 126.5."

CAPT (acknowledging): "Proceed to Romeo and 126.5."

Throughout the following minute, as the first officer apparently attempted to enter "Romeo" into the FMS keyboard, there were exchanges between the pilots concerning their present position and the specified minimum altitudes. Meanwhile the aircraft had continued the gradual turn to the right, completing a full circle and rolling out on a heading of 025°.

At 12.40pm, with the aircraft now 4nm southwest of the Kathmandu VOR, the captain called Area Control: "We are heading 025, maintain[ing] 11,500 – we like to proceed to Romeo to start our approach again."

A/C: "Confirm maintaining 11,500?"

Airbus: "Affirm – we like to proceed to Romeo – we got some technical problem concerned with the flight."

A/C: "Proceed to Romeo – maintain 11,500."

The crew's flightdeck exchanges continued over apparent difficulties

they were having with the FMS. It was clear from the CVR that they were still attempting to key in "Romeo" and other navigational information. Meanwhile the aircraft continued northeast on its new heading of 025°, passing 2nm to the west of the VOR.

A minute and a half later the area controller called the Airbus and asked for its DME distance. When the captain answered: "We are 5 DME," the controller replied: "Confirm 25 DME?" to which the captain retorted emphatically: "Five ... zero five!"

At this time the aircraft's position, as derived from the FDR, was indeed 5nm from the VOR, but to the north of it, rather than to the southwest, as the controller would have expected with the aircraft cleared to return to Romeo. But without radar surveillance, there was no way the controller could know this if the aircraft did not inform him.

Area Control (unconcerned): "5 DME, Roger – maintain 11,500, report over Romeo."

A few seconds later the captain asked the first officer to "please find Romeo for me," and the flightdeck exchanges regarding the FMS went on, including among other things: "Romeo 27 north", "near Simara", "direct Simara", "It doesn't show Simara at all", and the captain's question: "Romeo is how many miles from here?"

At 12.43pm the first officer exclaimed: "OK – it shows the way direct!" and the captain answered, "Romeo radial ... 220, 16 DME ... wait ... I will follow the line."

F/O: "It's coming – already come direct."

CAPT: "Wait ... wait ... we will return back, correct? We will return to Romeo again ... can you punch Romeo in again?"

F/O: "Here's Simara again, right?"

CAPT: "OK – we'll return to our initial approach point again ... punch in for position Romeo – load Romeo again."

Captain (transmitting to Area Control): "14 DME."

A/C: "Maintain 11,500, report over Romeo."

CAPT: "11,500, report Romeo."

At 12.40pm, at a distance of 16nm northeast of the VOR, the aircraft began a shallow turn to the left from 025° and rolled out on a heading of 005°.

F/O (still attempting to input data into the FMS): "This thing fails again ..."

(At this point the flightdeck conversation was interrupted for more than half a minute by transmissions to and from Flight RA206 concerning rain over the field.)

CAPT: "Transfer it from my side."

F/O: "Yes ... we had transferred it, but it is gone – same as before."

CAPT (transmitting to Area Control after overhearing advice to RA206): "Request visibility?"

A/C: "Standby for Tower observation and visibility."

F/O (loudly, in surprised tone): "Hey ... we are going ... we are going north!"

CAPT (calmly): "We will turn back soon." Three seconds later he transmitted to Area Control: "Request right turn back to the airfield."

A few seconds after 12.45pm, just as the controller was repeating, "... standby for visibility", the aircraft's Ground Proximity Warning System sounded: "Terrain!" "Terrain!", followed by "Whoop whoop, pull up! ... Whoop whoop, pull up!", and continued to sound. The captain immediately called "Level change!" and engine power was increased.

F/O (urgently): "Turn back ... turn back!"

CAPT: "It's false ... it's false!"

This was followed by an unintelligible exclamation, then one of the pilots cried out: "Oh my God!"

Two seconds later the recording ended as the aircraft and all its occupants were obliterated on the near vertical mountainside at a speed of 240 knots.

The flap failure

The investigators asked Airbus Industrie to provide assistance with the A310's flap system and to investigate reasons for the flap failure which led the crew to abandon their first approach.

In A310 aircraft, leading edge slats and trailing edge flaps are controlled by a single lever located on the first officer's side of the flightdeck centre pedestal. The lever has five gated slat/flap positions indicating de-

grees: 0/0, 15/0, 15/15, 20/20, and 30/40.

The fault was recorded on the FDR twice, first at 12.42pm after the slats and flaps were selected to 15/15. The fault then recurred after the slats and flaps were selected to 20/20. This time the flaps did not move, but the crew's selection of the lever back to 15/15 resulted in the problem clearing itself.

It was concluded that the flap extension failure resulted from activation of the screwjack torque limiters. Torque limiter operation normally indicates an increase in friction within the screwjack system, and could be caused by a number of factors, including increased air loads. Retracting the flaps resets the torque limiter automatically.

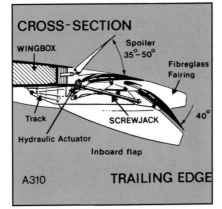

The 'fault' that wasn't – this sectional diagram of an A310 inboard trailing edge shows the screwjack mechanism which caused the initial distraction on the flightdeck of HS-TID. On a less demanding approach, recycling of the flap selection might not even affect the landing. By the time the crew had overcome the problem on the steep descent into Kathmandu however, the captain had no choice but to abandon the approach. (Matthew Tesch & Flight International)

ANALYSIS

In their official report, the investigators, displaying a degree of humility sometimes lacking in accident inquiries, prefaced their analysis with the rider that their comments were shaped with hindsight, an advantage available neither to the Airbus crew nor the Kathmandu air traffic controllers. As they also fairly pointed out, they were not time-limited in their analysis!

The initial approach

For the two pilots, the flight held the promise of being uneventful – a familiar trip to a familiar airport, and the seasonal weather did not appear to pose any untoward problems.

The captain began the usual approach briefing as the aircraft was on descent on autopilot. It was relaxed, and included the company re-

quirement to be in the landing configuration by 13 DME. But only then did Area Control inform them the weather had deteriorated, reducing visibility to the south of the airport. The wind from the south had also increased, producing a downwind component on Runway 02.

There was a moment of confusion because the first officer thought the controller gave the wind velocity as 150-180° at 18 knots, rather than 12 knots, which would have produced a downwind component in excess of the limit for a landing on Runway 02.

Now faced with reduced visibility and a requirement to circle, the captain said, "I guess we can't make it," and asked the first officer for the fuel required to divert to Calcutta. He replied they had enough fuel to go back to Bangkok, but the captain's next question "Calcutta – how much?" showed it was not the answer he wanted. A sigh by the captain possibly indicated frustration.

As the aircraft continued inbound on autopilot, the approach briefing was interrupted by an ATC instruction to report passing the Romeo fix, to expect the Sierra approach, and to call at 25 DME.

After completing the briefing, the captain asked the first officer to request the weather again. The area controller replied: "If you prefer Runway 02 also available" and repeated the requirement to report at 25 DME.

When the first officer failed to note their desired runway was now available after all, the captain took over the radio, repeating his unanswered question as to the visibility. But his question still went unanswered, the controller instead requesting the aircraft's DME distance. Replying "25 DME", the captain again asked for the visibility but was now told to contact the Tower. Meanwhile he slowed the aircraft below 240 knots and requested the first slat extension. The Tower then cleared them for the Sierra approach to Runway 02, reporting the visibility as 2500 metres.

The captain had so far been forced to resolve some aspects of the approach himself, his concerns having been deflected by inconclusive answers from both the first officer and the controller. The captain got his information – but only after repeated and frustrating exchanges.

On top of these difficulties there now came a more serious problem. As the aircraft neared 18 DME and the slats and flaps were in the process of extending to 15/15°, the flaps suddenly jammed. This occurred only 5nm from the point at which the aircraft needed to be established in the landing configuration – undercarriage down, slats/flaps at 30/40°.

The captain's remarks now betrayed further frustration – the fault meant that they would not be able to land at Kathmandu, with its steeper than normal descent requirements.

Communications

Radio communication was in English, and this requirement for both crew and controllers to speak in other than their first language created difficulty.

This was further compounded by the rapid succession of transmissions from the aircraft, first for a diversion to Calcutta, then an indication that "a problem" had been fixed, then for another approach. And when the controller responded by giving the aircraft a valid Sierra clearance, the crew rejected it, declaring they could not land and they wanted to return to Romeo. This not only seemed abnormal, but created confusion as to what the flight was doing. Crew and controllers were actually talking about the same approach – but were unaware of the other's interpretation.

The crew did not indicate that a flap problem made it impossible to complete their approach, and the controller did not question why the newly cleared approach could not be carried out, instead asking only for the aircraft's DME. The captain replied they were at 9 DME at 10,500 feet.

When the controller questioned this distance and height, seeking confirmation, the captain directed the first officer to answer. But the first officer's transmission: "We'll

maintain 10,500", did nothing to clarify the captain's left turn request, and was made without understanding what the captain was trying to resolve. But the first officer's next words about terrain clearance showed he was becoming concerned about the high ground around Kathmandu.

Obviously dissatisfied, the captain again asked for a left turn "now". Again the controller asked for the aircraft's DME and the reply was, "7 DME ... request left turn back". But the Tower's response, "... 10 DME copy sir, report 16 DME, leaving

11,500," was neither a correct readback nor an answer to the aircraft's request. The Airbus had in fact been given a valid Sierra approach clearance, but it was evident that the crew did not know they could carry out the Sierra approach from the 16 DME fix, only 6nm out from Sierra, as opposed to 31nm out, from Romeo.

This further misunderstanding, on top of the existing confusion, no doubt diminished the controllers' and pilots' estimate of each other's abilities – both on the flightdeck itself and outside the aircraft. So, after four unsuccessful requests for a

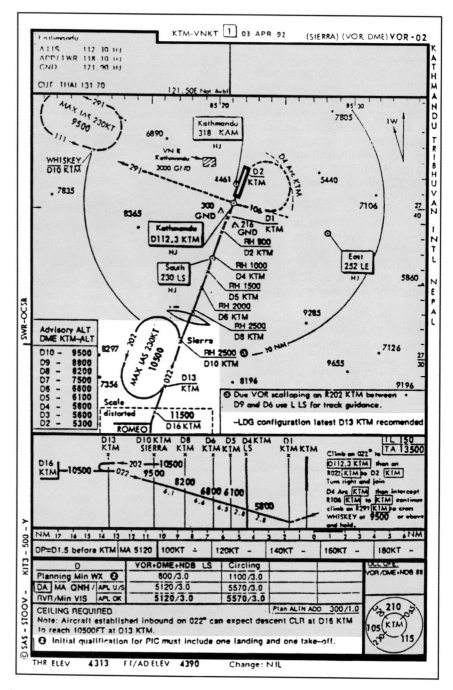

The role of the respective approach charts in both the Thai and PIA (see end of this chapter) accidents deserves careful study.
(right) Thai's company chart, like many other Thai operational procedures, owes much to its Scandinavian parentage, hence the SAS-Stoov copyright. A pale screen, not present on the original, has been overlaid here to help emphasise aspects of the layout. Despite the dashed line-box and "Scale distorted" notation (centre left), the misleading relationship between the 16 DME starting point of the Sierra approach and the Romeo fix is obvious. At the top right, in only minuscule type, is the title of the approach chart: "(Sierra) (VOR/DME) VOR-02".
(opposite) The commercially available Jeppesen-Sanderson counterpart, used by the Pakistani crew. Note by comparison the unequivocal title and description in the top right corner.

(centre left) The clear visual and typeset indications of the 16 DME starting point of the Sierra approach are equally unmistakable. The merits of the respective approach profile diagrams are discussed in the caption to the following full page diagram. Space precludes its reproduction here, but it is interesting that the ICAO standard chart produced by the Nepalese Department of Civil Aviation appears to combine the best design features of both these non governmental charts – while omitting their worst! (SAS-Thai, & Jeppesen-Sanderson Inc.)

left turn, the captain finally decided to begin a climbing turn to the right, still on autopilot.

Why back to Romeo?

The investigators posed two possible reasons for the captain's persistent requests for a left turn to the Romeo fix to rejoin the Sierra approach:

• He wanted more time to thoroughly deal with the flap problem and thought that backtracking 41nm from Kathmandu would provide this;
• His selection of Romeo was prompted by his misreading of the Thai Air-

ways approach chart as to the point where the approach commenced.

Going back 41nm just to ensure the was enough distance to extend the flaps seems highly improbable. Rather, the captain's transmission, "Romeo radial 202, 16 DME ..." suggests that, in requesting Romeo, he was in fact requesting clearance to the first point of the approach – and that he had misidentified Romeo as this point from his company chart.

It seems that the first officer also failed to resolve the disparity in the clearance, either not noticing, or being similarly misled by, the Thai ap-

proach chart. In view of the fact that both the captain and the first officer had flown into Kathmandu many times before, their lack of familiarity with the first point of the Sierra approach is surprising, to say the least.

Why left then right?

During the time that it took the captain to make his four requests for a left turn, the aircraft flew inbound from 11.5 to 7 DME on the 202 radial of the Kathmandu VOR. But when it had reached about 5.5 DME, it turned right.

The Kathmandu approach chart depicted a racetrack holding pattern, similar to that at Whiskey, between 13 DME and the Sierra fix at 10 DME, that required a left turn, and showed the approach could be commenced by following the pattern. So it is reasonable to assume the crew intended to turn left to conduct their second approach.

The controller, without radar equipment, was unable to approve turns in any particular direction. However, he knew the approach could be conducted using the Sierra racetrack holding pattern. In providing a clearance for the Sierra approach therefore, the controller had implicitly approved the request for a left turn, even though he did not specify a turn direction.

At this stage the crew were concerned about their height above terrain, so their third and fourth requests to turn back to the south are also understandable. The approach chart showed the missed approach track as a right turn from the VOR, and the missed approach procedure stored in the aircraft's FMS also showed this right turn. Probably frustrated by the continuing communication difficulties, now only 5 DME from the VOR, and probably uncomfortable that the flight was still continuing northwards, the captain decided to climb and turn right, thereby at least following the 'spirit' of the published missed approach procedure.

But although a right turn was now the only choice, the aircraft by this time was inside the Sierra 10 DME point, and the correct and safe course of action would have been to follow the full missed approach procedure as depicted on the approach chart.

Mutual misperceptions

To the air traffic controllers handling the Airbus, it would have seemed inconceivable that a crew would want to backtrack 41nm simply to reverse a turn and begin a new approach. So the pilot's nomination of

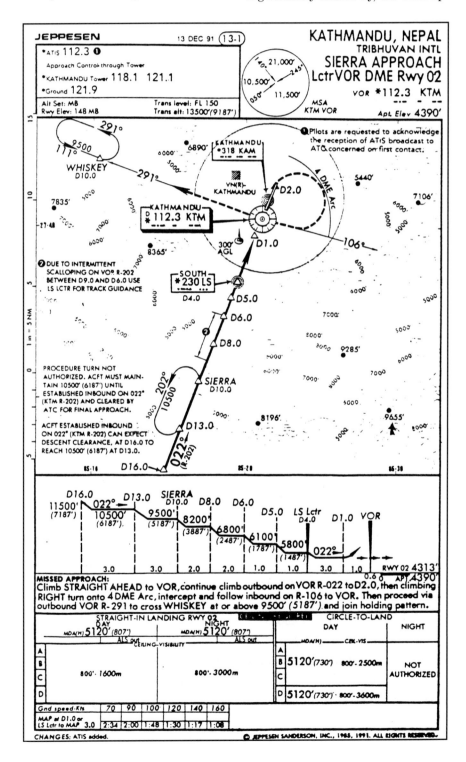

Romeo as the desired clearance point was confusing – the Romeo fix is not part of the Sierra approach and is a long way from Kathmandu. Moreover the aircraft would be going the wrong way on a one-way airway. But the controller's lack of response to the crew's request "to proceed to Romeo" was probably just as confusing to the pilots, particularly if they had already been misled by the layout of their company's approach chart.

This now led to further frustration for both crew and controllers. The lack of response by the Tower for a left turn no doubt gave the captain the impression the controller was having difficulties. And the repeated requests for left turns, which the controller was unable to grant with assurance of terrain clearance, made him doubt the judgement of the pilots.

ATC clearances – and misunderstandings

The crew began their right climbing turn on autopilot to FL180 without informing the Tower of their intended level. But they did transmit that the aircraft was climbing, prompting the controller to reiterate the requirement to report at 16 DME, leaving 11,500 feet for the Sierra approach.

The captain's reaction was "It's cleared – it's OK now", and he instructed the first officer to read back the controller's transmission. But the first officer seemed to have difficulty in doing so. To further compound the problem, the controller had difficulty understanding the first officer, stating a requirement to report at 10 DME, leaving 9500 feet. The first officer then read back the apparent new instructions, which were wrongly confirmed by the controller!

At this stage, the captain, realising the misunderstanding on both sides, again took over the radio, clarifying they could not make the approach now and that the aircraft was turning right and climbing to 18,000 feet "to start our approach again". But the Tower controller's reply, "Roger, ah ... standby, for the time being maintain 11,500 ..." still left the situation unresolved.

From the controller's point of view, it was also difficult to understand the Airbus's need for a climb to FL180. It would take the aircraft out of the Tower's airspace, requiring further co-ordination with Area Control, and it would conflict with inbound traffic. The controller was told the Airbus was in a turn; he had given it clearance for an approach, and adequate terrain clearance

should have existed at 11,500 feet. Romeo was not part of the approach, and the Airbus's continuing requests to proceed to Romeo were difficult to understand. What the controller of course did not know was that the approach chart being used by the crew could be misread to indicate Romeo as the starting point of the Sierra approach.

The crew, on the other hand, took the "Roger" to be an acceptance of their declared intention. But the controller's use of the ICAO standard phraseology "standby" ("wait and I will call you") was not clear, with the result that the first officer was now uncomfortable with the clearance. Again he transmitted that the aircraft was maintaining 13,000 feet, but again the controller's "Roger" prompted a further question from the first officer as to whether it was in fact "... OK".

The controller then reiterated that the aircraft was to maintain 11,500 feet because of conflicting traffic. The crew therefore stopped their climb, began a descent to 11,500 feet, reported the aircraft was descending, and gave their DME. They had established they had a valid clearance to maintain 11,500 feet – but the point to which they were cleared still remained uncertain.

After the Tower controller passed the position and ETA of the inbound traffic, he transmitted: "...understand you like to proceed to Romeo to make an approach". But when the captain confirmed this was so, the controller again merely replied "Roger".

Seeking clarification, the captain again transmitted "... confirm we can proceed to Romeo now", and the Tower replied: "Roger, proceed to Romeo and contact 126.5 [the Area Control frequency]". Though unusual, this now constituted a clearance to the Romeo fix an at altitude of 11,500 feet. But the tower controller was still thoroughly confused as to the crew's intentions – although technically for the time being they were now out of his hands!

At this stage the aircraft was still turning right on autopilot, with the crew preoccupied by their misunderstanding that the aircraft was not yet cleared for another approach, resulting in much unnecessary radio communication. They obviously did not realise the airspace jurisdiction of the Tower was limited to 11,500 feet and a clearance to a higher altitude was not possible without a change of controller and frequency. Apart from any other distractions, this led the captain to believe the controller was being neither helpful nor effective.

Terrain clearance

As the aircraft rolled out of the turn on autopilot on a heading of 025° – a direction almost opposite that required for the Romeo fix – at 11,500 feet, the crew again checked their terrain clearance, and after verifying their position, seemed satisfied. The aircraft was then about 5nm southwest of the VOR where the sector minimum altitude was 11,500 feet. But in only another minute on its present heading, it would cross the VOR where the minimum sector altitude would abruptly jump to FL210 (21,000 feet). Yet there was no more discussion by the crew on terrain clearance.

The 025° heading and the 5 DME report

The captain also reported to Area Control at this stage that: "... we got some technical problem concerned with the flight". But this was never questioned by the area controller, who merely reiterated the Tower's clearance to the Romeo fix, then broke the contact to talk to the inbound Royal Nepal flight.

(opposite) Cross section of a nation – literally. "Not only does Nepal's phenomenal topography range from near sea level to 8848m," declares one of the excellent guide books referred to in this chapter, "but it is contained within a country approximately the size of the US state of Iowa, or that of England and Wales together. The distance between the tropical lowlands and the realm under snow and ice is, in some places, less than 100km."
The truth of this statement is borne out by the plan view (top). The Indian border (and the southern boundary of the Kathmandu FIR), is on the left of the page, with Tibet on the right. The sectional elevation (bottom), taken through the extended centreline of Runway 02/20 at King Tribhuvan Airport, with the VOR/DME beacon as the "zero-axis", is to the same horizontal scale, shown at the foot of the page. The final 20 minutes of HS-TID's flight are depicted on each view. A 20nm section of the Kathmandu Valley has been enlarged for clarity, enabling the manoeuvres of both HS-TID and AP-BCP to be better assessed.
(centre left) This broader graphic enables a better comparison of the two approach chart profiles (the DME steps). Note the small but important differences in the presentation. The potential for confusion as to what height is required at what point may also be seen. Professional IFR pilots will have their own preference as to the style of presentation, but it is interesting that the 'smooth' profile and height/distance correlations of the SAS-Stoov/Thai chart are also those of the ICAO/Nepal DCA version. Yet the format of Jeppesen's Missed Approach instructions, with its clear prose, is obviously superior to the stilted abbreviations on the right of the SAS-Stoov profile. (Matthew Tesch & Mandala Maps, Nepal, with assistance from Lonely Planet Publications)

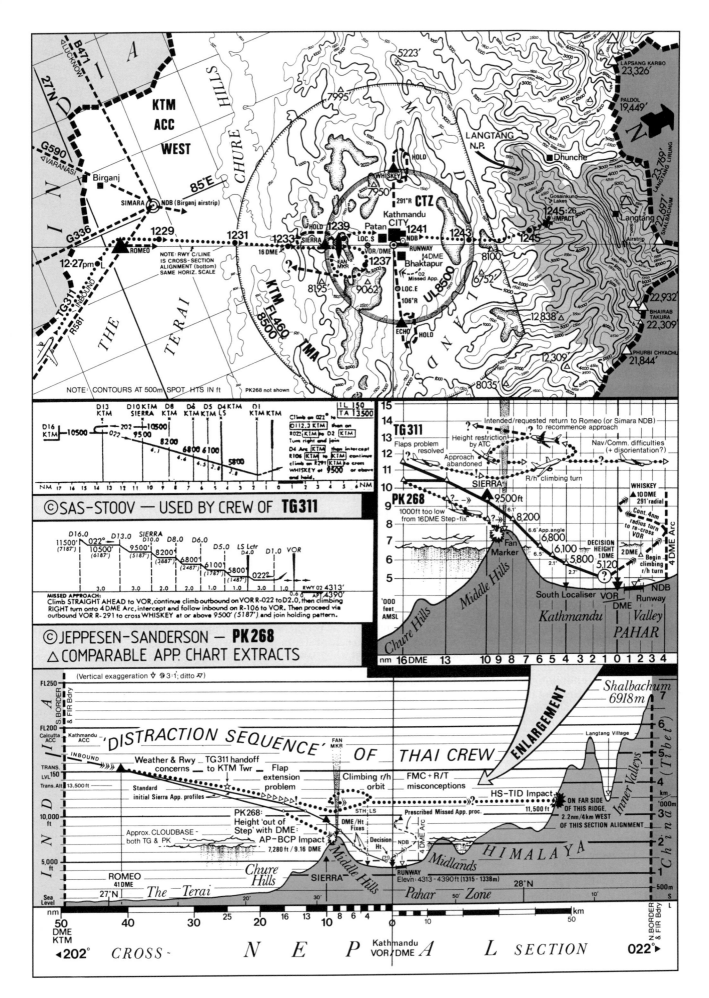

A minute and a half later the area controller called the Airbus and asked for its distance from Kathmandu. The captain reported: "We are 5 DME..." The controller queried, "Confirm 25 DME?" and the captain replied emphatically "Five – zero five!"

The previous DME report to the Tower at 9 DME was more than three minutes before, and because the controller believed the aircraft was to the south and heading towards Romeo, 5 DME was hardly what he expected. But he neither questioned the apparent anomaly nor asked for the aircraft's radial from the VOR.

Yet this exchange at 5 DME came at a critical point. Only a few questioning comments, from either the controller or the crew, might well have corrected the Airbus's flight towards the dangerous terrain to the north.

Indeed, had the crew begun a turn towards the Romeo fix within the following three minutes, they would have maintained adequate terrain clearance, though they would have been well below the minimum published sector altitude of FL210 on the Thai approach chart. Even so, considerable time remained to correct the flightpath. But several factors led to its continuation towards the treacherous, cloud enshrouded terrain of the Langtang National Park.

FMS distraction?

After the crew acknowledged the Tower's transmission to "proceed to Romeo and contact 126.5", nearly a minute elapsed before they contacted Area Control. The CVR showed their attention during this relatively long period was taken up with attempting to key in the Romeo fix as a navigation waypoint in their FMCs. Yet they were unsuccessful; meanwhile the aircraft continued northwards on autopilot. As it was passing the VOR, the first officer declared: "They are all gone – they have disappeared. We have to direct it again."

He could have been referring to the approach waypoints that would have disappeared after they were passed during the discontinued approach. Alternatively, it could have been that nothing could be seen when the Waypoints Navigation Display Map option was selected on the FMS. This would have been so for the aircraft's position. None of the waypoints such as Romeo (which would have been shown had the aircraft been heading south), would have been displayed while heading north – their non-display was simply a consequence of the aircraft's opposite heading.

But both the crew continued their efforts to bring up the Romeo waypoint on-screen, and to have the FMS calculate and display the track to Romeo. Yet without success. It is even possible that their unco-ordinated efforts led to confusing system outputs. It is a fact that if both pilots simultaneously attempt to place navigational data into their individual CDU keyboards, the computer systems will have difficulties accepting the inputs and the screens will present erroneous or meaningless information.

Further efforts were then made to use the Simara NDB, apparently as a reference for Romeo's position, but this was not successful either. "It doesn't show Romeo at all," the first officer said. After further exchanges, the captain asked, "Can you punch Romeo in again?" This attempt too was fruitless, for the first officer replied: "This thing fails again." More discussion followed about transferring the information to the FMS display on the captain's side, and finally the first officer said: "We had transferred it but it is gone – same as before."

It is not clear why the captain persisted so long with his attempts to navigate to Romeo using only FMS inputs. Other instruments were available to guide the flight with autopilot heading selections. Indeed, sufficient navigation information would have been available even if both FMC systems failed, including 'raw data' from the basic flight instruments.

Workload

The crew certainly had a higher than normal workload from the time of the flap deployment problem. Indeed, after the rollout from the climbing right turn, they seemed totally preoccupied with their efforts to input data into the FMS; both were doing so, but not in a co-ordinated manner. Simulator crew checks during the investigation showed that, in this situation, it was quite possible to lose track of time and the aircraft's position.

The northward flight that followed the 360° turn on autopilot may therefore have been unintentional, possibly as a result of transposing digits in selecting a VOR radial – eg 025° instead of 205°. In consequence, the captain's perception of direction could have been 180° opposite to the actual heading. In other words he could have believed the aircraft was heading southwest towards Romeo, He seemed content with the heading, there was no further request for a turn, and there was no indication that the crew were intending to initiate a turn.

It is even possible that the captain might not have consciously equated his verbalised "025" to Area Control with the dangerous flight to the north on autopilot. All the crew's efforts were being concentrated on finding Romeo and Simara in the FMS, and crosschecks of other instruments and navigation aid information were probably overlooked. In this situation, the captain could simply have read "025" from the Heading Select window of the Flight Control Unit without taking in its significance.

The area controller apparently did not note the heading either. At the time his supervisor was discussing with him the co-ordination of the inbound Royal Nepal flight. And without radar facilities, he was unable to provide heading clearances. In any case, there was some doubt as to whether the area controller had even heard the reference correctly.

Manoeuvring while heading north

At about the time of the 14 DME report, the Airbus began slowing to about 230 knots. And, as it neared 16 DME (the DME distance for joining the Sierra approach), it began a shallow left turn from its heading of 025° to rollout on 005°. These manoeuvres were consistent with preparing for an approach. The slats are extended below 240 knots, and the left turn of about 20°, followed by a right turn back on to a reciprocal, is consistent with a course reversal in accordance with Thai International procedures. The CVR dialogue at the time of the manoeuvre suggested that the captain was preparing for an approach and that his approach fix was at 16 DME.

About a minute before this reversal-type turn, the captain said "Romeo radial 202, 16 DME ... wait ... I will follow the line." The captain was apparently manoeuvring with reference to a line on his EFIS display. The aircraft was slightly to the west of the 022 radial at the time and, had the captain formed the impression that the aircraft was heading south-southwest towards Romeo and manoeuvring to the south of the airport instead of to the north, the left, then right turns would have been appropriate to establish the aircraft on the Sierra approach.

Altogether, it seems that the captain, in the absence of waypoint navigation, was guiding the flight using the VOR course on the Navigation Display, and was preparing to turn right for an approach. His actions, after the aircraft passed 14 DME, indicated he had somehow formed the impression the aircraft

The 16 year career of A300B4-2C [025], ultimately AP-BCP, which had taken it in diverse liveries from Cologne to Cairo and the Caribbean to Kuwait, finally came to an end on the 'fan marker hill' 9nm south of Tribhuvan on September 28, 1992. This Airbus, for early customer Bavaria-Germanair, was one of the first off the line at Toulouse. Delivered as D-AMAZ in May 1977 just as Hapag-Lloyd took over Bavaria-Germanair, it was immediately leased to Egyptair. The A300 then spent five years as SU-AZY, before passing on to Air Jamaica and Condor, among others. A Hapag-Lloyd fleet rationalisation in 1985-86 led to its sale to PIA – hence the aircraft's appearance here, fresh from the paintshop at Hannover, as it was being readied for its delivery flight to Karachi. Note the German flag and D-AHLZ registration, but the identifying 'CP' letters on the nose undercarriage doors. (ADC/ADNM Udo Weisse & HARS/MT)

was well to the south of the airport and was positioned for another Sierra approach – in essence where he *intended* it to be.

F/O's "north" comment

About 30 seconds before impact, the first officer suddenly exclaimed: "Hey – we are going ... we are going north!" But the captain replied calmly, "We will turn back soon."

This unconcerned response shows that the captain might have taken the first officer's remark as a prompt that it was time to turn towards the north. Had the aircraft been to the south of Kathmandu as the captain seemed to think, it would have indeed been time to turn back on to the inbound Sierra track. The fact that the captain merely asked the controller for a "right turn back to the airfield", rather than taking emergency action to avoid high terrain, supports the view that he had no idea of the desperate situation the aircraft was now in.

On the other hand, from the first officer's perspective, the captain's reaction to the "north" comment was that they would turn back – so the first officer did not press his obvious concern.

About eight seconds after the captain had requested the right turn, and 17 seconds before impact, the GPWS sounded: "Terrain ... Terrain!" followed by: "Whoop, whoop, pull up ...!"

The captain called "Level change!" and power was increased to climb,

but the first officer shouted: "Turn back ... turn back!"

"It's false ... it's false!" the captain replied. But then, only two seconds before impact, one of crew cried out: "Oh my God!"

It is uncertain whether a climb straight ahead following the "north" comment, would have cleared the high terrain. But it is possible that an immediate turn, climbing or otherwise, could have saved the aircraft.

AP-BCP, as delivered, wore the peacock green and metallic gold cheatline livery adopted by PIA with their introduction of Boeing 747s in mid 1976. Green is a traditionally Islamic colour and had been PIA's primary identifier since its formation with three Super Constellations in 1955. At the end of the 1980s, modifications smartened up the livery. The gold, and the word 'International' were omitted from the titling, and the green lowered to full-belly coverage, cut off forward by angled chevrons of peacock and bright emerald green, and sky-blue. AP-BCP wore this livery at the time of its loss. (Flight International)

Reaction to the GPWS warning

The warning came as the aircraft's height above terrain reduced to less than 2450 feet. But as this was only six seconds before impact, the steep slope of the rock face ahead made it utterly impossible to avoid the mountain.

The captain had probably experienced false GPWS warnings on previous occasions, thus reducing his sense of urgency about them. It is also possible he recalled that the flap fault rectification checklist included isolating the GPWS circuit to avoid spurious warnings. He might well have thought the "false" GPWS warning was a consequence of the earlier flap problem.

FINDINGS OF THE INVESTIGATION

• The Sierra VOR/DME approach into Kathmandu necessitates steep angles of descent. Aerodynamic performance requires that slats, flaps and undercarriage be fully extended by 13 DME.
• The flight profile was proceeding normally until the crew selected the slats and flaps to 15/15, when the flaps jammed. The flap fault was quickly rectified, but the aircraft was then too high and too close to the airport for the approach to continue.
• The aircraft made an unusual request for a clearance to the Romeo fix, specifying a direction of turn, to rejoin the Sierra approach for another attempt. The operator's approach chart was misleading, in that

it could be read as depicting Romeo as the start of the Sierra approach.

• The Tower controller issued a valid clearance to carry out the Sierra approach, but it did not include the Romeo fix or a direction of turn. The crew continued to ask for a clearance to Romeo, specifying a left turn, but did not receive a clearance satisfactory to them on either count.

• After four requests for a left turn, the crew initiated a climbing right turn from 10,500 feet, intending to climb to FL180. The Tower controller then instructed the aircraft to descend back to 11,500 feet. While nearing the 202 radial of the VOR, still in the turn, the Tower finally cleared the aircraft to the Romeo fix and instructed it to contact the Area controller.

• The aircraft continued its right turn, completing 360°. During the latter portion of this turn, the crew lost track of where the aircraft was going, with the result that they flew towards the north-northeast, the direction opposite the Romeo fix.

• Neither the area controller nor the captain succeeded in identifying the aircraft's actual position when it was five DME north of the VOR.

• When requesting the aircraft's position, the area and tower controllers asked only for its distance from the VOR, and not for its radial bearing. And when transmitting the aircraft's position, the crew gave only their DME distance, and not their VOR radial.

• The crew's use of the FMS for navigation was unco-ordinated, and may have led to confusing system outputs. As a result the aircraft did not turn south-southwest towards the Romeo fix.

• Communication difficulties – lack of radio clarity, language confusion and the use of non-standard phraseology – increased the crew's workload throughout the approach.

• There was no evidence that the crew had received simulator training for Kathmandu, even though the airline regarded it as an airport with unusual operational requirements. This led to an increased workload for the crew when confronted with a discontinued approach.

• The area controller on duty was a trainee with only nine months' experience. The controller supervising the trainee was simultaneously fulfilling other controller duties.

Recommendations

The Accident Investigation Report noted that communication between aircraft flying into Kathmandu and its controllers, with pilots and controllers speaking in a second lan-

A comparison between the two crew 'FFCC' of the Thai A310, and the 'traditional' three crew flightdeck of the PIA A300 is provided by this view of an Indian Airlines Airbus crew at work. Yet in the Kathmandu context, neither the former's advanced technology, nor the latter's 'third pair of eyes' were sufficient to avert their respective disasters. (Flight International & HARS/MT)

guage, required improvement. The investigation believed this problem, as well as worldwide communication difficulties at international airports, could be alleviated by:

• Emphasising the importance of effective communication, including the use of standard phraseology and complete position reporting by crews.

• Placing high emphasis in controller training on the ability to communicate in English, and in methods of effective communication to resolve potentially confusing situations.

• Licensing and rating controllers, as recommended by ICAO, as well as improving controller career incentives and motivation.

It was also recommended that manufacturers of FMS systems be made aware of the operational and technical aspects of the Kathmandu accident, and that operators and crew training centres be encouraged to emphasise the importance of co-ordinated use of the FMS.

Comment:

Although the Accident Investigation Report did not emphasise the fact, it is evident that the crew made a fatal error in electing merely to turn right and climb at 5.5 DME, after the captain's four requests for a left turn had not been met by the Tower controller.

Had the captain carried out the full, published Sierra missed approach procedure instead, this would have established the aircraft in a safe holding pattern at the Whiskey fix. There the crew would have had the opportunity to sort out their various operational problems without any constraints of time. Then, after any ATC misunderstandings had been clarified, they would have been able to safely reposition the aircraft for a normal Sierra approach.

Instead the captain, using an ad hoc procedure of his own and disregarding vital tenets of airmanship and air navigation, effectively turned back into a 'no man's land', where he placed all his reliance on the FMS to navigate the aircraft back to Romeo on autopilot.

The Tower controller meanwhile would have been expecting the Airbus to carry out the Sierra missed approach procedure, and when instead it reported making an unauthorised climb to FL180, probably became thoroughly alarmed at the possibility of it conflicting with the other inbound traffic.

Another notable omission in the Accident Investigation Report's recommendations was the absence of any reference to the need for crew training using 'raw data' navigational aid information only. The crew's action in relying entirely on the autopilot to fly the aircraft, while depending on 'blind' guidance from the FMS, would indicate a lack of basic instrument flying skills and the inability to quickly revert to instrument navigation techniques.

A second Kathmandu tragedy

History has a painful tendency to repeat itself. But rarely does it do so as swiftly it did in Nepal, only 59 days after the loss of HS-TID, when the Sierra Approach to the Tribhuvan International Airport's Runway 02 claimed another Airbus victim.

The pitiful scatter of Thai wreckage had been abandoned by the investigators on August 19, but the Nepalese Investigation Commission was still hard at work piecing together the events that led to the disaster.

Even while HS-TID's CVR and FDR were still yielding their data to investigators in Ottawa, on September 28, 1992, AP-BCP, an A300B4 be-

Resting amid the native rhododendrons, its smoking embers mixing with the misty cloudbase, the empennage of AP-BCP tells its own tragic story. The sharp gashes in the leading edges of the fin and starboard stabiliser attest to the violence of the disintegrating aircraft's passage through the dense canopy of the hillside jungle. (Wide World Photos)

longing to Pakistan International Airlines, was joining the Sierra VOR/DME 02 approach to Kathmandu. Operating as Flight PK268 from Karachi, this larger Airbus had a crew of 12 and carried 155 passengers.

The weather, even so late in the monsoon season, was similar to that of July 31, with a low overcast, drizzle, poor visibility and little or no wind. Descending in cloud on the 202° VOR radial at around 2.30pm local time that afternoon, the Airbus flew directly into the densely-wooded southern side of the fan marker hill at an elevation of 7300ft (3000ft above the airport), only a few hundred feet below its summit. There were no survivors.

The much less forbidding and far more accessible crash site of the PIA Airbus, only 9.16 DME short of the VOR on the Sierra approach track, enabled investigators to quickly determine that the A300 was established in its landing configuration, with slats, flaps and undercarriage fully extended, and that it was under power and on track.

In this instance the aircraft was an early model A300B4, with conventional control systems, traditional avionics, and a three crew flight-deck, and the investigators could find no technical reasons that could have contributed to the accident.

There was no CVR record of flight-deck conversation, but the crew had not reported any problems.

But having acquired the correct final approach track, which it subsequently maintained, the aircraft had begun its descent too early and then continued to descend in an altitude profile that was consistently "one step ahead" of the published DME decent profile.

As a result, the Airbus was more than 1000ft lower than the minimum altitude prescribed by the published DME steps for the Sierra approach when it struck the hillside. The A300's descent profile appears on the accompanying cross section diagrams, together with that of the Thai A310.

ATC recordings showed that at 16 DME the A300 crew misreported their height by 1000ft (the lower of the two aircraft's initial approach profiles shown in the diagram). A further transmission from the Airbus at 10 DME, the start of the Sierra Approach, advised they were at 8200ft – where the required safe minimum was in fact 9500ft. "Within seconds" an alert tower controller challenged the Pakistani crew for an altitude check – but it was already too late. That an error was made by the PIA crew seemed beyond dispute.

Final reports on both accidents were released within weeks of each

other in June and July 1993, and the part played by the Kathmandu controllers was perhaps best summarised in that on the PIA disaster: "Some air traffic controllers at Kathmandu had a low self-esteem and were reluctant to intervene in piloting matters such as terrain separation."

This was not the only reinforcement of conclusions drawn from the Thai crash. Misreading poorly-designed approach charts was obviously also a factor in the loss of the A300, viz: "... the pilots failed to follow the published approach procedure ...". And "... the inevitable complexity of the [Sierra VOR/DME] approach and the associated approach chart" were "contributory causal factors".

The flight profile diagrams in this chapter include extracts from the two different charts used in the Kathmandu disasters, showing the benefits and limitations of two varying interpretations of the DME descent steps. They provide a comparison of the graphic styles – and perhaps some understanding of how the PIA crew could misread a chart so fatally.

The approach chart used by the Pakistani crew was particularly criticised for its method of showing the vertical profile of the approach. "The minimum altitude at some DME fixes was not directly associated with the fix," the Nepalese Commission's report declared. And Pakistan International Airlines' own report recommended that ICAO "should review the conventions of commercial approach charts with a view to encouraging standardisation and reducing chart clutter".

Meanwhile Nepal, announced its Prime Minister at the time, would consider measures which "may even include building a new airport 80km south of Tribhuvan for use in bad weather".

Footnote:
Some resolution was required in deciding the spelling of Nepal's capital in this chapter: both "Katmandu" and "Kathmandu" are found in all manner of authoritative publications. The confusion results from different systems of translation from Sanskrit – the letter 'h' appears in some, but not in others. Standardisation with the "h" was adopted, to accord with the spelling used by the publishers of the approach charts and other materials in this chapter.

CHAPTER 7

"May I turn this – the control wheel – a bit?"

*– Captain's young son,
sitting in the left-hand seat*

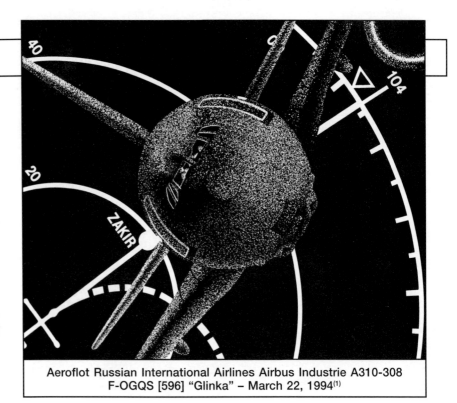

Aeroflot Russian International Airlines Airbus Industrie A310-308
F-OGQS [596] "Glinka" – March 22, 1994[1]

**The quiet Siberian flight sector in the dead of night was the crew's first break
in four hours of transiting busy airspace on the long haul from Moscow to the
Far East. So what better time for the captain's children to visit the flightdeck?**

The background

Isolated from 'Western' aviation by 70 years of separate political and operational development, Soviet flying, both military and civil, had grown up with its own traditions and operational procedures.

At variance in many respects from Western aviation industry concepts that are so basic and familiar to those involved in it, regardless of nationality, the result was an aviation system parallelling that of the West, with equivalent goals, but which was uniquely different in practice. To borrow a concept from science fiction, Soviet civil aviation was almost a "parallel universe".

With no less than 11,000 civil transport aircraft being operated throughout the Soviet Union by the USSR's giant Aeroflot – more an entire civil aviation industry than a single airline – not to mention huge numbers of military aircraft operations, a highly complex network of airways, route sectors, basic radio navigation aids, control centres, communications stations and reporting points was developed, covering the whole vast landmass that made up the USSR (see facing FIR map).

But, like most Soviet designed and built aero engines, these widespread airways facilities were for the most

part technically undemanding – for the same sound reason that this more simple technology was less likely to pose maintenance problems in remote areas huge distances away from well equipped workshops.

For flightcrews, airways flying in the settled western and southern USSR was thus hard work, with complicated procedures for aircraft separation and the avoidance of major population centres, short route segments, and a proliferation of reporting points. Unlike aviation practice in the West, navigation was fully metricated, with altitudes and flight levels measured and reported in metres, and flight distances in kilometres rather than nautical miles – familiar procedures to Soviet pilots and navigators, but operationally daunting to outsiders!

A new era

With the final overthrow of communist power in the Soviet Union in 1991, the majority of the 15 republics which made up the former USSR sought to establish regional identities independent of their past domination by a centralised Moscow government.

For Aeroflot, with thousands of aircraft, widely dispersed throughout the former USSR, and a total of

600,000 employees, the awesome political upheaval inevitably meant fragmentation, as great numbers of airports, ground installations, navigational services and radio aids, personnel and the aircraft themselves were shared out and transferred to new regional and local airlines and operators.

Even though 11 of the states, recognising the economic and practical advantages of continuing to work co-operatively in a country so vast and far flung, formed the Commonwealth of Independent States (CIS – still centred in Moscow), this had little effect on the dismantling of the former Soviet airline giant.

In Moscow however, the decision had been taken previously that the name Aeroflot should be retained for the newly formed Russian Federation's official flag carrier, now to be known as (to give it its full name in English) Aeroflot Russian International Airlines.

In the breakup of the former USSR Aeroflot, this much smaller Moscow-based Aeroflot was composed of the 103 civil aircraft actually based at Moscow's Sheremetyevo International Airport at the time of the radical political change. These included 29 long range Ilyushin Il-62s and 18 widebody Ilyushin Il-86s.

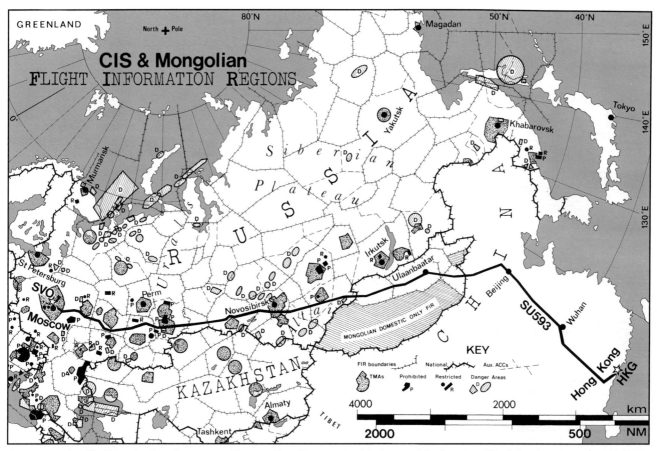

On a conventional world projection, the nonstop Moscow-Hong Kong track might seem oddly divergent. This Polar view gives a clearer Great Circle understanding of the SU593 route, as well as some idea of the vastness of the globe's biggest landmass, spanning more than 10 timezones. The entire Air Traffic Services system of the former USSR has recently been transformed to adapt to the surrounding world, but its basic elements would have still applied to the ill-fated Flight SU593. VORs remain scarce in a vast land sprinkled with more economical NDBs, and charts are still liberally annotated with restrictions and route advisories. Some sectors are "permitted with Russian escort crew only" (many Mongolian and Chinese routes also warn of "strict adherence to airway axis") and some NDB locations, while accurately mapped, carry the legend: "Frequency Unknown"!

Trans-Siberian sectors became available to selected airlines after the joint Aeroflot-JAL Tu-114 services of 1967, but only with the dismantling of the Soviet Union in 1991 have airlines generally been able to access more efficient flight planning options as alternatives to the southern Eurasian and Middle East routes of the 1970s and 1980s.

Aeroflot's scheduled Hong Kong services are quite recent. During frostier Sino-Soviet relations, there were few Aeroflot services to China, and Mongolia's airspace was similarly out of bounds as a buffer for both sides. With Korean Peninsula tensions to the east, and Chinese apprehensions about the Tibetan Plateau to the southwest, Aeroflot's commercial Asian presence was necessarily constrained. Moreover, until thawing relations with the West permitted the A310 order, Aeroflot had no equipment that could do justice to the long, thin Hong Kong route – let alone fly it nonstop from Moscow. (Matthew Tesch; Jeppesen-Sanderson Inc & British Airways)

A fine looking aircraft seating 350 passengers, the Il-86 was designed for the old Aeroflot's high density domestic routes from Moscow to the Black Sea, to Leningrad (now St Petersburg – again!(2)) Kiev, and other major destinations of similar distance. Traffic on Aeroflot's international routes at the time could not possibly justify an aircraft as big as an Il-86. In consequence, the Il-86 was never intended to operate long distance stages and its range was a relatively short 2500km (1500nm).

For the Russian Federation's "new" Aeroflot, it was now a source of embarrassment that its principal and most prestigious aircraft type was unable to operate most of its international routes without stops for refuelling. The Moscow/New York route, for example, would necessitate refuelling stops at both Shannon in Ireland and Gander in Newfoundland – shades of the 1950s and piston engined trans-atlantic air services!

But in the new political and economic climate, the airline was no longer under strictures to operate only former USSR-built aircraft. It was inevitable therefore that the airline should look to Western aircraft manufacturers as a solution to its range and capacity problems.

To make overtures to Boeing in the USA would have been unthinkable at this stage of the new Federation's life – such collaboration with the principal former Cold War foe was politically quite out of the question. But France was a different matter – it was European, and cultural ties between the two nations had endured over centuries.

Airbus Industrie's relatively new long range derivative of the wide-bodied A310 – the A310-300 – was the obvious choice. Although stubbier than the Il-86, which it resembled except for its two engines, and seating less than 200 passengers, its range was nearly three times that of the Il-86, making it eminently suitable for the airline's premier international routes and those to the Far East.

Late in 1989, Aeroflot announced it was ordering five A310-300s (with five options; see following page). In the event, after the aircraft were built and ready for delivery at Toulouse, the raising of finance for them ran into difficulties. As well, certain United States authorities had misgivings about some of the aircraft's computer technology, as well as that of its General Electric engine systems, being made available to the Russian airline.

But finally, after the A310-300s had

Sheremetyevo-2 was touted as a new "Olympic Airport" for the 1980 Games. In reality, it was a new international facility on the south side of the existing airport NW of the capital (see later map). This east-facing view shows the result of its DM230 million building contract, awarded to a West German firm in 1977. Framed by two Ilyushin Il-62s on the southern parallel taxiway, a Lufthansa 727, a TAAG-Angola 707, two Il-62s, an Il-86 and a Tu-154 stand docked at six of the 19 aerobridges which flank three sides of the eight storey administration building. Four of the aerobridges can handle 747s. (Matthew Tesch collection; Aviareklama)

as planned via a complex of route sectors and Control Areas on the R480 airway, the primary Trans-Siberian eastbound air route from Moscow to Novokuznetsk. The A310 was maintaining an IAS of 530kmh (286kt) with the engine power set at 87-89% N_1 and the autopilot engaged in the NAV (Navigation) mode.

As waypoints were passed over the next four hours, the aircraft's heading altered to the east and southeast. On the flightdeck after midnight, Captain Kudrinsky was occupying the left-hand seat, while aircraft commander Captain Danilov, having negotiated all the busy airspace that extends from Moscow eastward to the Ural Mountains, was

been held on the airfield at Toulouse for more than a year, the US relented and leasing finance was then guaranteed by the Russian Federation and negotiated with French bankers. Initial crews were trained by Airbus Industrie's Aeroformation training subsidiary, and Aeroflot took delivery of the first Western aircraft, incorporating state-of-the-art computerised avionics and flight management systems, in July, 1992.

The A310 entered Aeroflot revenue service a month later, shortly afterwards inaugurating a new, non-stop Aeroflot route from Moscow to Hong Kong. The other four A310s were delivered to Aeroflot subsequently. For the time being, all five leased Airbus A310s would retain their French registrations.

Flight to destruction

In the evening of March 22, 1994, Aeroflot's now regular service from Moscow to Hong Kong, designated as Flight SU593, was being operated by Airbus A310 F-OGQS, the last of the five aircraft to be delivered to Moscow from Toulouse, 15 months before.

The flightcrew for the long international trip comprised Captain A V Danilov (commander), Captain Ya V Kudrinsky (reserve commander),

and Second Pilot I V Piskarev. All three held the Russian designation of Pilot First Class.

In accordance with standard Russian aviation practice, medical checks of the crew for blood alcohol levels and blood pressure were made as they signed on for duty at Moscow's Sheremetyevo International Airport. The medical staff recorded no adverse findings.

The crew's preflight preparations at Sheremetyevo were then conducted under the direction of Captain Danilov. In addition to the three pilots, the A310's crew comprised nine flight attendants. Sixty-three passengers were on board the lightly loaded aircraft, plus 593kg (1307lb) of mail, baggage and cargo.

With a takeoff weight of 145 tonnes and its centre of gravity well within maximum allowable limits, the Airbus took off from Sheremetyevo's Runway 25 and, 12 minutes later, had climbed to a Flight Level of 9100m (30,000ft) and was maintaining an IAS of 555kmh (300kt). Half an hour later, after clearing the Moscow Terminal Area (see next map), the A310 climbed a further 1000m (3300ft) to reach its flight planned cruising level of 10,100m (33,000ft) at the Chernukha NDB.

The flight then proceeded normally

NO. 38

THE SOVIET BUSINESS WEEKLY ✦ OCTOBER 1, 1990

AEROFLOT IN LEASE-TO-OWN DEAL WITH AIRBUS

By SERGEI GORNOV

The Soviet airlines, Aeroflot, in a contract worth half a billion dollars, has leased five A-310 airbuses from the Western European aircraft manufacturing consortium, Airbus Industrie.

The deal, concluded with Airbus Industrie and a consortium of Western European banks was disclosed on September 25 during an A-310 demonstration flight as part of the international exhibition "Aviation-90".

Victor Kuskov, deputy chief of Aeroflot's passenger service, said that the five airbuses were to be supplied to the Soviet air company within a period of two years.

Kuskov also said the leasing arrangement was to last for ten years during which time Aeroflot hoped to pay the full price of the airliners and become a full-fledged owner of the machines.

An A-310 costs about US$70 million. But Kuskov said Aeroflot was paying $100 million for each of the five airbuses as part of the deal mediated by a consortium of Western banks led by Credit Lyonnais of France.

Despite such an extraordinary arrangement, Kuskov described the deal as extremely lucrative for Aeroflot. He said the planes would be bought from the manufacturer by the banking consortium, rather than the company itself, so the Soviet side would be spared the burden of massive lump-sum payments in hard currency.

The banks would then lease the planes to Aeroflot for ten years, receiving 10 percent of the price annually plus 12.5 interest on credit. As the banks' entitlements to the planes would diminish with every passing year, so would annual interest rates, bringing the average rate down to 7.5 percent.

Stuart Iddles, the senior vice-president for commerce of Airbus Industrie, said during the A-310 demonstration flight that five airbuses were not enough for a mammoth company like Aeroflot. He hoped other deals would follow for at least another 15 airliners.

The A-310 airbus is manufactured by Airbus Industrie, a consortium of four companies, including Aerospatiale of France, Deutsche Airbus GmbH of West Germany, British Aerospace of the UK, and CASA of Spain. The consortium has sold a total of 1,500 airbuses, including 118 in the first six months of 1990 at an estimated $7.5 billion.

During a demonstration flight of the US passenger airliner McDonnell Douglas MD-80 on September 26, Viesturs Zommers, McDonnell's vice-president, said that his company had

also offered a leasing arrangement to Aeroflot.

He said the price of one MD-80 that could take 170 passengers while flying over a range of 5,000 kilometers was about $32 million. Another model, the MD-11, for 300 passengers and with the flying range of 12,000 kilometers, would cost $100 million each.

Zommers admitted that his company had been negotiating a deal with Aeroflot since early 1990. He was adamant that Aeroflot was losing about 20 million potential passengers a year due to the shortage of airliners. He said Aeroflot should buy planes abroad instead of relying solely on the Soviet Ministry of Aviation, as no country in the world used passenger liners only of its own make, the United States included.

Asked to comment, Vitaly Goryachev, chief of the National Research Institute for Civil Aviation, said the Soviet side was negotiating deals with all of the world's major aircraft engine manufacturers as part of the effort to select the best option for contemplated imports.

He added that the question of importing MD airliners had not been raised on a practical plane, but he did not rule out such a chance.

Goryachev explained that import deals were precipitated by what he called a "process of de-monopolization" within Aeroflot. More autonomy is being granted to regional divisions of the company and even newly-emerging independent carriers.

He said such divisions were free to choose whatever planes they wanted to fly, including import options. But he said airliners of foreign make at this stage could only be leased for hard currency, so that 50-70 percent of airfares would have to be sold for hard currency. This means the imported aircraft could only be used for international routes.

taking a well-earned rest in the passenger cabin. Second Pilot Piskarev was on the right in the copilot's position, but had the seat slid back to its rearmost position.

At 12.40am, an off duty Aeroflot pilot travelling on the flight, Captain V E Makarov, brought Captain Kudrinsky's two children passengers – 13 year old daughter Yana and 15 year old son El'dar – to visit the flightdeck.

Shortly afterwards, Kudrinsky invited his daughter to sit at the controls. "Now, come and sit in my seat," he asked her. "Would you like to?"

Seating herself in the captain's position, Yana Kudrinsky first asked her father to raise the seat higher for her. After she had looked around for a few minutes, Captain Kudrinsky asked: "Well then, Yana, are you going to pilot the plane? Hold on to the control column ... hold on!"

Evidently standing behind the seat and using the autopilot's heading selector control while his daughter "followed through" with her hands resting lightly on the control yoke, Captain Kudrinsky first turned the aircraft gently a few degrees to the left and then to the right, before bringing it back on to its heading. Yana then vacated the left-hand seat after a few minutes.

As soon as she had done so, Captain Kudrinsky allowed his son El'dar to quickly re-occupy the seat. This event was apparently regarded as something of an occasion, for it was enthusiastically filmed by the off duty Captain Makarov with a video camera.

After briefly explaining the principles of aircraft control to his son, Captain Kudrinsky prepared to demonstrate a turning manoeuvre similar to the one he had carried out for his daughter. But El'dar, obviously far keener about the experience of handling the aircraft than his younger sister, asked his father: "May I turn this – the control wheel – a bit?"

Kudrinsky readily agreed, giving him further hints on what to do. "Yes ... look out to the left now, and watch for the horizon when you are turning," Kudrinsky told his son. "If we are going left, turn the controls to the left!"

Before Captain Kudrinsky could again turn the autopilot heading selector however, El'dar grasped the control yoke firmly and turned it 3-4° to the left. Only then did Captain Kudrinsky adjust the selector to al-low the autopilot to conform to the altered heading. After the aircraft had taken up this altered heading, he turned the heading selector back to the right and reselected the autopilot's NAV mode.

But undetected by either Kudrinsky or Piskarev, El'dar's enthusiastic overriding of the autopilot through the aileron controls had caused the autopilot servo to disconnect from the aileron linkage. Yet the autopilot itself remained otherwise as programmed to stabilise the aircraft's flight parameters.

There is no aural or visual warning system on the A310 to indicate an autopilot servo disconnection from the aircraft's control linkage, and the

The stately Il-62s that originally operated Aeroflot's "on off" Australian services were obviously wanting, compared to the 747-400s and 'Big Twins' that clustered with them around Sydney's International Terminal. But change was in the wind after F-OGQU [646] "Skriabin", the first of the Russian A310s, was delivered to Moscow in June 1992, entering service on the nonstop Trans-Siberian "Magistrale" to Tokyo. A310s appeared on the rejuvenated twice weekly Moscow-Bangkok-Sydney service in May 1993, F-OGQS "Glinka" (pictured) itself coming to Mascot not long afterwards. The new, Airbus inspired livery brightened the traditional Russian tricolours in "Eurowhite" style, accentuating the airline's break with the past. In 1992, stylised Imperial Russian double headed eagles replaced Aeroflot's winged hammer & sickle symbol on the upper fuselage and fin. Airbus Industrie won Aeroflot over with its short delivery times, as much as its unit price of $US70 million, and both the $US90m MD-11, with its 1994 delivery, and Boeing's $US170m+ 747-400, unavailable until 1996, were ruled out. The protracted financial arrangements which Airbus Industrie went to such lengths to negotiate proved the competition's last straw. Even if Russia's banking and financial systems could have coped with such figures on their own, aviation ministry and Aeroflot officials knew that, operationally, they would have to 'learn to walk before they could run'. The French lease-purchase arrangements gave Russia a face saving opportunity to begin more economical frontline international services, while progressively assuming more of the costs. A media interview in October 1989, reflecting Aeroflot's new commercial mood, reported that the first five A310s would permit the withdrawal of no less than 12 Il-62s. The Russian A310's F-Oxxx registrations denote the Overseas Department of the aircraft's French owner-financiers. (Australian Aviation/Julian Green)

instrument panel display continued to show the autopilot's previously programmed mode, even though it had ceased to control the aircraft in the rolling plane. As a result, the partial disengagement of the autopilot remained unnoticed.

Once the partial autopilot disconnection had occurred, with El'dar holding the control yoke slightly to the right, a gradual increase in bank began to the right. This also went unnoticed by either Kudrinsky or Piskarev. Within seven seconds, the bank had increased from 15° to 20°, and the aircraft was continuing to roll at a rate of about half to one degree per second. Yet such a slow rate of roll could hardly be sensed on the flightdeck at night without referring to the flight instruments.

From the 20° bank angle, the rate of roll began to increase to 5.5° per second – and the bank exceeded 30° (the limit for a fully operational autopilot manoeuvre), passing 45° about 40 seconds after Kudrinsky had selected the autopilot back to the NAV mode. Meanwhile El'dar had noticed "something strange" about the feel of the aircraft and,

with a keen eye, apparently discerned from the instruments in front of him that it was changing its heading. He interrupted his father, busy talking to Yana behind him, to draw it to his attention. "Why is it turning?" he asked him.

Kudrinsky: "Is it turning by itself?"
El'dar: "Yes it is!"

All three pilots on the flightdeck then began to discuss why the aircraft had started to "turn by itself" and to speculate on the reasons for it. Off duty Captain Makarov suggested that the aircraft had entered some kind of holding pattern, and Piskarev agreed.

Makarov: "It's still turning, lads – going into some kind of zone."
Piskarev: "We've gone into a zone – a holding pattern."
Kudrinsky: "Have we?"
Piskarev: "Of course we have!"

Despite the lack of any confirming data on the pilots' EFIS screens, both Piskarev and Kudrinsky apparently accepted Captain Makarov's observation without further comment.

Twelve seconds after the aircraft was seen to be turning, the bank angle

had increased to 50°, but neither the captain nor the second pilot apparently realised this fact, for they took no action to counter it. Yet, as this quite extreme bank angle continued to develop, the autopilot, with its autothrottle function still engaged, was attempting to maintain the aircraft's height and speed. As a result, g-loads and the angle of attack were both steadily increasing.

Captain Makarov, suddenly conscious of the increasing g-load as he stood on the flightdeck behind the control seats, realised the aircraft was in an unusual attitude and reacted with a spontaneous cry of exclamation. Moments later, the nose abruptly pitched up and the aircraft entered a pre-stall buffet, prompting Kudrinsky also to call out. "Hold on!" he cried. "Hold the control column – hold it!"

Kudrinsky's outburst, obviously intended for those at the controls to alert them to the rapidly steepening bank, was evidently understood by Second Pilot Piskarev, for he immediately turned his control yoke sharply to counter the roll. But El'dar apparently took his father's

(above) The rooftop parapet of the Sheremetyevo-2 terminal building on a damp summer's day in 1990 provided this panoramic montage which may be related to the inset airport map (below). From left to right across the distant northern horizon of this NNW-facing view are: the 07 runway thresholds, the hangar and headquarters of the capital's Polar Directorate, two maintenance hangars, a forlorn lineup of engineless Il-86s, the modern low-set Sheremetyevo-1 terminals, the older Krushchev era administration and ATC buildings, a 'boneyard' of stored and derelict airliners, many of them cannibalised for spares, and the Runway 25 thresholds. Beyond the southern parallel taxiway (mid foreground), Runway 07R/25L is visible, its Right counterpart (the original single runway) indistinct during resurfacing works. F-OGQS made its final, fateful takeoff from right to left across this view at 4.39pm local time on March 22, 1994. (Matthew Tesch photographs)

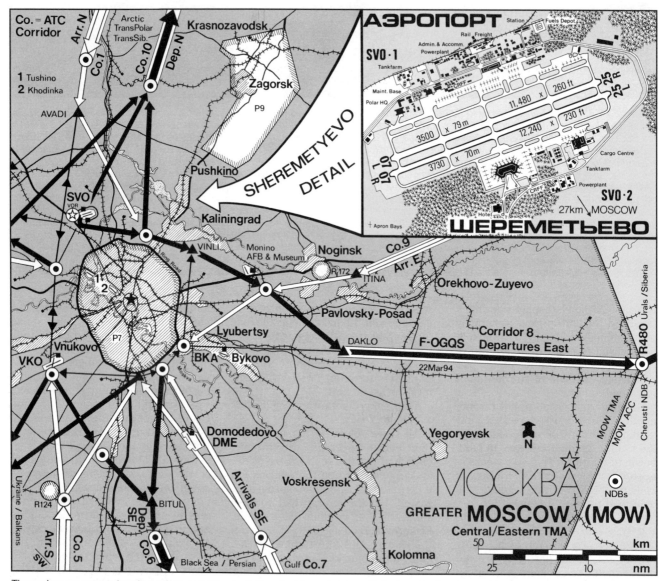

The main map covers barely a quarter of Moscow's Terminal Area, but is sufficient to display the capital's geography and four major civil airports, with the track of the departing F-OGQS indicated. Prohibited Area P7, a no-fly zone, overlies the whole of Moscow within its perimeter Ring Road. Sheremetyevo Airport, elevation 190m (623ft), set amid evergreen forest on a plateau to the northwest of the city, was opened in 1960 with one runway and a few northside buildings. To the southwest, Vnukovo Airport was a grass airfield before the 'Great Patriotic War' (WW2). Its later 3000m (10,000ft) Runways 02/20 and 06/24 received most visiting dignitaries during the Cold War era, although regular international traffic soon deferred to Sheremetyevo. Further out to the SSE, Domodedovo was long one of Europe's biggest airports, its main terminal and massive central pier bisecting its pair of 14/32 runways. Almost swallowed by expanding suburbs to the ESE, Bykovo's single runway remains operational for air freight and occasional, classified movements. Domodedovo has been proposed for redevelopment to offer long-haul Russian Federation and CIS trunk services, while Bykovo headquarters the troubled Yak-42 trijet fleet and other types used on domestic and local flights in European Russia. To the northeast, Prohibited Area P9 protects not only the iconic architecture and priceless treasures of Zagorsk – including the country's principal seminary and cathedrals, churches and monasteries dating back to the 14th century – but also "Star City", Russia's cosmonaut training and spaceflight control centre. Five pairs of arrival and departure corridors tightly channel traffic to and from the Moscow airports. At the Terminal Area's eastern corner, the Cherusti NDB marks the start of the eastbound R480 airway to Novokuznetsk – 3070km (1660nm), nine ACCs, 15 NDBs, and 12 reporting points away to the east! (Matthew Tesch; Jeppesen-Sanderson Inc)

words literally, and clutched the left-hand control yoke firmly at close to its neutral position, the disparity in the yoke positions being taken up by the heavy springs in the aileron circuit linkage.

In his attempts now to correct the aircraft's attitude, Piskarev was at a serious disadvantage. A man only 160cm (5ft 3in) in height, he was wearing his seatbelt and shoulder harness and, with his seat in its rearmost position, he could barely reach the control column, let alone the rudder pedals.

Piskarev's limited ability to manipulate the controls, the counteracting effect of El'dar's firm grip on the left-hand control yoke, with a resulting lack of control response, and the increasing angle of attack, all combined to reduce the lateral controllability of the aircraft and prevent any effective reduction of the steepening bank.

With the bank steepening so far, the A310 began to lose height. The autopilot, sensing this loss, applied nose-up elevator, further increasing the AOA towards a stalled condition. Attempts to control the aircraft's pitching manually, undoubtedly by Piskarev, then led to the complete disconnection of the autopilot. Adding to the confusion on the flightdeck, the "Autopilot Disengaged" alarm, the "Departure From Set Altitude" alarm, and the Stall Warning, all began sounding together, at about the same time as the aircraft began to buffet.

Realising all too late that the aircraft was in serious difficulties, Kudrinsky, Makarov and Piskarev all began shouting control instructions, apparently intended for El'dar, the only person on the flightdeck in effective touch with the flying controls:

Kudrinsky: "The other way!"
Piskarev: "The other way!!"
Makarov: "Turn to the left!!"
Piskarev: "Back!!"
Kudrinsky: "To the left!!"

Trying to follow these multiple, simultaneous instructions in the totally unfamiliar and bewildering environment of the aircraft's flightdeck,

The A310 flightdeck. Aeroflot's pilots, all with substantial jet transport experience, were well provided for by Airbus Industrie. The consortium's Aeroformation subsidiary undertook training for three crews per aircraft, then placed them with Western carriers for a period of line experience before they assumed their own Aeroflot A310 commands. But even senior Commander Danilov had gained less than 1,000hrs' experience on the type in more than two years since his initial training. For all the Russian aircrew, after a lifetime accustomed to Soviet design and performance philosophies, the computerised, CRT equipped flightdecks of the A310s must have seemed a revelation! Four of the six EFIS screens are visible here, the lower of each of the pilots' pairs obscured by the control columns. Both seats are approximately in their "hands-on" forward positions. Note the standby flight instruments, and the Flight Control Unit incorporating the autopilot controls on the central glareshield. The radio selectors on the centre pedestal below the thrust levers would have occupied much of Second Pilot Piskarev's attention during the flight, with almost continuous procedural reporting (most points averaging only 110km/60nm apart) and zone boundary frequency changes. His rearward seat position undoubtedly allowed easier access to these controls – a typical relaxed mid cruise monitoring position. But it is difficult to understand why neither the vivid electronic presentations on the Primary Flight Display screens, nor the coloured hemispheres of the standby Artificial Horizon, attracted any of the pilots' attention in time to avert the developing critically steep bank. (Airbus Industrie)

This majestically bleak Siberian panorama reflects both the weather and geography of the Kuznetsky region at the time of the accident. Once F-OGQS had passed the built-up areas in and around the "Kuzbas" coalfields (see adjacent map) and had overflown Novokuznetsk (10 minutes before 1.00am), the view through the A310's flightdeck windscreens would have been one of almost unbroken blackness. Isolated hamlets more than 50km (26nm) apart would have hardly pricked the darkness. The nearest major centre, Abakan, lay almost 300km (165nm) to the northeast. (Lufthansa)

with the three aural warnings sounding, and the added disorientation of the aircraft's steeply banked attitude, total darkness outside, and increasing g-force, El'dar probably felt utterly confused. Doubtless he was also thoroughly frightened, both by the situation that had developed, and what he had done to create it. He probably succeeded only in interfering with Piskarev's own limited attempts to bring the aircraft back to a level attitude.

After the autopilot disengaged, the computer controlled flight management system, designed to prevent the aircraft from attaining excessive angles of attack and stalling – the so-called 'alpha floor function' – began to take effect, automatically adjusting the tailplane trim to a nose-down setting, and deflecting the elevators nose-down from their nose-up position as well.

These actions, plus the efforts of Piskarev, although they succeeded in recovering the aircraft from its stalled condition, quickly nosed it over into a dive of about 40°. As it did so, the airspeed built up rapidly, increasing the rate of descent to a terrifying degree, and triggering the overspeed warning alarm. All the while the autothrottle continued to maintain its previously set cruising thrust on both engines.

As the aircraft dived away its height and Piskarev desperately attempted to recover, he called out, apparently to the boy in the left-hand seat: "Get it left – the ground is right here!"

Meanwhile Captain Kudrinsky was frantically trying to climb back into his seat, pleading desperately and repeatedly to his son to: "Get out! Get out!" But the boy's efforts to do so were obviously being hindered by

the extremely high load factors being imposed on the aircraft as Piskarev pulled back hard on the control column, and the narrow space between the seat and the left side of the flightdeck.

Piskarev, seeing the high indicated airspeed, called for the thrust of the engines to be reduced. But, in the extreme stress of the situation, as the aircraft responded to his hard back control column position, it appears that he might have failed to register that the Airbus had already assumed a nose-up attitude, for he seemingly continued to hold the control column fully back.

Now without any appreciable engine thrust, the aircraft pitched sharply nose-up, the airspeed fell off, it yawed to the right and then flicked into a spin to the left, with the nose-down attitude increasing to almost 90°. Piskarev now saw to his horror that the airspeed indicator, far from over registering, was showing less than 180kmh (97kt) and, in a highly agitated and emotional voice, he shouted: "Full throttle!! Full throttle!!"

Despite all his difficulties, Captain Kudrinsky had now at last managed to clamber back into his seat. But as he himself was only 170cm (5ft 7in) tall, with his seat now in its rearmost position too, access to the controls was only barely possible for him.

By the time the airspeed had risen again, the rate of spin had eased somewhat, with the bank to the left stabilised at about 20°. But with the control columns still being held fully nose-up, the aircraft again began to pitch up and the airspeed again began to decay. Half a minute later, the rate of spin began to increase once more.

With utter disaster now literally staring him in the face, Kudrinsky was probably "pumping" the rudder pedals to try to control the spinning and within a few seconds the rotation finally ceased. But the aircraft had now descended to only about 400m above the ground, and although the airspeed now rose again, there was insufficient height remaining for the plummeting A310 to recover from its dive.

Two seconds later, it struck a snow covered hillside in a near level attitude with an awesome, devastating impact.

The accident occurred less than eight minutes after the aircraft had last reported its position as over Novokuznetsk at 00.50am, and had passed its estimate for the ZAKIR reporting point, at 00.59am.

INVESTIGATION

Search and rescue action

After the A310's ETD from the Novokuznetsk (Auxiliary) Control Area had expired without any further radio contact from it, ATC at 1.01am began a number of attempts to call the Airbus, all without success.

Nearly two hours later, following information passed on to the Novokuznetsk ACC by local people in the nearby area, the Duty Controller informed airport officials that an aircraft had crashed and was burning near the tiny village of Maizas, about 100km to the east of Novokuznetsk. Ground parties and a helicopter were despatched to search the area and investigate.

At 3am, a small army team from the settlement of Little Maizas reached the scattered, burning

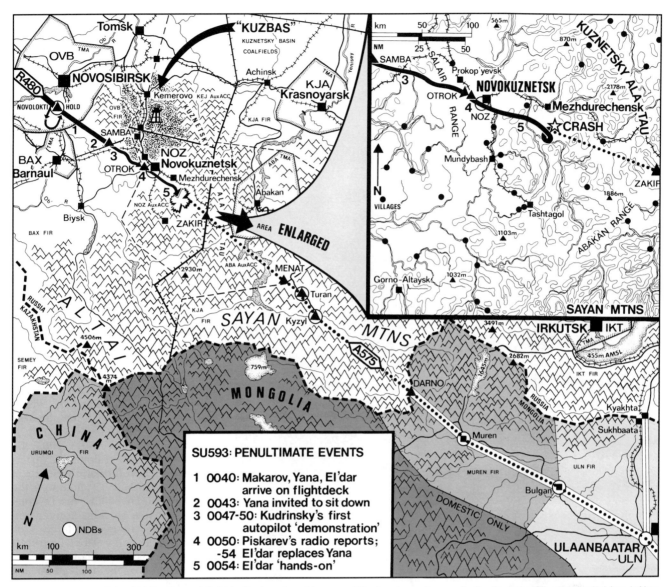

Around two hours of the A310's planned flight is displayed on this map of the border region crash site, from the Siberian capital (top left) to the Mongolian capital (lower right). From reporting point ZAKIR on the Novokuznetsk Auxiliary ACC boundary, Abakan's similar ATC unit would have taken SU593 until MENAT. Krasnoyarsk Control, the 11th Russian ACC of the flight, would have monitored the A310 as the crew began raising Mongolian controllers on HF, around Kyzyl, to receive their cross-border clearance and new Flight Level instructions.

Novosibirsk (population 1.5m) was founded in 1893 as the Trans-Siberian Railway pushed east across the swamps of the Ob' River. A major air traffic centre, its Terminal Area includes the Novolokti NDB and holding pattern, over which F-OGQS had passed just before the visitors entered the flightdeck. Two other major centres, in the hilly southern end of the "KUZnetsky BASin" (the USSR's second largest coalfields and heavy industrial area), which feature in this chapter, have coal mining associations that are centuries apart. Novokuznetsk (600,000) was founded in 1617, Mezhdurechensk (100,000) in the 1950s! The spot heights on both main map and inset are in metres, but may be converted to feet by multiplying by 3.28. (Matthew Tesch)

wreckage and began cordoning off the area. Three quarters of an hour later, the crew of a searching Mi-8 helicopter was directed to the site, and reported its co-ordinates to Novokuznetsk ATC. But because of the rugged, timbered and snow covered terrain in which the A310 had crashed, it was considered inadvisable for the helicopter to attempt a landing in the dark.

The site of the accident was in the foothills of Siberia's Kuznetsky Ala-Tau mountains, at a position 53°30'N, 88°15'E. The impact had occurred on the northeastern slope of a tree clad 600m hill, snow covered to a depth of 1.5m. The aircraft had completely disintegrated and its wreckage was largely destroyed by the explosive fire which occurred on impact. It was immediately obvious there could be no possibility of finding survivors.

Just before 7am, a four engined Antonov An-12 turboprop also reached the search area and, after its crew had located the burning wreckage visually, they were able to confirm the site's co-ordinates to ATC. Twenty minutes later, at 7.20am, another Mi-8 helicopter succeeded in landing a team to replace the initial ground search party. Other than the securing of the area, however, no examination of the wreckage was undertaken until after the arrival of the first investigators later in the morning.

Overnight, the Russian Department of Air Transport and the Ministry of Emergency Services called together a 238 strong combined response team from their own personnel, the Ministry of Defence, Air Traffic Control, the airline, various other aviation experts, and a local Novokuznetsk based operator. Together, the team mustered an Ilyushin Il-76 freighter and an An-12 transport aircraft, six helicopters, and a total of 34 vehicles for the combined investigation and recovery operation.

Evergreen and deciduous forests mix in the undulating, sometimes rugged countryside north of the Sayan and Altai regions on the Sino-Mongolian border. But as well as low bluffs and rolling hills, there are also 2100m (7000ft) mountains. This scene might almost be that of the A310 crash site, and was actually photographed in the Gorno-Altaysk area to its southwest. (via Dr M Kravchenko)

The wreckage

The accident investigators in the response team found that the A310 had struck the hillside in a nearly level attitude at an elevation of 400m (1310ft) AMSL, with the slats, flaps and undercarriage retracted, and both engines running. The impact was non survivable, all on board having died instantly from massive impact trauma. All evidence of burning was the result of post crash fire.

Over the following three days, all the remains of the A310's passengers and crew which could be recovered were taken by ground transport to hospital in Novokuznetsk.

From their detailed wreckage examination, and testing of identifiable components recovered from the debris, the investigation team established that, up to the moment that the aircraft's design load limits had been exceeded in the course of its final plunge to destruction, the operation of its engines and all its systems had been entirely normal.

The aircraft's DFDR and CVR were recovered from the wreckage and their decipherable records were subsequently analysed, including sound spectrum analysis of the CVR tape, in the laboratories of the Ministry of Internal Affairs and the Federal Counter-Intelligence Service.

Data from the two recorders not only confirmed the absence of any fault or irregularity in the operation of the aircraft, but provided a detailed account of the bizarre sequence of events which finally culminated in the catastrophe. This enabled the unfortunate human factors involvement in the development of the accident to be reconstructed with great accuracy.

Weather conditions

At the time of the accident, the regional weather was under the influence of a low pressure system, with a nearby warm front and a stable air mass. At Mezhdurechensk, only 17km from the crash site, the night was calm, with only a little high level cloud, and a visibility of 20km. The surface temperature was -5°C.

The crew

Aircraft Commander Andrei Victorovich Danilov, 40, graduated from the Sasovo College of Civil Aviation in 1973, and from the higher Academy of Civil Aviation in 1981. With a total of 9675 flying hours he was instrument rated to ICAO Cat II standard. In November 1992, he underwent A310 training at Airbus Industrie's Aeroformation centre in Toulouse. He had 950 hours on the A310 of which 895hr was in command. Prior to his conversion course, he had accumulated 4700 hours on Tupolev Tu-134 aircraft (the Soviet equivalent of the DC-9). He had not been involved in any previous accidents.

The Reserve Commander, Yaroslav Vladimirovich Kudrinsky, 39, graduated from the Kremenchug College of Civil Aviation in the Ukraine in 1975, and from the higher Academy of Civil Aviation in 1981 and was instrument rated to Cat I standard. He underwent A310 conversion training in Toronto, Canada, in 1992. He had a total of 8940 hours, 907 of which were on A310s, with 735 hours in command. He had previously accumulated 1636 hours on "pocket trijet" Yakovlev Yak-40s, 500 hours on Antonov An-12s (the Soviet equivalent of the Hercules), and 2265 hours on Ilyushin Il-76s (the Soviet Starlifter equivalent). He had not previously been involved in an accident.

Second Pilot Igor Vladimirovich Piskarev, 33, graduated from the Aktyubinsk Higher College of Civil Aviation in 1982 and was instrument rated to Cat II standard. He had a total of 5855 hours, more than 3000 of which was as a Tupolev Tu-134 Commander. He received his A310 conversion training with Aeroflot in April 1993 and at Lufthansa's simulator base in Frankfurt-Main, Germany. His line experience on A310s was 440 hours as Second Pilot, and like the other members of the crew, he had no previous accidents.

The aircraft

The Airbus A310-308, registered in France as F-OGQS msn [596], and owned by the European Bank, was on lease to Rossiiskie Aviatsionnye Linii (in English, Russian International Airlines) and had first flown at Toulouse on September 11, 1991. But at about this time, Aeroflot's planned lease of five A310 aircraft encountered difficulties. As a result, all five remained in open storage with Airbus Industrie for many months, and F-OGQS was not delivered to Moscow until December 11, 1992. In Russian service since that time, it had flown a total of 5375 hours and 846 cycles, during which it had required no unscheduled maintenance. No defects were recorded in the aircraft's logbooks, and the airworthiness of the aircraft, its engines, and its systems met all stipulated requirements.

ANALYSIS

Analysis of the accident flight was conducted using a broad range of data and spectrographic analysis from the aircraft's DFDR and CVR, as well as simulator reconstructions at Airbus Industrie in Toulouse. In addition, test flights were conducted in another A310 aircraft, and studies made of the accident aircraft's systems and components.

The chain of events which led ultimately to the accident had their beginnings when Captain Kudrinsky vacated his left-hand control seat to allow his young teenage children to sit in turn at the controls.

He did not formally hand over control to the second pilot before leaving his seat, and responsibility for the aircraft therefore still remained with him. In leaving his command position in this way, he was contravening both Russian and ICAO civil aviation requirements.

These requirements provide that "during the execution of a flight, flightcrew must be strapped into their seats ... when in their operating positions." Also that: "The captain must remain in his work position throughout the flight. Brief departures are permitted during favourable flight conditions. In such cases, the second pilot takes charge of the aircraft while the rest of the crew remain at their stations. Flightcrew

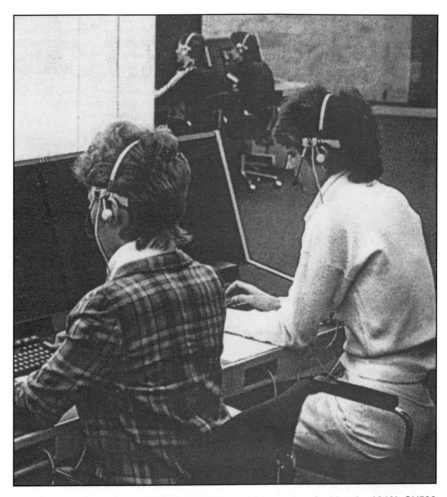

A typical Area Control room in the late Soviet era. Major centres flanking the A310's SU593 route would have been radar equipped, but the auxiliary ACCs – like Novokuznetsk – would almost certainly have been using procedural ATC methods. In the dead of a Siberian night, the unexpected silence and prolonged lack of response from F-OGQS would have created wonder, then concern and finally horror. (Matthew Tesch collection)

members must remain in their operating positions except when it is necessary to absent themselves for duties connected with the operation of the aircraft, or to satisfy personal needs."

According to the DFDR, after the captain's daughter Yana had been in his seat for about three minutes, the aircraft made a gentle turn of 9° to the left on to a heading of 102°M, achieving a maximum bank angle of 23°. It then banked 15° to the right and, after nearly three minutes more, resumed a heading of 102°M.

During the accident investigation, these heading deviations were found to correspond to the maximum

(right) Further to the east of the accident site, at a similar latitude, the settlement of Listvyanka by Lake Baikal provides a good approximation of the tiny villages of Maizas and Malyi (Little) Maizas, whose occupants were awakened by a crescendo of slipstream sound and jet engine noise, culminating in a ground shaking explosion, one minute 59 seconds before 1.00am. (Lufthansa)

(left) Another representative scene from the nearer Gorno-Altaysk area shows this hunting party making its way up a frozen river. In the early morning darkness, the dense forest and waist high snow covering rough ground would have made the going extremely hard for search parties scouring the area for the burning wreckage of the A310. (via Dr M Kravchenko)

(right) The name on the nose of F-OGQS, in red Helvetica capitals below each flightdeck side window. Mikhail Ivanovich Glinka (1804-1857) is popularly called "The Father of Russian Music". Tchaikovski (his own name graces the nose of F-OGQQ [592], the third A310) said that his contemporary "Russian symphonic school is all in 'Kamarinskaya' (Glinka's orchestral piece on two Russian folk tunes), just as the whole oak is in the acorn." All the A310s received names of famous composers – another break with past Aeroflot practice. (Encyclopaedia Britannica)

possible with the autopilot engaged in NAV mode. As the control forces applied were slight, the manoeuvres were probably executed by Captain Kudrinsky, using the autopilot's heading selector, regardless of the fact that his daughter's hands were lightly on the control yoke. Captain Kudrinsky was thus utilising the autopilot to show his daughter how the aircraft responded to the controls, while not actually in his seat.

Although the turns were no more than a demonstration for Yana, they could be regarded as a distraction for the crew from the responsibility of conducting the flight in a professional manner. Indeed, during the seven and a half minutes that Captain Kudrinsky's daughter was occupying the left-hand seat, the conversation between father and daughter did distract the crew from their monitoring of the flight. During the latter part of this time, Second Pilot Piskarev was transmitting position reports to both Novosibirsk and Novokuznetsk Area Controls, with an ETA for their next reporting point at ZAKIR, *with his right-hand seat slid back to its most rearward position.*

When Yana vacated the left-hand seat, her place was immediately taken by Captain Kudrinsky's more enthusiastic 15 year old son, El'dar. As Captain Kudrinsky spoke to him about carrying out a manoeuvre similar to the one he had shown his daughter, again using the autopilot's heading selector, the boy asked his father: "May I turn this – the control wheel – a bit?"

In agreeing so readily to his son's eager request, Kudrinsky was in effect "allowing an unauthorised person to control an aircraft for which he had neither the qualifications nor the right to do so".

His decision to do so, together with the preceding actions of both Kudrinsky and Piskarev while Yana was in the left-hand seat, demonstrated both a surprising lack of flightdeck discipline, and a startling lack of responsibility for the safe conduct of the A310's flight. The two pilots were in fact flagrantly disregarding Russian air regulations

This hangar scene from the north side of Sheremetyevo Airport shows two of the aircraft types that featured in the flying careers of the Russian pilots. In the foreground, a Tupolev Tu-134A displays the extensive nose glazing once derided by Western observers of this DC-9 counterpart. Readers might ponder the extent of the Siberian wilderness before making a judgement on the need for a navigator in the crew to maintain air schedules across such a vast and remote landmass. More than 700 Tu-134s have been Aeroflot workhorses since 1967. Unlike the DC-9, the Tupolev evolved without fuselage stretches, improvements being confined to systems and cabin arrangements. Passenger capacity has steadily increased from 56 to up to 96 on dense short sectors. For the claustrophobically inclined however, such a travel experience is hardly recommended! Behind stands Ilyushin Il-76TD SSSR-76474 [0033448409] (now RA-76474), the former Soviet equivalent of the USAF's "Starlifter" heavy transport. (ATW)

expressly forbidding "persons not connected with the execution of flight" being on the flightdeck.

Their actions as a whole were also entirely contrary to the spirit of the air regulation requiring that "... one of the pilots must keep control over the spatial position of the aircraft and maintain the predetermined flight level. When the autopilot is engaged, the crew member controlling the aircraft must warn the crew prior to carrying out a manoeuvre".

With his father's assent therefore, but before Captain Kudrinsky moved the autopilot heading selector, El'dar turned the left-hand control yoke 3-4° to the left, deflecting the port aileron upwards about 0.7°. As he held the controls in this position, the aircraft's highly sensitive autopilot immediately reacted with a countering control input, deflecting the starboard aileron upwards by about 1°. The overall result was that the force El'dar was applying to the control yoke increased to about 10kg. But it then decreased about three seconds later when Captain Kudrinsky adjusted the heading selector to the left, enabling the autopilot to conform to the altered heading.

The A310's flightdeck control columns have a spring-loaded interconnection, with a tension greater than the control forces that are normally applied during flight. The resistance encountered by the autopilot, in aileron inputs that were being changed

Mikhail Mil's design bureau specialises in helicopters, including many of the world's biggest capacity lifters. The twin Izotov turbines of the Mi-8 give it a MTOW of 12 tonnes (26,400lb) – the loaded weight of a DC-3. Sliding doors forward give entry to a 28 seat cabin, while clamshell rear doors provide a diverse cargo capability. More than 1000 Mi-8s operate in Siberia's diverse terrain and temperature extremes. Several of them logged almost 22 hours on recovery operations between the impact site and Novokuznetsk after the A310 accident. The Mi-8 shown is actually a Chinese example, its cowls open in between tourist flights. (ADC/WAFM/Stephen Simns)

This diagram depicts the two intervals during which Captain Kudrinsky was "demonstrating" flying the A310 by adjusting the autopilot – or thought he was. (The viewpoint is that of an observer beneath the A310's flightpath). On the left are the key elements of the first set of manoeuvres, with Kudrinsky using the autopilot heading selector while his daughter timidly holds the control yoke. His reengagement of the NAV mode resulted in the Airbus automatically recovering its previously set heading. A few minutes later Kudrinsky set out to repeat Yana's experience for his son (right-hand sequence), but apparently overlooked El'dar's more literal interpretation of the 'hands-on' advice. After again reselecting the NAV mode, Kudrinsky was distracted from checking that the aircraft was stabilising – as it had only minutes before. The inset sketch provides an impression of the likely positions of the children and crew at this crucial interruption. The extent of El'dar's control inputs having gone unnoticed, the holding zone proposal, so positively affirmed by both Makarov and Piskarev when the headings projected on the A310's navigational displays began to veer to the right, seems to have persuaded Kudrinsky, perhaps against his better judgement. But hadn't they overflown the Novolokti beacon and such a pattern just a short time before? (Matthew Tesch)

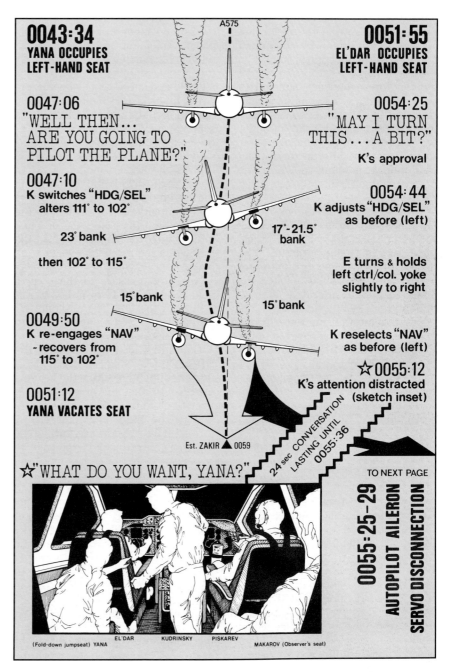

0043:34
YANA OCCUPIES
LEFT-HAND SEAT

A575

0051:55
EL'DAR OCCUPIES
LEFT-HAND SEAT

0047:06
"WELL THEN...
ARE YOU GOING TO
PILOT THE PLANE?"

0054:25
"MAY I TURN
THIS...A BIT?"

K's approval

0047:10
K switches "HDG/SEL"
alters 111° to 102°

23° bank

then 102° to 115°

17°-21.5°
bank

0054:44
K adjusts "HDG/SEL"
as before (left)

E turns & holds
left ctrl/col. yoke
slightly to right

15° bank

15° bank

0049:50
K re-engages "NAV"
- recovers from
115° to 102°

K reselects "NAV"
as before (left)

☆ **0055:12**
K's attention distracted
(sketch inset)

0051:12
YANA VACATES SEAT

Est. ZAKIR ▲ 0059

☆ "WHAT DO YOU WANT, YANA?"

24 sec CONVERSATION LASTING UNTIL 0055::36

TO NEXT PAGE

**0055:25-29
AUTOPILOT AILERON
SERVO DISCONNECTION**

(Fold-down jumpseat) YANA   EL'DAR   KUDRINSKY   PISKAREV   MAKAROV (Observer's seat)

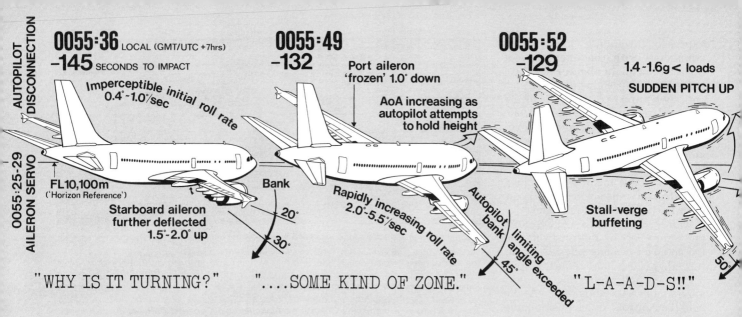

0055:36 LOCAL (GMT/UTC +7hrs)
-145 SECONDS TO IMPACT

Imperceptible initial roll rate
0.4°-1.0°/sec

FL10,100m
('Horizon Reference')

Starboard aileron
further deflected
1.5°-2.0° up

Bank
20°
30°

"WHY IS IT TURNING?"

0055:49
-132

Port aileron
'frozen' 1.0° down

AoA increasing as
autopilot attempts
to hold height

Rapidly increasing roll rate
2.0°-5.5°/sec

Autopilot bank limiting angle exceeded
45°

"....SOME KIND OF ZONE."

0055:52
-129

1.4-1.6g < loads
SUDDEN PITCH UP

Stall-verge
buffeting

50°

"L-A-A-D-S!!"

---

in both magnitude and direction, apparently led to fluctuating, contradictory signals from the electronic sensors of the autopilot computers and the restrained control yoke.

Thus, when the opposing control column forces had accumulated to between 11-13kg, they automatically triggered the aileron circuit's torque limiter, disconnecting the autopilot servo from the aileron linkage. After the inadvertent aileron disconnection, the forces being applied to the control column promptly decreased to between 5-7kg.

The Flight Crew Operations Manual for the A310 warns that overriding the autopilot is not a normal procedure and is to be avoided: "The means of overriding the autopilot are to allow for safety outside the limits of normal aircraft operation. Should there be any suspicion of abnormal behaviour in the aircraft when the autopilot is engaged in the Command mode, disengage the autopilot immediately.

"WARNING: Do not make any attempt to correct the trajectory of flight by exerting force on the control column if the autopilot is not first disengaged."

Disengagement of the autopilot servo from the aileron linkage by restraining the control column, the investigation found, occurs at an exerted force of between 11-13kg. Exerting force, either by restraining or displacing one of the control columns, allows the precise moment of disconnection to be determined. *When both control columns are restrained or displaced at the same time, the forces may be distributed in such a way that pilots may not notice the moment of disengagement.*

After the autopilot servo's discon-

nection from the aileron linkage, the aircraft's instrumentation continued to display the autopilot's previously programmed mode. But the autopilot itself remained otherwise fully functional, stabilising the aircraft's altitude and speed.

The investigators believed that the operational status of the autopilot's selected mode should be displayed on the instrument panel. The display should indicate if there is any rejection of a selected mode, or when there is an accidental variation in the selected mode.

In summary, it was evident to the investigation that, after the boy had moved into the captain's seat, the following sequence of events took place:
• Applying pressure to the control yoke, El'dar tried to turn the aircraft a little to the left. The autopilot resisted this control interference to counter the resulting bank.
• Captain Kudrinsky engaged the HDG/SEL (Heading Select) mode of the autopilot, and turned the heading selector to the left more than 15° from the initial heading of 105°M.
• With the bank angle increasing through 17-19°, Kudrinsky turned the selector control back to the right to re-acquire the 105°M heading, and the A310 rolled through a wings-level position and began to bank and turn to the right.
• As the aircraft reached a right bank of between 3-5°, Kudrinsky re-engaged the NAV mode of the autopilot, and the aircraft promptly increased its bank angle from 6° to 15° as it continued rolling to the right in an attempt to return to its commanded heading of 105°M. At this stage on the flightdeck, continuing comments by Yana, sitting or standing behind her brother's

position, distracted her father from monitoring both El'dar's actions and the aircraft's attitude.
• With the aircraft already banked 15° to the right, and with the control yoke being held 3-5° to the right, the autopilot's attempts to reduce these values, as the aircraft approached its commanded heading of 105°M, resulted in the exerted control column forces increasing to between 11-13kg. Automatically, and without any instrument indications, the autopilot servo disconnected from the aileron linkages.

Had Second Pilot Piskarev been holding or restraining his control column *on his own* at this stage, he could not have failed to notice the autopilot disconnection.

There was evidence on the DFDR of an application of force on the right-hand control yoke which showed that both El'dar and Piskarev were holding their respective control yokes at this time. The control forces could have been distributed between the two in such a way that the moment of disengagement went unrecognised by Second Pilot Piskarev – either because of the light pressure he might have been applying, or because he might have assumed that the changes in control force were inputs from El'dar.

The partial disengagement of the autopilot thus went unnoticed – by either Kudrinsky or Piskarev. The absence of any reference to the autopilot in the CVR recording of flightdeck conversation at this stage of the flight is further evidence of this fact.

Altogether, several factors could explain why the pilots did not notice the autopilot disconnection, either at the time it occurred or subsequently.
• Ignorance, on the part of Kudrinsky

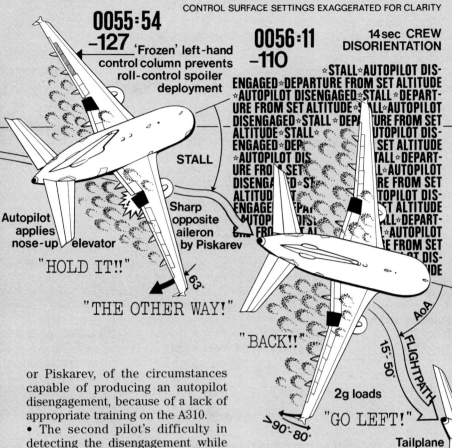

0055:54
–127

'Frozen' left-hand control column prevents roll-control spoiler deployment

STALL

Autopilot applies nose-up elevator

"HOLD IT!!"

"THE OTHER WAY!"

63°

0056:11
–110

14 sec CREW DISORIENTATION

☆STALL☆AUTOPILOT DIS-ENGAGED☆DEPARTURE FROM SET ALTITUDE ☆AUTOPILOT DISENGAGED☆STALL☆DEPART-URE FROM SET ALTITUDE☆STALL☆AUTOPILOT DISENGAGED☆STALL☆DEPARTURE FROM SET ALTITUDE☆STALL☆AUTOPILOT DIS-ENGAGED☆DEP...SET ALTITUDE ☆AUTOPILOT DIS...STALL☆DEPART-URE FROM SET...LL☆AUTOPILOT DISENGA...D☆ST...URE FROM SET ALTITUD...ALL☆DEPART-ENGAGE...AL...ST ALTITUDE ...AUTOP...DIS...ALL☆DEPART-...FRO...A...☆AUTOPILOT...RE FROM SET...T DIS-...DE

Sharp opposite aileron by Piskarev

"BACK!!"

AoA

FLIGHTPATH

15° 50°

2g loads

>90° 80°

"GO LEFT!"

Tailplane reset nose down

On this and the following double page spread, a spectacular sequence of Matthew Tesch drawings reconstructs the final two and a half minutes of F-OGQS's flight. By assessing DFDR traces and timings against previous research data, Russian investigators demonstrated that the accelerating rate of change in angle of bank, heading and g-forces, in the critical situation that was developing, was initially of "sub-threshold cognitive levels". In other words, the insidious change in these values began too imperceptibly for even sensitive human inner ear mechanisms to detect in the visually-referenceless Siberian night. By this time, the illegalities of the children's 'demonstrations' had given way to more disastrous lapses of airmanship – Kudrinsky's failure to hand over responsibility for the aircraft to Piskarev when he vacated the left-hand seat, and Piskarev's negligence, even in these circumstances, in not repositioning his seat forward where he could monitor the aircraft's manoeuvres while the children were occupying the left-hand seat and the 'demonstrations' were taking place. Even without prompting from Kudrinsky, sound airmanship would have dictated that Piskarev did so as his senior was unbuckling himself from his command seat. From this point on, the late and inadequate crew reactions were insufficient to avert the fatal loss of control.

0056:18
–103

'ALPHA-FLOOR' FUNCTION

AoA reduces to ≤7.0°

0056:28
–93

Full nose-up elevator by 0056:38

200m/sec (39,870fpm) dive

740kmh 400kIAS

4.6~4.7g

"GET OUT! GET OUT! GET OUT! GET O..."

"THRUST LEVERS TO SLOW!"

or Piskarev, of the circumstances capable of producing an autopilot disengagement, because of a lack of appropriate training on the A310.

• The second pilot's difficulty in detecting the disengagement while handling his own control column, either because of force on it, or because he assumed that the feel of it was the result of El'dar's handling of the controls.

• The absence of any aircraft warning system drawing attention to the disconnection.

With both control yokes still being held slightly to the right, the bank to the right then began to increase further. But this was so gradual at first that the pilots also failed to notice it.

Within seven seconds, the bank had increased from 15° to 20° and at this stage the rate of roll increased slightly. Tests established that, with the autopilot disconnected from the aileron linkages, an additional force as small as 1-2kg on one of the control yokes would have been enough to produce such an increase in roll rate. The total force on the control yokes would then have been of the order of 5-7kg.

The roll rate continued to increase to 5.5° per second – and the angle of bank exceeded 30°, the limit for a fully operational autopilot manoeuvre, passing 45° about 40 seconds after Kudrinsky had selected the autopilot to the NAV mode. This 45° angle was significant as it is an operational limitation on the A310 – on reaching this bank angle, part of the data displayed on the pilots' EFIS screens disappears.

Meanwhile El'dar, still at the controls in the left-hand seat, had finally become aware that something about the flight was changing, prompting him to ask his father, "Why is it turning?" The question prompted speculation and discussion between all three pilots on the flightdeck as to the reason why the aircraft appeared to be "turning by itself".

Despite the lack of any confirming data on the pilots' EFIS screens, both Piskarev and Kudrinsky apparently accepted off duty Captain Makarov's suggestion that the aircraft's autopilot had "captured" a holding pattern.

Unlikely though this may seem to Western readers, much of Russian airspace fairly bristles with reporting points, short sectors, and a great number of NDBs, and such a "capture" could be quite possible with the A310's highly computerised Flight Management System. Indeed, the aircraft had overflown the Novolokti NDB, and its published holding pattern south of Novosibirsk, only moments before the visitors had arrived on the flightdeck (see previous map).

It is also possible that a false route

The feelings of the cabin crew and sleepy passengers, undoubtedly bored by the long night flight over dark, almost featureless terrain, can barely be imagined as the widebody aircraft suddenly nosed up, stalled and flicked into a spin, followed by a high speed dive and extreme g-forces. After the autopilot disengaged fully, the aircraft nosed down steeply, quickly reaching its terminal velocity and a decent rate of almost 40,000fpm before being subjected to excessive load factors as the crew made attempts to recover. Even the DFDR recordings were distorted by aerodynamic loads. The CVR tape made it clear that Piskarev, then Kudrinsky, fought to bring the aircraft back under control all the way down. Even so, the A310's descent rate was still around 14,000fpm when it struck the ground. (Matthew Tesch)

AIRSPEED FALLING BELOW
13+sec DIVE
185–220kmh
100–119knots
THRUST REDUCED

0056:41
–80

or course line could have unexpectedly appeared on the Horizontal Situation Indicator EFIS screens. In such an event, Piskarev could have taken it to be a "holding zone". Subsequent to the accident, investigators found that false tracks or extended heading lines had occurred on EFIS navigational displays several times in the past – during a simulator experiment, during a test flight, and during normal operation of another Aeroflot A310. Further enquiries established that the developers of the FMS and its software were themselves unable to rule out the possibility of such false trajectories appearing on the screens on rare occasions.

By the time the aircraft's angle of bank had increased to 50° some 12 seconds later, the autopilot, with its autothrottle function still engaged, was no longer able to maintain the aircraft's programmed flight level and airspeed, despite the fact that both its angle of attack and g-loading had been steadily increasing, and the A310 began to lose height.

A load factor of 1.6g was recorded on the DFDR as the aircraft began to buffet, indicated by high frequency oscillations of both lateral and vertical loads, as the aircraft verged on the stall. During the investigation, a similar DFDR recording was obtained on an A310 during a test flight at Mach 0.8.

At the same time as the buffeting began, the aircraft abruptly pitched up, steepening its attitude from 4.5° to 10° nose-up in only two seconds, with almost no change in either tailplane or elevator settings. At this stage of the flight, fuel burn had reduced the aircraft's all-up weight to 122 tonnes, and its CofG had moved aft to around 36% MAC. The same post accident A310 test flight, with an identical CofG and a similar AUW of 116 tonnes, also produced this same aircraft response.

About this time, probably as the aircraft's load factor increased past 1.4g, the crew at last reacted with surprised concern. Had the A310 been fitted with a warning system which drew attention to the extreme

bank angle, the aircraft's attitude might well have been recognised much earlier – and corrected before it developed so dangerously.

The pilots' failure to detect the aircraft's steep bank could be attributed to a combination of factors:
• They were preoccupied with finding reasons why the aircraft was turning.
• Captain Kudrinsky, standing behind the left-hand seat, could have failed to notice the indications of the artificial horizon, perhaps because they were obscured from his position, or possibly because his attention had been diverted by another remark from Makarov: "Set the gyro to normal for him".
• The lack of crew readiness generally, resulting in delay in recognising and reacting to the aircraft's developing unusual attitude.

Numerous investigations into flightcrew behaviour have established that, even after a brief distraction from a monitoring or control task, it takes no less than three seconds for a pilot to fully re-adapt his concentration. Prolonged distractions of attention require considerably longer – up to 10 or 11 seconds for the necessary pilot re-adaptation. In the case of Captain Kudrinsky, one distraction occupied at least 24 seconds – from when he responded to his daughter: "What do you want, Yana?", until El'dar asked: "Why is it turning?"

Finally however, the increasing g-forces, as much as the aircraft's aerodynamic buffeting on the threshold of its stall, became the trigger for the crew's shocked reaction to the aircraft's extreme attitude.

With the A310 now banked 63° to the right, a vigorous deflection of the starboard aileron to 14° down, consistent with a sharp turn of the right-hand yoke to the left to counter the roll, was recorded on the DFDR, while the left-hand yoke remained firmly gripped in position for 3-4 seconds, the disparity in the yoke positions being taken up by the heavy springs in the aileron circuit linkage.

As a consequence of the left-hand

yoke being "frozen" in this almost neutral position however, neither the port aileron, nor the three roll-control spoilers of the outboard five on the port wing, deflected at all. The increasing angle of attack, combined with this lack of control response on one side, reduced the lateral controllability of the aircraft, preventing any effective reduction of the steepening bank which, 19 seconds after Piskarev had turned his yoke sharply to the left, finally reached a full 90°.

Aerodynamic analysis of this evidence showed however, that the blocking of the left-hand control yoke did not really have a decisive effect on lateral control, because the aircraft had already exceeded its 45° limiting bank angle and was now at such a high angle of attack.

Six seconds had elapsed between the time the aircraft passed its 45° bank angle limit (indicated by the deletion of some of the data on the pilots' EFIS screens), and when Piskarev attempted to counter the increasing bank – and this itself was two seconds after the onset of the pre-stall buffeting. Yet Piskarev's reaction time, including the process of detection, recognition, assessment and decision making, was typical of measured pilot response times, especially considering the conditions then prevailing on the A310 flight-deck.

About two seconds after Piskarev turned his control yoke sharply to the left, the DFDR recorded a short, sharp turn of it to the right, further, if momentarily, increasing the bank, before the yoke was returned to the left. This brief movement probably resulted from the second pilot's failure to understand the aircraft's apparently sluggish response to full left aileron deflection, and his need to check what he was doing.

Had the second pilot corrected the increasing bank with a control input six seconds earlier, before the bank angle exceeded 40°, the ailerons

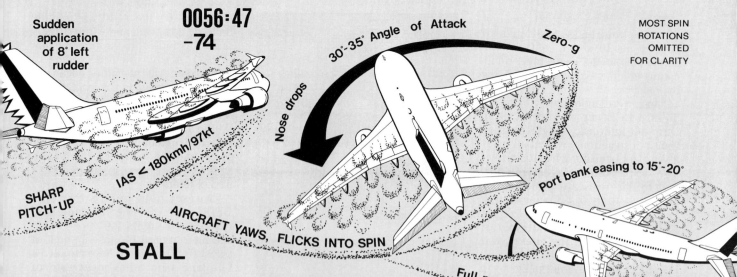

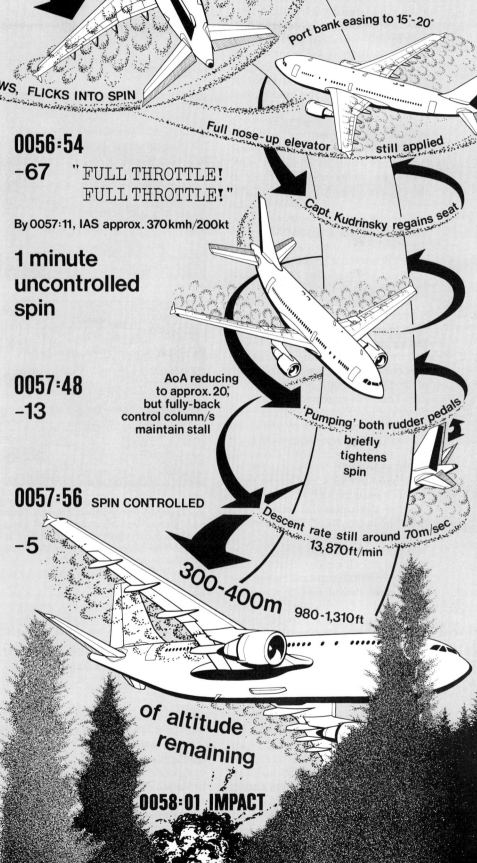

would still have had sufficient effect to roll the aircraft back towards a wings level attitude. Piskarev's attempted correction thus came too late – and one of the reasons for this was the absence of any warning system on the flightdeck that the limiting bank angle had been attained.

It also has to be said that the crew's reactions as they were attempting to correct the bank were, on the whole, inadequate in the circumstances. In the situation that was developing, the appropriate action to bring the aircraft back under control should have been:
• full disengagement of the autopilot, either by the control column switch, or by applying strong forward pressure on the control column, thereby completely overriding the autopilot;
• pushing the control column forward would also have countered the pitch-up and decreased the AOA – correcting the roll and restoring the aircraft to balanced flight before the onset of the buffeting;
• decreasing the engine thrust as a last resort.

As the bank steepened further and the aircraft began to lose height, the autopilot deflected the elevators into a 6.5° nose-up attitude. This, following the sudden pitch-up that occurred earlier, dramatically increased the AOA, and the aircraft began to stall.

On the flightdeck, the "Departure from Set Altitude" alarm sounded twice, together with the "Autopilot Disengaged" and Stall Warning alarms. It is likely that the Stall Warning was drowned out by the other two signals, and although it sounded for only four seconds, the onset of the buffeting at about the same time was itself an unmistakable indication that the aircraft was about to stall.

Throughout the next 21 seconds, Captains Kudrinsky and Makarov both began to shout control input commands at the same time, duplicating commands being called out by Piskarev.

These were undoubtedly being addressed to El'dar who, in trying to carry out Kudrinsky's and Makarov's frantic instructions, was in all probability interfering with Piskarev's own desperate efforts, severely limited by his rearward seat position and reach, to try to bring the aircraft back under control.

During the 14 second interval that followed, in which the aircraft was banked nearly 90° to the right, with load factors of the order of 2g, and a descending flightpath varying from 15° to 50° nose-down, it is likely that the pilots became disorientated. There are no exercises or drills in the course of normal airline flight-crew training programs on the recovery of aircraft from complex, unusual attitude situations with bank and pitch angles as extreme as those encountered by this A310 crew.

Subsequent elevator deflections – from 6.5° to 2.5°, then to 7.5° nose-up – were apparently the result of El'dar's inadvertent interference with Piskarev's attempts to control the aircraft's pitching. As a result, the control column forces increased to more than 15kg, leading to a complete disconnection of the autopilot and the three alarms sounding. Second Pilot Piskarev did not react to this disengagement by operating the autopilot disconnect switch on his control column, with the result that the Autopilot Disengaged warning continued to sound every three seconds until impact.

After the autopilot disengaged fully, the automatic flight system designed to prevent the aircraft from attaining excessive angles of attack (the 'alpha floor function'), came into play, initially trimming the tailplane nose-down, and at the same time moving the elevators from their 7.5° nose-up position to 2.5° nose-down as well.

With Piskarev's own attempts to recover from the stall, the cumulative effect of nose-down control application certainly reduced the aircraft's AOA – but increased its rate of descent to 200 metres per second (39,370fpm!), sharply increased the load factor being imposed on the aircraft, and triggered the overspeed warning alarm. Throughout this time, the autothrottle system continued to maintain cruising speed thrust levels on both engines.

Whatever systemic flaws or shortcomings the Soviet air transport industry may have had, aircrew education and actual flying skills were not among them. Indeed, it is probably fair to observe that Aeroflot pilots were better and more fully informed aeronautically than many of their Western counterparts. Equally, the type of airline flying that was done so routinely over vast and diverse terrain, in sound but unsophisticated aircraft, with limited ground facilities, demanded pilots that were "aviators" in the old sense of the word. Deficiencies of equipment, rather than differences of method or lack of ability, feature more often in the air safety records of the USSR and Russia. (MT; Aviareklama)

Piskarev's exclamations – "Get it left!" and "The ground is right here!" – seven seconds after the autopilot disengaged completely, suggest he had regained some sense of attitude orientation, and that the aircraft was being brought out of its steep bank.

However, now diving at an angle of about 40°, the A310 was rapidly building up speed, and within 10 seconds was indicating around 750kmh (420kt). At this time, according to DFDR data, the elevators began deflecting upwards as the control columns were pulled back in an attempt to recover from the steep dive. Within another 10 seconds the elevators had reached the limit of their travel and the load factor had risen to 4.7g – in excess of the aircraft's design limits.

Two seconds before this, the DFDR recorded the tailplane trim resetting from its 3.5° nose-down setting to its full 14° nose-up limit of travel. Yet this would have entailed a tailplane trim adjustment rate of more than five degrees per second, which is technically impossible on the A310. The only explanation is that the extremely high aerodynamic loads being developed had deformed the airframe in the vicinity of the tailplane position sensor.

As a result, the sensor could have provided unreliable data on the tailplane settings to both the DFDR and the elevator control system, and the actual position of the tailplane trim was probably considerably less. The forces being developed in the elevator control system were thus lower than normal, enabling Piskarev to pull his control column almost fully back into the maximum nose-up position. This, together with his subsequent call to reduce engine thrust, was without doubt a desperate response to the high airspeed and rate of descent.

Yet, although the aircraft was now recovering into a steep nose-up attitude, the control columns continued to be held fully back. The reason for this can never be known. But it seems possible that, in the situation of extreme stress, and because he had not fully regained orientation, Piskarev might have failed to realise just what the aircraft's true attitude was at this stage.

It is also possible that the continuing rearward position of the control columns could have a more mundane explanation: with the aircraft now so wildly out of control, and his own seat so agonisingly far back that he could do little about it, Piskarev might have been making a desperate effort to haul himself forward, using the only object within his reach – the control column itself! It is also possible of course that El'dar's overwhelmingly confused reactions to the nightmare that had suddenly engulfed him could have contributed to the situation.

Whatever the reason, the aircraft was now pitched sharply nose-up, with almost full up elevator. So, with the thrust reduced to flight idle, the airspeed quickly fell to around 200kmh (107kt). At this point, a sudden application of rudder yawed the aircraft steeply to the right, still with Piskarev's control yoke deflected to the left.

Thus, only 13 seconds after its recovery from the high speed dive began, the aircraft was placed in a classic stall-spin situation: full nose-up elevator, low airspeed, opposite aileron, and a sudden rudder input. Inevitably, the aircraft stalled, reaching an AOA of more than 30°, and flicked into an uncontrollable spin to the left, with the nose-down attitude increasing to almost 90°, and the load factor reducing to zero (weightlessness).

It was not possible to determine exactly how the rudder input occurred at this point. The left rudder pedal could have been trodden on by El'dar in his frantic efforts to vacate the left-hand seat under his father's desperate urgings. Similarly, it could have been an accidental push by Captain Kudrinsky as he hastily clambered into the seat, or it could have been the result of an involuntary extension of Kudrinsky's foot or leg as he quickly applied aileron.

All that can be said with certainty is that the rudder input did not come from either Piskarev, whose feet could not reach the pedals from his seat's rearmost position, or from the autopilot, which by this time was fully disengaged.

And, although Captain Kudrinsky was now back in the left-hand seat, the aircraft had already been in an extremely high rate of descent for 10 seconds and, at the moment Piskarev shouted for full power, was almost vertically nose-down and accelerating again.

Despite the fact that Kudrinsky's slid-back seat allowed him only limited control, the rate of spin had slowed within 15 seconds, the bank angle was evening out at about 20° to the left, the angle of attack had decreased and the airspeed was rising to 370kmh (200kt).

There is every reason to believe that, had the control column been relaxed even to a neutral position at this stage, the aircraft could have been brought under control. However, because the elevator remained deflected fully nose-up, the aircraft again began to pitch up, and the airspeed began to fluctuate and decay once again.

Half a minute later, with the left bank still around 20°, opposite aileron, the nose pitched up 20° under the effect of full nose-up elevator, the sudden application of opposite rudder resulted in the rate of spin increasing again.

But further coarse applications of rudder, obviously made in an attempt to stop the spin, were successful after about eight seconds and the aircraft's airspeed again increased through more than 370kmh (200kt) as it once more came out of the spin into a dive. This time the rate of descent was not quite so extreme, but it was still about 70m per second – a terrifying 13,800 feet per minute!

But only 300-400m of height now remained above the snow covered ground and, five seconds later, even as the A310 was finally beginning a recovery, it plunged with an enormous impact into the snow-covered hillside.

CONCLUSIONS

The loss of the A310 resulted from its stalling, spinning, and ground impact, as a consequence of a combination of the following factors:

1 Captain Kudrinsky permitting an unauthorised person, who had neither the right nor the qualifications, to occupy his command seat and to interfere with the control of the aircraft.

2 His demonstration, using the autopilot, of manoeuvres that were neither authorised in the flightplan, nor warranted by any operational reason, while not occupying his control seat.

3 Forces applied to the control columns that interfered with the normal operation of the autopilot and led to the disconnection of the autopilot servo from its aileron linkages.

4 The failure of the captain and the second pilot to notice the autopilot servo's disconnection from the aileron linkages, probably because of:

• The lack of any warning system on the A310 indicating that the autopilot had disconnected. Such a warning system, in accordance with the recommendations of international practice, could have ensured the autopilot's disengagement was noticed at the time and prevented the dangerous situation from developing.

• Possible ignorance on the part of the second pilot and the captain of the factors capable of triggering an autopilot disconnection, and of the action to be taken in such a situation. This information was included

If the costs of a fleetwide livery change can daunt airlines like United or Delta, then the changed circumstances of Aeroflot made such considerations unaffordable luxuries. The sudden focus of attention on the already conspicuous Russian Airbuses after the accident probably hastened their livery reversion. Interestingly, the winged hammer & sickle emblem has returned, balanced against the fin's Russian tricolour. F-OGQR [593] "Rachmaninov" is seen here, rolling out after landing on Sydney's Runway 34, not long after the loss of "Glinka". After its initial five orders, Aeroflot not only replaced "Glinka" but went on to build its fleet to more than 10 A310s. Four ex Delta and PanAm A310-300s with PW4152 engines have also been leased in Aeroflot's 12xFirst, 35xBusiness, 136xEconomy configuration. Even well into 1998, few Il-96/Ms and Tu-204s had yet entered revenue service. (Rob Finlayson)

neither in the airline's A310 Flight Crew Operations Manual, nor in its crew training program.

• The difficulty experienced by the second pilot in identifying the autopilot disconnection physically, either because of his lax grip on the control column, or because he took the changes in column feel to be the result of El'dar's actions.

• The captain's absence from his control seat, and his distraction from monitoring the aircraft during conversation with his daughter.

5 The unintentional, slight turning of the controls after lateral disconnection of the autopilot, which led to a further increase in right bank.

6 The failure of both the captain and the second pilot to notice the bank was increasing beyond the normal operating limit, because they were distracted by trying to determine the cause of the roll, and because they took this manoeuvre to be typical of an entry into a holding pattern. A warning system to alert the crew that the maximum permitted bank angle had been exceeded could have facilitated earlier recognition of the developing roll.

7 The autopilot, in continuing to attempt to maintain its preset height and heading after disconnection of its servo's aileron linkage, caused the aircraft to attain steep angles of attack and the onset of buffeting.

8 The inadequate action of the second pilot in not pushing his control column fully forward and disengaging the autopilot when the aircraft began buffeting in a steep turn. The resulting stall and spin could have been caused by:

• the unauthorised occupant of the

left-hand seat delaying the captain's access to the controls;

• the second pilot's difficult control position, with his seat slid back to its rearmost setting;

• the initiation, two seconds after the onset of buffeting, of a sharp nose-up pitch and an abruptly increased angle of attack, and the resulting deterioration in lateral controllability of the aircraft;

• the crew's lack of preparedness in reacting to these situations, because of training program inadequacies;

• a temporary loss of attitude orientation in the dark, featureless conditions.

DEFICIENCIES

• A general absence of regulations or statutory guidelines concerning the certification of foreign manufactured aircraft for civil aviation operations in the Russian Federation, and deficiencies in training and operational documentation for such types.

• Inadequate provision by Aeroflot of specialised monitoring equipment, particularly that relating to foreign manufactured flight recorder readouts.

• A lack of primary and recurrent training for Russian airline pilots on recovery from unusual attitudes or manoeuvres.

• Insufficient supervision of Aeroflot operations by the Ministry of Transport and Department of Air Transport regional offices.

RECOMMENDATIONS

• With a view to improving State supervision of flight safety, State inspection units should be strengthened and adequate provision made

to staff them with suitably qualified specialist personnel.

• Technological and disciplinary measures should be taken to improve the monitoring and control of flights, and their observance of flight regulations, with more adequate use of flight recorders to record audio and parametric data.

• Flightcrew training should be improved, taking particular account of the deficiencies in instrument flight and operational techniques for recovery from unusual attitudes, revealed in this accident investigation.

• Specific statutory regulations and procedures should be developed for Russian Federation certification of foreign manufactured aircraft and their accompanying documentation.

• The possibility of establishing a system of Russian training centres, dedicated to the operation of foreign manufactured airliner types, should be examined.

• With the co-operation of aircraft manufacturers, and the participation of scientific research specialists from Russian Federation organisations, investigations should be conducted into the operation and inadvertent disconnection of autopilots.

Comment:

This was a totally unnecessary tragedy – so what more can be said of such an amazing exercise in flightdeck mismanagement?

"How small are the seeds of disaster," a highly experienced Australian air safety investigator once commented of a complex fatal accident on which he was preparing a final report. His discernment has continued to ring true – time and again, major aviation catastrophes have had their origin in events that, at the time, probably seemed minor or insignificant.

The loss of the Aeroflot A310 is surely such a case. The chain of events that ultimately led to the complete destruction of a superb, near new, high technology airliner, and took the lives of 63 trusting passengers, not to mention the innocent crew members involved, could so easily have been countered at its beginning. With only a modicum more vigilance and attention to basic airmanship, the small 'drama' on the flightdeck which set off that fatal chain of events would have become no more than a passing minor incident.

This is far from being the first time "an unauthorised person" has been allowed to occupy a "command seat and to interfere with the control of the aircraft". Certainly, to permit a

15 year old boy to do so in the course of a regular public transport flight carrying fare-paying passengers was highly irregular and a gross abrogation of flying discipline by a senior airline pilot. But this breach of professional conduct *did not in itself cause the accident*, and it has to be admitted that such unauthorised "flying demonstrations" have taken place elsewhere at other times without seriously endangering the safety of an aircraft.

Rather, it seems that what really set the stage for the accident was the captain's failure to hand over responsibility for the aircraft to the second pilot when he vacated his left-hand seat, and equally, the second pilot's failure to reposition his seat further forward where he could safely monitor the aircraft's manoeuvres while the "demonstration" was taking place. Had these elementary precautions been observed, the aircraft attitudes that developed so unexpectedly and unobserved could have been easily checked before they became extreme.

But even though Captain Kudrinsky neglected to formally hand over to Piskarev before he left his seat, Piskarev himself seems to have been inexplicably negligent in not taking matters into his own hands to properly monitor the aircraft while the left-hand seat was occupied by the children. Piskarev was certainly the junior of the three pilots rostered to crew the A310 to Hong Kong, but he was by no means just a raw first officer.

The Russian designation of 'second pilot' on Aeroflot aircraft conveys an authority greater than that of the West's concept of 'first officer', and Piskarev, like his colleagues aboard the A310, was a 'Pilot First Class'. He also had more than 3000 hours' experience in command of Tupolev Tu-134 twinjet aircraft. That such a capable and experienced pilot was content to let his seat remain at its most rearward position, while untutored children fiddled with the controls, seems to defy rational explanation.

It is perhaps understandable in the circumstances that Piskarev did not notice the autopilot's aileron disengagement when it occurred. What is less comprehensible is the apparent oversight, or even the disregard, by both pilots of the clear warning contained in their Aeroflot A310 operations manual that overriding the autopilot was to be avoided. Yet Kudrinsky was in effect allowing his son to do just this when he agreed to

Two points distinguish this photograph. Foremost is the Ilyushin Il-62 itself, and this angle shows why aviation writers have diplomatically ascribed its similarity to the VC-10 as the result of "an equivalent design paradigm". In fact, Sergei Ilyushin's flagship was at least partly the product of GRU (military intelligence) espionage at Vickers and BAC. With its economics more subsidised than the VC-10's and for much longer, it has been a good all-round performer for Aeroflot, and has become as difficult to retire as to replace. When pushed to its maximum load and range capabilities however, its trim and CofG become sensitive and its takeoff climb and landing approach profiles noticeably flatter. At high all-up weights, the Il-62 has little available in handling margins, and many of the type's losses over the years have been the result of engine failure in such a condition.
Noteworthy in the picture too, is the Sheremetyevo-1 apron position of SSSR-86606 [71402]. As the first USA-USSR air services agreements were being prepared for joint operations by Pan American and Aeroflot between New York and Moscow, the elliptical, six-bay "Jet Clipper" terminal at JFK was being developed. Its soaring overhanging roof design was promptly matched by a circular extension at Sheremetyevo, with an even more dramatic covering and a first floor enclosed walkway linking it with the low set terminal halls. But by the end of the 1980s, Soviet airport officials were privately admitting it to be an eyesore, hindering to apron operations and passenger flows, and were planning its demolition. (Matthew Tesch collection)

let him turn the control yoke with the autopilot engaged.

The other aspect in the development of this accident which defies understanding is how all three experienced pilots on the flightdeck could have failed to notice the aircraft's bank was becoming excessive. Had they done so before it became extreme, there would surely have been time for Piskarev to move his seat forward, take the controls, and correct the aircraft's attitude before it stalled.

The reader can only wholeheartedly agree with the official Russian conclusion that the crew exhibited a woeful lack of preparedness in reacting to the situation that was developing.

Could this possibly have been because of their relatively recent experience with the A310's highly sophisticated Flight Management System? Had that system's very effectiveness lulled them all into the belief that the aircraft would continue to fly safely as programmed – and they had all 'mentally switched off' as a result?

The total flightdeck preoccupation with the fact that the A310 was turning for an unknown reason, to the detriment of any apparent awareness of its developing attitude, recalls a night accident to an Eastern Air Lines Lockheed L-1011 TriStar in the Everglades National park, Florida, at the end of 1972 (see *Air Disaster*, Vol 1, Chapter 9).

In that instance, the TriStar was flying in total darkness at 2000ft on autopilot under the guidance of its Avionic Flight Control System (an earlier version of the A310's FMS). The AFCS had been placed in the Altitude Hold mode while the three flightcrew gave their full attention to determining why the green 'down' indicator lamp for the noseleg had not illuminated when the undercarriage was lowered prior to landing at Miami.

Undetected by the crew however, the Altitude Hold function disengaged when the captain inadvertently pushed his control yoke lightly as he turned round to speak to the flight engineer. From that moment on, as the crew continued to investigate the undercarriage indication system fault, the TriStar gradually lost height. Four and a half minutes later, as the radio altimeter warning began beeping, both the first officer and the captain finally saw the altimeter indications were reading almost zero. "Hey – what's happening here!" the captain exclaimed, a remark almost exactly echoed by Captain Kudrinsky 21 years later.

But it was too late – seconds later the TriStar gouged into the soft ground of the Everglades swampland and broke up, killing 99 of the aircraft's 176 occupants.

During the investigation of that accident – one of the first involving an advanced technology aircraft with a computerised automatic flight control system – it was found that crews were relying more and more on such systems to fly their aircraft, particularly as the reliability of the new technology increased.

The A310's advanced technology flight control system was still relatively novel to the Aeroflot pilots, and a similar crew attitude might well be the underlying explanation for the events which finally led to the disastrous loss of control.

Footnotes:
(1) As customary in this book, local times have been used throughout this chapter (GMT/UTC + 7hrs), the accident to F-OGQS thus occurring two minutes before 1.00am on March 23, 1994. Yet official aviation records document the loss of this A310 by reference to Greenwich time – 5.58pm GMT/UTC on March 22, 1994.
(2) Although every effort has been made to use names in accordance with post Soviet nomenclature, some confusion may remain. "Soviet" or "Soviet Union" may be taken to refer to the 1917-1991 era, or to Bolshevik or Communist influences before or since those years. From 1991, with the demise of the USSR and the formalisation of the CIS, "Russia" and "Russian Federation" resume their correct meaning.

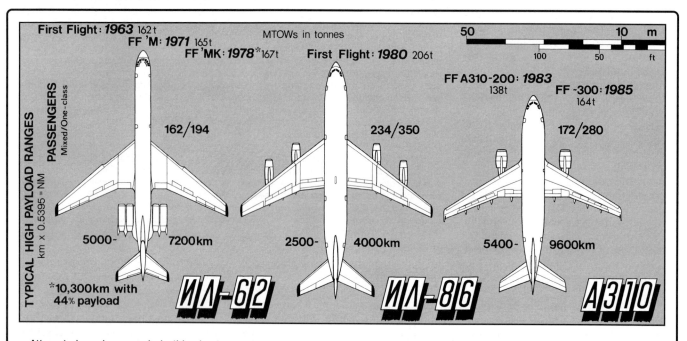

Attempts have been made in this chapter to give the reader a political and operational perspective on the A310's presence in post Soviet Russia. These same-scale plan drawings encapsulate the relative merits of the three airliners discussed, yielding some interesting insights. Simply put, the A310 could do the job of an Il-62 with half the engines and twice the aisles. Although the Ilyushin's published range came to be a respectable 10,000km (5400nm), in practice its four thirsty Soloviev turbofans limited its maximum payload range, with reserves, to 7200km (3900nm) or less. (And then only with the hope that the aircraft had sufficient runway for takeoff!) By contrast, even the A310-200 could manage that range with a typical one class capacity of 230, compared with the Ilyushin's 186. The A310-300 further extended this to more than 8500km (4600nm), or over a third more payload with the same range as the Il-62M/MK. Even Airbus Industrie was surprised by the performance of what was designed as an A300 derivative. Any direct comparisons with the Il-86, however, require qualification

– and the first DC-10-10 is a better yardstick. Both were tailored for high-traffic regional domestic operations; both are of similar size, weight and thrust. In fact, McDonnell Douglas had to re-engine its trijet as its Series 15/30/40 marques to overcome these limitations and offer international sales appeal. Unlike the DC-10, the not so fortunate Il-86 was designed from the outset with a centre main undercarriage bogie, not for ultimately handling more power and weight, but simply to accommodate sub-standard airport pavements.

But what cannot be denied in any direct A310-Il-86 assessment, is that, as early as the first flight of the A310-300 on July 8, 1985, the A310-200 was operating economically on routes ranging from Frankfurt-Stuttgart (Lufthansa: 160km/90nm) to Singapore-Mauritius (Singapore Airlines: 6000km/3250nm). Even before this, one commentator had noted that "gestation of state-of-the-art aircraft [in the USSR] in the mid-1970s was taking three times as long as the first generation jet airliners of the 1950s." (Matthew Tesch)

CHAPTER 8

"If this goes on it'll stall!"

*– Captain to First Officer,
1000ft above runway threshold*

GO AROUND
ALT

MAN THR

FD 1

40 — 40

China Airlines (CAL) Airbus Industrie A300B4-622R B-1816 [580]
– April 26, 1994

The flight was almost over, with the aircraft cleared to land in fine night conditions. But an unintentional triggering of a critical flight mode by the young first officer led to a sequence of manoeuvres that, within seconds, had destroyed the aircraft and killed nearly all on board.

The flight

From its Taipei base in this politically sensitive part of Asia, China Airlines (CAL) operates a route network fanning out from the northeast, clockwise around to the west, with an arterial route connecting Hong Kong with Taiwan and Japan generating much traffic for the dynamic national carrier. The makeup of the airline's fleet reflects its long standing relationships with both Boeing and Airbus Industrie, and also includes McDonnell Douglas built aircraft.

On April 26 1994, the late afternoon service from Taipei to Nagoya, some 140nm (260km) southwest of Tokyo on the main Japanese island of Honshu, was scheduled to be flown by one of the company's Airbus A300s, B-1816. Just over three years old (see Endbox), the A300B4-622R, powered by two Pratt & Whitney PW4158 engines, had flown only a little over 8500 hours.

In command for the two and a half hour flight to Nagoya was middle aged Captain Wang Lo-chi, who had been with the airline for the past five years and had a total of 8000 hours' experience. Having spent 19 years as a pilot with the Taiwanese air force, he had gained nearly 5000 hours

command experience on piston engined C-47s (the military version of the DC-3), before joining China Airlines as a Boeing 747 first officer in 1989. After more than three years in the right hand seat of both 747-200s and 747-400s, he was promoted to a command on A300s late in 1992.

His first officer for the trip to Nagoya, Chuang Meng-rong, was a much junior pilot. In his mid 20s, First Officer Chuang had joined the airline as a cadet in 1990 and, after training to commercial pilot standard in the United States, had gained

around 500 hours on light twins. He was then sent to Toulouse to attend Airbus Industrie's training subsidiary, Aeroformation, for simulator and flying training on the A300-600 (see Sidebox). He was promoted to first officer on the type just over a year previously and now had a total of 1600 hours' flying experience.

Designated as CAL's Flight CI140, the A300 took off from Taipei's Chiang Kai Shek International Airport at 5.53pm (Japanese Summer Time). On board were 256 passengers, including two infants, and an

The bustling departure hall at Taipei's Chiang Kai Shek International Airport. This showcase facility, on flat coastal plain 40km west of the capital, was opened in 1979, improving safety and relieving pressure on Sungshan Airport in Taipei's hilly northeastern suburbs. Twenty-one million Taiwanese live politically delicate but industrious lives on an island only half the size of Tasmania. (via Ian Allan Ltd)

A300B4-220 B-190 [193], slats and flaps set for its maiden flight, poses for the camera at Toulouse on April 28, 1982. First of a China Airlines order for four, B-190 remains the most photographed CAL Airbus. The A300s proved such a success CAL took two more from Airbus Industrie storage in 1985-87. Following the lead of Korean Air Lines, an enthusiastic A300 customer since the mid 1970s, CAL went on to order the improved A300-600R as well. The first two CAL A300B4-622Rs were to be lost in tragically similar circumstances, four and eight years respectively after their first flights in October 1990. (Airbus Industrie)

experienced cabin crew of 13. The aircraft's flightplan showed that it would be cruising at Flight Level 330 (33,000 feet) at 465 knots TAS, and that its total estimated flight time was two hours 18 minutes.

The en route flight was uneventful and at 7.47pm Tokyo Control cleared the A300 to commence descent from cruising level and instructed it to call Area Control on 125.7 MHz.

Area Control then cleared the Airbus to continue descent to 9000ft on QNH.

At 7.57pm the aircraft, now flying in darkness, reported "Approaching 9000" and was instructed to contact Nagoya Approach Control on 120.3 MHz. Reporting its altitude a minute later, the aircraft advised that it had received Nagoya's "Information Bravo", and the descent continued,

the aircraft gradually slowing in accordance with Approach Control's further traffic separation clearances.

At 8.04pm, Approach instructed the aircraft, now at 5000ft, to turn left on to a heading of 010°. Three minutes later, when the Airbus had descended to 2500ft, the controller reported that its radar position was now 14nm from the Outer Marker for Nagoya's Runway 34. Clearing the aircraft for an ILS Approach, the controller instructed the crew to call Nagoya Tower on 118.7 MHz.

Contacting the Tower, the aircraft reported passing over the Outer Marker at 8.12pm. The Tower controller instructed the A300 to continue, and a minute later cleared it to land, reporting the wind as 290° at six knots.

The Airbus was now fully configured for the night landing, with the undercarriage and flaps extended and the landing lights on. But when just over 3nm from the runway threshold at about 1000ft, the aircraft briefly levelled off, diverging slightly above the glidepath as this flat approach continued.

After about 15 seconds the descent continued again, but with

Although now dated by the closure of the infamous Kai Tak airport, this busy Hong Kong scene provides an apt context for the CAL A300B4 in the foreground. During the years of phenomenal Asian economic growth before 1998, the Hong Kong-Taiwan-Japan artery generated revenue rivalling the traditional trans-Atlantic link between the UK and the USA. The A300 was CAL's first regional widebody – as it was for Garuda, Malaysian and others in East Asia – and distinguished itself on such high density, 500-2500km route sectors. The Dash 600R's enhanced capabilities rendered the third engine of the ageing DC-10s and TriStars unnecessary – even for later Airbus converts like Cathay Pacific, two of whose L-1011s can also be seen in the picture. Interestingly, Cathay's final TriStar revenue service, on October 15, 1996, was Nagoya-Taipei-Hong Kong. (Airways magazine; David Riley photograph)

TPE - NGO : 2 hr 20 min
2015 km / 1087 nm

A background view of B-190 taxiing for departure from Kai Tak's Runway 13 is overlaid by a map of northeastern Asia, with national and political references omitted. CAL's regional routes and trans-Pacific services are shown, set against the airways that are the primary links between these populous islands. The flightplanned A1-V52 route of the ill-fated Flight CI140 is drawn in bold. Both Tokyo and Fukuoka have been CAL destinations since April 1967, when the airline received its first Boeing 727; Nagoya is a more recent substitute for Osaka, the third inaugural Japanese port, now no longer served. CAL's "hockeystick" stripes of dark blue and bright red have been a feature since the days of its Super Constellations in late 1966. The company's 30th anniversary commemoration saw the unveiling of the new pastel "plum blossom" livery in October 1995. (Matthew Tesch; Osprey Books)

decreasing speed, and an increasing noseup pitch. The pitch increased as the aircraft continued to slow, and when it was on short final, less than 1nm from the runway at a height of about 500 feet, the engines were suddenly heard being opened up to high power. But the burst of power was brief, and the engines closed down again.

Several seconds later, high power was applied again, and the Airbus nosed up into a steep climb. At the same time the crew called: "Going around!" on the Tower frequency. But even as the Tower acknowledged the crew's call, telling them to

Accident aircraft B-1816 rolling out after landing at Naha, Okinawa. Although obviously an A300, the -600R is more than a generational derivative, quite literally being a new aircraft from the inside out (detailed later this chapter). The deletion of the A300B's long dorsal ADF fairing gives the Dash 600 a sleeker look – and, wingtip fences notwithstanding, the easiest means of recognition. (Matthew Tesch)

standby for further instructions, the climb steepened sharply and the A300 rapidly gained height.

As it continued to climb at angles that rapidly became alarmingly steep, the aircraft's speed fell off and, after gaining more than 1500 feet in a few seconds, it stalled. The nose dropped and the widebodied aircraft began diving, equally steeply, with increasing speed towards the ground.

Then, as though recovering from the dive, the nosedown attitude began progressively changing to slightly noseup. But the high vertical rate of descent remained seemingly unchecked. Thirty seconds after the crew's "going around" call, the A300 struck the ground on its extended undercarriage with tremendous force, close to the airport boundary. So violent was this impact that the whole aircraft instantly disintegrated, its scattering wreckage at once exploding into a raging fire. The time was just after 8.15pm.

Firefighting vehicles reached the crash site within three minutes, with ambulances following two minutes later. Sixteen occupants, still alive but badly injured, were pulled from the burning wreckage and rushed to hospital. Six were found dead on arrival, and another three died later from their injuries. Seven passengers survived, all suffering trauma to varying degrees.

INVESTIGATION

The investigation of the accident was conducted by a Commission of Japan's Ministry of Transport (JMT). It commenced on the night of the accident and continued until January

1994, when the Commission's comprehensive and detailed accident report was published. The investigation included visits by members of the Commission's team to China Airlines in Taiwan, to Airbus Industrie in France, and to the National Transportation Safety Board in the USA.

The airport

Administered by the Ministry of Transport, Nagoya Airport serves the country's heavily industrialised and third biggest city, with more than 6.5 million people in its 500km² greater metropolitan area. On the city's northern outskirts in Aichi Prefecture, the airport has an elevation of 49ft AMSL. Its single paved Runway 16/34, 2740m (8990ft) long and 45m (148ft) wide, separates civil operational facilities on its western side from a major Japanese Self Defence Force base to the east. Well equipped with navigational aids, even including the now rare Precision Approach Radar because of its joint military use, the airport was

operating normally on the night of the accident.

Weather

At the time, a region of high pressure covered most of Japan, producing fine weather throughout the country, except in the north, where it was cloudy. At Nagoya Airport at the time of the A300's approach, the wind was from 280° at 6-7kt, visibility was 20km, the temperature 20°C, and the QNH 1011.

Wreckage

The aircraft had struck the ground with its undercarriage extended on a flat, unpaved area 100m immediately to the right of the Runway 34 threshold, close to the perimeter road and airport boundary. It was evident that the A300 had recovered from its steep nosedown attitude and, though still descending at a steep angle at a high rate in a stalled condition, was in fact slightly nose up, port wing down in an almost level attitude.

As a result, the initial extremely

The scene illuminated by portable floodlights, rescue workers at the crash site continue sifting through the carnage on the night of April 26, 1994. Miraculously, 16 people were found still alive amongst the wreckage. But only seven were ultimately to survive their traumatic injuries. (JMT)

heavy impact was taken on the port main undercarriage, followed almost instantaneously by the starboard bogie and nose leg. All three undercarriage assemblies were bent and broken into several pieces. All had compression damaged oleo struts and buckled cylinders. The rear bogie beam of the port main undercarriage was sheared off, while the rear inner column, with the tyre still inflated, and its accompanying brake assembly, had been hurled 190m from their initial impact points.

With the exception of the tailcone, the remains of the centre and aft fuselage were scattered over an area 140m long and 60m wide, extending from where the port main undercarriage had struck the ground. This wreckage was almost entirely destroyed by fire. Some 120m further away in the direction of impact, the remains of the nose and forward fuselage were similarly strewn, but these showed no evidence of fire damage.

Both wings and both engines had been torn off, and their broken and burnt wreckage lay 80m from the initial point of impact. It was evident that the wing slats and flaps were selected to the 15°/15° position when the aircraft crashed. The fan hubs of both engines were broken and detached.

The least damaged sections of the aircraft were the tail surfaces. The tailplane and tailcone, broken and torn from the fuselage, lay 30m from the initial impact point. The adjustable tailplane was trimmed to fully noseup. The broken and burnt fin, together with a piece of the upper rear fuselage, was lying across an open drain 65m from the first point of impact.

The cargo on board was scattered between where the aircraft hit the ground and the vicinity of the drain, as were nearly all the damaged passenger seats.

The aircraft

The twin engined Airbus A300B4-622R had been in service with China Airlines for three years and had flown a total of only 8572 hours. Its weight at the time of the accident was approximately 131,951kg (290,900lb), well within its maximum, and its CofG was also within its permissible limits. For the flight to Nagoya, all but eight seats in its Business Class section were occupied.

Automatic Flight Control System

Like the Airbus A310, the A300-600 series aircraft is designed to be flown by two pilots only, and is equipped with a sophisticated, computer controlled Automatic Flight Control System (AFCS), incorporating two autopilots. The AFCS enables the crew to operate the aircraft in the most efficient manner in all phases of flight. The flight condition selected is indicated on the flight-deck's Electronic Centralised Aircraft Monitoring system (ECAM) and on the Flight Mode Annunciators (FMAs), along the top of each pilot's Primary Flight Display, while the aircraft's various flight parameters are displayed on the PFDs in the normal way.

Each of the two autopilots is engaged by selecting the corresponding switch on the FCU below the glareshield. They can be disengaged either by turning the appropriate switch off, or by pressing the autopilot disconnect button on each of the control yokes.

The different flight modes are also selected with their appropriate push button on the FCU. When one or both autopilots are selected to Command mode (CMD), the aircraft is controlled automatically according to the selected flight mode. Both autopilots cannot be engaged simultaneously in CMD, except in the LAND or GO AROUND mode.

According to the particular flight mode selected, the autothrottle system continuously computes the required engine thrust and applies it through an electric actuator to the thrust levers. The settings applied by the autothrottle can be overridden by controlling the thrust manually.

The various flight modes, some of which are used in conjunction with one another, are as follows:

BASIC Mode: The autopilot maintains vertical speed and heading.

ALT Mode: Selected to level off at a particular altitude, the aircraft's speed being controlled by the autothrottle.

LVL/CH Mode: Automatically engaged when an altitude different from the current altitude is selected on the FCU.

PROFILE Mode: The Flight Management System (FMS) controls vertical navigation and thrust.

HED/SEL Mode: Used to change heading, with the inner knob selecting the required heading and the outer knob setting the maximum bank angle.

NAV Mode: Horizontal navigation is conducted by the FMS.

VOR Mode: Enables the aircraft to capture and maintain a VOR track. Automatically disengaged when GO AROUND, NAV or LAND are modes selected.

LOC Mode: Captures and maintains a Localiser track.

TAKEOFF Mode: Engaged with the Go Around lever.

LAND Mode: Captures and maintains an ILS path (localiser and glidepath), then aligns the aircraft with the runway centreline and flares it for an automatic landing. Engaged with the LAND mode button on the FCU when radio altimeter height is greater than 400ft, and an ILS frequency and runway heading have been selected.

GO AROUND Mode: Performs a go around with the autopilot controlling engine thrust. Engaged by triggering one of the Go Around levers, provided the slats/flaps are extended at least 15°. Disengaged by selecting modes *other than* the LAND mode.

In any but LAND or GO AROUND modes, the autopilot automatically disconnects when a pilot applies force to the control yoke. But although the elevator control can be *overridden* in LAND or GO AROUND mode, *the autopilot does not disconnect, regardless of the force applied manually*. If this manual control input is opposing the autopilot's elevator control, the autopilot will adjust the tailplane jackscrew to maintain the aircraft on the scheduled flightpath, creating an out-of-trim situation. A caution against this hazard is included in the Flight Crew Operating Manual.

In LAND mode, if there is any malfunction of instruments being used for an automatic approach which changes the programmed landing category, the "Landing Capability Change" warning sounds. When GO AROUND mode is engaged during a manually flown ILS approach, the landing capability is lost and the warning will sound.

As in the Airbus A310 and A320, the A300-600's AFCS includes a flight envelope protection system – the Alpha Floor Function – designed to prevent the aircraft from stalling by automatically applying maximum engine thrust if an excessive Angle of Attack (AoA) is detected. When the Alpha Floor function is activated, the symbol THR L (Throttle Latched) is displayed on the FMA and the thrust levers move forward to their maximum positions.

Engines

Examination of the aircraft's two Pratt & Whitney PW4158 engines showed that both had been running at high power when the aircraft crashed.

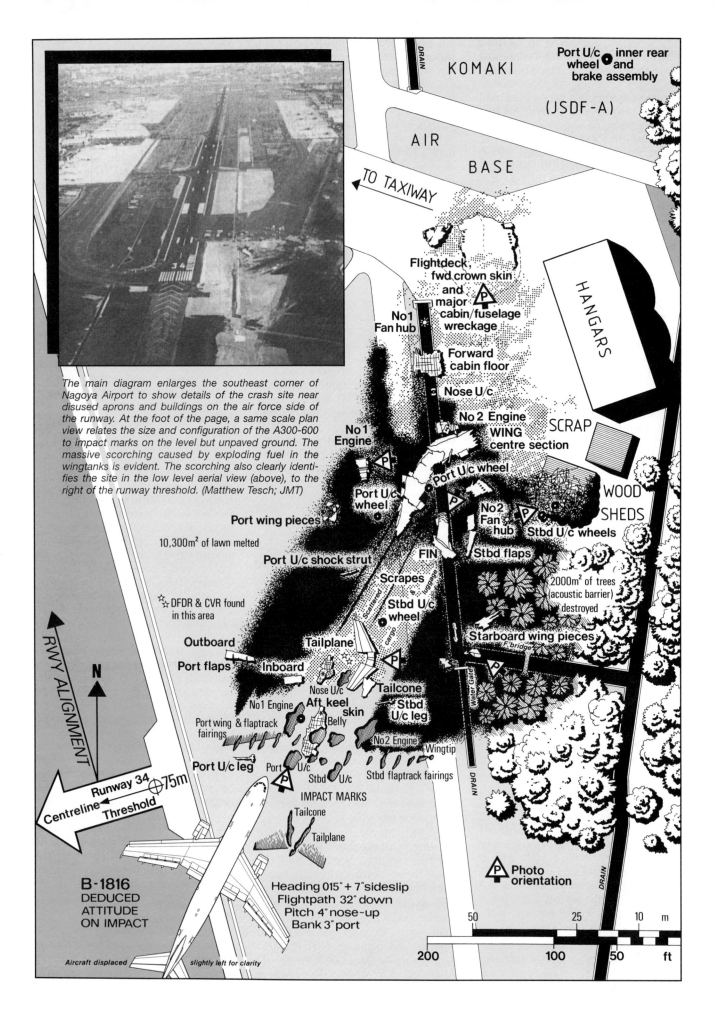

KOMAKI

Port U/c inner rear
wheel and
brake assembly

(JSDF-A)

AIR

BASE

DRAIN

TO TAXIWAY

HANGARS

Flightdeck,
fwd crown skin
and
major
cabin/fuselage
wreckage

No1
Fan hub

Forward
cabin floor

Nose U/c

No 2 Engine

WING
centre section

SCRAP

No1
Engine

Port U/c wheel

WOOD
SHEDS

Port U/c
wheel

No2
Fan
hub

Stbd U/c wheels

Port wing pieces

10,300m² of lawn melted

Port U/c shock strut

Stbd flaps

FIN

☆☆ DFDR & CVR found
in this area

Scrapes

Stbd U/c
wheel

2000m² of trees
(acoustic barrier)
destroyed

Outboard
Port flaps

Tailplane

Inboard

Starboard wing pieces

Nose U/c

Tailcone

No1 Engine

Aft keel
skin

Stbd
U/c leg

Port wing & flaptrack
fairings

Belly

No2 Engine

Wingtip

Port U/c leg

Port   U/c

Stbd   U/c

Stbd flaptrack fairings

Runway 34 ⊕ 75m

Centreline   Threshold

IMPACT MARKS

Tailcone

Tailplane

RWY ALIGNMENT

N

Ⓟ Photo
orientation

B-1816
DEDUCED
ATTITUDE
ON IMPACT

Heading 015° + 7° sideslip
Flightpath 32° down
Pitch 4° nose-up
Bank 3° port

50   25   10   m

200   100   50   ft

Aircraft displaced   slightly left for clarity

*The main diagram enlarges the southeast corner of
Nagoya Airport to show details of the crash site near
disused aprons and buildings on the air force side of
the runway. At the foot of the page, a same scale plan
view relates the size and configuration of the A300-600
to impact marks on the level but unpaved ground. The
massive scorching caused by exploding fuel in the
wingtanks is evident. The scorching also clearly identi-
fies the site in the low level aerial view (above), to the
right of the runway threshold. (Matthew Tesch; JMT)*

No 1 engine's FADEC computer unit remained attached to the engine core, surviving the accident unscorched.

Scalped from its fragmented fuselage frames, this area of outer skin from the forward upper section of the passenger cabin paradoxically preserved both the company livery and cabin windows.

Near inverted, its composite leading edge melted, the fin was charred by blazing fuel pouring into the open airport drain. The fin is still attached to the upper section of the tailcone, indicating the shattering nature of the initial impact. (All photos JMT)

Photo layout approximates wreckage diagram opposite: arrowheads keynote locations and angles.

(above) A shed containing scrap wood was demolished by hurtling components of the starboard main undercarriage bogie. (below) Pieces of spoiler from the starboard wing, lying in an open airport drain.

The tailplane broke off on impact almost in one piece, and was the first major item on the wreckage trail. The screwjack assembly can be seen in the centre of the picture.

The port main undercarriage (intact view left), which took the A300's initial impact, was driven more than half a metre (2ft) into the ground. Only the engines gouged deeper craters.

INITIAL IMPACT

Flight recorders

The DFDR and CVR, together with their mountings, were found separated from the fragmented airframe near the tail surfaces. Their outer cases were deformed by impact forces and sooted by fire, but the recording mediums in both units were capable of being read out. An analysis of the DFDR, in combination with that of the CVR, enabled investigators to reconstruct a highly detailed history of the flight, particularly over its last 30 minutes, including the flightdeck actions that so suddenly led to the disaster during the final stage of the Airbus's approach to land.

The DFDR established that the aircraft reached its cruising level of FL330 20 minutes after takeoff at about 6.14pm, and continued towards Nagoya in accordance with its flight planned track along the primary A1 airway (refer route map).

Together, the DFDR and the CVR showed that, at 7.47pm, still cruising at FL330, with First Officer Chuang at the controls, the No 2 autopilot engaged, and Captain Wang handling the radio communications, Tokyo Area Control cleared the aircraft to descend to FL210 and, after a change of frequency to 125.7 MHz, cleared it to continue down to 9000ft on QNH.

As the descent proceeded, the captain spent the time briefing the first officer on the approach to Nagoya and on landing technique in general. At 7.58pm, with the Airbus nearing 9000ft, the captain again changed frequency, reporting to Approach Control on 120.3 MHz that they had received Nagoya ATIS's "Information Bravo". Nagoya Approach then cleared the aircraft to descend and maintain 6000ft, and instructed the crew to reduce speed to 200kt.

As they completed the Approach Checklist, Captain Wang, discussing the actual night landing, encouraged First Officer Chuang to handle the aircraft himself at his own discretion. "Do it by yourself," he told the first officer. "Don't ask me – you make the decisions."

The leading edge slats were extended by selecting the slat/flap lever to the first detent for 15°/0° and, immediately afterwards, when Nagoya Approach instructed the aircraft to turn on to a heading of 050° and to further reduce speed to 180kt, the slats/flaps were further selected to 15°/15°. Minutes later, Approach then instructed the Airbus to turn left on to a heading of 010°.

Advising the crew they were now 14nm from the Outer Marker, the approach controller then cleared the aircraft for an ILS Approach to Runway 34, and instructed them to contact Nagoya Tower on 118.7 MHz. The No 1 autopilot was then engaged in addition to the No 2, and the approach continued.

8.07:37pm: CAPT (to Tower): Good evening – Runway 34 approach.
8.07:42: TWR: Good evening, report Outer Marker, Runway 34.
8.07:50: [First Officer exclaims as Airbus encounters turbulence]
8.08:26: F/O: It seems aircraft often pick up another's wake turbulence here, doesn't it? Is it because of the terrain? Today it seems we are in wake turbulence from beginning to end.

With the first officer expressing his concern about wake turbulence, the captain gave him advice on how to deal with it, then adjusted his own seat in preparation for the approach.
8.08:35: CAPT: Step firmly on the rudders ... it will not sway so hard.
8.08:41: CAPT: OK – Localiser is alive ... runway heading [is the] inbound course.
8.08:55: CAPT: ... that one [aircraft] in front – you'd better kill the speed a little bit.
8.08:59: F/O: Sir – isn't it a 747?
8.09:00: CAPT: I can't tell ... but you'd better kill the speed a little more. Kill it to 170 ... otherwise, if we follow too closely, we'll be turned over!

Over the next two minutes or so, as they continued their final approach leg in the dark, the captain gave the first officer general advice on low altitude aircraft handling at night.
8.11:20: F/O: We are in it [the turbulence] on glideslope!
8.11:24: CAPT: We can do nothing about it – there are too many aircraft.
8.11:34: F/O: Then I'll disengage it [the autopilot].
8.11:35: CAPT: OK – fly manually.
[First officer disengages both autopilots]
8.11:45: CAPT: Glideslope alive!
8.11:46: F/O: Yes sir – go around altitude 3000ft.

The go around altitude was then set in the glareshield ALT SEL (Altitude Selector) window, shortly before the aircraft passed the Outer Marker, gradually decreasing speed.
8.12:23: CAPT: Nagoya Tower, Outer Marker!
8.12:26: TWR: Continue approach – No 1 for touchdown.
8.12:41: F/O: Flaps 20! [sound of slat/flap lever]
8.12:56: F/O: Gear down! [sound of undercarriage extending]
8.13:13: CAPT: Gear down – three greens!
8.13:14: F/O: Flaps 30/40, Speed V approach 140 – landing checklist please.

At this, the captain made a further selection of the slat/flap lever from 15°/20° to 30°/40°.
8.13:21: CAPT [calling landing checklist]: Landing gear down, three greens, anti-skid normal, slat/flaps 30/40, spoilers armed, landing lights on – landing checklist completed!
8.13:39: TWR: Cleared to land Runway 34, wind 290° at 6kt.
8.13:49: CAPT (to F/O): There is a small crosswind from the left – all lights are on!

Living up to their design specifications, both the DFDR (left) and CVR (right) survived the shattering impact and escaped the worst of the fire. Photographed as they were found, the DFDR's picture was taken by flashbulb during the night. Daylight brought the discovery of the CVR, the solitary playing card lying beside it (top) providing an idea of the scale of the so-called "black box". (JMT)

Ten seconds later, as the aircraft was descending through 1070ft on QNH, the engine thrust suddenly began to increase, the Landing Capability Change warning sounded as the Flight Mode Annunciator display changed to GO AROUND, the aircraft tended noseup, and the Airbus began to deviate above the glide path.

The first officer immediately countered the noseup tendency by pushing forward on the control column, but succeeded only in levelling the aircraft off at about 1040ft.

8.14:10: CAPT: [surprised exclamation]! You've – you've triggered the GO lever!

8.14:11: F/O: Yes, Yes – I touched it.

8.14:12: CAPT: Disengage it! .... you what ... you watch ... watch outside ... outside!

The first officer continued to push forward hard on the control column, deflecting the elevators about 3.5° nosedown. But as he attempted to trim the aircraft nosedown to reduce this force on the control column with his pitch trim switch, both autopilots became engaged in the Command mode almost simultaneously. The first officer's action thus had no effect on the adjustable tailplane, because the pitch trim switch on either control column is inhibited when one or both autopilots are engaged.

Furthermore, because the Flight Director was now in Go Around mode, the autopilots also became engaged in the Go Around mode, and the adjustable tailplane began moving noseup from minus 5.3° – directly opposite to the trimming effect the first officer was attempting to apply.

8.14:23: CAPT: Push down! Push it down! Retard those throttles!

8.14:29: F/O: Uh ... too high.

At this stage the captain saw that the Flight Mode Annunciator was still displaying GO AROUND.

8.14:30: CAPT: You're ... you're [still] using the Go Around mode ... it's OK ... disengage again slowly ... with your hand on.

The first officer evidently took action to change from Go Around, but for some reason this was not achieved. The pitch trim switch was activated several times, apparently in the nosedown direction but, as before, it had no effect. Instead, the adjustable tailplane progressively moved to a setting of minus 12.3° (noseup).

8.14:41: CAPT: Push more! Push more! ... Push more!

F/O: Yes!

8.14:43: CAPT: Push down more! ... it's [still] in the Go Around mode!

Remarkably, the shattered shell of B-1816's flightdeck (above) retains intact windscreen panels, cleanly separated from the A300's demolished nose. A fortnight after the accident, the Japanese investigators had completed their cataloguing of the wreckage in situ, and it was removed to a nearby air force compound for more detailed examination. The interior view (below) offers not only a 'before' contrast, but also an interesting comparison with the other Airbus Industrie flightdecks pictured in this volume – the A320 in chapter 1, the early A300B in chapter 6, and the A310 in chapters 6 and 7. The photograph was taken on board only the second Dash 600 built, F-WZLS [284], earmarked for Saudia as HZ-AJA. (JMT and Airbus Industrie)

Although the first officer apparently took some further action, again no change from Go Around mode actually took place. With the aircraft's pitch angle and AoA still increasing and its speed decreasing, the first officer now increased the thrust slightly.

8.14:49: [Sound of autopilot disengagement] F/O: Sir – autopilot disengaged!

Whether this action was taken at the first officer's discretion or at the captain's instruction remained unclear, because the CVR record was masked by another ATC transmission just beforehand.

8.14:51: F/O: Sir – I still can't push it down!

8.14:58: CAPT: I ... well ... Land mode?

The aircraft's pitch angle and its AoA were still increasing, while its speed was continuing to decrease. When the AoA reached 11.5°, as the Airbus was descending through about 570ft, the Alpha Floor function automatically activated, suddenly increasing the engine thrust and airspeed. As a result, the Airbus's descent was checked and it began to climb. Activation of the Alpha Floor function also displays the symbol

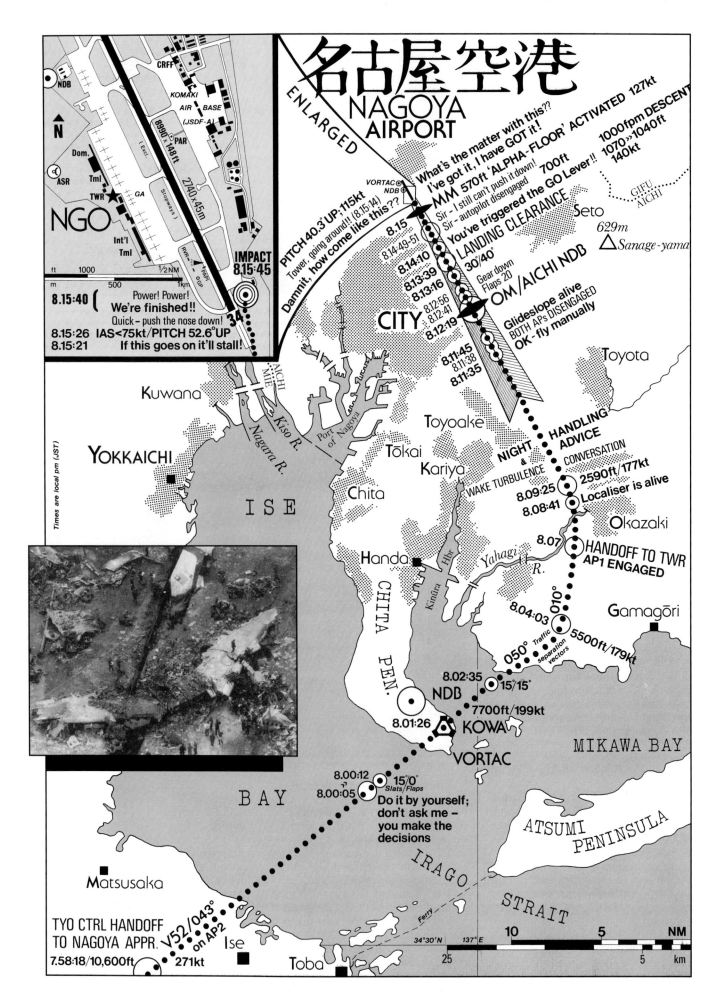

(opposite) The greater Nagoya metropolitan region, in Aichi, Gifu and Mie Prefectures, at the head of Ise Bay, is the setting for the inbound track of B-1816 and its Runway 34 ILS approach. Data from ATC tapes, and the aircraft's DFDR and CVR, provide references relating to the main text. The destination airport and crash site are detailed in the inset enlargement (top left). Beneath it, a low level aerial photograph of the main wreckage shows the near complete wing inspar and centrebox sections (middle foreground, looking aft). On the left, the starboard wing has been fragmented outboard of the aileron, which is still in position. On the right, an investigator stands on the upper port wing directly behind the No 1 engine pylon. Although covered in the burnt remains of the cabin, the central section, with its carry through spars and main undercarriage bays, has remained substantially intact. Further evidence of the strength of this section is provided in the following diagram, showing the seat positions of the seven fortunate survivors. (Matthew Tesch; JMT; Rand McNally; Wide World Photos)

THR-L on the Flight Mode Annunciator.

8.15:02: F/O [urgently]: Sir – throttle latched again!

8.15:03: CAPT [firmly]: OK – I've got it, I've got it ... I have got it!

Taking over the controls, the captain pushed his control column to its forward limit, and retarded the thrust levers, but the aircraft continued to climb.

8.15:04: F/O [becoming unnerved]: Disengage, disengage!

8.15:08: CAPT [concerned and puzzled that the powerful noseup tendency was persisting]: What's the matter with this?

8.15:09: F/O [still apparently urging the captain to disengage the autothrottle]: Disengage! Dis....

Nonplussed that the pitch angle was continuing to increase, the captain reapplied thrust, at the same time using the pitch trim switch to trim the tailplane nosedown.

8.15:11: CAPT: Go Lever! ... damn it, how come like this? [Sound of pitch trim]

But the aircraft's climb steepened further, and its airspeed, which had increased, began to decrease again.

8.15:14: F/O [urgently]: Nagoya Tower, going around!

8.15:17: (GPWS, as glidepath tolerances exceeded): Glideslope!

8.15:18: TWR: Roger – standby for further instructions.

[Sound of slat/flap lever selections]

In a normal go around, the slat/flap lever would be reselected back from the 30°/40° position to 15°/20°. But from the number of times the lever's sound was recorded, it could have been moved back to 15°/0° or even the 0°/0° position. Seconds later, at 8.15:27, the sound of the lever's downward movement was again recorded on the CVR, and the DFDR showed it was reset at the 15°/15° position.

At 8.15:20, both thrust levers were retarded almost simultaneously, No 1 to its idle position but No 2 only slightly.

8.15:21: CAPT [shouting desperately]: If this goes on it'll stall!

8.15:23: [Sound of master caution – probably caused by tripping of yaw damper]

8.15:26: F/O: Quick – push the nose down! [Sound of slat/flap lever – and both thrust levers are pushed to their full thrust positions again]

8.15:28: [Sound of master caution – probably caused by tripping of pitch trim]

8.15:31: [Sound of master caution – probably caused by tripping of autothrottle]

F/O [seeing CAUTION message on ECAM display – probably pitch trim – resets it]: Set, set ... push the nose down!

8.15:34: CAPT: It's OK ... It's OK. Don't hurry, don't hurry!

F/O [loudly and fearfully]: Power!!

8.15:35: Captain, still applying nosedown elevator, pulls control column back in response to stall and steep descent.

8.15:37: (GPWS): "Terrain! Terrain!"

CAPT: Ahhhhhh!

F/O: Power! Power! Power!

8.15:40: [Continuous sound of Stall Warning]

CAPT: Ahhhh!

F/O: Power!

CAPT: We're finished!!

F/O: Power!

CAPT: Ahh!

F/O: Power! Power!

8.15:45: END OF RECORDING [Moment of impact]

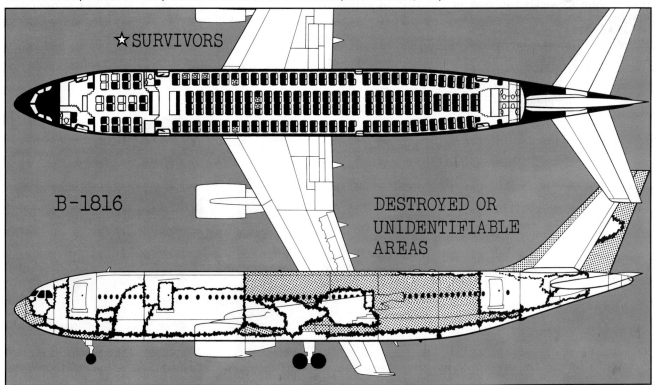

Portside profile and interior cabin arrangement of B-1816. The profile drawing not only defines the tears and fractures identified by the Japanese investigators, but also parts of the fuselage utterly destroyed by impact or fire. Aboard the Airbus, all but eight Business Class seats were occupied and the seat positions of the survivors are notable. (Matthew Tesch; JMT)

★SURVIVORS

B-1816

DESTROYED OR UNIDENTIFIABLE AREAS

ANALYSIS

It was evident to the investigators that the flight of the Airbus had been entirely normal in every respect until it was descending through about 1000ft on short final approach.

The weather was fine and clear and played no part in the development of the accident, there were no radio communication problems with the aircraft, and all radio navigation aids, both aboard the aircraft and on the ground, were functioning correctly.

Similarly, it was evident that the operation of the aircraft was entirely normal, and the investigation could find no evidence of any fault or malfunction in the aircraft, its engines or its various mechanical and electronic systems that could have led to the accident.

But examination and analysis of the data recorded on the DFDR and CVR showed conclusively that the problem that had led to the sudden and unexpected catastrophe in the very last minute of the flight was one involving the interface between the aircraft's AFCS (Automatic Flight Control System) and the pilots themselves.

Indeed, all had been perfectly normal, with the final stages of the approach to land proceeding as expected, until the first officer unintentionally triggered the Go Around lever on the thrust lever quadrant.

Activation of the Go Around lever

Up to 8.14:05pm, the aircraft's approach was proceeding as expected. Already cleared to land by the Tower, the Airbus was continuing its descent normally on the 3° ILS glidepath with the undercarriage down and the slats/flaps fully extended to 30°/40°. Both EPRs were set at about 1.1, the airspeed was about 140kt, the pitch angle 4°, and the tailplane trim was at minus 5.3°.

But at this moment on short final, as the aircraft descended through 1070ft, the first officer somehow inadvertently triggered the Go Around lever, resulting in an immediate, automatic increase in engine thrust to 1.21 EPR. At the same time, the Landing Capability Change warning sounded and the display on the Flight Mode Annunciator changed to GO AROUND, doubtless prompting the captain's exclamation of surprise a second later.

On the A300-600R, the small Go Around levers are positioned just below the thrust levers' knobs and operate by being moved rearwards – a similar action to retarding the thrust levers themselves. Because of this juxtaposition, some possibility exists for an inadvertent movement of one of the Go Around levers with the fingers when thrust is being reduced manually (see photograph).

Judging from the smooth movements of the thrust levers recorded by the DFDR up to that time, it seems that the first officer had his left hand on the levers during autothrottle operation and, as he went to select manual thrust, he might have momentarily confused the Go Around lever with the autothrottle disconnect button on the thrust lever knobs. Or he might simply have moved the Go Around lever accidentally as he adjusted the thrust levers.

Almost immediately, the captain ordered him to: "Disengage it".

Four seconds later, according to the DFDR, both autopilots were engaged in the Command mode. But with the AFCS already in Go Around mode, this brought the autopilots into Go Around mode also. Although no verbal exchange on autopilot engagement was recorded on the CVR at the time, the crew's intention might have been to regain the ILS glidepath by selecting Land mode and re-engaging the autopilots.

The first officer quickly retarded the thrust levers from their Go Around position, but not far enough and, although he was also pushing forward on the control column to return the aircraft to the glidepath, the A300 increased its airspeed and pitch slightly, deviating above the ILS glidepath and levelling off at about 1040ft.

With the first officer continuing to push on the control column, the autopilots, in Go Around mode, were attempting to move the elevators noseup. But this overriding of the elevators resulted in the tailplane trim beginning to move noseup from minus 5.3°. Even so, the first officer's nosedown elevator initially cancelled the aerodynamic effect of the tailplane, and the aircraft temporarily continued level flight.

The sound of the pitch trim switch was recorded on the CVR three times in the 20 seconds after the autopilots were engaged. The first officer would have known the pitch trim switch is inhibited while the autopilots are engaged, so it is possible that the captain engaged the autopilots without the first officer's knowledge. On the other hand, the first officer could have moved the trim switch involuntarily while pushing forward hard on the control column.

Despite the captain's three successive instructions to him to disengage the Go Around mode, the aircraft's AFCS remained programmed that way. To disengage Go Around mode, both the lateral and longitudinal modes (except the Land mode) have first to be selected. Directly accessing the Land mode button cannot disengage the Go Around mode, so the first officer's selection of the

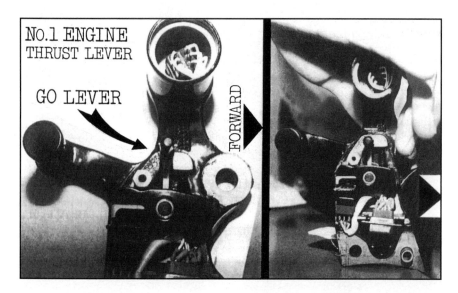

Details of the flightdeck's left thrust lever, showing the relationship between the thrust lever knob and the smaller Go Around lever immediately beneath it. The Go Around lever is triggered by being selected rearwards. The picture at lower right shows how the fingers can reach the Go Around lever with the pilot's hand resting on the thrust lever knob. The position of the springloaded pushbutton autopilot disconnect switch can also be seen on the side of the thrust lever knob itself. The corresponding controls on the right thrust lever are positioned as a mirror image, so that the two Go Around levers and autopilot disconnect switches lie between the pair of thrust levers. (JMT)

Land mode button on the Flight Control Unit was ineffective.

From the captain's comment "I ... well ... Land mode?" a few seconds later at 8.14:58, the captain apparently intended to select Land mode after the Go Around mode was disengaged. To say the least, it is unusual to attempt to disengage the Go Around mode once it has been engaged in the final phase of an approach, and then to engage the Land mode.

Although the first officer took some action to change modes, he was unable to do so, but he neither told the captain he could not, nor that he did not know how to. Overall, this indicated a lack of understanding of the A300-600's AFCS.

Flight profile

To try to correct the descent path, the first officer retarded the thrust levers further, reducing the EPRs from around 1.17 to about 1.00. As a result, the airspeed began to decrease from 146kt, resulting in the noseup tendency also decreasing. The pitch angle reduced to 1.2° and, at 8.14:26, the aircraft began to descend again.

But four seconds later, the aircraft's pitch began to increase again. The surface area of the tailplane is considerably greater than that of the elevators, and its aerodynamic effect proportionally more. As a result, the noseup tendency being generated by movement of the tailplane progressively overcame the nosedown elevator force being applied by the first officer. As the pitch angle increased, the AoA also began to increase as the airspeed decreased further.

As the aircraft descended through 880ft at 8.14:37, the tailplane reached its fully noseup setting of minus 12.3°, and the nosedown elevator being applied by the first officer reached 8.5°. The rate of descent was 1000fpm, and although the first officer was still pushing on the control column, the pitch angle and AoA continued to increase, while the airspeed continued to decay. In an effort to correct the decreasing airspeed, the first officer increased the thrust slightly to 1.04 EPR.

Twelve seconds later, because he was still unable to maintain airspeed, the first officer disengaged both autopilots. This increased the mobility of the control column a little, enabling him to push the elevators further nosedown.

Now at an altitude of 700ft, the aircraft's pitch angle and AoA decreased, but a few seconds later at 8.14:51, as the first officer relaxed his forward pressure on the control column a little, the pitch and AoA increased again, prompting him to exclaim to the captain: "Sir, I still cannot push it down!"

Out-of-trim situation

In the half minute or so that had elapsed since the first officer had mistakenly placed the aircraft in the Go Around mode, the captain had repeatedly been urging him to push the nose down with the control column.

Yet until this moment, the first officer, probably because he was under stress, had not told the captain of the abnormally strong noseup resistance he was experiencing in the control column. As a result, the captain was not fully aware of the situation.

With the aircraft's AFCS selected to any flight mode, elevator control by the operative autopilot can be overridden with the control column. But when Land or Go Around modes are selected, with one or both autopilots engaged, the autopilot will adjust the tailplane trim to maintain the aircraft on flightpath. Overriding the elevators manually can thus lead to an out-of-trim condition.

The aircraft's AFCS *does* incorporate a supervisory override function to allow pilots to assist the autopilot *when capturing a glideslope, localiser or VOR heading*. Possibly the captain's experience in using this function led to the mistaken belief that the autopilots could be overridden *during all phases of an approach*. It is also possible that his experience on Boeing 747-200s and 747-400s led him to believe he could safely manually override the autopilot.

A caution against overriding the autopilots in Land or Go Around modes is included in the A300-600's Flight Crew Operating Manual. It can only be presumed the crew did not fully understand these cautions.

Takeover

At 8.15:02pm, as the aircraft descended through 570ft, its airspeed was 127kt and pitch angle 8.6°. At this point, the AoA exceeded the threshold angle of 11.5° for the slats/flaps 30°/40° configuration, and the aircraft's Alpha Floor function activated. The engine thrust suddenly increased again, causing a large pitch up moment, and the Airbus began to climb steeply. At the same moment, the symbol THR-L appeared on the Flight Mode Annunciator, and the first officer exclaimed: "Sir – throttle latched again!"

Until this time, the captain did not appear to have fully grasped the developing situation and, even at this point, still seemed unaware the tailplane trim was at its noseup limit. But now, with the approach so obviously getting out of hand at an

The thrust lever quadrant, mounted on the forward section of the flightdeck centre pedestal between the crew seats. In the centre are the two thrust levers themselves. Assymmetrically positioned in the picture, the right hand lever for the starboard engine is at a higher thrust setting than that for the port. The spigot of the right hand Go Around lever can be seen protruding between the two thrust levers. To the right and left of the thrust levers, respectively, are the speedbrake lever and the slat/flap lever, while on either side of the quadrant are the trim wheels for manual adjustment of the tailplane screwjack. The tailplane is normally trimmed electrically, either by the autopilots if they are engaged, or through switches on either pilot's control yoke.

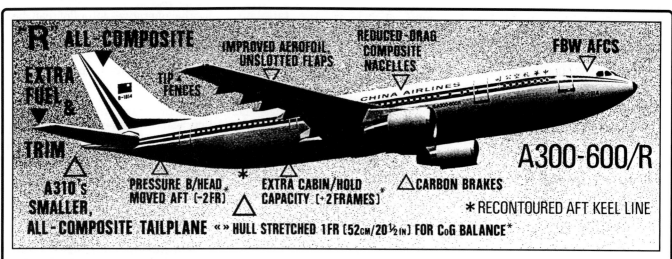

The second of the two CAL Airbuses lost in fatal accidents, B-1814 [578], serves here as the 'vehicle' to summarise some of the major structural differences between the early A300B and the Dash 600.

The latter is indeed a development of the A300 which first flew as long ago as 1972, but it is a much more efficient aircraft. Incorporating the A310 rear fuselage into the design increases its capacity by two seat rows. Its two crew flightdeck – now regarded as standard – and the A310's scaled down, all composite tailplane, with additional trim balancing fuel capacity, has reduced the A300-600's empty weight and drag, despite its improved payload and range.

The reference in an earlier caption to flightdeck comparisons with other Airbus Industrie types is also pertinent. "If the A310 and A300-600 represent Airbus Industrie's first generation of digital avionics," commented Flight International as long ago as February 1987, "then the A320 is its second generation, and the A330/340 its third".

This observation reflects the Dash 600's role as more than a simple upgrade of the ageing A300B design, and emphasises not only the interlocking design threads at Toulouse, but also a technological turning point for the world airline industry. "The underlying trend," concluded Flight International, is towards increasing integration and, through it, improved efficiency." Boeing's longstanding family of narrowbody types (707-727-737), with their commonality of design, spares, and flightdecks, was an industry standard which Airbus Industrie in fact overtook with an electronic revolution.

Much of the sophisticated computerisation evolved through the tandem development of the A310 and A320 has already been covered in earlier chapters in this volume – and much of it came to be applied to the A300-600. Advances in composite materials also provided substantial weight and drag savings, and advantages in strength.

But as Airbus fought hard to gain technological supremacy, Boeing steadfastly maintained its conservative views of aeronautical evolution. Yet the spate of early A320 accidents, which at first appeared to vindicate the traditionalists, has only underlined the sometimes inexplicable behaviour of the human operators of high technology equipment.

While McDonnell Douglas dithered away its once well earnt primacy in airliner manufacture – and indeed its very existence – Airbus and Boeing have continued to fight a drawn-out battle for sales. The days of "either-or" evaluations by airlines of the A300 and 767, or the A310 compared with the 757, for instance, have gone, superseded today by more practical, common sense attitudes.

China Airlines itself, regarded as "a Boeing airline", with its first 727-109 joined by others and, subsequently, 707s and 737s is an example. For when Airbus sales teams were beginning to find fertile ground in Asia in the late 1970s, CAL was tempted to buy four – but made aviation history by ordering two 767-209s as well!

In the long run however, political ties and commercial influences across the Pacific were found to count for less than the economic appeal of the A300s; the 767s departed and the A300-600/Rs became an almost inevitable succession. Nearly 40% of A300 production has now been sold in Asia.

Even Boeing's briefly pioneering "EROPS" lead was swiftly matched by the Dash 600's "R" marque, and no less a standard setter than American Airlines stunned the world industry in 1987 by simultaneously ordering 25 A300-600Rs as well as 15 767-300ERs!

---

altitude of only 500ft, he finally took over the controls himself.

Although he immediately felt the unusually powerful nose-up force on the control column, he clearly still intended to continue with the landing. Pushing the control column to its forward limit, he retarded the thrust levers to try to reduce the increasing noseup pitch and steep climb. But despite his efforts, the pitch continued to increase.

"How come like this?" he cried, as he realised he was unable to reduce the pitch angle. With the aircraft now climbing through 600ft, pitched noseup at 21.5°, he gave up his attempt to land, calling "Go Lever" in urgent tones, while himself pushing the thrust levers to their forward limit as he attempted to go around.

But the large further pitch up moment, again generated by the sudden increase in thrust in the aircraft's out-of-trim condition, increased its pitch angle even more, and the airspeed began to decrease from 137kt.

In a normally executed go around in this type of aircraft, the pilot handling the controls calls "go around flap" as he activates the Go Lever. The pilot not flying then reduces the slat/flap setting from 30°/40° to the 15°/20° detent, and after confirming and calling "positive climb", retracts the undercarriage on the other pilot's command.

In this case however, doubtless because of the stress of the moment, it was not until about seven seconds after the captain called "Go Lever" that the slat/flap lever was retracted. While the lever should only be moved up to the next detent, it seemed possible from the CVR that the lever was moved to 15°/0° or even higher to the fully up 0°/0° position, before being lowered again to 15°/15°. The undercarriage was left extended. The aircraft's noseup pitching moment would have been further increased by this slat/flap retraction.

The captain continued to hold the control column fully forward, intermittently operating the pitch trim switch, and the tailplane setting slowly returned from its noseup limit angle of minus 12.3° to minus 10.9° over the next seven seconds.

Over the following five seconds the tailplane setting moved again from minus 10.9° to minus 7.4°, where it remained until impact. Because of the fact that the captain used the pitch trim only intermittently and so little during his go around attempt, the investigators believed he did not realise the tailplane's setting had become so far out-of-trim.

Climbing so steeply with the airspeed decreasing so alarmingly, the captain evidently hesitated to reduce the engine thrust. But when the aircraft's noseup pitch had reached a grossly abnormal 40.3° and the airspeed had fallen to only 115kt, he finally did so in a desperate attempt to reduce the steep noseup attitude.

Yet although the No 1 thrust lever was retarded to almost idle, the No 2 lever was retarded only slightly. The investigators believed this was because the captain's right hand probably came off the No 2 lever as he desperately tried to retard the power while continuing to push hard on the control column with his other hand.

Four seconds later, either the captain or the first officer pushed the thrust levers back to full thrust in a vain attempt to recover lost airspeed.

The time of the accident was determined to be 8.15:45pm when the CVR and DFDR simultaneously stopped recording.

Crew co-ordination

It was evident to the investigators that, apart from any shortcomings on the part of the crew in their understanding of the aircraft's AFCS, their flightdeck co-ordination also left something to be desired. This was not only evident as the emergency developed.

Well before this, at 7.59pm, the captain had read out the Approach Checklist at the request of the first officer. And at 8.11pm he had read out the Landing Checklist. But neither of these were performed as required, the captain reading aloud the items only to himself, including those to which the captain and first officer should respond together.

During the approach descent, crossing Ise Bay, the captain instructed the first officer to control the aircraft at his own discretion for as long as he could. But as soon as the first officer inadvertently triggered the Go Lever on final approach, the captain began firing rapid instructions at him one after another.

This not only completely negated the autonomy the first officer had just been given for the approach, but also simultaneously disregarded the company's standardised crew operating procedures. The captain's authoritative manner and succession of unquestioning instructions clearly 'rattled' the young first officer, probably intimidating him to the extent of being unable to think clearly for himself – or from even conveying the true nature of the developing out-of-trim problem to the captain.

Had the captain taken control of the aircraft himself to correct the situation immediately the first officer triggered the Go Lever, instead of trying to do it indirectly through the well intentioned but obsequious young junior pilot, himself all too conscious of the status and authority of the captain, the lack of communication and crew co-ordination that so quickly set the scene for the accident might have been avoided.

The investigators believed another factor leading to the accident was that the text of the Airbus Flight Crew Operating Manual was not always clear to non European pilots. Yet another was that flightdeck systems or warnings to alert pilots to an out-of-trim condition of the tailplane were not effectively incorporated into the aircraft's AFCS.

CAUSE

The Japanese investigators determined that, as a result of the extreme out-of-trim configuration of the aircraft, brought about by the combination of maximum power and the fact that the tailplane setting had moved automatically and undetected to the maximum noseup position, the aircraft climbed uncontrollably steeply until it stalled. Entering a steep descent at below flying airspeed, it then struck the ground within the confines of the Nagoya airport.

An unhappy sequel

How well the lessons of this sudden, needless tragedy were learned remains an open question. For even as this volume was being written four years after the accident, another A300-600 belonging to China Airlines crashed fatally during an approach to land at Taipei Airport, Taiwan, on February 16, 1998.

The circumstances of this second accident appear almost identical – an attempted go around, a rapidly steepening climb culminating in a stall, a steep nosedown dive, a partial recovery and a devastating noseup impact close to the airport boundary. This time all 196 occupants of the Airbus were killed – plus six people on the ground.

As this book went to press, the accident was still under investigation (see Endbox, next page).

Displaying typical Airbus Industrie panache, the former TAA's first A300B4-203, VH-TAA [134] "James Cook", makes a spectacular pre-delivery takeoff as F-WZEJ in the northern summer of 1981. This rare photograph illustrates almost exactly the aircraft attitude in which the bewildered crew of CAL's B-1816 found themselves in their ill-fated landing attempt at Nagoya. (Matthew Tesch; Air Pictorial)

TAIPEI: THE BIGGER PICTURE

History's tendency to repeat unheeded or forgotten lessons of bitter experience was never more apparent than in this third volume of *Air Disaster*.

In Taiwan, the aftermath of the Nagoya disaster led to recriminations harsher and more peremptory than that of the fallout from Bangalore, Colorado Springs, Pittsburgh or Kathmandu. Media speculation fixated on minute traces of alcohol discovered during the post mortems of Captain Wang and First Officer Chuang. (Far more likely pathological than suspicious; the possible contributory effects certainly irrelevant.) Taiwanese authorities announced their own investigation into China Airlines, threatening punitive repeal of some of CAL's route rights.

The airline itself temporarily banned the "manoeuvring" of its aircraft by its first officers, and began "special but unspecified checks" on its five remaining A300B4-622Rs. The traditional Oriental customs of "face" and personal accountability – manifested in the Japan Air Lines 747 catastrophe in 1985 (see *Air Disaster*, Vol 2, Ch 10) – were revealed even in the provocative politics of Taiwanese democracy. The CAA director general promptly resigned – although reportedly commenting he didn't think he "should take responsibility for the crash". On a more practical operational note, the succeeding minister immediately ordered simulator checks for all 440 CAL pilots.

Now, with the strikingly similar accident at Taipei in February 1998 – even as this book was being written – hindsight would suggest the only tangible result of that seemingly sensible precaution was the resulting chaotic disruption to CAL's schedules! Around 170 mostly international services were abruptly cancelled in the weeks following the Nagoya tragedy.

The degree of similarity – almost virtual replication – of circumstances, data and aircraft, between Nagoya and Taipei, less than four years apart, is nothing less than breathtaking.

On the evening of February 16, 1998, a few minutes after 8.00pm local time, A300B4-622R B-1814 [578], operating Flight CI676, was making an ILS approach to Taipei's 3658m (12,000ft) Runway 05L. In a gentle northerly wind with a visibility of 1km, the Airbus was for some reason 1000 feet above the glideslope, only 1nm from the runway threshold.

Initial analysis of B-1814's DFDR data, read out by Australia's Bureau of Air Safety Investigation (asked to assist the Taiwanese CAA), outlined a sequence of events uncannily like those which preceded B-1816's crash at Nagoya – complete autopilot disengagement just after Taipei Tower's landing clearance; a manually flown attempted go-around, with a falling airspeed varying between 150 and 100 knots, and pitch up angles exceeding 40°; a sharp gain in height of almost 1000 feet, followed by a total stall at almost unregisterable airspeed; and a more than 40° pitch down dive, with scant recovery in aircraft attitude before impact.

All 196 passengers and crew died as the Airbus exploded just beyond the Chiang Kai Shek Airport boundary, flinging burning debris across a road to kill another six people in an adjacent residential area. V-shaped impact marks made by the A300's tailcone, disintegrated PW4158 engines, and a short (400m) splay of wreckage, aligned more than 30° away from the runway centreline, were all disturbing evocations of Nagoya.

Data interpretation revealed few significant differences between the two manoeuvre sequences. The B-1814 crew at Taipei had retracted the A300's undercarriage early in their intended go-around, whereas Captain Wang's CVR comments at Nagoya indicated that, at least initially, he believed B-1816 could be recovered to effect the landing.

Also, B-1814's gyrations above and to the west of the Taipei runway, demonstrated more wildly erratic bank angles – from 40° left, to 90° right, then through 38° left to an incredible, almost wings-vertical 78° before rolling back to more than 20° starboard wing down. Both A300s, however, impacted in a near level, slightly noseup attitude.

Not surprisingly, the operational and disciplinary ramifications that followed the Nagoya accident were even more severe within CAL after such a disaster at its own capital city home base. Taiwan's CAA immediately grounded China Airlines' nine other A300-600s for thorough technical and avionics checks. And CAL's dedicated A300 aircrew complement – 140 pilots – were once again swiftly despatched to intensive, week-long, simulator re-evaluations.

The two destroyed A300-600s had led effectively identical service lives. B-1814 first flew from Toulouse on October 16, 1990, B-1816 a fortnight later, on the 30th. B-1814 was delivered on December 14 that year, B-1816 following it on January 28, 1991. On an incidental note, many of the Dash 600s in CAL's much expanded Airbus fleet, in the later half of the 1990s, are leased-in aircraft with their American owned registrations pointedly composed of the Orient's "lucky number eight". A300B4-622R N8888P [555], which joined China Airlines in February 1998, is one such (hopefully lucky!) example.

Apart from their cultural standing, such omens carry the legacy of the all too frequent blemishes on CAL's safety record. In the past 20 years alone, China Airlines has lost two Boeing 707s, two 737s and a 747-400 less than six months old. In addition there have been half a dozen turbo-props and sundry types – plus the two A300s.

The treachery of the weather at Hong Kong's former Kai Tak Airport might explain, if still not excuse, the unfortunate skidding overrun of a brand new 747-400 into the harbour in November 1993, five months before the Nagoya disaster. Coincidentally, it could also be mentioned that the inshore waters around the island of Taiwan have claimed, through various causes, the remains of both the 737s, a 707 on a training flight, and one of four early, secondhand CAL Caravelle IIIs in 1971.

Another fatal loss – like the training 707 that went into the Formosa Strait just after takeoff from Taipei – was that of Taiwanese regional carrier FEAT (Far Eastern Air Transport), on August 22, 1981. The corrosion induced, explosive inflight decompression of FEAT's Boeing 737-222 B-2603 [19939] is documented in *Air Disaster* Vol 2, Ch 11. (Another coincidence, of more relevance to this volume's fourth chapter, is this aircraft's Model 222 suffix, this 1969 veteran Boeing only the eighth United Air Lines 737, the one-time N9058U "City of San Diego".)

It is ominous enough that the undistinguished Taiwanese air safety record hints at periodic outbreaks of aberrant operational behaviour, interspersed with apparently short-lived calms of lessons learnt and warnings heeded.

It is perhaps even more disturbing that China Airlines has managed – not once, but twice – to repeat other crews' errors, made no less than four times on Airbus Industrie flightdecks, since 1989 alone!

Emulating the type of investigation work for which the NTSB is justly renowned (see *Air Disaster* Vol 2, Ch 9 Endbox), the Japanese Ministry of Transport's Nagoya report detailed not only these prior examples of conflict between crew and computer – and every one in a critical approach phase of flight – but also Airbus Industrie's responses.

One of the first Dash 600s, in March 1985, as well as a late model A300B4 fitted with an FFCC flightdeck, in January 1989, were the first to record the conflicting inputs and pre-landing upsets, twice repeated so fatally by CAL years later.

Airbus Industrie's resulting communications to its customers between 1985 and 1994 included Technical Notes, Service Bulletins, FCOM procedure revisions and cautionary warnings, avionics modifications, and Operations Engineering Bulletins. The second incident in fact even prompted Airbus Industrie to the unusual step of conducting an "Operators' Conference" at Toulouse in May 1990.

But the airport and aircraft type featured in the previous chapter were to attract even more serious attention on February 11, 1991. On this occasion, a German A310-304, making an automatic ILS approach to Moscow's Sheremetyevo Airport, was instructed by the Tower to go around as it descended through 1550ft AGL on final approach.

The resulting radio exchange and AFCS reprogramming occupied a further 300 feet of the aircraft's descent, before the A310 pitched up in a high power climb. Just as the two China Airlines crews were to do later at the cost of their lives, the German pilots applied control column pressures that were resisted and countered by the AFCS. The conflicting sequence, now familiar to readers, then led to a severe out-of-trim condition.

Zooming back up through 1500ft AGL, the A310 crew found themselves pitched up to an almost vertical 88°, with the Indicated Air Speed a heartstopping 30 knots! The full thrust of the engines somehow carried the lightly loaded Airbus on up to more than 4300ft, before it fell back in a stall. Worse still, the continuing control conflict then caused the aircraft to repeat the same violent pitching cycle a further three times! Peaking at an amazing 11,755ft, the A310 fell back to 8700ft before the hapless crew, finally realising their trim condition, took corrective action to recover the aircraft.

Happily, the crew were ultimately able to make a safe landing, but the bewilderment of the Sheremetyevo tower controllers can only be imagined!

The fact that an international airline had to reacquaint itself with such frightening and well documented incidents – in the form of two disastrous accidents costing more than 450 lives – almost defies belief.

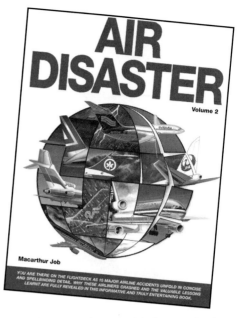